# The Collected Works of
# Marie-Louise von Franz

## MLvF

## Volume 4

**General Editors**
Steven Buser
Leonard Cruz

Marie-Louise von Franz
1915-1998

Volume 4

# Archetypal Symbols
# in Fairytales

## Opposition and Renewal

## Marie-Louise von Franz

Translated by Mark Kyburz

CHIRON PUBLICATIONS • ASHEVILLE, NORTH CAROLINA

**Logo of the Foundation for Jungian Psychology, Küsnacht, Zürich, Switzerland:**
*Fons mercurialis from Rosarium Philosophorum*, 1550 (*Fountain of Life*).

Original title: *Symbolik des Märchens – Versuch einer Deutung*
Copyright © 1952, 1960, Bern; revised edition 2017
Verlag Stiftung für Jung'sche Psychologie, Küsnacht, Zürich, Switzerland

www.ChironPublications.com
Interior and cover design by Danijela Mijailovic
Translated by Mark Kyburz
Cover image by Martina Ott
Printed primarily in the United States of America.

ISBN  978-1-68503-590-7 paperback
ISBN  978-1-68503-591-4 hardcover
ISBN  978-1-68503-592-1 electronic
ISBN  978-1-68503-593-8 limited edition paperback
ISBN  978-1-68503-594-5 limited edition hardcover

# A Note on the Compilation of
# The Collected Works of
# Marie-Louise von Franz

Marie-Louise von Franz was blessed with a keen intellect and an outstanding memory. As a classical philologist with a doctorate in Latin and Greek, she was familiar with the writings of the ancient philosophers. She was exceptionally well read. Her private library alone contained over 8,000 books and writings. She was also both diligent and conscientious in her work. She met C.G. Jung in her youth and found him to be an excellent teacher and mentor. She went on to become a close confidant and collaborator, particularly in his work on alchemy. Jung's psychological observations and the conclusions and hypotheses he drew from them about the structures of the unconscious psyche increasingly coincided with her own observations. Marie-Louise von Franz was imbued with an inexhaustible creativity that inspired her well into her old age. She devoted her last lecture to the rehabilitation of the feeling function, a subject that was of great importance to her and to C.G. Jung. Her unconditional devotion to the manifestations of the unconscious psyche was exemplary for all who met her during her lifetime, and for many who came to know her from her writings or their own dreams.

Only a few of her works survived in the form of finished manuscripts. Many of her books derived from transcriptions of her lectures, some of which were delivered in German, though most were in English. The English transcriptions were later translated into her native German. Her primary focus was always on the psychological context and background of her books, and less on their linguistic delivery. Some publishers therefore took the liberty of adding or changing certain things in her texts to make it easier for the reader, as they thought. After realizing what they had done, Marie-Louise von Franz indignantly insisted on her original text being used, claiming that what she had written was what she had wanted to express. Since then, many of her works have been translated into 23 languages, with editions of varying quality being used as the basis for translations into local languages.

In addition to the publishing rights, Marie-Louise von Franz left to the Foundation for Jungian Psychology a handwritten list in which she noted which editions of her books she considered to be the best and most accurate. After her death in 1998, the members of the Foundation decided to republish all of her works in German in accordance with her list. We have respectfully endeavored to remain as close as possible to her original tone, to correct obvious audio or transcription errors, to add footnotes to facilitate understanding, and to supplement texts when written records or tape recordings of her lectures were available. In some instances, this has resulted in greatly altered and revised publications, which we consider to be the basis for all new translations.

For the publication of the Collected Works of Marie-Louise von Franz by Chiron Publications, the Stiftung commissioned Alison Kappes-Bates, Hirzel, a professional translator who knew Marie-Louise von Franz for over 30 years and was a close companion until her death, to translate into English the newly-revised texts in German. Mark Kyburz, Zürich, an experienced translator of Jungian texts, re-edited the first three English volumes of Archetypal Symbols in Fairytales, translated Volumes 4 and 5, and will translate further volumes. The Foundation for Jungian Psychology is responsible for the content and the design, the latter having been created in close consultation with Chiron Publication, Asheville.

On behalf of the Foundation for Jungian Psychology,
Küsnacht, April 24, 2023
PD Dr. Hansueli F. Etter

◆

# Table of Contents

# The Problem of Redemption

Ever will He be to you the One who does into Many
Sunder Himself, and remains: One, the ever unique.
Find in the One the Many, and feel the Many as Oneness,
And the inception you'll have, have the completion of art.

Goethe, *The Soothsayings of Bakis*[1]

---

[1] Goethe, *The Soothsayings of Bakis*, ed. and trans. Harald Jantz (Baltimore: Johns Hopkins Press, 1966), p. 52.

◊

# A.
# The Redemption of the Enchanted Prince

¹ Fairytales are images of the archetypal events that shape reality. As such, they reflect a process in which both men and women participate through their unconscious. What follows explores a theme that forms part of this process and is frequently depicted in fairytales: the liberation or redemption of one's companion or partner from distressing circumstances.

² The unfolding drama is even more fascinating because the female figure is both the image of the woman in the man's soul and the ideal image of the female being in the woman's soul, just as the male figure is both the image of the spiritual being in the woman's soul and the higher being in the man's soul. Put slightly differently: A feminine archetype appears in the soul of both man and woman, and likewise a masculine one. When, as the fairytale plot unfolds, the characters representing these archetypes relate to each other and influence each other's fate, one of them is more conscious and actively strives to redeem the other, while the other is more unconscious, more bound to their plight.

³ As our discussion of the fairytales considered in Volume 1 has shown, their characters, as images of psychic forces, were described as nonhuman entities and confined to that sphere. In part, they were described as suffering great distress from which they had to be redeemed by a higher, human consciousness. Redemption here means transformation into a free human being who consciously determines his or her fate and who is more independent of any enslavement to the demonic forces of matter: a transformation, then, from demonic nature into a humanity superior to it.

4     This problem of redemption is depicted in fairytales so manifoldly and with such profound symbolism that it might be said to encapsulate the most essential psychological truths, which are presented as images in fairytales.

5     Without overly condensing this rich material, we can divide fairytales into two groups: In the first group, a female protagonist redeems an animus-figure that has been turned into an animal or has been otherwise bewitched or enchanted; in the second group, a man frees his anima from the spell of the unconscious. This separation, however, as we will see, and as the previous remarks on the common "reality" of the soul suggest, is a conscious, ordering principle by which matter, even if not completely understood, is made somewhat accessible. A third group of fairytales, in which this reciprocal relationship between man and woman also becomes formally evident within the symbolic action, and where one or the other interpretation prevails, will establish the interpersonal reality of these fairytales even more clearly at the end of this book.

6     The material presented here raises several questions: Why and how did this plight of the soul-image in need of redemption arise? And through which human stance and action can be it be liberated?

7     Let us begin with a fairytale which, some minor differences aside, resembles a group of fairytales that we discussed in the last section of Volume 1. This tale, in which a woman serves an old forest demon, is the Grimm's "The Hut in the Forest":

8     A poor wood-cutter lived with his wife and three daughters in a little hut on the edge of a lonely forest. One morning … he said to his wife … "Let our eldest daughter bring me my dinner into the forest." … The girl could not find the path … Then in the distance she perceived a light which glimmered between the trees. It was not long before she came to a house whose windows were brightly lit. She knocked, and a rough voice from inside cried: "Come in." The girl stepped into the dark entrance … an old gray-haired man was sitting at the table, supporting his face with both hands, and his white

beard fell down over the table almost as far as the ground. By the stove lay three animals, a hen, a cock, and a brindled cow. The girl told her story to the old man and begged for shelter for the night. The man said:

9

> "My pretty hen,
> My pretty cock,
> My pretty brindled cow,
> What do you say now?"

10 "Duks," answered the animals, and that must have meant: "We are willing," for the old man said: "Here you shall have shelter and food, go to the fire, and cook us our supper." The girl found in the kitchen abundance of everything, and cooked a good supper, yet had not thought of the animals … When she had had enough, she said: "But now I am tired, where is there a bed in which I can lie down, and sleep?" The animals replied:

11

> "Thou hast eaten with him,
> Thou hast drunk with him,
> Thou hast had no thought for us,
> So find out for thyself where thou canst pass the night."

12 Then said the old man: "Just go upstairs, and you will find a room with two beds" … The girl went up … After some time the gray-haired man came, held his candle over the girl and shook his head. When he saw that she had fallen into a sound sleep, he opened a trap-door, and let her down into the cellar.

13 … The second daughter went out … and everything happened just as it had happened the day before.

14 On the third morning the youngest daughter [took the same path. At the hut everything happened as it had before] … The girl went to the stove where the animals were lying, and petted the cock and hen,

…, and caressed the brindled cow … when the animals were fed, the girl seated herself at the table by the old man …

15

> Then said the girl: "Ought we not go to bed?
> The animals answered: "Duks,"
> Thou hast eaten with us,
> Thou has drunk with us,
> Thou hast had kind thought for all of us,
> We wish thee good-night."

16 She slept quietly till midnight, and then there was such a noise in the house that she awoke. There was a sound of cracking and splitting in every corner, and the doors sprang open, and beat against the walls. The beams groaned as if they were being torn out of their joints, it seemed as if the staircase were falling down, and at length there was a crash as if the entire roof had fallen in. When, however, all grew quiet once more, and the girl was not hurt, she … fell asleep again. But when she woke up in the morning with the brilliancy of the sunshine, what did her eyes behold? She was lying in a vast hall, and everything around her shone with royal splendor; on the walls, golden flowers grew up on a ground of green silk, the bed was made of ivory, and the canopy of red velvet, and on a chair close by, was a pair of slippers embroidered with pearls … three richly clad attendants came in and asked what orders she would like to give. "I will get up at once and make ready some soup for the old man, and then I will feed the pretty hen, and the pretty cock, and the pretty brindled cow." She thought the old man was up already and looked round at his bed; he, however, was not lying in it, but a stranger … he awoke, sat up in bed, and said: "I am a King's son, and was bewitched by a wicked witch, and made to live in this forest, as an old gray-haired man; no one was allowed to be with me but three attendants in the form of a cock, a hen, and a brindled cow. The spell was not to be broken until

a girl came to us whose heart was so good that she showed herself full of love, not only towards mankind, but towards animals—and that you have done, and by you at midnight we were set free, and the old hut was changed back again into my royal palace." ... the King's son ordered the three attendants to set out and fetch the father and mother of the girl to the marriage feast. "But where are my sisters?" inquired the maiden. "I have locked them in the cellar, and tomorrow they shall be led into the forest, and shall live as servants to a charcoal-burner, until they have grown kinder, and do not leave poor animals to suffer hunger."[2]

17   This plot resembles that of two other fairytales: "The Stepdaughter's and the Maid's Reward" (Finland, no. 53) and "The Moon on the Forehead," a Persian tale.[3] In both tales, the heroine must bathe and delouse an old man. Their close resemblance (see also "Vun'n Mannl Sponnelang")[4] makes detailed interpretation unnecessary. The motif, however, is significant: The old man not only shows his gratitude with gifts, but is transformed into a king's son and into the heroine's bridegroom. He first appears as a father-imago, as found, for example, in "King Thrushbeard,"[5] in "Allerleirauh,"[6] or in "The Magic Horse" (Turkestan, no. 9),[7] where the effect is negative, or in "The Moon on the Forehead," where the father-imago appears in its double aspect. His second guise represents that soul-image on which the life-enhancing bonds of love are based.

---

[2] Translator's note: This tale has been abridged and slightly adapted from *The Complete Grimm's Fairy Tales* (New York: Pantheon Books, 1944), pp. 698–704. This edition of the fairytales collected by the Brothers Grimm is used throughout this volume.

[3] For these tales, see August von Löwis of Menar, ed., *Finnische und estnische Volksmärchen*, collected in *Märchen der Weltliteratur* [hereafter *MdW*], eds. Fr. v. d. Leyen and P. Zaunert (Jena: Eugen Diederichs, 1922); see also Arthur Christensen, trans., *Märchen aus Iran* [*MdW*], ed., v. d. Leyen (Jena: Eugen Diederichs, 1939), p. 90.

[4] Paul Zaunert, ed., *Deutsche Märchen seit Grimm*, collected in *MdW*, vol. 1, ed. v. d. Leyen (Jena: Eugen Diederichs, 1922), p. 404.

[5] *The Complete Grimm's Fairy Tales*, pp. 244-248.

[6] *Ibid.*, pp. 326–331.

[7] Gustav Jungbauer, ed., *Märchen aus Turkestan und Tibet*, in *MdW*, eds. v. d. Leyen and Zaunert (Jena: Eugen Diederichs, 1923).

18     Thus, in hindsight, the two figures presumably also shared a secret identity in the fairytales discussed previously. Intrapsychically, rather than the figures *changing*, their psychic potency was *transformed*,[8] from the manifestation of the father into that of the son. In terms of the woman's psyche, the archetype common to both manifestations is the "animus" (i.e., the image of her soul's masculine-spiritual component). This also corresponds to the unredeemed father-figures in other fairytales (e.g., "The Golden Bird"[9]), where such processes tend to be reflected in the man's (rather than in the woman's) soul. Ultimately, we are dealing with the father-archetype as an underworld demon, which can take effect in every person's soul. This "divine spirit" manifests in nature and therefore participates in its imperfection and blind striving for development. We have already witnessed the transformation of this father-image from an old man into a young one in "The Red Swan" (North America, no. 14).[10] This widespread archetypal motif underlies the ideas of royal or divine regeneration in many peoples across the world.

19     As in "The Red Swan" (North America, no. 14), and analogous to the views of medieval alchemy, this dark *spiritus mundi* (world-spirit) requires human redemption. In the present fairytale, the redemptive act is performed by a woman and thus involves loving affection. Significantly, the three animals must be looked after with utmost care, because the dark spirit of nature is strangely related to the essence of animals, plants, and even inorganic things. The actual meaning of this careful attention to animals, however, will only fully transpire when we consider fairytales in which the companion or partner who must be redeemed is an animal.[11] As human beings, we

---

[8] The substitution of the seven dwarfs—in some variants, they are *an* old man—by a prince in "Little Snow-White" (*The Complete Grimm's Fairy Tales*, pp. 249–258) illustrates the same process.

[9] *The Complete Grimm's Fairy Tales*, pp. 272–279.

[10] Walter Krickeberg, ed., *Indianermärchen aus Nordamerika*, in *MdW*, ed. v. d. Leyen and Zaunert (Jena: Eugen Diederichs, 1924).

[11] For a transitional figure to the animal aspect, see "The Old Rattlebag" (Sweden, no. 27), Klara Stroebe, trans. *Nordische Volksmärchen*, vol. 1: Dänemark und Schweden, [*MdW*], ed. v. d. Leyen and Zaunert (Jena: Eugen Diederichs, 1922). This fairytale was cited as a parallel to "King Thrushbeard" (*The Complete Grimm's Fairy Tales*). See also Novalis, *Fragmente*, 1st complete edition, ed., Ernst Kamnitzer (Dresden: Wolfgang Jess Verlag, 1929), no. 653: "If God could become man, he can also become a stone, plant, animal, and element, and perpetual redemption in nature might occur thus."—Trans.

should "show consideration" for animals and "look back" at these psychic components, at the animal souls in our genetic, hereditary material, or we will be consigned to a cellar or dungeon. Thus, suppressing such part-souls does not contribute to human freedom but binds human beings to their darkness. The cellar is an image of the chthonic regions of our inner being and the unconscious forces at work there,[12] in whose power those who have no relationship to their own nature are held captive, without any hope.

20     In "The Hut in the Forest," spending the night together implies that the heroine should take kindly to the old man despite his unsightly appearance. Characteristically, women are tasked with performing such redemptive acts in fairytales. In our present tale, it is also significant that a woman must break the spell: After all, as we are told, it was cast by a woman, namely, by a witch, the archetype of the terrible mother. Psychologically, the harm inflicted by this archetype in the man's soul is often compensated solely by the anima's related archetype. Otherwise, the children may need to continue bearing the problem like a curse. That is, suffering continues.[13]

21     The connection between the motif of the generational curse and that of bewitchment (i.e., the enchantment by a witch) is described both poetically and revealingly in "The White Cat":

22     A grieving widowed King also turned down a witch who appeared as a deeply veiled woman covered in diamonds and thus incurred her wrath. In revenge, she transformed the castle into a large "rock furnace" set in deep mounds of snow and the King, his son, and his servants into ravens circling the rock. Water flowed from a hole in the rock, covering the gardens and forming an ice-cold lake. "And thou shalt remain

---

[12] See the sorceress's and the grandfather's cellar in "Die Jungfrau Zar" (Russia, no. 41); see August von Löwis of Menar [trans.], *Russische Volksmärchen*, collected in *MdW*, ed. v. d. Leyen and Zaunert (1921). For a published English translation ("The Maiden Tsar"), see Alexander Afanas'ev, *Russian Fairy Tales*, trans. Norbert Guterman (Toronto: Pantheon Books, 1945), pp. 229–234.

[13] On the eternal, i.e., never-ending curse, see "The Ghosts of the Hanged" (China, no. 66); Richard Wilhelm. [trans.], *Chinesische Märchen*, collected in *MdW*, ed. v. d. Leyen (Düsseldorf-Cologne: Eugen Diederichs, 1958).

bewitched," said the wicked witch, "Till a maiden drives an extraordinary carriage across the lake into the rock and kisses the old raven."

23  The old witch had a daughter who was as evil as her mother; but she was very stupid and had never learned witchcraft. And thus it happened that she didn't receive a prince as a husband, but a poor woodcutter. The man had a little girl from his first marriage, and the witch's daughter became the child's evil stepmother. When the woodcutter's cat gave birth to "four snow-white, very dear cats" and died, the witch ordered the girl to drown the animals in the frozen pond. The girl punched a hole in the ice but could not commit the murder. Overcome by grief and sadness, she fell asleep by the hole and dreamed that someone were calling to her: "Get in, get in!" When the girl awoke, a lovely golden sleigh lay before her, with the four snow-white cats harnessed to it. She drove this miraculous vehicle to the rocky cave on the shore and got out. The sleigh and the cat disappeared. Deep inside the cave, she found two little lights and an old screeching raven, whose neck was tied with a cloth. "Well," she said, "there is a dear little bird, so poor and sick!" She picked up the sick animal and kissed it. But there followed a loud crashing noise, as if the world were falling to pieces and the rock were about to collapse. Before she knew what had happened, she was standing in the middle of a large, bright hall, and a King stood before her. Solemnly, he kissed the astonished child and said: "You have saved us! Be thou my son's bride and our kingdom's queen!"[14]

24  This fairytale spans two generations and presents in rare detail the background of a tale of redemption. As in "The Hut in the Forest," the predicament is caused by a witch's curse. This, however, is

---

[14] Paul Zaunert, ed., *Deutsche Märchen aus dem Donaulande*, collected in *MdW*, ed. v. d. Leyen and Zaunert (Jena: Eugen Diederichs, 1926), p. 37—Trans.

justified: The witch is a rejected "false bride." We should probably interpret the death of the first queen, a natural process beyond human influence, as the end of a stage of development. However noble, the king's refusal to remarry therefore contravenes the law of living inner progress. The king's adherence to the past also indicates his advanced age, his blindness and sickness, albeit in terms of guilt, as a willful splitting-off from the law of nature.

25   As our discussion of the "magical marriage" (in Volume 1) revealed, when the concrete woman dies, the feminine soul-image emerges in the man particularly clearly and, as it were, demands realization (see, for instance, "Una, The Elf Maiden"; Iceland, no. 10).[15] When the king rejects this sphere, the anima becomes negative, consistent with the law that what is rejected by consciousness exerts a negative effect in the unconscious. Or, put differently: The luminous aspect of the anima "died," and the king rejects the dark aspect without any confrontation, without inquiring what has caused the change; anticipating the curse, this process already reflects the king's aversion to emotional and psychic life.

26   And yet, the two worlds, that of the conscious ego and that of the unconscious realities, represented here by man and woman, are mutually dependent: The king, despite or as a result of rejecting the anima's world, depends on a woman's redemptive act. Just as the harsh fate of the wicked witch's step-grandchild turns only after she reaches the enchanted royal court. The girl has been assigned a task, and as long as she does not recognize it and therefore does not fulfill it, she, too, remains governed by the world of witches. Like many women who are spellbound by the archetype of the terrible mother, and who compensate for this curse with a profound motherliness, the heroine's tender motherliness forms the bridge to the man's darkened soul, which is beaten down by the terrible mother and alienated from life.

27   Here, the tormenting aberrations in which the man, turning away from feeling, becomes entangled, are expressed in the king's

---

[15] Hans Naumann and Ida Naumann, trans., *Isländische Volksmärchen*, in *MdW*, ed. v. d. Leyen and Zaunert (Jena: Eugen Diederichs, 1923).

appearance as a raven. This transformation reflects the king's fate: He must circle his bewitched castle (i.e., his inner home), and his paralyzed psychic life, in an eternal, senseless quest. Ice symbolizes the paralysis of emotional life and in general of psychic life. Here, this is caused by the witch's curse, that is, by the mother-anima in her negative aspect. As a raven, the king is adapted to the archetype of the chthonic father-god, whose despondent restlessness he shares. By way of a brief digression: In Germanic paganism, the raven was one of Wotan's animals; in ancient Mediterranean culture, ravens were attributed to the sun-god and thus embodied the darkened midnight sun, which sometimes also represents the spirit of nature; and in alchemy, as mentioned, the raven's head symbolizes decomposition, or *nigredo* (blackness), and spiritual darkness. Thus, the king, whose archetype is symbolically closest to the sun, may be said to have fallen into the state of the dark sun—alchemically, the *sol niger* (black sun).[16] Psychologically, this image means a supremacy of the "shadow," a devouring of the personality by the psyche's dark components. The unconscious has a decomposing effect: It deadens life, which disintegrates as a result; and it governs, as a dark force, the king's soul.

28     In terms of the woman's psyche, the dark raven symbolizes the masculine-spiritual part of being, which remains in the unconscious and appears as a gloomy father-imago. In "The Princess in the Tree,"[17] an evil sorcerer who forces himself between the maiden and her future bridegroom first turns into a thirsty crucified raven. In this tale, the man's soul-image, which manifests in two different

---

[16] C.G. Jung, *Psychologie und Alchemie*, CW 12, fig. 34. See also the important juxtaposition of the king and the raven as two aspects of one and the same being in "The Boy and the Large Human-Headed Beast" (France, vol. 2, no. 55; see Ernst Tegethoff [trans.], *Französische Volksmärchen 2: Aus neueren Sammlungen*, in MdW, eds., v. d. Leyen and Zaunert, 1923): After the hero had answered the questions of the human-headed beast that stood guarding the gold, and it was now his turn to ask questions, the beast was unable to say what lay at either end of the world, so that the young man answered the question himself: At one end, a king wearing a crown and purple and golden robes "was preparing for battle and wielding a great sword"; he looked at heaven, earth, and sea, yet saw nothing coming. At the other end, a large 7,000-year-old raven sat perched atop a mountain. It knew and saw all that was happening and would happen yet was reluctant to speak. In "How Wildcat's Sons Became the Sun and the Moon" (North America, no. 17), the raven temporarily replaces the as-yet "uncreated" sun, so that the earth grows very cold. Thus, the raven is the *sol niger* (black sun). See also Krickeberg, *Nordamerika* (Jena, 1924), p. 391, footnote on "The Raven's Birth" (no. 27a).
[17] Zaunert, *Deutsche Märchen seit Grimm* (Jena, 1922), p. 1.

figures (i.e., the true lover and hero; and the false, dark-demonic suitor), is described as one and the same figure. This, however, appears in two successive states: enchantment and redemption (the king's son, who is bewitched at the same time as the father, is said to form a unity with him).

29       Thus, the raven represents a dark spirit, whose unconsciousness and abstract essence, which eludes feeling, is expressed by the image of ice, which separates everything from the surrounding world. Belonging to both the man's and the woman's soul, it negatively affects the former as a "shadow" and the latter as a dark spirit-imago. The lights in the cave indicate the illumining function of this psychic component. The duality of these lights suggests that the content has begun to split into a pair of opposites as a precondition of conscious realization. As in "The Stepdaughter's and the Maid's Reward" (Finland, no. 53), and in "The Moon on the Forehead" (Persia), the woman is freed from the overpowering mother-imago by developing a relationship with the husband-imago. The man's psyche, on the other hand, seems completely dependent on the "other's" initiative: Because after the sick king succumbs to an excessive ego-emphasis, passively accepting the psychic events remains the only redemptive attitude. Her clarity enables the maiden to reconnect the king and his emotional life, which has been split off from existence. This event is expressed in the image of the heroine driving a team of cats across the ice. As the cat represents to a considerable extent the woman's instinctual life, and also the feminine in general, the four kittens symbolize the heroine's maternal instinct.

30       The fact that these kittens appear in a group of four also indicates that inner wholeness is still slumbering in the instinctual realm. Moreover, the fact that the kittens (which belong to the woodcutter's cat and thus to a simple, ancillary sphere) are described as little and harmless, young and white, and the fact that they can be "yoked," suggests that these qualities also characterize the heroine's instinctual life: Her womanhood is still youthful, yet also plain and uncorrupted. But because she is persecuted by her mother, her delicate femininity is threatened with immersion in a freezing lake

and thus, like the king's emotional life, with paralysis. And yet, their respect for life keeps the youthful instincts alive. The girl follows the inner voice, which offers her clear guidance, and lets herself be drawn by those instincts in a golden chariot. Recalling the miraculous sledges in "Ivan the Simpleton" (Russia, no. 8), and in particular in "The Miraculous Sledge,"[18] the chariot symbolizes a bearing, mothering force. The girl is transported deep into the interior of the world, her world. There, her compassion, based on a sense of affinity, makes her pity the creature. She now attends to the raven, which represents the spirit suffering in her own soul. The girl's action breaks the witch's spell for both man and woman.

31      One fairytale that repeats some of the above motifs, albeit more weakly, while depicting the redemptive transformation more richly, is "The Werewolf" (Sweden, no. 11):

32      A scheming woman with two daughters persuaded a King's daughter with false promises to induce her widowed father to make her his wife. This he did, but he told his daughter not to complain if she became disappointed later. At first, the stepmother was kind; but when the King's daughter found a valiant young King's son as a suitor, the stepmother transformed the young man into a werewolf when the King was away. The princess searched for her lover in the dark forest and, without the stepsister, who had been sent along to supervise the undertaking, noticing, she came to an old woman in a hut. The woman advised the girl to pick, if she could, a magnificent lily, which she would discover on her way, and someone would appear who would tell her what to do.

33      Things happened as the old woman predicted, yet whenever the King's daughter found the magnificent white lily, it had disappeared and stood a little further away. "Now the King's daughter was most eager and no longer listened to her

---

[18] Alexander Afanas'ev, *Russian Fairy Tales*, trans. Norbert Guterman (Toronto: Pantheon Books, 1945), pp. 142–145; Alfred Loepfe, *Russische Märchen* (Olten: Verlag Otto Walter, 1941), p. 130.

stepsister's calls, but just kept running; but every time she wanted to pick the lily, it had vanished and stood a little farther away. Events continued like this for a long time, and the princess got farther and farther into the deep forest. But the lily always stood there and disappeared and moved further away, and every time it seemed larger and more beautiful than before. Eventually, the princess reached a high mountain. When she looked up to the summit, the flower was standing at the top of the bare rock, shining white and beautiful like the brightest star." When she reached the summit, the princess reached for the flower, plucked it, and fell into contemplation. When the sun had set, a little old man was standing next to her and offered his help if she obeyed him completely. She must light a large fire with the help of his lighter, bring a nearby cauldron full of tar to boiling point and, despite her reluctance, throw the lily into it, which she did with her face averted. At that moment, the muffled roar of a wild animal was heard from the forest, a howl and a crashing noise, and a large gray wolf ran straight toward the mountain. The frightened princess wanted to run away, but the old man said: "Hurry up, jump to the edge of the mountain and pour the cauldron over the wolf when he passes by." Almost senseless with fear, she obeyed, and "no sooner had she done as she had been told, the wolf changed, threw off its thick gray fur, and instead of the hideous wild beast there stood a handsome young man looking up at the mountain." It was her beloved, with whom she sat happily all night on the mountain.

34 When the new day broke, they saw a straight path to her father's castle ahead of them, but the old man stopped them from returning home and showed them how one could see everywhere from the mountain. As if in a play, the princess, prevented time and again by the man from intervening, saw how her father returned home from warfare, how her stepmother and her daughters pretended that she was dead,

how they are caught and convicted when the empty coffin was opened, and how everyone now set out to search for her. Then, at the little man's behest, she threw the wolf's skin down from the mountain to the stepmother and the daughters, who ran away howling, like werewolves, and rushed with her beloved to meet her father. When she wanted to thank the little man, he had disappeared, "and since that day no one knows who he was or where he is." But the princess went on to celebrate her wedding with her beloved.

35  As in "The White Cat,"[19] the stepmother is the old king's "false bride." Unlike the king in the Danube tale, this king, after losing his spirited, ensouled companion (i.e., queen), marries a scheming, treacherous woman. Although she, too, belongs to him, he succumbs to her power. The protagonist is the king's daughter. After her mother's death, she becomes his real soul-image. And yet, she reflects the fate of a woman who, as a result of her father's incorrect attitude, is forced to seriously consider the man's soul-image dominating her.

36  While, for instance, in "King Thrushbeard," the animus-figure (i.e., Thrushbeard) at first appears to be a difficult character, although for no apparent reason, here this trait is linked to the father-problem postulated there. The actual cause is the father's demonic and domineering psychic component, which is embodied in the stepmother. At the same time, however, we must also see the stepmother—like Aunt Bîbî in "The Moon on the Forehead" (Persia)—as the heroine's shadow-figure. Thus, she, too, is secretly governed by a pseudo-being; and the stepsister, who embodies this aspect in particular, even accompanies the heroine on her way into her inner being (forest). The need for redemption is thus portrayed as a generational curse. Behind the human figures, however, stand the father- and mother-archetypes, and thus the conflicts and also their resolution extend beyond ordinary human life. Behind the stepmother stands, as suggested, the image of the Great Mother in her terrible aspect. Behind the personal father, who has gone to fight

---

[19] Zaunert, *Märchen aus dem Donaulande* (1926), p. 37.

a war (i.e., engage in conflict!), and who thus appears as a passive and ensnared figure in terms of the plot, stands the father-archetype, which later even reveals its magical aspect by appearing as a little old man. The positive aspect of the Great Mother is hinted at by the helping old woman in the forest.

37     The path leading out of all these entanglements resembles an alchemical mystery of transformation. The individual symbols merit more detailed explanation. First, the heroine must try to pick the white lily that keeps eluding her. In popular belief, the lily symbolizes the pure soul.[20] Beyond that, however, it is, like flowers in general, a symbol of the self, an expression of the self in a state that has yet to become conscious. According to Martin Ninck, lilies also symbolize royal power and the transportation into the magical realm[21]; in sum, that is, the sense of calling created by encountering the self.

38     In the Grimm's "The Gold-Children,"[22] two lilies growing at home and originating in the same fish indicate the fate of the brothers who went out into the forest. The lilies are related to the brothers in *participation mystique* and represent, as it were, their vegetative souls. Similarly, in "The Twelve Brothers,"[23] lilies bear the brothers' fate. In popular belief, lilies blooming on a grave manifest the souls of the dead; in fairytales, however, they ordinarily return to life,[24] just as, in the present fairytale, the enchanted prince emerges from the lily. Thus, the lily represents not only the soul of the enchanted lover, which has remained pure, but also the center of the girl's psychic life. Here, they have become one.

39     The lily gradually abducts the girl up onto a mountain, where she remains standing and shines "like the brightest star." The ascent is an image of the laborious and gradual process of becoming conscious. In many cults, the deity reveals itself on mountain

---

[20] Hanns Bächtold-Stäubli, *Handwörterbuch des deutschen Aberglaubens*, ed. with the special assistance of E. Hoffmann-Krayer and numerous specialists, vols. I–VII (Berlin and Leipzig: W. de Gruyter & Co., 1927–1936); vols. VIII–X (Berlin, 1936–1942), under *Lilie* (lily).
[21] Martin Ninck, *Wodan und germanischer Schicksalsglaube* (Jena: Eugen Diederichs, 1935), pp. 196–197 and 287–288. Translator's note: Here "transportation" means entrallment and enrapturing (German *Entrückung*).
[22] *The Complete Grimm's Fairy Tales*, pp. 388–393.
[23] *Ibid.*, pp. 59–64.
[24] See Bächtold-Stäubli under *Lilie* (lily).

peaks.[25] Thus, scaling the mountain out of the dark forest represents the continuous struggle to attain a position above human embroilment.[26] The lily guides the heroine like a light. In mythological terms, it is often a symbol of light and fire.[27] In this fairytale, it acts as a guiding, sensemaking *lumen naturae* (light of nature): It stems from the unconscious and offers guidance. When the princess contemplates the luminous flower at her destination, we can see this beautiful image as a meditative turning to this psychic center as an "immersion" through which the self, preformed on a vegetative level, is enlivened.

40    Hence, the mysterious little man stands before her and draws her out of her absent-mindedness; in a certain sense, he should thus be understood as the plant's spirit, as a personification of the unconscious. Unlike the plant, this figure has a human voice and thus appears not only as a guiding light, but also as a counselor and as an interpreter of events. The little man, who, mythologically, belongs to mountain and leaden men according to medieval belief, is a psychopomp, as depicted especially in alchemical parables. Already the Greek philosopher Zosimos is advised in the alchemical mystery of transformation by a homunculus, who calls himself "the leaden man."[28]

41    Such figures are frequent in medieval literature. Lead is associated with the planet Saturn.[29] The ore or leaden man also fits the lily insofar as in alchemical symbolism it belongs to Saturn, who is considered the "lord of purification … from all that is heavy, dull, and laden; his mischief becomes the purifier (lily)."[30] On the other hand, the lily points to the alchemical *quinta essentia* through

---

[25] See Mount Sinai and Persian mountain cults.

[26] *The Complete Works of Meister Eckhart*, ed. and trans. Maurice O'C Walshe, rev. Bernard McGinn (New York: Crossroad Publishing, 2009), p. 46: "… that is a light above all lights: there the soul outgrows all light 'on the mountain's peak, where there is no light. Where God breaks forth into His Son, the soul is not caught up there. If we catch something of God when He is outflowing, the soul is not detained there: all is higher up, where she outgrows all light and all knowledge."

[27] Johann Jakob Bachofen, *Die Sage von Tanaquil: Eine Untersuchung über den Orientalismus in Rom und Italien* (Heidelberg: Mohr, 1870), p. 318.

[28] Jung, "The Visions of Zosimos," *CW* 13, § 86, III, V, 3.

[29] Herbert Silberer, *Probleme der Mystik und ihrer Symbolik* (Vienna and Leipzig: Hugo Heller & Co., 1914), pp. 77, 101.

[30] Gustav Friedrich Hartlaub, "Signa Hermetis. Zwei alte alchemistische Bilderhand-schriften," *Zeitschrift des deutschen Vereins für Kunstwissenschaft*, vol. 4 (Berlin, 1937), pp. 110–111.

the fivefold division of its flower. It was also equated with the realm of the blessed and with heavenly Jerusalem.[31] Thus, while the lily is an initial image of the process of awakening, it already contains the symbolism of the ultimate goal.

42     After a lofty goal (mountain, illumination) seems to have been reached in the present fairytale, only now does transformation begin, initially at its darkest level: The white lily, as an intuitive anticipation of the wholeness to be attained, must be sacrificed in a cauldron of boiling pitch. Alchemically speaking, pitch or tar symbolizes the stage of *nigredo* (blackness), of inner dissolution and decomposition, a state of melancholy and overpowering by dark psychic contents. The leaden demon relentlessly drives the heroine to advance ever further, beyond the attained level, to the actual reality of her psychic foundations. There, at the bottom of her soul, she must first recognize, as a reality within herself, all the darkness and all the evil that had previously only affected her from the outside in the guise of the evil stepmother. Thereby, however, the spirit in her soul, which in reality manifested as her beloved and as a flower was nothing but a ghost, is embodied and revived anew, so that it reappears, at least initially, as a wolf. Casting the lily into pitch thus symbolizes a first *coniunctio*, an immersion into the darkness of the womb (cauldron = mother's womb) and leads to rebirth.[32]

43     The king is generally regarded as a ruling figure, as a symbol of power, illumination, and life, and as the earthly parallel of the sun. In contrast, the wolf symbolizes a demon that is hostile to light (in Germanic myth, he devours the sun at the end of the world[33]), a destroyer, and a messenger of death. Thus, as a psychic image, he symbolizes the king's shadow. The wolf is the passion that exists behind ordinary human consciousness as a driving force; when this

---

[31] Hartlaub, "Signa Hermetis," p. 110; see also Silberer, *Probleme der Mystik*, p. 119.

[32] See the related ideas of alchemy in Silberer, *Probleme der Mystik*, pp. 81–82: "The red man and the white woman, also the red lion and the white lily, which are assigned many other names, are commingled and cooked in a vessel, the philosopher's egg. In the process, matter gradually turns black (and is called raven or raven's head), later white (swan); now subjected to stronger heat, the substance in the vessel sublimates (the swan flies up); with further heating, a vivid play of colors appears (peacock's tail or rainbow); finally, the substance turns red, bringing to conclusion the main *opus*. The red substance is the philosopher's stone (also called our king, red lion, great elixir, etc.)"—Trans.

[33] See Ninck, *Wodan*, pp. 53ff.

passion becomes predominant, it dissolves the personality and casts it into a state of obsession or fanatical zeal.

44     In terms of the man's psychic structure, the old king, who loses contact with life (after his wife's death) and adopts a negative attitude toward it (appearance of the "false bride"), might be said to become involved in a serious conflict (war); as a result, his future personality (prince) is also transformed into an animal of Mars (wolf) and expresses itself as greed and compulsion. Personified by the daughter, the positive psychic force, however, causes an inner mystical transformation, from which ensues the king's renewal (motif of succession). This fairytale can be interpreted in terms of both sexes and thus might be said to represent psychic processes that have symbolic meaning and hold true for both man and woman.

45     The disenchanting of the wolf, by pouring the contents of the cauldron over it, represents another stage of alchemical transformation, so-called *similia similibus* (i.e., darkness by darkness). Once more, this process is not simply destructive but represents a union of opposites: the lily's marriage with the wolf in the dark bath of renewal. Morally, the achievement leading to this nocturnal transformation lies in overcoming fear, which all natural persons initially experience when encountering the predators in their soul and their saturnine, havoc-wreaking shadow side. And yet, from this darkness comes a voice (the little man), which calls to action; that is, the unconscious is not merely a corrupter but also a helper, in particular amid the greatest distress.

46     After the heroine and her lover have overcome the nightly horror, they may once again remain on the human level, where they are no longer affected inside or outside by the principle of evil. What had previously appeared as an unclear involvement from outside, as persecution by the family, as a dark aberration in the forest, now dissolves. The rising sun is an image of this sudden illumination of consciousness, through which the law of life now becomes visible.

47     Symbolically, the straight path, which lies unexpectedly ahead of the couple, and on which it can return home, means that as a result of the higher consciousness attained in the conflict, "the paths

become level." In other words, the guidelines for outer action fall into place of their own accord. The little man, however, prevents the heroine from returning home immediately. He compels her, although she wishes to intervene, to witness the spectacle of the evil women unmasking themselves through their machinations. The little man advises the princess, who has overcome herself and found her inner center beyond the opposites, not to abandon her superior vantage point and descend to the moral level of the opposing powers, but instead to view the actions of the inimical women "from above" and to characterize and defeat their essence when the time comes by donning the werewolf's coat. In this way, she rejects, as it were, the projection of evil emanating from the women, which consequently falls back on the projectors. The stepmother had projected (literally: cast) her own wolfish nature onto the heroine's masculine soul-image; and because the king's daughter was temporarily fascinated by the evil woman, the bewitchment succeeded. Through the laborious path of development, however, the dross, which enables bewitchment, has fallen from the couple back onto the originator. The old father-king realizes that his present wife, symbolically his attitude toward the world, was to blame for the disappearance and the bewitchment of his true personality. The positive, conscious elements of the soul merge, as represented by the couple marrying when it returns home.

48 From this moment, the little man is no longer to be found. The fact that the magical helper disappears after the happy ending is a frequent motif. Thus, the two horses escape in "The Rose Girl" and in "The Boy and the Serpent,"[34] just as the wolf does in "Prince Hassan Pascha" (Turkestan, no. 4),[35] while in other variants this figure is redeemed (see the Grimm's "The Golden Bird").[36]

49 This motif therefore merits closer scrutiny. The Danube fairytale "The Little Red Man"[37] might help illumine the present fairytale: A knight, coldly rejected by a duke's daughter, avenges himself by

[34] Zaunert, *Märchen aus dem Donaulande* (Jena, 1926), pp. 269 and 288.
[35] See also "Lasse, My Servant!" (Sweden, no. 2).
[36] *The Complete Grimm's Fairy Tales*, pp. 272–279; see also "The Princess in the Tree" (Zaunert, *Deutsche Märchen seit Grimm*, p. 1).
[37] Zaunert, *Märchen aus dem Donaulande*, p. 10.

hiring on (unrecognized, of course) as a shepherd at her castle and by seducing her, so that she becomes pregnant. By playing the flute while herding the sheep, he befriends a little red man who has emerged from the ruins of an enchanted castle and who once stole sheep from other shepherds. The duke has since no longer slept badly (!). A tournament is announced: The winner is to marry the duke's daughter, since by God's judgment, he will transpire to be the child's father. The hero wins three times, riding a brown, a black, and a white horse and wearing magnificent armor, which the little red man has given him. Wounded in the third victory, he is recognized, and the duke gives him his daughter. A loud clamor ensues, "as if the whole world were about to collapse," and the bewitched castle is freed from the evil spell.

50    Many years ago, the old little man was a great king and as such he was quite proud. One day, a neighboring prince, the father of the duke, asked for the king's daughter, but was rejected by the king with scorn and derision. And so the young suitor enchanted the castle, which shall not be redeemed until a shepherd marries a prince's daughter. And so it happened and the minstrel became a great king. Yet whenever he entered the old castle, he did so affectionately and very timidly.

51  In this tale, the little red man is obviously the proud duke's *doppelgänger*. Like the heroine's father-king, he must also atone for being too arrogant. Significantly, the duke sleeps better as soon as the redeemer approaches the little red man. Apparently, the latter had tormented the duke at night and had stolen his sheep. Thus, he represents the duke's unconscious shadow brother. On the one hand, the color red indicates his underworldly, demonic character, while on the other it symbolizes suppressed emotions, which could not participate in life due to the vain supremacy of consciousness. If we apply this interpretation to the fairytale about the werewolf, then the little man would also be an unconscious *doppelgänger* of the king, who is away fighting a war. The image of war symbolizes an

intrapsychic conflict, through which the king, who represents the conscious personality, is paralyzed (he is absent).

52    The little man pointing the way to the redemptive act indicates that this concerns his own redemption. Hence, the impulse for transformation and the guidance received on the way stem from the unconscious, as we have seen repeatedly. For the same reason, it follows that the little man disappears when the king returns and is liberated from the influence of the "false bride." Why? Well, because, psychologically speaking, the discord between the king's conscious behavior and his unconscious is eliminated, in a process that parallels the union of opposites represented by the young couple. The reunification of the king and the little man represents, in a different way, the recovery of the sick king, which expresses the "healing" effect of the symbolically represented unconscious processes on consciousness.

53    Comparing the ending of this fairytale with that of "The Golden Bird"[38] shows that the fox prince, who must be redeemed, is a parallel figure to the little man and thus part of the old and sick father-king's soul that has been split off in the unconscious. Thus, he corresponds to the dominant of consciousness, which has become unconscious, from which the king's renewal proceeds and that points the way for the new personality (hero and anima). He is the shadow brother of both the old king and the hero, as well as of the anima and ultimately also of the anima's father, who is also suffering.[39] As such, he is the *mediator* between all psychic components and therefore represents inner unification. Given that he is both the old king's and the hero's *doppelgänger*, the hero is closely related to the old king. Once again, this justifies considering him an intrapsychic component belonging to the old father-king.

54    The same also applies to the hero in "The Maiden Tsar" (Russia, no. 41): We can now interpret the tearing asunder of the raven, and its rebirth through the water of life, not only as an experience

---

[38] *The Complete Grimm's Fairy Tales*, pp. 272–279.
[39] On other animal figures that must be redeemed, see "Ferdinand the Faithful and Ferdinand the Unfaithful" (*The Complete Grimm's Fairy Tales*, pp. 566–571) and "The Golden Castle That Hung in the Air" (Norway no. 35, Klara Stroebe [trans.], *Nordische Volksmärchen*, vol. 2, Norwegen, collected in *MdW*, ed. v. d. Leyen and Zaunert (Jena, 1922).

mirrored by the hero, as mentioned above, but also as a mirroring of the old tsar's later healing. The mortified raven also represents the archetype of the demonic father in "The Princess in the Tree" and in "The White Cat."[40] Ultimately, the question about the cause of suffering, and about the intrapsychic figures' need for transformation, leads to the conclusion that the demonic primordial spirit inherent in nature must be redeemed.

[55] One of the most interesting figures amid these highly diverse fairytale characters is the aforementioned mediator. Often functioning as a psychopomp, he emerges as a figure that must sometimes be interpreted as a shadow brother, or *doppelgänger*, of the father-king, who represents consciousness, sometimes as a mirror-image of the hero, who represents the new personality, sometimes as the animus, that is, the heroine's soul-image, and sometimes as an image of the chthonic god. In particular the latter aspect, which so far we have only managed to infer, will become clearer in what follows. This mysterious psychic phenomenon has been called the spirit Mercurius by most alchemists, and its phenomenology has been described in detail by Jung. Drawing on alchemy, Jung characterizes this figure as follows:

[56] Mercurius consists of all conceivable opposites. He is thus quite obviously a duality, but is named a unity in spite of the fact that his innumerable inner contradictions can dramatically fly apart into an equal number of disparate and apparently independent figures ... He is the process by which the lower and material is transformed into the higher and spiritual, and vice versa ... He is the devil, a redeeming psychopomp, an evasive trickster, and God's reflection in physical nature.[41]

[57] In one group of fairytales, this archetype appears as a so-called "animal prince." Psychologically, he is a symbol of the self and

---

[40] Zaunert, *Deutsche Märchen seit Grimm*, pp. 1 and 37.
[41] Jung, "The Spirit Mercurius," *CW* 13, § 284.

therefore dominates the unconscious of man *and* woman: in the former as a demonic-superior shadow figure, in the latter as the representative of the ghostly bridegroom.[42]

58 One tale in which this figure appears almost devoid of human features is "Hans the Hedgehog":

59 There was once a country man who had money and land in plenty, but however rich he was, his happiness was still lacking in one respect—he had no children. Often when he went into the town with the other peasants they mocked him and asked why he had no children. At last he became angry, and when he got home he said: "I will have a child, even if it be a hedgehog." Then his wife has a child that was a hedgehog in the upper part of his body and a boy in the lower, and when she saw the child, she was terrified, and said: "See, there you have brought ill-luck on us." Then the man said: "What can be done now? The boy must be christened, but we shall not be able to get a godfather for him." The woman said: "And we cannot call him anything else but Hans the Hedgehog."

60 When he was christened, the parson said: "He cannot go into any ordinary bed because of his spikes." So a little straw was put behind the stove ... His mother could not suckle him, for he would have pricked her with his quills. So he lay there behind the stove for eight years, and his father was tired of him and thought: "If he would but die!" He did not die, however.

61 Now it happened that there was a fair in the town, and the peasant was about to go to it, and asked his wife what he should bring back with him for her ... At last he also said: "And what will you have, Hans my Hedgehog?" "Dear father," he said, "do bring me bagpipes." ... When Hans the Hedgehog has the bagpipes, he said: "Dear father, do go to

---

[42] On animal marriages, see *Archetypal Symbols in Fairytales*, vol. 3 ("The Maiden's Quest"), pp. 4ff.

the forge and get the cock shod, and then I will ride away, and never come back again." At this, the father was delighted ... and had the cock shod for him, and when it was done, Hans the Hedgehog got on it, and rode away, but took swine and asses with him which he intended to keep in the forest. When they got there he made the cock fly onto a high tree with him, and sat there for many a long year, and watched his asses and swine until the herd was quite large, and his father knew nothing about him ... he played his bagpipes, and made music which was very beautiful. Once a King came traveling by who had lost his way and heard the music ... So Hans the Hedgehog descended from the tree, and said he would show the way if the King would write a bond and promise him whatever he first met in the royal courtyard as soon as he arrived at home. Then the King thought: "I can easily do that, Hans the Hedgehog understands nothing, and I can write what I want." ... when he had done it, Hans the Hedgehog showed him the way, and he got home safely. But his daughter ... was so overjoyed that she ran to meet him ... [He] told her what had happened ... but instead of writing that [Hans the Hedgehog] should have what he wanted, he had written that he should not have it. Thereupon the princess was glad ...

62 Hans the Hedgehog ... was always merry and sat on the tree and played his bagpipes. Now it came to pass that another King ... also had lost his way ... He likewise heard the music [and they exchanged the same words as before]. This King said: "Yes" ... [the beautiful daughter] was delighted to have her old father back again ... she promised that, for love of her father, she would willingly go with this Hans if he came.

63 Hans the Hedgehog ... took care of his pigs, and the pigs became more pigs until there were so many ... that the whole forest was filled with them. Then Hans the Hedgehog resolved not to live in the forest any longer, and sent word to his father ... for he was coming with such a great herd that all

might kill who wished to do so … and drove the pigs into the village, and ordered the slaughter to begin … After this Hans the Hedgehog said: "Father, let me have the cock shod once more at the forge, and then I will ride away and never come back as long as I live."—Hans the Hedgehog rode away to the first kingdom. There the King had commanded that whosoever came mounted on a cock and had bagpipes with him should be shot at, cut down, or stabbed … When, therefore, Hans the Hedgehog came riding thither, they all pressed forward … but he spurred the cock and it flew up over the gate in front of the King's window … and Hans cried that the King must give him what he had promised, or he would take both his life and his daughter's … So she dressed herself in white, and her father gave her a carriage with six horses and magnificient attendants together with gold and possessions. She seated herself in the carriage, and placed Hans the Hedgehog beside her with the cock and the bagpipes, and they took leave and drove away … when they were at a short distance from the town, Hans the Hedgehog took her pretty clothes off, and pierced her with his … spikes until she bled all over. "This is the reward of your falseness," said he … he chased her home again, and she was disgraced for the rest of her life. Hans the Hedgehog … rode to the dominions of the second King. But this one had arranged that if any one resembling Hans the Hedgehog should come, they were to present arms, give him safe conduct, … and lead him to the royal palace.

64 But when the King's daughter saw him she was terrified, for he really looked too strange … When the evening came and they wanted to go to sleep, she was afraid of his quills, but he told her she was not to fear, for no harm would befall her, and he told the old King that he was to appoint four men to watch by the door of the chamber, and light a great fire, and when he entered the room and was about to get into bed, he would creep out of his hedgehog's skin and leave it lying there

by the bedside, and that the men were to run nimbly to it, throw it in the fire, and stay by it until it was consumed ... When the fire had consumed it, he was saved, and lay there in bed in human form, but he was coal-black as if he had been burnt. The King sent for his physician who washed him with precious salves, and anointed him, and he became white, and was a handsome young man. When the King's daughter saw that she was glad, and the next morning ... the marriage was properly solemnized, and Hans the Hedgehog received the kingdom from the aged King.[43]

65 Like "The White Cat," this tale first only describes the man's fate, but then considers the female figure, who becomes the redeemer. Once again, psychic transformation takes place between man and woman, or between the masculine and the feminine soul-image as a distinct, self-existent psychic reality. This process focuses on Hans the Hedgehog, who represents the shared unconscious content. Corresponding to the hero-archetype, his birth is magical, because mythologically the hero comes from the otherworld. Psychologically, he emerges from the unconscious, through wishful thinking or rather, as the farmer's wife says, through "ill-luck" (i.e., a curse). The fact that the boy is not given a godfather because of his appearance implies that he is regarded as the child of a devil or ghost or as a changeling. He thus possesses the mercurial quality of a *filius macrocosmi*: He embodies the god-hero archetype, which has earthly-maternal and pagan traits.[44] He is conceived by the father's wishful thinking, by a curse.[45] This amounts to prophesizing an inevitable fate, where the one who curses knows the laws of magic, that is, of the unconscious. Growing up behind the stove in the straw, Hans the Hedgehog resembles Ivanko in "Ivan the Simpleton"

---

[43] Slightly abridged and adapted from *The Complete Grimm's Fairy Tales* (New York: Pantheon Books, 1944), pp. 497–502. See also the weaker parallel "The Hedgehog and the King's Daughters" (Lithuania, no. 24): Max Boehm and Franz Specht, eds., *Lettisch-litauische Volksmärchen*, collected in *MdW*, eds. v. d. Leyen and Zaunert (Jena, 1924).

[44] Jung, *Psychology and Alchemy*, CW 12, Introduction § 1–43.

[45] On the meaning of curses and blessings, see Gerardus van der Leeuw, *Phänomenologie der Religion: Neue theologische Grundrisse*, ed., R. Bultmann (Tübingen: Mohr & Siebeck, 1933), pp. 384ff.

(Russia, no. 8), who sat on (rather than behind) the stove.[46] Despite the reasons adduced in the present fairytale, Hans the Hedgehog thus spends a very long time with his mother.

66   Here, remaining unconscious or even being attached to the unconscious is expressed in particular by the half-animal form. The symbol of the hero, if considered to be part of a personality, coincides with the unconscious psychic function (see the discussion of the hero's journey in Volume 1). Its stage of development is archaic, and its nonhuman (not conscious) and emotional character is expressed in the hero's animal form. This suggests that in the instinctual sphere of the total personality an essential, yet still indistinct psychic tendency has arisen and begins to develop, without, however, reaching consciousness. The birth of Hans the Hedgehog therefore symbolizes the hidden emergence of a spiritual nucleus of the personality, which encompasses the man's higher spiritual essence, his self, and at the same time the spiritual component in the woman's soul; this intrapsychic process becomes destiny and is recognized by consciousness only much later.

67   The upper half of this tale's hero is a hedgehog. Zoologically, hedgehogs belong to the family of porcupines and thus of pigs in general; it is therefore no coincidence when Hans the Hedgehog becomes a swineherd.[47] He is a spirit-being from the realm of pigs. In primitive belief, he would belong to the pig totem. We should also understand the animal herds as a part of him. A famous parallel, "King Porco" (Italy, no. 24),[48] therefore describes the hero literally as a pig, which rummages through garbage, behaving as pigs do. (According to Hanns Bächtold-Stäubli under *Wildschwein*, wild boar, superstitions about "werewolves and berserkers ... are accompanied by ones about wild boars").[49] Two princesses, both

---

[46] Afanas'ev, *Russian Fairy Tales*, pp. 142–145.

[47] See also Johannes Bolte and Georg Polívka, *Anmerkungen zu den Kinder- u. Hausmärchen der Brüder Grimm*, vol. 2 (Leipzig: Dieterich'sche Verlagsbuchhandlung, 1915), p. 483.

[48] Walter Keller, trans., *Italienische Märchen*, collected in *MdW*, ed. v. d. Leyen (Jena, 1929).

[49] Dölger points out that in antiquity pigs were said to have a chthonic character; see his *"Ichthys": Der Heilige Fisch, in den antiken Religionen und im Christentum*, vol. 2 (Münster: Verlag der Aschendorff-schen Verlagsbuchhandlung, 1922), p. 370. In *Die Thiere in der indogermanischen Mythologie*, trans. M. Hartmann (Leipzig: Grunow, 1874), De Gubernatis discusses the dæmonic character of the wild boar (pp. 341–345). Bächtold-Stäubli's comprehensive summary reveals that in India the wild boar is an incarnation of Vishnu and Rudra, in Egypt of Seth, and in Persia of Behram (corresponding to the

"profane brides," are killed by him, while the third, a devoted woman, redeems him. A group of parallel tales describes the same animal prince as a donkey, just as Hans the Hedgehog herds both pigs and asses. These tales include "The Donkey," which, as Johannes Bolte and Georg Polívka note, seems to go back to "Asinarius," a medieval Latin poem from either France or the Netherlands.[50]

68

The pig, which in the East symbolizes sensual pleasure, in the ancient Western world symbolized fertility, as the animal of the mother-goddess Demeter. In Egyptian mythology, the evil Seth, among others, transforms into a black pig to harm the sun-god Horus.[51] These traits, together with those of donkey symbolism, place the animal prince in a bleak, swamplike maternal realm.[52] The hedgehog differs from the pig insofar as it is a nocturnal animal and therefore is associated less with the notion of dirt; it is, after all, also considered unchaste in popular superstition and a witch's animal, and therefore was burned alive[53] (just like the hedgehog's skin in our present tale). Unapproachable due to its quills, it symbolizes a highly sensitive and therefore aggressive person. As the psychically vulnerable often hurt others, Hans the Hedgehog, being attached to the unconscious, makes himself inaccessible to the harsh outer world. It is also significant that in the parallel tales ("King Porco" and "The Donkey"), the disenchanted youth is ashamed of his

---

Roman Mars). "Among the Siamese, a boar-shaped giant kills the sun," just as luminous heroes fight the boar in the Greek sagas (Heracles, Meleager, Theseus). The Athenians swore "by the gods of Orkus and took the oath on the skin of a boar." Bächtold-Stäubli also discusses the relationship between the boar and the *magna mater*, as well as with demons that appear as boars (e.g., the devil).

[50] *The Complete Grimm's Fairy Tales*, pp. 632–635. See Bolte and Polívka, *Anmerkungen*, vol. 3, pp. 154–165, where this poem is reproduced in full. See also "Donkey Cabbages" (*The Complete Grimm's Fairy Tales*, pp. 551–558). In world literature, Apuleius's *The Golden Ass* is worth mentioning in this regard. See also Hermann Hamann, "Die literarischen Vorlagen der Kinder- und Hausmärchen und ihre Bearbeitung durch die Brüder Grimm," *Palaestra XLVII, Untersuchungen und Texte aus der deutschen und englischen Philologie*, vol. 47, eds., Alois Brandl, Gustav Roethe, and Erich Schmidt (Berlin: Mayer & Müller, 1906), p. 45; Johannes Bolte and Lutz Mackensen, *Handwörterbuch des deutschen Märchens*, vols. 1–2 (Berlin and Leipzig: W. de Gruyter & Co., 1930/1934), esp. under *Esel* (ass, donkey) and *Eselmensch* (human-donkey).

[51] Günther Roeder, "Urkunden zur Religion des alten Ägypten," *Religiöse Stimmen der Völker*, ed. Walter Otto (Jena: Eugen Diederichs, 1923), p. 271. See also the boar as the god of storms in Bächtold-Stäubli under *Schwein* (pig), who notes that in Bavaria whirlwinds are believed to be pigs because they are incited by devils and witches. Pigs are called *Sauwedel, -zagel, -kegel, -arsch, -dreck, Windsau*. Often, they are dead people who find no rest in their grave; or revenants; or "cursed" souls who were turned into pigs as a means of punishment; or murdered or guilt-ridden folk; or who had committed suicide; some were even believed to be "unnatural sons."

[52] On donkey symbolism, see *Archetypal Symbolism in Fairytales*, vol 2., p. 260f.

[53] See Bächtold-Staubli under *Igel* (hedgehog).

humanity and wishes to escape, yet without giving any reason. His humanity is so delicate and vulnerable that it fears the world. The upper half of Hans the Hedgehog is that of a hedgehog, which suggests that his body does not belong to the animal world. Instead, he wears a face mask, which also makes sense considering his sensitive nature. Unwelcome in his family, and not adapted to ordinary human life, the hero becomes unapproachable, a child of the night. And yet, his parents call him Hans *my* hedgehog; they cannot deny that he belongs to them.

69    Hans the Hedgehog becomes a magnificent bagpiper. In the parallel tale "The Donkey," he even becomes a famous lute player and thus is invited to the royal court. In "The Devil's Flute" (Russia, no. 47), the hero owns a flute. Given to him by the devil, the instrument makes everyone dance and means the hero is acknowledged by the tsar's court. As an expression of feeling, music comes easily to the "stupid," to those who do not think profanely. To the father, who is a peasant or later a king, Hans the Hedgehog therefore embodies the shadow personality; to the princess, he is an animus-figure, which fits into the group of music-making animus-figures like King Thrushbeard in the eponymous fairytale.[54]

70    Hans the Hedgehog rides a rooster, which he has shod, and which probably merely serves to underline his capricious nature. We have discussed the rooster as a sun-animal, as a guardian of the hereafter, as a shadow representative, and as an admonisher of conscience elsewhere.[55] The rooster, however, is not merely related to the gods of the realm of the dead. As a sacred symbol, he also belongs to Hermes, who accompanies the souls of the dead into the underworld. Hermes has even been portrayed as a human-headed rooster.[56] This is significant insofar as the alchemical spirit Mercurius can be traced to Hermes and also because Hans the Hedgehog, the mighty animal prince to be redeemed from his entanglement in

[54] *The Complete Grimm's Fairy Tales*, pp. 244–248.
[55] See *Archetypal Symbolism in Fairytales*, vol. 1, p. 353, and vol. 3, p. 191.
[56] Dölger, "Ichthys," vol. 2, pp. 406 and 430–431; see also Georg Weicker, *Der Seelenvogel. In der alten Literatur und Kunst. Eine mythologisch-archäologische Untersuchung* (Leipzig: Teubner, 1902), pp. 35 and 156.

matter, is a parallel fairytale figure.[57] Thus, the rooster's attributes underscore the hero's mercurial nature in this fairytale, in particular as we can easily imagine the "admonisher of conscience" as a guide of souls, as the "guardian of the hereafter" who points the way. Hans the Hedgehog riding the rooster strikes profane consciousness as ridiculous. However, this aspect is sometimes part of the sublime nature of the unconscious, as well as of its pagan nature and its meaning, which reaches into both subhuman and superhuman worlds.[58] Endowed with these characteristics, Hans the Hedgehog points a king who has lost his way in the right direction. At first unseen, and only manifesting himself through magical music (i.e., feelings), he appears to the king as his inner self, which the latter, however, still fails to recognize due to Hans's grotesque appearance.

71    The fairytale about Hans the Hedgehog describes various facets of consciousness. Its first representative is the peasant, who embodies a profane conscious attitude. In contrast, the symbol of the king represents the dominant of consciousness, which is also profane to begin with. The second king, however, symbolizes that dominant of consciousness that, despite some difficulties, can now acknowledge the new content—Hans the Hedgehog—as superior. Accordingly, the second king is also the only form of consciousness that is not stripped away as the plot unfolds, but which passes over into the new personality. We can also see the path from the peasant

---

[57] On the nature of Hans the Hedgehog, see also *Archetypal Symbolism in Fairytales*, vol. 5 (forthcoming).

[58] See "The Snail Man," the charming Japanese parallel collected in Fritz Rumpf, *Japanische Volksmärchen*, ed. v. d. Leyen (Jena: 1938), p. 157, which mocks the animal prince's smallness. The fairytale is poetic and worth reading, yet does not further elucidate matters. On the hedgehog riding a rooster, see Bolte and Polívka, *Anmerkungen*, vol. 2, p. 483: "The hedgehog riding the rooster and playing the bagpipes recalls the popular amusing images of the rooster rider ... and of the finch riding the goose... It also recurs in Slavic and Lithuanian versions"; see also p. 484: "Taking a large hedgehog, or perhaps even our fairytale, as its starting point, a fifteenth- or sixteenth-century satirical song depicts a duel between a hedgehog and a linen weaver ...:

> The hedgehog was an angry man,
> He put on two bright spurs...
> He was not idle for long,
> The swords began sounding,
> The linen weaver wanted to stoop,
> And had to proffer himself before the hedgehog:
> "Oh dear hedgehog, let me live,
> I will give you my sister,
> My sister Grete."

to the second king (one parallel has three kings[59]) as a gradual transformation of consciousness.

72      The development of Hans the Hedgehog parallels this implied transformation while being its actual cause. First, he undergoes an incubation period in the forest, as it were, during which his swineherd multiplies immeasurably. The profane world was hostile toward him, because he embodies an unconscious, irrational content. Thus, displacement makes him stronger and subsequently enables him to enter the sphere of consciousness. When Hans the Hedgehog drives the pigs toward his father, and thus gives them away, he demonstrates, contrary to widespread belief, his usefulness to the profane world; at the same time, these events signify that he has overcome being a shepherd in the animal world.

73      While the first stage symbolizes the confrontation between the animal prince—the nucleus of the soul—and the profane-human sphere (peasanthood), there now follows the struggle for royal inheritance. In other words, the tendency dominating consciousness thus far needs to be modified or even replaced. Consciousness defends itself with its own means in association with the "false bride," who symbolizes an attitude that rejects what really matters. She prevents any connection with the self: Her calculating nature, aimed solely at benefitting herself, is repelled by the "spikiness" (i.e., inaccessibility) of the nucleus of the soul.

74      This disruption on the path of development does not discourage Hans the Hedgehog. In the second kingdom, he finds a female figure who is willing to accept him despite his ugliness for the sake of her "old father." In terms of the man's psyche, here a conscious attitude (royal court) is described in which the soul is actively involved, so that a willingness exists to accept new unconscious contents, which initially cause suffering. If, however, the princess is understood as a real female figure, then the same situation arises as in "King Thrushbeard": At her father's behest, she takes in the despised suitor; and because she is attached to her father, she accepts the confrontation with the man's soul-image as her task. (In another

---

[59] See Bolte and Polívka, *Anmerkungen*, vol. 2, p. 483.

fairytale about an animal prince, the heroine commands the man-eating snake prince to "Rise and devour me!"; she later redeems him through her acceptance and devotion[60]).

75     In "Hans the Hedgehog," the animal prince is transformed by *four* men, who burn his animal skin at his request. This motif expresses the idea that the self realizes itself in a human being only if all four elements of consciousness or if all four psychic functions actively participate in the process of becoming conscious. Human beings must, however, activate their conscious functions and devote their soul to this task; everything else is left to the demon at work in the unconscious. The self thus frees itself, enlisting the human being as its servant, from the shrouds of animal unconsciousness and becomes recognizable as what it has always been: the eternal image of the human being.

76     The animal clothing is burned. Closely related to this motif in the present fairytale is the burning of the skull in "The Maiden and the Skull" (Siberia, no. 36).[61] As in that tale, here it probably also means the transformation in the fire of passion, which explains why fire is transformed in the bridal night. Fire not only burns but also enlightens. Thus, setting oneself on fire, as the myths of Phoenix and Heracles show, leads to immortality. Fire purifies from all corruptible substance and transforms the burned into a spirit-being, which is no longer subject to physical decay. In this tale, the corruptible is symbolized by the animal skin, which represents the material nature of humankind that prevents it from realizing its spiritual essence.

77     Although only the animal skin is supposedly thrown into the fire, the animal prince is also completely burned. The animal skin was more than simply a covering or mask: It was an essential part of the animal prince and remained, even when removed, connected to him

---

[60] See Bolte and Polívka, *Anmerkungen*, vol. 2, p. 240 for the Armenian variant of "The Singing, Soaring Lark." According to Bolte and Polívka, *ibid.*, p. 31, this tale is a counterpart to "The Three Feathers" (*The Complete Grimm's Fairy Tales*, pp. 319–322), as mentioned in *Archetypal Symbols in Fairytales*, vol. 1, p. 414; in that tale, the hero is redeemed by heeding the anima's call: "Embrace me and immerse your-self."

[61] Hugo Kunike, ed., *Märchen aus Sibirien*, collected in *MdW*, ed. v. d. Leyen (Jena: 1940). See also "A Head" (Finland, no. 39) where the parallel figure to Hans the Hedgehog is nothing other than a head.

by *participation mystique*. In fact, it is Hans the Hedgehog who was burned and who emerges from the ashes as a new, real human being freed from his shadow aspect. We find the same idea in the myth of Phoenix, the bird that sets fire to itself and rises anew from the ashes. This myth is a parable of the image of God in the human soul, which, when a human being is on the path to themselves, is transformed in the fire of the inner struggle.

The old king instructs his physician to anoint and embalm Hans the Hedgehog until he has turned white. Now "a handsome young man," he becomes the ruler of the kingdom: Consciousness endeavors to help the new dominant, which has appeared almost fatefully from the unconscious, to attain full splendor. It subsequently steps back from the intrapsychic transformation—figuratively from its exponent—that has occurred.

The heart of the plot, the burning of the animal skin, features prominently in "The Young Wolf," a tale from the Danube region:

A poor weaver could not find a godmother for his twelfth child, and a rich merchant's wife, whom he finally asked, scornfully rejected him: "Your wife will give birth to a wolf, and it will feed itself." But the weaver returned her curse and exclaimed: "Let it come back to thee, because thou mockest the poor so." The weaver's wife gave birth to a normal girl, but the merchant's wife gave birth to a young wolf who hid under her bed for seven years and behind the stove for seven. When this time had lapsed, he became ever grimmer, demanding that he be married off, but his parents were rejected everywhere. Eventually, the merchant's wife went to pray at the church and dreamed that the first woman her servants encountered would be her son's proper bride. This turned out to be the weaver's twelfth child, who responded to the pleas of the merchant's wife and the weaver's wooing. She asked the parson for advice, and he said: "She should put on nine gowns and light nine candles in the room where the wolf is behind the stove and pray nine rosaries; but after each rosary she should take off one gown and extinguish one candle. After the last rosary, however, the fire will be extinguished and something will fall through the door. She should take this object, throw it into the piping hot oven, and look behind the oven. The girl followed the parson's instructions. She put on nine gowns, heated the oven so that the tiles glowed, and lit nine candles. Thereafter, she began to pray, and after each rosary she took off a gown, until after the last rosary she stood there in nothing but her undershirt; when she extinguished the ninth candle, there was a loud crash, as if the whole house were about to collapse, and something heavy fell against the door. Quickly she tore open the door, grabbed the whimpering bundle from the doorstep into her shirt without looking at what it was, and shoved it into the stove. Then she looked at the wolf, and behind the stove sat a beautiful youth. He joyfully thanked his savior, and when he had also shown himself to his parents, he celebrated a great, happy wedding feast with the youngest weaver's daughter."[62]

As in "The White Cat,"[63] the guilt that necessitates redemption must also be sought in the previous generation: With the merchant's wife, it is arrogance; with the weaver, it is vindictiveness. Thus, the children are forced to compensate for their parents' misconduct. Both impressively and meaningfully, those for whose sake guilt was incurred are brought together by a dream (that of the merchant's wife), that is, by the unconscious. In folklore, the tale about the young wolf belongs to the many werewolf stories that have been handed down in particular from the Germanic regions. For the meaning of the berserker and the werewolf, please refer to the seminal and comprehensive accounts in Wilhelm Hertz's *Der Werwolf*[64] and Martin Ninck's *Wodan*. The first volume of our own study [*Archetypal Symbols in Fairytales*] has explained this phenomenon on various occasions as the state of being possessed.

81

---

[62] Zaunert, *Märchen aus dem Donaulande*, p. 1.—Trans.
[63] *Ibid.*, p. 37.
[64] Wilhelm Hertz, *Der Werwolf. Beitrag zur Sagengeschichte* (Stuttgart: Kröner, 1862).

In the present case, the connection between animal skin, covering, caul,[65] and placenta with werewolves and berserkers is also important. As Ninck observes:

82

> Thus transformation is one of several older forms of going berserk. The other expression for "going berserk" is *skipta homum*, literally "changing form," or *hamast*, "changing one's covering." *Ham-ramr* means both "able to change form" and "possessed by a berserk-like rage." *Ham-far* and *ham-hleypa* mean *Gestaltfahrt*, *Gestaltlauf* (the jumping or movement of shapes) or, more precisely, "the capacity to leave one's body transformed," while *ham-fong* denotes *Gestaltfang* (the arresting or catching of shapes), obsessive rage, form-changing frenzy." *Hamr* means "skin, shadow, shape, guardian spirit," while *hamingja*, the feminine derivative, means "guardian spirit, luck." *Hamo*, the corresponding Old High German word, means "skin, covering, clothing" and has survived as *Hemd*, "shirt" ... Middle High German *ham* and *hamel*, English *heam*, signifies "afterbirth (placenta)," Wallonian *ham* is "caul, uterus skin," in which darlings of fortune are born, and which was carefully preserved or buried, because it was regarded as the child's guardian spirit (see Icelandic *fylgja*, "afterbirth (placenta)," originally "protective spirit").[66]

Commenting on the semantic development of these expressions, Ninck points to the widespread idea of a person's image or shadow leaving them while they are asleep or in a frenzy, and that person changing shape as a result. He also mentions an Icelandic custom, according to which the originally sacred placenta was burned or else the child would be plagued by an evil, ghostly being.[67]

83

In our present tale, the werewolf is also tormented by such a

---

[65] Translator's note: Caul is the large fatty membrane covering the intestines (as of a cow, sheep, or pig).
[66] Ninck, *Wodan*, p. 43—Trans. See also p. 280 and esp. pp. 48–49: "Belief in berserkers considers predators (i.e., bears and wolves) to be more important. The word *berserkr* has been interpreted as 'bear skin' ( < *beri*, 'bear,' preserved in the ancient feminine form *bera*, and *serkr*, 'shirt'). This corresponds to the expression *úlfhepnar*, 'wolf fur or pelt' ..."—Trans.
[67] See Ninck, *Wodan*, p. 44, fn. 1; see further Bolte and Polívka, *Anmerkungen*, pp. 288ff.

84 shadow demon, which has grown on him as a wolf's skin; consistent with psychological experience, that the tormented torment others, he threatens his surroundings. In the transformation scene, he is obviously a deplorable, whimpering bundle, which is tossed into the oven (note that in the eponymous fairytale, the redeemed Hans the Hedgehog has burn marks, although apparently only his skin was burned). Thus, he would have been born as a *human being* only now, freed from his berserker's clothing by fire or reborn from the oven. The fact that it is unclear that the werewolf, detached from his animal skin, nevertheless seems to form a unity with it, makes sense insofar as the berserker's clothing corresponds to the shadow or alter ego and also because the obsessed are to some extent identical with their shadow.

85 Presumably, this duality will puzzle the profane observer. The fact that animal skin is a symbolic form of the shadow is illustrated by the Grimm's "Bearskin," whose hero wears his mask as commanded by the devil. A mythological relation also exists to the motif or theme of golden hair (i.e., goldilocks): According to several versions, the hero hides his golden hair by covering his head with animal skin to feign baldness or scabbiness.[68] Once again, this indicates that the future dominant of the personality first approaches the sphere of consciousness as a shadow-figure. This is the case because, to reach its goal, the mystery of renewal emerging from the depths of the unconscious makes use of the undeveloped, irrational psychic function, whose behavior is archaic and inferior to rational consciousness and therefore initially unacceptable, although it alone contains the germ of development.

86 In the present fairytale, purification by fire separates the shadow aspect (the animal clothing) from the actual personality, which corresponds to becoming conscious. The shadow (i.e., the wolf's skin) stems from the curse of the merchant's wife, a mother-figure (just as it does from the stepmother in "The Werewolf"; Sweden, no. 11). In male initiation rites in primitive societies, initiates are

---

[68] See, e.g., "The Witch and the Golden-Haired Prince" (Turkestan, no. 6) and "The Black Filly" (Christensen, *Iran*, Jena 1939, p. 77).

sometimes wrapped in animal furs, casting them back, as Richard Thurnwald suggests, to a kind of embryonic stage. After consecration, the initiate's father characteristically says: "My son, you have now left the mother's vesture."[69] Thus, the animal skin also signifies the hero's infantile attachment to the indistinguishable, unconscious primordial ground of the prenatal world, from which he must detach himself as an individual. In "An Underworld Journey" (Siberia, no. 77), a hunter who has been transformed into an animal once again becomes a human being by throwing himself, in a dream and at a god's advice, from a pine tree. He breaks into two parts and awakens as a human being. His animal skin lies next to him. Here, conscious realization happens by means of shock, whereas in the burning motif, it follows an emotional outburst. Only the greatest convulsion seems to make higher consciousness attainable for the human being.

87    A famous fairytale where redemption is caused by shock is the Grimm's "The Frog-King, or Iron Henry"[70]:

88    … there lived a king whose daughters were all beautiful … the youngest … went out into the forest and sat down by the side of the cool fountain; … when she was bored she took a golden ball, and threw it up on high and caught it …

89    on one occasion the princess's golden ball did not fall into the little hand … but rolled straight into the water … she began to cry … and as she thus lamented, someone said to her: "What ails you, King's daughter?" … She looked round to the side from whence the voice came, and saw a frog stretching forth its big, ugly head from the water. "Ah! Old water-splasher, is it you?" …

The frog answered: "I do not care for your clothes, your pearls

---

[69] Richard Thurnwald, "Primitive Initiations- und Wiedergeburtsriten," *Eranos-Jahrbuch 1939: Die Symbolik der Wiedergeburt in der religiösen Vorstellung der Zeiten und Völker*, ed. Olga Fröbe-Kapteyn (Zurich: Rhein-Verlag, 1940), p. 391; see also pp. 333 and 341, fn. 2.
[70] *The Complete Grimm's Fairy Tales*, pp. 17–20. Two parallel versions are "Ode und de Slang" (Zaunert, *Deutsche Märchen seit Grimm*, p. 113) and "The Little White Dog" (Latvia, no. 16).

90 and jewels …; but if you will love me and let me be your companion and play-fellow, and sit by you at your little table, and eat off your little golden plate, and drink out of your little cup, and sleep in your little bed—if you promise me this I will go down below, and bring you your golden ball up again."

91 "Oh, yes," said she, "I promise you all you wish, if you will but bring me my ball back again." But she thought: "How the silly frog does talk! All he does is to sit in the water with the other frogs, and croak! He can be no companion to any human being!"

92 But the frog when he had received his promise, put his head into the water and sank down, and in a short while came swimming up again with the ball in his mouth … The King's daughter was delighted to see her pretty plaything once more, and picked it up, and ran away with it … She did not listen to [the frog] and soon forgot the poor frog.

93 The next day when she had seated herself at the table with the King and all the courtiers …, something came creeping splish splash … up the marble staircase … knocked at the door and cried: "Princess, youngest princess, open the door for me" … she opened the door, there sat the frog … she slammed the door to … sat down to dinner again, and was quite frightened.

94 [The King asked his daughter]: "What does the frog want with you?" … In the meantime it knocked a second time, and cried:

95
"Princess! Youngest princess!
Open the door for me!
Do you not know what you said to me
Yesterday by the cool waters of the well?
Princess! Youngest princess!
Open the door for me!"

96 Then said the King: "That which you have promised must you perform. Go and let him in." She went and opened the door, and the frog hopped in and followed her, step by step, to her chair. There he sat and cried: "Lift me up beside you." She delayed, until ... the King commanded her to do it. Once the frog was on the chair he wanted to be on the table, and when he was on the table he said: "Now, push your little golden plate nearer to me ..." She did this, but it was easy to see that she did not do it willingly ... At length he said: "... carry me into your little room and make your little silken bed ready, and we will both lie down and go to sleep."

97 The King's daughter began to cry, for she was afraid of the cold frog ... But the King grew angry and said: "He who helped you when you were in trouble ought not afterwards to be despised by you." She took hold of the frog with two fingers, carried him upstairs, and put him in a corner. But when she was in bed he crept to her and said: "I am tired, I want to sleep as well as you, lift me up or I will tell your father." At this she was terribly angry, and took him up and threw him with all her might against the wall. "Now you will be quiet, odious frog," said she. But when he fell down he was no frog but a king's son with kind and beautiful eyes. He by her father's will was now her dear companion and husband. Then he told her how he had been bewitched by a wicked witch, and how no one could have delivered him from the well but herself, and that tomorrow they would go together into his kingdom. Then they went to sleep, and next morning when the sun awoke them, a carriage came driving up with eight white horses, which had white ostrich feathers on their heads, and were harnessed with golden chains, and behind stood the young King's servant, faithful Henry ... The carriage was to conduct the young King [and the princess] into his kingdom ... when they had driven a part of the way, the King's son heard a cracking behind him as if something had broken. So he turned round and cried: "Henry, the carriage is breaking."

98  "No, master, it is not the carriage. It is a band from my heart, which was put there in my great pain when you were a frog and imprisoned in the well."

99  Again and once again … something cracked … it was only the bands which were springing from the heart of faithful Henry because his master was set free.[71]

100  We can interpret the heroine of this fairytale in two ways: either as the soul-image that faces prevailing consciousness (represented by the royal father; this interpretation is supported by the fact that in older versions she is the youngest of three daughters, and thus the fourth within the royal group[72]); or as an independent female personality (just like the heroines of most of the fairytales considered in this section). In this case, her sisters would be shadow-figures and her father the first image of the animus. Both interpretations are equally feasible because central to the plot is a problem that is common to man and woman: the confrontation with the nucleus of the soul that has been transfixed into animal form.

101  The ball or golden ball with which the heroine plays on the edge of the fountain at the beginning of the tale is, as explained previously, an image of the self.[73] In the ancient world, the ball or spherical object was considered not only an image of the individual soul, but also of the world-soul (*anima mundi*), and thus in part also an image of the godhead.[74] As Bachofen has emphasized, the role of the *sphaira*, "the image of the universe conceived in the perfect form of

---

[71] Abridged and slightly adapted from *The Complete Grimm's Fairy Tales* (New York: Pantheon Books, 1944), pp. 17–20. Compare the Grimm's final version of this fairytale with the stylistically and, in terms of the following interpretation, more expressive older version collected in Panzer's *Die Kinder- und Hausmärchen in ihrer Urgestalt* (Munich: Beck, 1913), pp. 14ff.; see also his Preface, p. XLIVff.

[72] Albert Wesselski, "Versuch einer Theorie des Märchens," *Prager Deutsche Studien*, No. 45, eds. E. Gierach and H. Cysarz (Reichenberg i. B.: Sudetendeutscher Verlag Franz Kraus, 1931), pp. 116–117. In the Grimm's version, the older sisters are also mentioned, yet are meaningless.

[73] On the spherical shape of the soul, see Marcus Aurelius, *Selbstbetrachtungen*, trans. Wilhelm Capelle (Leipzig: Alfred Kröner Verlag, 1933), Book XI, Aphorism 12: "The spherical soul gives itself its shape when it neither extends outward to anything nor shrinks inward and neither rises nor contracts, yet is illumined by the light through which it recognizes the truth of all things and those within itself." See also Book VIII, Aphorism 41: "... Nothing can obstruct the powers peculiar to the spirit. For neither fire nor iron, neither the tyrant's wrath nor blasphemy nor anything else touches it when it is 'clenched into a circular sphere'"—Trans. See also "The Crystal Ball" (*The Complete Grimm's Fairy Tales*, pp. 798–801).

[74] Jung, *Psychologie und Alchemie*, CW 12, § 108 f. and fn. 41, § 433.

a ball," as a Bacchic mystery symbol, and as a plaything for Zeus, Dionysus, and Aphrodite, is probably also based on this meaning.[75] As Jung points out, psychologically such a geometric structure symbolizes that part of the self that is removed from consciousness.[76] In the present fairytale, the sphere is made of gold, assigning this symbol the highest value.

102   It is more common for two or more people to play with a ball than for one person to do so alone. In this case, the symbol of the ball as the self expresses the idea that this does not merely belong to the isolated individual, but that several people are involved, so that it essentially signifies relationship and appears as such. The ball flying from one person to another symbolizes the mystical relationship within a transpersonal wholeness. We should also consider this meaning in the present fairytale, as the ball initiates the relationship to the animal prince.[77] Relationship is thus willed, and also conditioned, by the self. We also need to consider another aspect of the ball: Like the wheel, it moves by itself; it rolls away from itself of its own accord, symbolizing psychic activity that is independent of consciousness, as is the case with the self.[78]

103   When the girl plays with the ball somewhat self-indulgently, but lets it slip away carelessly, this suggests that the relation to the self (still represented as an inorganic entity completely separated from consciousness) is playful, irresponsible; the princess's attitude also makes her not keep her promise to the frog. Incidentally, Sanskrit *las, lásati* (to play) is related to *láshati* (to desire) and to Greek

---

[75] Johann Jakob Bachofen, *Die Unsterblichkeitslehre der orphischen Theologie auf den Grabdenkmälern des Alterthums. Nach Anleitung einer Vase aus Canosa im Besitz des Herrn Prosper Biardot in Paris*, illustrated by Dr. J. J. Bachofen with a plate reprinted in color (Basel: Felix Schneider's Buchhandlung, 1867), pp. 15–16.

[76] Jung, "The Psychological Aspects of Koré," *CW* 9/I, § 315.

[77] The same image occurs, albeit with a negative meaning, in a ballad cited by Lincke in "Das Stiefmuttermotiv im Märchen der germanischen Völker," *German. Studien*, no. 142, ed. E. Ebering (Berlin: Verlag Dr. Emil Ebering, 1933), p. 108ff. In that version, a young boy's ball falls into a maiden's chamber, and from there into her lap. She curses the youth, saying that he may never sleep nor rest until he has freed a maiden being held captive in a foreign land.

[78] Jung, *Nietzsche's Zarathustra, Notes of the Seminar Given in 1934–1939*, ed. James L. Jarrett, vol. 2 (Princeton NJ: Princeton University Press, 1988), pp. 783f. See also the many wayward balls or spheres in fairytales, e.g., "The Princess with the Twelve Pairs of Golden Shoes" (Denmark, no. 18), "The Golden Castle That Hung in the Air" (Norway, no. 35), "The Bird that Says Everything" (France, vol. 2, no. 21), and "The Seven Brothers" (France, vol. 2, no. 58).

*lastauros* (lustful) and to New High German *Lust*.[79] The etymological connection is even more significant when considered in terms of the events in this fairytale: because, as mentioned, in antiquity, young Eros played with a ball; if, however, he threw a ball to someone else, this meant not only a summons to love, but also to death—to immortality,[80] the deepest mystery containing both states.

104    In the older version cited by Panzer,[81] the scene about losing the ball begins as follows: "On one occasion, the ball soared very high." Throwing the ball implied devotion, stepping out of oneself at the risk of losing oneself to the unknown, a surging of greater determination. In such moments, the unconscious takes effect, at first, however, by assaulting the sphere of consciousness. The ball rolling away implies a "loss of soul," as is described vividly in "The Woman Who Wanted Something for Her Button" (Iceland, no. 28). The present version of the motif resembles that in "Childe Rowland,"[82] where a girl runs after a lost ball and falls into the world of fairies—that is, into the clutches of the unconscious. Thus, in the Grimm's tale, playing with the ball also leads to encountering another world: All of a sudden, playing on one's own becomes a game for two, in which the image and its function are transformed; the ball, thus far the only aspect of the self, slips away into an unattainable psychic layer and thereby establishes the connection with what is no longer merely a geometrical embodiment of the soul-image but a living one: the frog prince.

105    The frog's strange appearance and way of life have always exercised the human imagination. Franz Lukas suggests that the frog was born directly from the earth and emerged as one of the first creatures from primeval, chaotic mud.[83] Mythologically, the frog has not always been harmless. In Iranian mythology, it is considered the

---

[79] Jung, "The Transformation of Libido," *CW* 5, § 234.

[80] Bachofen, *Orphische Theologie* (Basel, 1867), pp. 15ff. See also "Connla's Sea-Journey" (Ireland, no. 2), collected in Käte Müller-Lisowski, ed., *Irische Volksmärchen*, [MdW], ed. v. d. Leyen and Zaunert (1923) and the meaning of the apple thrown to the hero in that tale.

[81] Panzer, *KHM in Urgestalt* (Munich, 1913), p. 14; for a comparison of these versions, see Panzer's preface, pp. XLII–XLVI.

[82] F. A. Steel, ed., *English Fairy Tales* (London: Macmillan, 2016; originally published 1918).

[83] Franz Lukas, *Die Grundbegriffe in den Kosmogonien der alten Völker* (Leipzig: Verlag von Wilhelm Friedrich, 1893), p. 62.

animal of Ahriman, who attempted to destroy the immortality-bestowing plant in Lake Vourukaša.[84] Bächtold-Stäubli mentions its devilish nature but also that it protects the house in whose cellar it dwells against misfortune. "The frog must not be despised; for it does not decay, yet merely dries up, while man decays and is eaten by worms (Posen)." "The croaking of frogs is interpreted as the crying of unborn children"; frogs are also a manifestation of the impoverished soul. Rudolf Meyer emphasizes[85] that, biologically, the frog represents an intermediate stage between gill breathing and pulmonary respiration. It therefore mediates between two realms: Although frogs can remain underwater, they cannot live completely submerged. According to Johann Jakob Bachofen, frogs belong to both water and light, "the two basic creative elements from which everything originates." [86] Psychologically, frogs thus symbolize primordial animal life and the unpredictable reactions of the depths of nature. These, however, also express the will to live inherent in primordial nature. If in the present tale playing with the ball is meant to result in a marriage with the immortal inner human, then the subterranean powers so readily despised by consciousness must be respectfully accepted as the basis of human life, even if this appears as the wholly "other"—as a cold-blooded animal in this case.

106    Accordingly, the process perceived by consciousness as a "loss of soul" animates the unconscious, which manifests first as a "voice" and then as a frog. The latter seeks a connection with the conscious sphere in order, as later becomes evident, to be redeemed. Presumably, the frog also deflects the ball. One variant emphasizes that the frog takes the initiative: There, too, the plot unfolds on a hot summer's day, when the king's three daughters are drawing water from a well. The water, however, is opaque. A frog jumps onto the edge of the well and says:

---

[84] Hermann Güntert, *Der arische Weltkönig und Heiland. Bedeutungsgeschichtliche Untersuchungen zur indoiranischen Religionsgeschichte und Altertumskunde* (Halle a. S.: Max Niemeyer, 1923), p. 397, fn. 1; for a more general account, see Bolte and Mackensen, *Handwörterbuch* (Berlin 1930/1934) under *Frosch, Kröte* (frog, toad).
[85] Rudolf Meyer, *Die Weisheit der Schweizer Märchen* (Schaffhausen: Columban-Verlag, 1944), p. 183.
[86] Bachofen, *Orphische Theologie*, p. 21.

107
> If you wish to be my sweetheart,
> I will give you bright, bright water.
> But if you do not wish to be my sweetheart,
> I will give you dark, dark water.[87]

108 Here, water, the primordial substance of life, is the "water of life." Depending on the conscious attitude, the unconscious will either cloud surging life or enable it to flow clearly.[88] While the heroine recklessly represses the self-evident humility toward that power (she finds it quite acceptable that the frog, which is left in the lurch, returns back into the well), the father-king, out of a sense of entitlement, enforces the association.

109 In terms of the man's psyche, this king represents male consciousness. Unlike the capricious anima, it adopts a truly reliable attitude toward the unconscious. On the other hand, interpreting the tale in terms of the woman's psyche leads to the same situation as in "King Thrushbeard," where the king may be said to represent the first animus-figure in the woman's soul; correspondingly, here this powerful image bestows an inner uprightness on the woman.

---

[87] Bolte and Polívka, *Anmerkungen*, vol. 1, p. 1, esp. fn. 1, according to which the last two lines "were added only in the extract given in the notes of 1856, p. 3."

[88] In a Scottish variant cited by Bolte and Polívka, *Anmerkungen*, vol. 1 (1913), pp. 4–5, the well appears as a "barely reachable" well of the world, which contains the treasure. "In the 'Complaynt of Scotlande,' published in 1549 (ed. J. Leyden, 1801, p. 234; ed. J. Murray, 1872, p. 63. LXXIII), 'the tayl of the volfe of the varldis end' is mentioned among other tales, which probably does not mean the legend of the Norse Fenrir (Grimm, *Myth.* 3, p. 224), but that of the well of the world (volle = well). Leyden has heard fragments sung in which the fountain of the world's end occurs and is called 'the well Absolom' and 'the cald well sae weary.' He relates this to our present fairytale: 'According to the popular tale, a lady is sent by her stepmother to draw water from the well of the world's end. She arrives at the well, after encountering many dangers, yet soon realizes that her adventures have not reached a conclusion. A frog emerges from the well and, before it makes her draw water, obliges her to betroth herself to the monster, under the penalty of being torn to pieces. The lady returns safely; but at midnight the frog lover appears at the door and demands entrance, according to promise the great consternation of the lady and her nurse:
> Open the door, my hinny, my hart,
> Open the door, mine ain wee thing.
> And mind the words that you and I spak
> Down in the meadow at the well-spring!
The frog is admitted and addresses her:
> Take me up on your knee, my dearie,
> Take me up on your knee, my dearie,
> And mind the word that you and I spak
> At the cauld well sae weary!
Eventually, the frog is disenchanted and appears as a prince in his original form.' In this variant, the significant mythical and psychic background of the fairytale is also expressed atmospherically and enables the whole mysterious meaning of the well as a source of life in the unconscious to emerge.

Elevating her beyond the purely feminine, this righteousness compels her to engage in a fruitful confrontation with the spiritual principle in order to deepen her childish, playful, and therefore insecure relationship to the unconscious (playing with and losing the ball) in favor of another form.[89]

110     Like the father, however, the frog also admonishes the heroine to keep her promise. Time and again, it reminds her in no uncertain terms of its existence and asserts its claim to union.[90] The frog thus demands ever greater closeness and eventually *conjunctio*. Coerced by the masculine-spiritual principle, the princess's defense becomes highly emotional: She slings the frog violently against a wall. This motif is difficult to interpret. In many variants, it is missing and replaced by kissing, the burning of animal skin, or decapitation; or the prince is simply redeemed by the passage of time and by his union with the heroine. Presumably, throwing something against a wall is partly a projection. It seems that the contents of the unconscious and thus also its highest value can, as Jung remarks, be found "only by the circuitous route of projection."[91] Consciousness in particular tends to "project" what it cannot accept beyond the personality, making tangible what is rejected. "Throwing against the wall" might imply something along these lines. For what was strangely beleaguering becomes, when projected, a recognizable "counterpart," an "encounter," in which the assailing, harassing force can reveal itself.

111     Consciousness distances itself emphatically from the given relationship to the unconscious, thus creating space for transformation. At the same time, we recognize a connection with the motif of fixation, frequently mentioned by Laistner, in which the demon is clamped, held captive, or nailed down. Consequently, it loses its protean, intangible nature and becomes tangible or even controllable for consciousness.[92] This makes it possible to "behold

---

[89] In a Hungarian parallel collected in Bolte and Polívka, *Anmerkungen*, vol. 1 (1913), p. 7, the frog even turns directly to the father to achieve his goal.
[90] See below for the motif of the purchased nights, which has a similar meaning.
[91] Jung, "The Psychology of the Transference," *CW* 16, § 383.
[92] Ludwig Laistner, *Das Rätsel der Sphinx. Grundzüge einer Mythengeschichte* (Berlin: Verlag von Wilhelm Hertz, 1889), vol. 1, p. 109; this motif also occurs in "Snow-White and Rose-Red" (*The

the demon,"[93] and thereby to recognize its essence. (In German, *betrachten*, "to behold," means *trächtig machen*, "to make pregnant": From contemplation thus arises a productive relationship between the beholder and the beheld).

112   Another central aspect of the present fairytale is affect. Also in "The Mouth Organ Player" (Norway, no. 56), the shepherd banished the female troll in the heat of the moment. This lightning intuition reveals the nature of the mysterious counterpart to consciousness. In this respect, as Lüthi points out, throwing against the wall, as an act of understanding, corresponds to disenchanting decapitation in other fairytales.[94] This distancing equals the demand to "Embrace me and immerse yourself!" in "The Three Feathers," the Hessian variant, and also to a legend mentioned by Laistner,[95] where the hero is meant to embrace a snake until it turns into a beautiful maiden. Embracing expresses accepting what arises from the unconscious and concentrating on it; in contrast, distancing—in the heat of the moment or not—denotes "confrontation," during which consciousness also engages intensively with the unconscious content.[96] Here,

---

*Complete Grimm's Fairy Tales*, pp. 664–671), "The Story of the Youth who went forth to learn what Fear was" (*ibid.*, pp. 29–39), and "The King and his Three Sons" (Balkans, no. 36, August Leskien, ed., *Balkanmärchen aus Albanien/Bulgarien, Serbien und Kroatien*, collected in *MdW*, ed. v. d. Leyen and Zaunert, 1919).

[93] On visual fixations, see also "The Bridegroom and the Revenant" (Iceland, no. 29).

[94] Max Lüthi, *Das europäische Volksmärchen. Form und Wesen. Eine literaturwissenschaftliche Darstellung* (Bern: Francke, 1947), p. 78; for a variant on the above fairytale, see Bolte and Polívka, *Anmerkungen*, vol. 1 (1913), p. 5, where the frog must be beheaded.

[95] On the Hessian parallel, see *Archetypal Symbols in Fairytales*, vol. 1, p. 414; for the legend, see Laistner, *Das Rätsel* (1889), vol. 1, p. 228f.

[96] The Siberian fairytale "Pondandi" (no. 30) vividly illustrates the transforming effect of distancing in the heroine's confrontation with her husband's image, even if this occurs less violently than in the previously mentioned Grimm's tale: A master died and Pondandi, his servant, remained with his daughter and worked for her as he had done for her father. One morning, he sat motionless on the other side of the river and did not seem to hear any question or request, so that she had to light the fire, fetch water, cook, and eat alone. The next day, she asked him whether he wanted her to be his wife, whereupon he jumped up and danced around, only to sit down again and look at her as steadfastly as before. Hoping to rid herself of him, and thinking of the wedding, she sent him to hunt bears (from which she would make a blanket), then to hunt elks (to replace her clothes), and eventually to hunt mountain sheep (to procure the wedding roast). He performed each of these tasks before sitting down again, motionless. Thereafter, she asked him to find a large stone as a plaything for their future children, and so he moved a mountain. Next, she ordered him to shoot an arrow to the sky and follow its course. When he did not return for a long time, she was sad. Then a handsome man arrived with a team of reindeer and sat down in her encampment. She turned him away, as otherwise her bridegroom would scold her. Hearing her words, he revealed himself as Pondandi, whose old dress and old skin were hanging on a tree. His parents owned herds larger than the maiden's. In the end, they celebrated their wedding. Pondandi evidently takes the place of the father, yet retreats to the "other" side of the "river," from where his spellbinding gaze besets the maiden. Although she offers to marry him in recognition of their relationship, she repeatedly sends Pondandi away until she is able to recognize his beauty and

the psychic process in which forcible distancing, projection, and fixation strangely coalesce thus provides a clear view and a surprising understanding of the true essence.

113    The redeemed prince drives the heroine to his kingdom in a carriage drawn by eight white horses: The animus thus accompanies the soul into the inner center, toward which all forces (horses) flow. The eight horses already indicate wholeness, while their whiteness affirms that even the natural energies now serve the spiritual principle; the somewhat unclearly appended final episode,[97] about the bands "springing from the heart" of the faithful servant Henry, points in a similar direction.

114    In fairytales, the hero's servant almost always symbolizes his shadow. He is the more undifferentiated and thus more unconscious companion, at times assisting and at others adversarial, and as such is suited to representing the shadow-figure. As a shadow, he is also the prince's *doppelgänger*, such that his liberation also sets free his servant. Just as the prince broke out of his animal skin, so the shadow breaks out of its iron fetters. The redemption of the royal figure, which, as the ruling principle, can only be spiritual, also liberates that side of the soul lying closer to matter. Nature is included in the process of transformation.

115    Certain variants cited by Bolte and Polívka seem to make more psychological sense. In those tales, the same episode refers not to a hitherto unknown servant but instead to the bride, whom the redeemed animal prince initially left yet again or forgot about. When the bands (i.e., fetters) begin springing, he recognizes her again.[98]

---

wealth; typically, her capacity is preceded by grief. He hangs his old "skin" on a tree, returning it to Mother Nature, which shows that development has helped overcome the original situation.

[97] This episode is missing in an older version collected by the Brothers Grimm. See Wesselski, "Versuch einer Theorie des Märchens" (1931), p. 117.

[98] See Bolte and Polívka, *Anmerkungen*, vol. 1 (1913), pp. 2–3: According to a Paderborn version, the redeemed prince temporarily leaves the bride, who later realizes (by means of a prearranged signal) that he is either dead or unfaithful. Disguised as horsemen, "the bride and her two sisters sought out the king's son, into whose service they entered. ... When the king's son set off with the false bride, the three sisters had to follow the carriage. On the way, the king's son heard a loud crash and shouted: 'Stop, the carriage is breaking'; the true bride exclaimed from behind the carriage: 'Oh no, a band is breaking from my heart.' Two further crashes occurred as a result, and on each occasion the king's son received the same answer. He remembered the true bride, recognized her as one of the horsemen, and married her." See further Bolte and Polívka, *Anmerkungen*, p. 3, fn. 3: "In an East Prussian fairytale, ... the forgotten bride rides with the prince disguised as a hunter; 'the knight's band,' which he had given her to pledge his loyalty, snaps in two under her hunting coat. 'What was that?' asks the prince. 'Has the

Psychologically, this means that after the demon-lover has become human, the woman is also no longer bound to a certain fate. Thus, her convulsive attitude also eases, so that her feminine nature is only now able to realize itself, as those variants show in which the iron bands had prevented her from giving birth.[99]

116   A certain affinity may be said to exist between the motif of the iron bands falling off the bride and the shirts discarded by the heroine in "The Young Wolf."[100] The importance of the shirt motif becomes apparent when we consider "King Lindworm" (Denmark, no. 1), which dwells extensively on this theme[101]:

117   A childless Queen was advised by an old hag to take a bowl in the evening after sunset "and to place it upside down in the northwestern corner of the garden. In the morning, at sunrise, she should remove the vessel. Two roses would appear underneath, a red one and a white one. 'If you take the red one and eat it, it will be a boy; if you take the white one, it will be a girl; but you must not take both together.'" The Queen took this advice and ate the white rose, thinking that a boy might be taken from her during a war. But it was so delicious that she also ate the red rose. While her husband was away, she gave birth to a lindworm, which crawled under her bed and later greeted the King, who was returning from the war, as "father," and said: "If you do not want to be my father, I will destroy you and the castle!" He coveted a woman and made the same threat, "whether she is young or old, tall or short, rich or poor." On the wedding night, however, he devoured the princesses, who were not permitted to see him before the wedding, unconcerned about the threat of war

saddle torn?' "On the bands placed around the pregnant woman's body, see also Theodor Benfey, *Pantschatantra: Fünf Bücher indischer Fabeln, Märchen und Erzählungen* (Leipzig: Brockhaus, 1859), Part I, p. 267, and R. Köhler, *Kleinere Schriften*, vol. I, p. 316." See also Bolte and Polívka, *Anmerkungen*, p. 7 f. On the the motif of the bride disguised as a servant, see "The Twelve Huntsmen" (*The Complete Grimm's Fairy Tales*, pp. 334–336) and "Siebenschön" (Zaunert, *Deutsche Märchen seit Grimm*, p. 146).
[99] See, e.g., Bolte and Polívka, *Anmerkungen*, vol. 2 (1915), p. 255.—Trans.
[100] Zaunert, *Märchen aus dem Donaulande*, p. 1.
[101] One weaker parallel is "The Snake" (Zaunert, *Deutsche Märchen seit Grimm*, p. 164); see further "The Story of the Black Snake" (Turkey, no. 14, collected in Friedrich Giese, ed., *Türkische Märchen*, [MdW], ed. v. d. Leyen and Zaunert, 1925, p. 164).

with their fathers. When he demanded, for a third time, a wife, the King forced his poor shepherd to give up his only daughter. But an old woman in the forest advised her: "When the wedding is over and you are sent to the chamber, you must wear ten shirts; if you do not possess so many, you must borrow them. Then you must ask for a bucket of lye, a bucket of sweet milk, and an armful of rods. All this you must take into the chamber. When he enters, he will say: 'Beautiful maiden, take off your shirt!' Then you must say: 'King Lindworm, take off your skin!' And he will say this to you and you to him, until you have taken off nine shirts and he nine skins; eventually, he will have no skin left, but you will still be wearing a shirt. Thereafter, you must take him, for he will be nothing other than a bloody lump of flesh. You must dip the rods into the lye and beat him with the liquid until he almost falls to pieces. Then you must bathe him in the sweet milk and wrap him in the nine shirts and take him in your arms; then, however, you will fall asleep, if only for a little while." And so it happened. Already after he had taken off the nine skins, he lay on the ground and could barely move. When she fell asleep, it was late. "When she awoke, she found herself in the arms of a beautiful King's son." There was great joy at the court and a wedding was celebrated. (In the second part of the story, the Queen is slandered and banished; she later redeems two princes who were bewitched and turned into a crane and a swan, and eventually returns home, rehabilitated).

118 In this fairytale, the cause of the enchantment is described in new images. It stems from a selfish mother, who from the outset regards her future children as possessions that can be "taken" from her and which she therefore chooses not to release into the world but instead keeps within her sphere of influence. The tragic consequences of such instinctual maternalism for the children thus affected are well known. The archetype of the terrible mother as the cause of

bewitchment is depicted quite dramatically in "The Knight with the Sinister Laugh" (Ireland, no. 32). The same figure, which appears as the father's "false bride," also caused the enchantment in "The White Cat."[102]

119    In these cases, the enchantment consists in a state of un-consciousness created by the overpowering influence of an archetype. An archetype that becomes particularly effective in the psyche determines the actions of those concerned and makes the unconscious become overwhelmingly powerful within the personality. In this fairytale, the supremacy of the maternal principle means that the son, who is conceived in a magical way, does not become a human being; instead, he remains, as it were, in the mother's womb, which he carries with him as a dragon's skin (dragon = mother). In the Danube tale "The Young Wolf,"[103] the wolf's skin refers to the placenta (i.e., the skin of the uterus), thus also indicating the hero's attachment to the mother. In our present tale, the son is also completely enveloped by the mother, by the unconscious. The fact that he hides under the bed has the same meaning in both tales; in the Danube variant, the wolf also hid there first and then behind the oven.

120    The story of the red and white rose lends the motif of the supreme mother yet another nuance. Red and white, a primordial pair of opposite colors, have a particular symbolic meaning in

---

[102] Zaunert, *Märchen aus dem Donaulande*, p. 37. For further evidence, see Lincke, "Stiefmutter" (1933), pp. 67ff., 112–115. On the motif of the dark aspect of the father's anima as the wicked stepmother, see also "Queen Rose or Little Thomas" (Spain, no. 45, Harri Meier, trans. and ed., *Spanische und por-tugiesische Märchen*, [MdW], ed. v. d. Leyen, 1940): One day, a King brought back a white rose for his wife, who put the flower in a box. A voice from inside the box woke the King at midnight; when he opened the box, a princess emerged. She called herself Queen Rose and forced the King to throw his wife, whose eyes he would first have to blind, into the cellar and marry her instead. Now a stepmother, she was intent on ridding herself of 14-year-old Thomas by repeatedly sending him on life-threatening ventures, during which, however, an old man warned him of the dangers and thus saved his life. Finally, the stepmother grew so angry that she completely disowned the boy. But the old man led the boy to her sisters' castle, where he succeeded in taking the lives of these women and his stepmother. He killed the sisters himself while his father eliminated Queen Rose, thus saving the mother. — In "The Horse with the Golden Mane and the Sword" (Iceland, no. 42), the young prince's stepmother is split into a luminous and a dark aspect (her sisters are three man-eating giantesses). From this double aspect ensues the stepson's fate: He would rather not leave until the sister's curse compel him to do so. He must un-dergo a great journey, whose various tests he passes.—In "Hans Wunderlich" (Zaunert, *Deutsche Märchen seit Grimm*, Jena 1922, p. 37), the hero's animal form is created by a magic potion given to his mother by her stepmother. See also "Arsuman" (Caucasus, no. 16, Adolf Dir, selected and trans., *Kauka-sische Märchen*, [MdW], ed. v. d. Leyen and Zaunert, 1922), "The Fighting Brothers" (Finland, no. 83), and "The Helpful Animals" (Iceland, no. 49).
[103] Zaunert, *Märchen aus dem Donaulande*, p. 1.

alchemy. They express the primordial opposition between male and female, just as the old woman's words in the present tale do. By eating both flowers, the queen gives birth to a monster, which should be understood as a hermaphrodite. This idea dovetails with "Mercurius," whom the alchemists considered to be both a dragon and a "twin."[104] The alchemical opus mostly involves dismembering this dragon.[105] Psychologically, this is a process of differentiation: For life to continue, a disparity must exist between the diverging opposites, which coexist in the unconscious. A supremacy of the unconscious—the mother—prevents differentiation, because the maternal tendency strives to persist and preserve. Holding together the opposites inhibits the son's development. Enveloped by the unconscious, in the present tale he therefore appears as a hermaphroditic monster that has remained on the animal level. Only suffering, which breaks asunder the opposites, can liberate those affected from this predicament.

121     The lindworm demands, irrepressibly and threateningly, to be married. This suggests that if the unconscious is adhered to, its instinctual aspect initially emerges in an unruly manner (just as Hans the Hedgehog in the eponymous fairytale was first accompanied by pigs). Enveloped in the unconscious, in the mother-dragon's skin, thus causes nonhuman, indeed inhuman behavior.[106] Those women who either accept these psychic circumstances in the enchanted one or who, as in "King Porco" (Italy, no. 24), contemptuously reject them, are killed by him (i.e., perish psychologically). He senses that they cannot redeem him because they do not realize that he is human.

---

[104] On the dual nature of Mercurius (i.e., his appearance as a dragon and as a hermaphrodite), see Jung, "The Spirit Mercurius," CW 13, § 267–269; on this image in relation to "original matter," see Silberer, *Probleme der Mystik* (1914), p. 83ff., esp. p. 85.

[105] Silberer, *Probleme der Mystik*, p. 128f.: "One of the manuscripts cited by Berthelot (orig., p. 60) states: 'The dragon is the guardian of the temple; if you sacrifice him, strip off his skin, and separate the flesh from the bones, then thou shalt find what you seek.'"

[106] On the son's mother complex, see Jung, "Psychological Aspects of the Mother Archetype," CW 9/I, § 162–166. According to Persian belief, whoever eats a dragon's heart and hangs his skin around a loved one will have their love reciprocated (see Jungbauer, *Turkestan*, Jena, 1923, p. 297, appendix). Transposed to the above fairytale, the mother would thus have attempted to bind the son to herself, just as Prince Lindworm is bound to the maternal-magical world.

122     The heroine, who eventually redeems the animal bridegroom, does this either, as in "Hans the Hedgehog," through genuine love, that is, by actively (and not merely passively) accepting his animal nature. Or she, too, resorts to a ruse and even a certain harshness. The old woman, who advises the heroine in the present tale, symbolizes natural female knowledge, which enables the girl to cope with the problem. She acquires as many shirts as the lindworm has skins (well, actually, one more; see also "The Young Wolf"), except that here the motif is more obvious: to force him, or so it seems, to take off all his skins and to avoid having to expose herself to him prematurely and defenselessly. She counteracts his inappropriate behavior toward her, which is due to his state of possession (and therefore does not correspond to his actual nature). As in "The Young Wolf," he is a "blood-drenched lump of flesh." As a human being, he is still, so to speak, unborn and unformed, and therefore extremely sensitive and vulnerable. This, in turn, requires him to don an aggressive, animal mask.[107]

123     The heroine first beats this "lump of flesh" with twigs dipped in lye, before bathing it in sweet milk and wrapping it in her discarded nine shirts. In the morning, the lump has turned into a beautiful king's son. The lye, with which the formless "embryo" is treated, as well as the beating, symbolize harsh and even cruel psychological treatment, by which the still unformed inner person is immersed, as it were, in bitterness, tears, disappointment, and pain.[108] This suffering hence becomes salvific because it stems from a loving, redemptive intention.

124     The animal aspect is defeated, as it were, according to the law that similar things should be fought with similar things.

---

[107] On the vulnerability of the unconscious, see Carl Gustav Carus, *Psyche: Zur Entwicklungsgeschichte der Seele* (Kröners Taschenausgabe, no. 98), ed. R. Marx (Leipzig: Alfred Kröner Verlag, 1931, pp. 435–436): "Although it rests entirely on a divine and eternal principle, the unconscious is, because its revelations tend to be transient, easily wounded and easily becomes diseased ... Matters are quite different with the conscious spirit, once it has reached maturity: It is as invulnerable as air, can endure severe suffering and pain, and can struggle amid the greatest trials and tribulations. And yet, it has, insofar as it is a divine idea that has attained self-awareness, realized that it is eternal, and thus its revelations also become immortal. With regard to what concerns us here, it therefore also exists beyond disease. It is only in this sense, therefore, that what has been revered since time immemorial as the higher power of the spirit can be fully understood."—Trans.
[108] On beating the "half" to make it whole, see "The Half" (Malay, no. 29; collected in Paul Hambruch, ed., *Malaiische Märchen aus Madagaskar und Insulinde*, [MdW], ed. v. d. Leyen and Zauner, 1922).

Unconsciousness becomes painfully perceptible by being immersed in the "bitter water" of the unconscious. The antithesis is "sweet milk." (Once more, this idea might also be based on alchemical thinking, according to which vinegar has a transforming and ennobling effect as living water). At the same time, milk is equated with the water of life.[109] (Thus, both symbolize a spiritual power that flows from the unconscious.) In popular superstition, milk, to which a particularly magical and mystical quality is attributed, was used in aphrodisiacs and fertility rites, as well as in lustration rites (for its alleged cathartic effect). In the ancient Mediterranean world, milk was considered to be the nourishment of the spiritually reborn and a means of attaining immortality. In the Orphic mysteries, baptism in milk denoted a rite of renewal[110]; it represents the archetype of baptism, which symbolizes purification, rebirth, and admission into a spiritual realm.[111] The alchemists formulated the twofold effect of this process in their concept of paradox: Its solution (dissolution), which is also its coagulation (clotting), occurs through water, which is a "means of the soul." This water is also a fire.[112]

125     This perspective enables regarding the fire that redeemed Hans the Hedgehog as a correspondence between lye and milk in the present fairytale. The motif of flaying is also evident in alchemical symbolism. Jung refers to the ancient parallels in his discussion of the flayed Marsyas and of the legendary flaying of Mani.[113] Thus, the cruel transformation of the lindworm ultimately rests on the archetypal motif of the sacrificed god-man[114]; killing this figure of

---

[109] Silberer, *Probleme der Mystik*, p. 88.
[110] See Bächtold-Stäubli under *Milch* (milk) and *Milchopfer* (milk sacrifice); Richard Reitzenstein, *Die hellenistischen Mysterienreligionen: nach ihren Grundgedanken und Wirkungen*, 3rd ed. (Leipzig and Berlin: Teubner, 1927), p. 83; Ernesto Buonaiuti, "Die Erlösung in den orphischen Mysterien," *Eranos-Jahrbuch 1936: Gestaltung der Erlösungsidee in Ost und West I*, ed. Olga Fröbe-Kapteyn (1937), p. 180.
[111] On the significance of baptism, see also v. d. Leeuw, *Phänomenologie der Religion* (1933), pp. 322–327.
[112] Silberer, *Probleme der Mystik*, p. 103; on the symbolism of the whirling sea of milk and the origin of the deathless potion in Indian myth, see Heinrich Zimmer, *"Maya" der indische Mythos* (Stuttgart and Berlin: Deutsche Verlags-Anstalt, 1936), pp. 121–142.
[113] Jung, "The Visions of Zosimos," *CW* 13, § 92; "Transformation Symbolism in the Mass," *CW* 11, § 348; *Symbols of Transformation*, CW 5, § 595.
[114] In *Symbols of Transformation*, CW 5, § 503, Jung also mentions that ancient Mexican flaying rites served divine renewal; on this theme, see esp. Theodor-Wilhelm Danzel, "Zur Psychologie der altmexikanischen Symbolik," *Eranos-Jahrbuch. 1937: Gestaltung der Erlösungsidee in Ost und West II*, ed. Olga Fröbe-Kapteyn (1938), pp. 234–236.

the self is a necessary step on the path toward inner maturation. Insofar as the bath, as a vessel, and as water or milk, also signifies the "mother," immersion here symbolizes the union with the mother and the subsequent rebirth. What the concrete mother was guilty of, only the symbolic mother can make amends for. Therefore, the heroine also receives instruction and advice about this deed from a mother-figure.

126    We find a milk bath also in "Padischah's Three Sons" (Turkey, no. 18) and "The Boy and the Serpent."[115] Sometimes, this bath is scalding, at others poisonous, or sometimes also rejuvenating or beautifying. In these two tales, the double aspect is preserved, whereas in the present one it fragments into two images. In the above fairytale, the milk bath in which the hero immerses himself was prepared by a virgin and might thus be understood as symbolizing her Eros. Something similar is thus also true here: The bride (in King Lindworm's view) lovingly envelops him, so that his hitherto undifferentiated, yet hypersensitive nature is protected. Symbolically, this is expressed by her wrapping him in her shirts. This transformation of his nature enables him to assimilate with humankind.

127    Psychologically, clothing symbolism has highly diverse meanings. First of all, it expresses that part of a person that they display to the world and by which they wish to be recognized. As such, it is adopted and therefore easily cast off again. And yet, this symbol also expresses a considerable part of the psychic totality, in that being related to the world is a condition of human life; indeed, insofar as human beings become recognizable only in their actions, through which they realize themselves in the world, their clothing can express their truest essence and even the self. Fairytales therefore contain the motif of wonderful garments concealed either in a nut (see, e.g., "Allerleirauh") or in a ball.[116] This establishes the connection between clothing and the symbol of the self: the manifestation of the individual and its activity in the world, based

---

[115] Zaunert, *Märchen aus dem Donaulande* (1926), p. 288.
[116] *The Complete Grimm's Fairy Tales*, pp. 326–331. See also Bolte and Polívka, *Anmerkungen*, vol. 2 (1915), p. 314.

on the law of the self. This important symbolic meaning of clothing is particularly evident in the imagery of the mysteries of late antiquity. Reitzenstein has described their manifold forms in detail. The mystics put on twelve garments one after the other as an expression of inner transformation.[117] The Pauline expression (Galatians 3:27) of clothing oneself with Christ in baptism also goes back to the same idea. The symbolism of the so-called hymn of the soul from the Acts of Thomas, where the king's son, immersed in the filth of the world, encounters the garment of his soul left behind in heaven when he is summoned again, very aptly illustrates the connection between garment and self:

128

> ... so suddenly the robe, when I saw it facing me, appeared to me to become a mirror of myself. I saw it completely in me, and I saw myself completely in it, because we were two, different from each other, and yet again only One, in the same form ... And it was skillfully woven in its height, and its seams were fastened with diamonds, and the image of the King of kings was painted all over it, and its colors shimmered like sapphire. Above it, I saw the stirrings of gnosis, and also that it was preparing to speak. I heard its sound, which it produced with its ...: "I am what acts in actions ..." And in its royal movements it poured over me ... And its love pressed itself on me, urging me to meet it and to receive it, and I reached out and seized it. I adorned myself with its beautiful colors and wrapped myself completely in my brightly shining toga. I clothed myself with it and came up to the gate of salutation and homage."[118]

---

[117] Reitzenstein, *Hellenistische Mysterien* (1927), pp. 263–264, and *Das iranische Erlösungsmysterium. Religionsgeschichtliche Untersuchungen* (1921), pp. 95–97, 159, 164, 167. On the idea of clothing in Gnostic and New Testament apocryphal thinking (Acta Thomae, Book of Enoch II, Mandaeism), see Wilhelm Bousset, "Die Himmelsreise der Seele," *Archiv für Religionswissenschaft*, vol. IV (Tübingen and Leipzig, 1901), pp. 233–234, fn. 2. On changing clothes as an expression of psychic transformation, see v. d. Leeuw, *Phänomenologie der Religion* (1933), p. 179.
[118] Hans Leisegang, *Die Gnosis*, Kröners Taschenausgabe, vol. 32 (Stuttgart: Alfred Kröner Verlag, 1941), p. 369.—Trans. The omissions are von Franz's.

129    Here, the garment becomes an inner image and symbolizes a person's inner essence, untouched by the filth of the world.[119]

130    In most mystery cults, such a luminous garment is contrasted with the clothing worn previously, which the myst (i.e., initiate) must remove and thus enter the sanctuary naked.[120] In the Mithras mysteries, the myst, when ascending through the planetary sphere, places before or returns to each celestial lord a spiritual quality in the form of a garment.[121] Here, clothing thus denotes the horoscopic character traits, a multitude of inherited passions, which must be overcome. This latter meaning of clothing does not contradict the former: Here, too, it is a matter of psychic realization, except that garments symbolize more unconscious, natural, and not self-governed traits. Therefore, their meaning is more negative than the destiny that a person unconsciously weaves from all their desires, cravings, and impulses, only to find themselves imprisoned in that fabric one day.[122] (The iron bands that spring from the heart of Henry, the loyal servant in "The Frog-King, or Iron Henry," who is also redeemed, are also of this kind).

131    Insofar as realization in the here and now is conditioned by bodily life, clothing symbolism is also closely related to ideas of the body.[123] For example, a Mandaean text describes the baptism of

---

[119] See also Reitzenstein, *Hellenistischen Mysterien* (1927), pp. 53–55, 60–62, 179, 350f.; see further van der Leeuw, "Immortality," *Eranos-Jahrbuch Band XVIII: Aus der Welt der Urbilder*, ed. Olga Fröbe-Kapteyn (1950), pp. 196–199, who refers to Petersen's "Theologie des Kleides" (*Bened. Monatsschrift* 16, 1934), pp. 347ff.

[120] Leisegang, "Das Mysterium der Schlange: Ein Beitrag zur Erforschung des griechischen Mysterienkultes und seines Fortlebens in der christlichen Welt," *Eranos- Jahrbuch 1939: Die Symbolik der Wiedergeburt in der religiösen Vorstellung der Zeiten und Völker,* ed. Olga Fröbe-Kapteyn (1940), p. 214f. In German, the expression *den alten Adam* ausziehen ("to cast or put off old Adam," i.e., to change one's ways) also derives from this idea.

[121] Franz Cumont, *Die orientalischen Religionen im römischen Heidentum.* Lectures delivered at the Collège de France. See Gehrich's translation (of the fourth French edition), ed. A. Burckhardt-Brandenberg (Leipzig and Berlin: Teubner, 1931), pp. 115 and 145.

[122] On the evil demon as a "shroud" or "imprisoner," see Güntert, *Weltkönig* (Halle a. S., 1923), p. 21ff. See especially Zimmer's interpretation of "Abu Kasem's slippers" in his *Weisheit Indiens: Märchen und Sinnbilder* (Darmstadt: Wittich Verlag, 1938), pp. 53–71; see also his *Maya* (1936), p. 398: "All forms and persons are merely garments, which the imperishable God, who divides himself manifoldly in Mayan belief, puts on and playfully changes when they have worn thin."—Trans.

[123] See Bächtold-Stäubli under *Hemd* (shirt): "Since the actual shirt *lies directly on the body*, it is better suited than any other piece of clothing to *represent its wearer's person*, whose qualities adhere to the shirt, as it were, just as his life very often does. Thus, the shirt almost also appears as *human skin*, as a mere *covering of the soul*, which can also assume any other covering." See also the rich material on magic and feather shirts and the shirt in folklore, including the widespread ancient custom that the bride gives the bridegroom the bridal shirt, who is subsequently adopted by her clan. In Turkey, the child about to be adopted is pulled through a shirt (which thus represents the mother or maternal clan). See also the

Manda d'Haije, the Mandaean savior, by Johānā, the Son of God, as follows: "He stripped him of his garment in the Jordan, he stripped him of his vestment of flesh and blood, he clothed him with a robe of splendor and covered him with a pure, good turban of light."[124]

132    The equation garment = body covering = body, for which Lucien Lévy-Bruhl cites several examples, is also found among primitive peoples. Thus, for example, the inhabitants of the Trobriand Islands report that witches can leave the human body as bats or nocturnal birds, leaving either their skirts or skin or even their body at home. The primitive, however, is unable to clearly define what remains behind, nor what leaves the body; what remains behind is sometimes called a "shadow" or is a wild animal.[125] Thus, what remains is not a body in the natural sense, but an imagined, essentially psychic figure, which can only be described symbolically. Psychologically, this might be most aptly described as that part of the unconscious totality that most strongly coalesces with the bodily functions or which psychically animates the body and is expressed by it.

133    Regarding its inner wholeness, however, human existence, which is conditioned by the life of the body, is—just like ego-consciousness, insofar as this has arisen only from bodily feeling—merely one half of human essence. In "The One-Sided Man" (Siberia, no. 24), the protagonist therefore has a skin, instead of an animal skin, which makes him appear one-sided. If we relate these various meanings to the motif of animal skin (in fairytales, that of the so-called animal prince), then burning skin means clarification, that is, becoming conscious of precisely that part of the psyche that is bound to this

---

belief that treating the shirt cures its owner's illness. Under *Kleid* (garment), Bächtold-Stäubli notes that its magical power also emanates from the human body: "Sometimes clothing and the skin are equivalent … The close connection between clothing and people is emphasized by the belief that a reversal into human form becomes impossible if the clothes that were taken off before the transformation were taken away."—Trans. See also various other sagas.

[124] Reitzenstein, *Hellenistischen Mysterien* (1927), p. 231 f.; see also his commentary, p. 353f. On the kabbalistic meaning of the sephirot as vestments, as instruments of God's working, as the fingers on his hands, as the manifestation of his spirit, see Erich Bischoff, "Die Elemente der Kabbalah," Erster Teil: Theoretische Kabbalah, *Geheime Wissenschaften. Eine Sammlung seltener älterer und neuerer Schriften über Alchemie, Magic, Kabbalah, Rosenkreuzerei, Freimauerei, Hexen- und Teufelswesen usw.* Unter Mitwirkung namhafter Autoren, ed. A. v. d. Linden, vol. 2 (Berlin: Hermann Barsdorf Verlag, 1913), p. 180f.

[125] See Lucien Lévy-Bruhl, *The "Soul" of the Primitive*, trans. Lilian A. Clare (London: Allen & Unwin, 1922), pp. 136–141.

world. This is profoundly liberating, as it marks a deliverance from the coercion or duress to become entangled, unknowingly and unwillingly, in fate. Only now does serving the higher principle in the world become possible. The fairytale about the transformation of the animal prince expresses, archaically and profoundly, the liberation from the obscuring envelopment by the unconscious. Being a numinous inner process, this liberation can, however, be represented only in images.

134     The symbolism of changing skins or garments also implies the transformation of a mortal being into an immortal one. Worth mentioning in this respect are the numerous primitive tales according to which people lost their immortality when they no longer shed their skin, often in contrast to snakes. The latter were considered immortal because they shed their skin—because only constant renewal safeguards against paralysis or death.[126] This meaning of changing skins and garments probably also resonates in the present fairytale.

135     After his agonizing liberation from the animal skin, King Lindworm is wrapped in the heroine's shirts (paralleling the hero's treatment by the king's physician in "Hans the Hedgehog"). The above amplifications of clothing symbolism reveal that these shirts correspond to the luminous garment, which the myst receives after removing the animal fur or the earthly, protective clothing and which represents his true self. In antiquity, this luminous garment

---

[126] For examples, see Wesselski, "Versuch" (1931), p. 44ff. See also the conclusion of "The Great Flood" (South America, no. 84, Theodor Koch-Grünberg, ed., *Indianermärchen aus Südamerika*, [MdW], ed. v. d. Leyen and Zaunert, 1921). See further the Scottish ballad recounted by Wilhelm Mannhardt, *Wald- und Feldkulte, vol. 2: Antike Wald- und Feldkulte aus nordeuropäischer Überlieferung* (Berlin, 1877), p. 63: A knight who had been enchanted into a rosebush near a spring appeared to Janet, Countess of March, who wanted to pick some roses. He forbade her to pick the flowers and told her that he was Tamlane, Earl of Murray, who had been abducted by elves as a child and was now about to be given to the devil, who demanded a sacrifice every seven years. If she wished to save him, Janet should expect the procession of the elves to hell at midnight, pull him from the white horse, embrace him tightly, even if he turned into a snake, newt, fire, and red-hot piece of iron one after the other. Thereafter, she should throw him into a barrel of milk, then into water and continue to hold him tightly, for he would become an eel, a toad, a dove, and a swan; "thereafter, however, she should throw her green cloak over him because he would once again turn into man and would be naked, just as when he came into the world."— Janet redeems the knight. The transformations occurring here are interesting. From the mandala-shaped plant, symbolizing vegetative-unconscious existence, a ghostly horseman escapes, to become a glowing metal (chthonic-demonic) via the form of lower animals and thereafter, ascending until he becomes a swan, as a luminous symbol of the spirit, becomes a naked human being, who is eventually redeemed and returned to life by the anima-figure's "green" (natural) mantle, which mediates between the previously opposite forms.

was nothing other than the soul.[127] This conception of clothing as the *psyche* explains why in the present fairytale the bride dresses the animal prince in nine shirts: She is, as it were, identical with them. The soul envelops the self with its essence.[128] Thus, the anima-figure brings about relationship, inwardly and outwardly, and as such she is the medium through which the self realizes itself—and therefore she gives the garment.

136   If we consider the same process with regard to the woman's psyche, we realize that while she finds creating reality natural, she struggles to properly incorporate the spiritual aspect into her life, as the spirit emerges in her as semi-corporeal and demonic, as a mixture of spirit and instinct. Helping this soul-image to attain clarification and become fruitful is one of the main tasks in a woman's development. The overlapping of images plainly shows the interpersonal, or indeed the transpersonal, meaning of the figures and their relation to each other. However, we will only grasp this meaning if we consider the peculiar symbol of the animal prince in greater detail. Some fairytales offer very detailed accounts of his redemption.

137   First of all, the burning of the animal skin is not always as unproblematic or depicted as positively as in the fairytales discussed above. For instance, in "The Hedgehog Bridegroom" (Balkans, no. 33), a parallel to "Hans the Hedgehog," the hedgehog becomes human only to utter some enigmatic words to his bride, who denies redeeming him: "Don't deceive me. I know you burned it (the animal clothing) and did well; yet if you had persevered a little longer, I would have been fortunate." We can understand this unclear statement only if we realize that a large group of tales about animal princes does not enable redemption to happen without detours: "Premature illumination" or other motifs of betrayal interrupt and

---

[127] See Reitzenstein, *Iranische* (1921), pp. 35ff., 39, and 41, fn. 2.

[128] Especially the problem of redemption links—other factors aside—fairytales to Gnosis. Unfortunately, Otto Huth's *Märchen und Gnosis*, which discusses this relationship in detail, has not yet been published. Therefore, we refer to his shorter "Wesen und Herkunft des Märchens," published in *Universitas, Zeitschrift für Wissenschaft, Kunst und Literatur.* Offprint from vol. 4, no. 6, ed. S. Maiwald (Stuttgart: Verlag Dr. Roland Schmiedel, 1949), pp. 651–654.

endanger the initiated redemption, whose success also seems to be bound to a particular time.

138     Violent intervention, the burning of the animal skin, is therefore not desired under all circumstances to liberate the bewitched. One example is "The Bristle Child"[129]: The cursed hero, who appears as a pig, performs impossible tasks for the father of a princess whose favor he wishes to gain: He must transform the king's castle into a silver edifice and erect a golden castle opposite; between the castles he must build a bridge of diamond crystal (i.e., mandalas and symbols of the self made of gold and silver, the masculine and the feminine metals, and in between the bridge as the union of opposites). By performing these tasks, the pig receives the princess. She, however, betrays his nocturnal human form to the mother, who prematurely burns the animal skin, whereupon the animal hero disappears to the end of the world, from where the princess must bring him back in a long quest. In some fairytales, the animal prince even dies as a result of his animal skin being burned, and the story ends tragically as a result.[130] This burning amounts to consciousness invading the unconscious. Therefore, some fairytales point to the subtle conditions whose observance alone ensures a successful outcome.

139     As mentioned, a number of fairytales having the same main theme describe the incursion of consciousness as "premature illumination," as in Apuleius's famous "Cupid and Psyche" (collected in his *Metamorphoses*). One representative tale in this respect is the Grimm's "The Singing, Soaring Lark," which has numerous variants, in particular European ones.[131] Unfortunately, we cannot do enough justice to their importance; some, however, are referred to occasionally along the principal thematic line of the Grimm's version. The tale goes like this:

---

[129] Zaunert, *Deutsche Märchen seit Grimm*, p. 286.
[130] Bolte and Polívka, *Anmerkungen*, vol. 2 (1915), pp. 238ff.
[131] *The Complete Grimm's Fairy Tales*, pp. 399–404; on this tale, see Bolte and Polívka, *Anmerkungen*, vol. 2 (1915), pp. 229ff.

140    There was once upon a time a man who was about to set out on a long journey, and on parting he asked his three daughters what he should bring back with him for them. Whereupon the eldest wished for pearls, the second wished for diamonds, but the third said, dear father, I should like a singing, soaring lark. The father said, yes, if I can get it, you shall have it, kissed all three, and set out. Now when the time had come for him to be on his way home again, he had brought pearls and diamonds for the two eldest, but he had sought everywhere in vain for a singing, soaring lark for the youngest, and he was very unhappy about it, for she was his favorite child. Then his road lay through a forest, and in the midst of it was a splendid castle, and near the castle stood a tree, but quite on the top of the tree, he saw a singing, soaring lark. Aha, you come just at the right moment, he said, quite delighted, and called to his servant to climb up and catch the little creature.

141    But as he approached the tree, a lion leapt from beneath it, shook himself, and roared till the leaves on the trees trembled. He who tries to steal my singing, soaring lark, he cried, will I devour. Then the man said, I did not know that the bird belonged to you.

142    I will make amends for the wrong I have done and ransom myself with a large sum of money, only spare my life. The lion said, nothing can save you, unless you will promise to give me for my own what first meets you on your return home, and if you will do that, I will grant you your life, and you shall have the bird for your daughter, into the bargain. But the man hesitated and said, that might be my youngest daughter, she loves me best, and always runs to meet me on my return home.

143    The servant, however, was terrified and said, why should your daughter be the very one to meet you, it might as easily be a cat, or dog. Then the man allowed himself to be persuaded,

took the singing, soaring lark, and promised to give the lion whatsoever should first meet him on his return home.

144   When he reached home and entered his house, the first who met him was no other than his youngest and dearest daughter, who came running up, kissed and embraced him, and when she saw that he had brought with him a singing, soaring lark, she was beside herself with joy. The father, however, could not rejoice, but began to weep, and said, my dearest child, I have bought the little bird dear. In return for it, I have been obliged to promise you to a savage lion, and when he has you he will tear you in pieces and devour you, and he told her all, just as it had happened, and begged her not to go there, come what might.

145   But she consoled him and said, dearest father, indeed your promise must be fulfilled. I will go thither and soften the lion, so that I may return to you safely. Next morning she had the road pointed out to her, took leave, and went fearlessly out into the forest. The lion, however, was an enchanted prince and was by day a lion, and all his people were lions with him, but in the night they resumed their natural human shapes.

146   On her arrival she was kindly received and led into the castle. When night came, the lion turned into a handsome man, and their wedding was celebrated with great magnificence. They lived happily together, remained awake at night, and slept in the daytime. One day he came and said, to-morrow there is a feast in your father's house, because your eldest sister is to be married, and if you are inclined to go there, my lions shall conduct you. She said, yes, I should very much like to see my father again, and went thither, accompanied by the lions.

147   There was great joy when she arrived, for they had all believed that she had been torn in pieces by the lion, and had long ceased to live. But she told them what a handsome husband she had, and how well off she was, remained with

them while the wedding-feast lasted, and then went back again to the forest.

148 When the second daughter was about to be married, and she was again invited to the wedding, she said to the lion, this time I will not be alone, you must come with me. The lion, however, said that it was too dangerous for him, for if when there a ray from a burning candle fell on him, he would be changed into a dove, and for seven years long would have to fly about with the doves. She said, ah, but do come with me, I will take great care of you, and guard you from all light. So they went away together, and took with them their little child as well.

149 She had a room built there, so strong and thick that no ray could pierce through it, in this he was to shut himself up when the candles were lit for the wedding-feast. But the door was made of green wood which warped and left a little crack which no one noticed. The wedding was celebrated with magnificence, but when the procession with all its candles and torches came back from church, and passed by this apartment, a ray touched him, he was transformed in an instant, and when she came in and looked for him, she did not see him, but a white dove was sitting there. The dove said to her, for seven years must I fly about the world, but at every seventh step that you take I will let fall a drop of red blood and a white feather, and these will show you the way, and if you follow the trace you can release me. Thereupon the dove flew out at the door, and she followed him, and at every seventh step a red drop of blood and a little white feather fell down and showed her the way.

150 So she went continually further and further in the wide world, never looking about her or resting, and the seven years were almost past, then she rejoiced and thought that they would soon be saved, and yet they were so far from it. Once when they were thus moving onwards, no little feather and

no drop of red blood fell, and when she raised her eyes the dove had disappeared. And as she thought to herself, in this no man can help you, she climbed up to the sun, and said to him, you shine into every crevice, and over every peak, have you not seen a white dove flying.

151    No, said the sun, I have seen none, but I present you with a casket, open it when you are in sorest need. Then she thanked the sun, and went on until evening came and the moon appeared, she then asked her, you shine the whole night through, and on every field and forest, have you not seen a white dove flying.

152    No, said the moon, I have seen no dove, but here I give you an egg, break it when you are in great need. She thanked the moon, and went on until the night wind came up and blew on her, then she said to it, you blow over every tree and under every leaf, have you not seen a white dove flying. No, said the night wind, I have seen none, but I will ask the three other winds, perhaps they have seen it.

153    The east wind and the west wind came, and had seen nothing, but the south wind said, I have seen the white dove, it has flown to the red sea, where it has become a lion again, for the seven years are over, and the lion is there fighting with a dragon, the dragon, however, is an enchanted princess. The night wind then said to her, I will advise you, go to the red sea, on the right bank are some tall reeds, count them, break off the eleventh, and strike the dragon with it, then the lion will be able to subdue it, and both then will regain their human form. After that, look round and you will see the griffin which is by the red sea, swing yourself, with your beloved, on to his back, and the bird will carry you over the sea to your own home. Here is a nut for you, when you are above the center of the sea, let the nut fall, it will immediately shoot up, and a tall nut-tree will grow out of the water on which the griffin may rest, for if he cannot rest, he will not

be strong enough to carry you across, and if you forget to throw down the nut, he will let you fall into the sea.

154   Then she went thither, and found everything as the night wind had said. She counted the reeds by the sea, and cut off the eleventh, struck the dragon therewith, whereupon the lion conquered it, and immediately both of them regained their human shapes. But when the princess, who hitherto had been the dragon, was released from enchantment, she took the youth by the arm, seated herself on the griffin, and carried him off with her.

155   There stood the poor maiden who had wandered so far and was again forsaken. She sat down and cried, but at last she took courage and said, still I will go as far as the wind blows and as long as the cock crows, until I find him, and she went forth by long, long roads, until at last she came to the castle where both of them were living together, there she heard that soon a feast was to be held, in which they would celebrate their wedding, but she said, God still helps me, and opened the casket that the sun had given her. A dress lay therein as brilliant as the sun itself. So she took it out and put it on, and went up into the castle, and everyone, even the bride herself, looked at her with astonishment.

156   The dress pleased the bride so well that she thought it might do for her wedding-dress, and asked if it was for sale. Not for money or land, answered she, but for flesh and blood. The bride asked her what she meant by that, so she said, let me sleep a night in the chamber where the bridegroom sleeps. The bride would not, yet wanted very much to have the dress, at last she consented, but the page was to give the prince a sleeping-draught.

157   When it was night, therefore, and the youth was already asleep, she was led into the chamber, she seated herself on the bed and said, I have followed after you for seven years. I have been to the sun and the moon, and the four winds, and

have enquired for you, and have helped you against the dragon, will you, then quite forget me. But the prince slept so soundly that it only seemed to him as if the wind were whistling outside in the fir-trees.

158     When therefore day broke, she was led out again, and had to give up the golden dress. And as that even had been of no avail, she was sad, went out into a meadow, sat down there, and wept. While she was sitting there, she thought of the egg which the moon had given her, she opened it, and there came out a clucking hen with twelve chickens all of gold, and they ran about chirping, and crept again under the old hen's wings, nothing more beautiful was ever seen in the world. Then she arose, and drove them through the meadow before her, until the bride looked out of the window.

159     The little chickens pleased her so much that she immediately came down and asked if they were for sale. Not for money or land, but for flesh and blood, let me sleep another night in the chamber where the bridegroom sleeps. The bride said, yes, intending to cheat her as on the former evening. But when the prince went to bed he asked the page what the murmuring and rustling in the night had been. On this the page told all, that he had been forced to give him a sleeping-draught, because a poor girl had slept secretly in the chamber, and that he was to give him another that night. The prince said, pour out the draught by the bed-side.

160     At night, she was again led in, and when she began to relate how ill all had fared with her, he immediately recognized his beloved wife by her voice, sprang up and cried, now I really am released. I have been as it were in a dream, for the strange princess has bewitched me so that I have been compelled to forget you, but God has delivered me from the spell at the right time.

161     Then they both left the castle secretly in the night, for they feared the father of the princess, who was a sorcerer, and they

seated themselves on the griffin which bore them across the red sea, and when they were in the midst of it, she let fall the nut. Immediately a tall nut-tree grew up, whereon the bird rested, and then carried them home, where they found their child, who had grown tall and beautiful, and they lived thenceforth happily until their death.

162  In his extensive "Studien zum Märchentype von Amor und Psyche" (Studies on Fairytales like Cupid and Psyche"), Ernst Tegethoff has compiled the variants of this tale, which are scattered across Europe, thus greatly facilitating efforts to interpret them.[132]

163  This tale begins with a group of four people, in whom we recognize the psychic constituents of human consciousness. Unlike the group of four, for instance, in "The Golden Bird,"[133] this one represents both sexes. The four figures can be understood as constituents of both a male and a female personality, depending on whether we identify the ego with the father or the daughter. As far as the female figure is the protagonist and takes the initiative, she can be considered to be the ego (without refuting the opposite interpretation, i.e., that she represents the anima-figure in relation to the ego [father]). We can explain the paradox that, depending on our vantage point, the father sometimes symbolizes the most differentiated function, yet at others the fourth, inferior function, by pointing out that the relation between consciousness and the unconscious can be seen from two sides: On the one hand, the most differentiated function of consciousness is the oldest figure insofar as it has already matured and grown old by the middle of life compared to the inferior function, which inwardly remains archaic and young, so that their relationship can be expressed aptly in the image of father and son. On the other hand, however, the

---

[132] Ernst Tegethoff, "Studien zum Märchentypus von Amor und Psyche," *Rhein. Beitr. u. Hülfsbücher z. germ. Philologie u. Volkskunde*, vol. 4, eds., Th. Frings, R. Meissner, J. Müller, Kurt Schroeder (Bonn and Leipzig, 1922). For an overview of the mythical, literary, and formal connections, see Bolte and Mackensen, *Handwörterbuch* (1930/1934), esp. under "Amor und Psyche" (Cupid and Psyche) and "Belle et la Bête" (Beauty and the Beast). For a general discussion, see Reitzenstein, "Das Märchen von Amor und Psyche bei Apuleius," Inaugural lecture at the University of Freiburg on June 22, 1911 (Leipzig and Berlin: Teubner, 1912). Reitzenstein places this tale in the context of the history of religion.
[133] *The Complete Grimm's Fairy Tales*, pp. 272–279.

unconscious is again that part of the soul that brings forth consciousness and as such its father or mother. The latter view is valid if the daughter is regarded as the female ego, which she is meant to be here. In this case, the father represents the fourth function. This is related to the unconscious and at the same time, as observed in "King Thrushbeard" and "The Magic Horse" (Turkestan, no. 9), the first level of the man's soul-image.[134]

164 In the present fairytale, the emphasis placed on the special love between father and daughter subtly points to the psychological incest that is plainly evident, for example, in the Grimm's "Allerleirauh." It indicates, as it were, that the relationship between consciousness and the unconscious has become problematic, and that consequently the process of development and clarification begins fatefully. In this story, the archetype of the animal prince appears as a result of the woman's extraordinary wish. Although manifoldly modified in the variants, this symbol always remains significant. Thus, in "The Lame Dog" (Sweden, no. 13), a king's three daughters all wish to have a husband: The first daughter wants her husband to have golden hair and a beard; the second one longs for a husband with silver hair and a beard; yet the third one, at her sisters' insistence, says that she will settle for that husband whom fate assigns her, "even if it were only a lame dog." Her wish is soon fulfilled: She must tearfully follow her doggish husband.

165 The Irish parallel, "The White Hound of the Mountain" (no. 38), begins similarly: On her deathbed, a queen makes her husband promise not to let anyone into her chamber until she has lain in her grave for one year and one day. On one occasion, however, when their father is away, the couple's three daughters find the key to the forbidden room. The eldest daughter sits down on her mother's chair and says: "I ask God and this wonderful chair that the son of the western king may set me free!" Likewise, the second daughter wishes to be liberated by the son of the eastern king. The youngest daughter,

---

[134] On the father as an animus-figure, see De Gubernatis, *Thiere i. d. indog. Mythologie*, (Leipzig, 1874, p. 631ff.), who cites a variant from the region of Livorno. In that tale, the heroine does not encounter misfortune at her sisters' wedding, but when she loses her enchanted husband's ring at her father's funeral.

who obeys her father, sits down on the chair only because her sisters force her to and says: "I ask God and this wonderful chair that the white dog of the mountain may set me free!" The two elder daughters are immediately collected by the sons of the western and eastern kings, who drive up in their carriages. On the third day, the youngest daughter must also follow the white dog of the mountain, who meets her at the gate with a horse and carriage. We have previously discussed how wishful thinking shapes reality in the primitive psyche.[135]

Contriving fantastic plans and dreams is a characteristic function of the masculine-spiritual component in the woman's soul. In many variants, the motif of wishful thinking is therefore related to that of the father's journey. As observed, the father embodies the animus. Just as Cinderella (in the eponymous fairytale[136]) asks her father to give her the first thing that brushes and knocks off his hat, and subsequently receives the hazel twig that later helps to realize her inner destiny as a tree on her mother's grave, so in the present fairytale, the heroine wishes to receive an object whose special essence is hidden behind an inconspicuous exterior and whose numinous character distinguishes it as a most valuable symbol.

The Norwegian fairytale "King Valemon, the White Bear" offers a poetic account of this episode: The heroine dreams of a golden wreath, and since she cannot have it, she grows despondent. One day, she sees a white bear in the forest that is playing with this wreath. He is willing to give it to her only if she becomes his wife, to which she agrees. Three days later, the bear forces through the marriage, despite the king's armies standing by. As a round object of crucial importance to the heroine, the golden wreath (in this tale, the desired object has quite a conspicuous exterior) is a symbol of the self. In a Russian variant, "The Scarlet Flower,"[137] the daughter longs for a scarlet flower, the most beautiful of all. The flower symbolizes the self, which is still hidden in the unconscious. In "East of the Sun and West of the Moon" (Norway, no. 31), the father gives

---

[135] See *Archetypal Symbols in Fairytales*, vol. 1, p. 361.
[136] *The Complete Grimm's Fairy Tales*, pp. 121–128.
[137] See Loepfe, *Russische* (1941), p. 86.

his daughter to a bear, who promises to make him wealthy. This links this tale of redemption to the initial motif of the greedy father who sells his child to a demon (see "The King of the Golden Mountain").[138] The acquisitive, profit-seeking stance becomes a source of distress, which eventually leads to the inward path. The profound meaning of distress and hardship as a starting point for psychic development is vividly expressed in "Worry and Sorrow" (Norway, no. 25): The first daughter wants her father to give her a ring that promises her immortality; the second daughter desires a wreath that will bring her eternal joy; the heroine, however, wants "worry and sorrow." The father, who cannot find the latter, is offered a squirrel, which calls itself "worry and sorrow," and which becomes the heroine's animal bridegroom.

In the latter variants, the father brings all of these desired symbolic objects back to his daughters from his travels or military campaigns in distant lands. He thus acts as a mediator or represents the relational function toward the unconscious (distant lands). He raises from the unconscious that goal that should henceforth become the heroine's overriding destiny.

The archetypal image of the animal prince, which now replaces that of the father as the animus-figure, corresponds somewhat to both the magic horse and the *div* (i.e., desert demon) in "The Magic Horse" (Turkestan, no. 9). In other words, the animal prince has both positive and negative traits and embodies the unconscious or the self. This figure is so important that its meaning can only be revealed by illumining its various facets. As a goal and prevailing fate, what the heroine desires is identical with the animal bridegroom. In "The Lame Dog" (Sweden, no. 13) and "The White Hound of the Mountain" (Ireland, no. 38), the wishes concern the future husband. In "King Valemon, the White Bear" (Norway, no. 29) and in "The Scarlet Flower," they are jewels owned by the enchanted and from which arises the connection with the animal bridegroom. The identity of the desired one with the husband is plainly evident in "Worry and Sorrow" (Norway, no. 25), where the

---

[138] *The Complete Grimm's Fairy Tales*, pp. 425–430.

peculiar description of what the father should bring home corresponds to the animal prince's name. In the German version of "The Singing, Soaring Lark," the bird's name (*Löweneckerchen*) expresses the fact that the animal bridegroom appears as a lion. The meaning of this peculiar word has yet to be clearly established.

Based on the existing parallels, Jakob Grimm argued that it means *Lerche* (English "lark"), Westphalian *Lauberken*, Lower Saxon *Leverken*, and Middle New German *lewerike*.[139] Bolte and Polívka assume, however, that it denotes a singing leaf, in particular as some fairytales are about a "singing or resounding little tree" (or "leaf") or a "clinging-clanging lion's leaf."[140] The recurrence of the same motif (a hazel twig brushing against the father's hat) in "Cindarella," in the Russian parallel "The Scarlet Flower," as well as in a variant where the daughter wishes to have "a twig with three acorns on one stem,"[141] further supports the assumption that we are dealing with a twig, leaf, or flower. While Bächtold-Stäubli's comments on *Eckerken* throw further, indeed considerable, light on the possible background of the designation conferred on this animal prince, they only marginally extend Grimm's and Bolte and Polívka's assumptions. The parallel expressions for *Eckerken* are *Eckerle, Eckermännlein, Eckele*, and *Egglegeist*. This dwarfish devil or gnome is a benevolent and helpful household spirit but also a nuisance or tormentor, which demands travelers to pay tax, hauls them off their horses, or overturns their carriages. He is a sort of mountain demon or succubus.[142] *Eckerle* is also the name of a goblin in an Alsatian lullaby. "The *Eckermändle, Eckermännlein* who sports a pitch-black hat is a forest spirit in the *Eckernwäldlein* near Rottweil. *Ecker* (Gothic *akran*) is a beech or acorn." In southeastern Thuringia,

[170]

---

[139] "Kleine Schriften," vol. 2, p. 124, cited in Bolte and Polívka, *Anmerkungen*, vol. 2 (1915), p. 229. See also Wilhelm and Jakob Grimm, ed., *Kinder und Hausmärchen gesammelt durch die Brüder Grimm*, vol. 3 (Göttingen: Verlag der Dieterich'schen Buchhandlung, 1856), p. 152.

[140] Translator's note: This is one of the common names given to the flower known in Latin as *leontice leontopetalum*.

[141] Bolte and Polívka, *Anmerkungen*, vol. 2, p. 241.

[142] *Ibid.*, p. 241, fn. 1: "... Grimm's derivation of the name from North German *ekerken* [Translator's note: squirrel] is doubtful."

*Eckele* is a little gray man, a gnome, or a vegetation demon who escapes human deceitfulness by rushing into a forest.[143]

171    Accordingly, this figure refers to a small nature demon or forest spirit, whose name (*Eckerken*) applies to squirrels (see "Worry and Sorrow"; Norway, no. 25), as well as to beechnuts or acorns, whose falling (which can also be associated with falling "leaves") can easily frighten or even strike ramblers or travelers. Its personification as a dangerous demon seems obvious, in particular because the loneliness of the dark forest easily induces projections. Relating the name of the animal prince to *Eckerchen* (or acorn) seems feasible, since fruit, here that of the tree, is an important symbol of the self. On the other hand, *Löweneckerchen* is clearly related to the lion appearing later in the tale. In some variants, it is replaced by other demonic animals and thus might represent a combination of ideas.

172    As explained, the jewels desired by the daughter belong to the animal demon. Their plant or animal nature emphasizes that the self is still deeply unconscious or merely intuited; it still belongs to an instinctual spirituality of the psyche. That part of the animus that is represented by the father, which belongs to consciousness and might be described as a traditional attitude toward life, becomes dangerously dependent on the animal demon by striving for the highest value. Psychologically, this means that consciousness is shaken, even overwhelmed, by the fears swelling up from the unconscious. If the father first brings home the desired object, and if its demonic previous owner later demands to marry the heroine in return, then this represents an attempt to assimilate the symbol of the self with the help of the previous attitude toward life—without, however, taking into account the threatening emotional background, which violently enters the sphere of consciousness—in some variants even quite menacingly—as the animal prince.

173    Symbolizing the self, the animal prince reveals its dual nature. As a psychic being, he comprises both spirit and instinct, demonic possession and nature. In this fairytale, the lion prince in a certain

---

[143] See also Wilhelm Mannhardt, *Wald- und Feldkultte, vol. 1: Der Baumkultus der Germanen und ihrer Nachbarstämme. Mythologische Untersuchungen* (1875), pp. 75ff.

sense represents the mysterious reality of the self as the spirit that is bound in time, space, and matter, yet also becomes manifest and takes action. In some fairytales about animal princes, the animal demon and the object of desire are sometimes distinct, while in others they are identical. This reveals the unity of the self, which takes effect through images or embodiments while at the same time serving as both the starting point and the goal.

In the present fairytale, the archetype of the animal prince is represented by a lion. In Mediterranean culture, the lion symbolizes the sun at its zenith (highest point). For this reason, Aion, the god of time, was also depicted as half-lion and half-serpent (the latter represented the sun at its nadir).[144] Psychologically, the lion, as a symbol of the all-consuming August heat, represents instinctuality and unbridled desire.[145] One medieval author comments on the lion as follows:

174    This beast is neither unfaithful nor false ... it is so fiery that one wishes it were sweet-tempered or feverish ... at the same time it perishes from its own anger, so hot-tempered does it become when angry beyond measure ... the lion is hotter at the front and colder at the rear; when the sun is in the sky, the lion is hot ... the lion is feverish in bright summer, but even-tempered in winter. He also grows feverish at the sight of man.[146]

175    One Manichaean text describes the principle of evil as

176    the filthy, stinking, consuming, corrupting body ... not only the block, the fetter, the ropes and nooses (of the soul), but

---

[144] On the lion and the sun-god in ancient Egypt and Greece, see Albrecht Dieterich, *Abraxas: Studien zur Religionsgeschichte des spätern Altertums* (Leipzig: Teubner, 1891, p. 52); Leisegang, "Schlange" (1940), pp. 243ff. and 172f.; Reitzenstein, *Iranische* (1921), pp. 192ff. and 201; Karl Abraham, "Traum und Mythus, eine Studie zur Völkerpsychologie," *Schriften zur angewandten Seelenkunde*, no. 4, ed. Sigmund Freud (Leipzig and Vienna: Franz Deuticke, 1909), p. 53.

[145] C.G. Jung, *Seminar über Kinderträume und ältere Literatur über Traum-. Interpretation*, a. d. ETH Zürich, ed. Hans H. Baumann (Zurich, printed privately, 1936/37), pp. 34 and 58. On the lion as a symbol of evil, see Reitzenstein, *Iranische*, pp. 79 and 267f.

[146] Bächtold-Stäubli under *Löwe* (lion).—Trans. See also Jung, *Symbols of Transformation*, CW 5, § 425, 600, fn. 190, § 671 and fn. 76.

the ravenous lion, the unfathomable sea, the unbridgeable chasm, the corrupting fire, even the dragon that circles the earth and whose power is unrivalled; these are all designations of matter or its ruler.[147]

177   As the animal king, the lion symbolizes power and the paternal principle in the sense of passionate mastery. He combines the nature of matter and the demonic nature of the mercurial dragon (according to alchemical thinking), the essence of the beast. This also inhabits the human soul ("la bête humaine"), and at the same time "the titanic aspect of our instincts."[148]

178   The lion, however, also has a positive aspect: The wild desire that it embodies "means the wholeness of man ... [He] is ... indeed a roaring monster, a ravenous wild animal, but *he loves the light, the sun*."[149] In the alchemical process, the lion represents a *sol inferior*,

179   a light, a day star, which is, as it were, under our feet, an illumination which does not come from heaven, but from the earth. And so the lion is just this *mysterious earth, which contains the germ of light*. In psychological terms, this means: this devouring desire contains light in itself. It is not completely dark, but light can arise from it, namely, an illumination, expansion, and intensification of consciousness.

180   Thus, the animal bridegroom in the fairytale about the singing, soaring lark might be said to bear traits of the chthonic father-god (and thus of the father-animus), of dark fervor and enlightening spirituality. Both traits make him recognizable as a symbol of the

---

[147] Reitzenstein, *Iranische*, p. 51.—Trans.

[148] Silberer, *Probleme der Mystik* (1914), pp. 83, 99, 160, and 202. On the lion as a symbol of the father, see *ibid.*, esp. pp. 47ff. Thus, at least for this fairytale, we might conclude that the animal aspect of the animus is linked to the heroine's attachment to the father. See also Jung, *Psychology and Alchemy*, CW 12, § 277: "Lions, like all wild animals, indicate latent affects. The lion plays an important part in alchemy and has much the same meaning. It is a 'fiery' animal, an emblem of the devil, and stands for the danger of being swallowed by the unconscious"; see also *ibid.*, § 518: "Lion and unicorn are both symbols of Mercurius." See further fn. 11.

[149] Jung, "Psychologische Interpretation von Kinderträumen und älterer Literatur über Träume. Seminar a. d. ETH Zürich," eds. Liliane Frey and Riwkah Schärf, private offprint (Zurich 1938/39), p. 173 f. See *ibid.*, p. 174, fn. 1: "Caussinus: Polyhistor. Symb.: Leo est animal lucis amicum." See *ibid.*, pp. 171–176.—Trans.

self, albeit in a double, even predominantly negative aspect, which suggests that the symbol is still removed from consciousness.

While melancholy, which often precedes suffering, is not depicted in the present fairytale, it is hinted at in "Worry and Sorrow," the Norwegian variant (no. 25), where the squirrel is called "worry and sorrow." Even if the squirrel appears as a harmless representation of the animal bridegroom compared to the lion, it should be noted that squirrels were sacred to Donar in Germanic mythology[150]; once again, the demonic power is intimated—at least in the background. Bächtold-Stäubli mentions the following folkloristic facts in his entry on "squirrel": Because of their red color and swiftness, squirrels are said to personify lightning and are considered sacred to Thor (i.e., donar), the god of thunder. They also played an important role in cults and rites, as demonstrated by the fact that they were hunted on Maundy Thursday, at Easter, and on Ascension Day (in the regions of Pomerania, Harz, and Waldeck). If a squirrel scuttles across a roof, fire breaks out. In Swabia, squirrels are said to be cursed people and to suffer epileptic seizures. This trait, like their red color, "indicates that they are one of Donar's animals." In Silesia, squirrels haunt people as ghosts, in the Voigtland as fiends, while in Baden they are considered to be cursed white maidens or domestic spirits.

Closely related to the lion, and taking its place in most Norse mythology, is the bear. It appears as the animal bridegroom in two Norwegian tales: "The White Bear King Valemon" (no. 29) and "East of the Sun and West of the Moon" (no. 31). In the former tale, it appears on a Thursday, to fetch the king's daughters, again implying a relation to Donar (i.e., in Norse culture), who embodies untamed natural forces; psychologically, therefore, bears represent instinct and emotionality. In "East of the Sun and West of the Moon," the bear appears in a wild storm, which underscores this connection. In one of her visions, Hildegard von Bingen attributes the bear to the North Pole, the place of greatest darkness[151]; it therefore often

---

[150] See Bächtold-Staubli under *Bart* ("beard").
[151] Leisegang, *Die Gnosis* (1941), pp. 20–23. See also Bächtold-Stäubli under *Bär* ("bear") for a discussion of the bear as a transformed human being in folk belief, as a *Seelentier* (soul animal), as a manifestation

symbolizes the principle of evil. In Germanic myth, it embodies a lack of restraint and also the berserker's blind rage.[152] Psychologically, it thus symbolizes forces similar to those associated with the lion.

The dog, a parallel figure to the bear (e.g., in "The Lame Dog" and "The White Hound of the Mountain"), also represents the instinctual world, albeit in a domesticated form. It embodies that world as instinct and thus as unconscious knowledge (therefore, Anubis, the Egyptian Hermes, also has a dog's head).[153] Like the lion, it is associated with the scorching sun, and hence with the Dog Star (Sirius), which shines brightest on the hottest days.[154] At the same time, it is an image of "the hetaeric earth, which enjoys every kind of fertilization."[155]

Comparing the symbolic meaning of the animals that appear as suitors (i.e., the ram and goat,[156] the fox, wolf, and steed,[157] the ox, "which has a pig's head," the hedgehog, raven, *roi des corbeaux*, swan, bird, snake, worm, toad, frog, *serpent volant*, viper, and voice, "a rough thing like the fiery devil") reveals a common denominator: They all represent the unconscious in its manifestation as a life force, impulse, instinct, emotion, and as vitality. It is a realm of life which, in terms of human morality, is regarded as low or as threatening due to its chthonic nature. And yet, higher consciousness can be gained there (see the animal prince as a swan).

---

of the devil, as one of Thor's animals, and as a vegetation demon.

[152] Ninck, *Wodan* (1935), pp. 48–49.

[153] According to Bernhard Schweitzer, *Herakles: Aufsätze zur griechischen Religions- und Sagengeschichte* (Tübingen, 1922), p. 229, the white hound (of an Irish fairytale) is a manifestation of the ruler of the underworld.

[154] For a Scottish variant in which the white, red-eared dog is called Summer-under-dew, see Bolte and Polívka, *Anmerkungen*, vol. 2, p. 249.

[155] Bachofen, *Das Mutterrecht: Eine Untersuchung über die Gynaikokratie der alten Welt nach ihrer religiösen und rechtlichen Natur* (Stuttgart: Krais & Hoffmann, 1861), p. 11.

[156] Tegethoff, "Amor und Psyche" (1922), p. 17.

[157] See also "The White Wolf" (Wilhelm Wisser, ed., *Plattdeutsche Volksmärchen*, [MdW], vol. 1, ed. v. d. Leyen and Zaunert, 1922, p. 266), "Green Cap" (Christensen, *Iran*, 1939, p. 31), and "The Story of Batim" (Roma, no. 9, Walther Aichele, ed. *Zigeunermärchen*, [MdW], ed. v. d. Leyen and Zaunert, 1926). Although these fairytales do not present the motif of the animal prince in an essentially new way, they do so quite vividly.

185    In some variants, therefore, the symbol of the self, be it the golden wreath or the scarlet flower, appears only in the realm of wild animals (in one parallel, the demon is even called "re Kristallu," the realm of crystals).[158] A Swabian variant reports that the daughter asks for a rose at the height of winter, which the father finds in a "black beast" to whom he must promise his daughter. In another variant, three lilies are guarded by a dragon.[159] In a Swalmian variant, "The Summer and the Winter Garden," the rose is found in a castle garden where summer rules one half and winter the other. The rose is part of summer, the black animal part of winter. The garden symbolizes psychic wholeness, which encompasses the two opposites; yet whoever strives for one of the opposites will also come upon the other—within themselves. Self-knowledge therefore involves encountering one's own darkness. In one variant, the animal prince is literally called a "shadow."[160]

186    In most parallel versions, the animal bridegroom assumes human form at night. Thus, the unconscious realm of instincts and emotions seems to be nonhuman only in terms of daytime consciousness. At night and in dreams, however, the two worlds draw closer, revealing the value and meaning of the unconscious figure.

187    The marriage with the animal prince, who becomes human under the cover of night, is ruined by the woman's misdemeanor; according to Tegethoff, she violates various precepts:

188    In a small number of fairytales, the prohibition to see things is replaced by a warning not to inquire about the elf's name: This is the Lohengrin motif ... that is, not to divulge the name of the elf. It amounts to artifice when the prohibition is not declared outright, but the departing woman is instead warned to heed her mother's counsel / not to become insincere / not to bring anything from the parental home / not to speak to the parents alone / not to talk to them / to tire

---

[158] Tegethoff, "Amor und Psyche," p. 40.
[159] Bolte and Polívka, *Anmerkungen*, vol. 2 (1915), pp. 232ff., esp. p. 230.
[160] Tegethoff, "Amor und Psyche," p. 17.

of him or not to have any confidence in him / to leave this house / not to do anything without first asking / not to forget anything at home /. More widespread is the prohibition to speak, which has displaced the prohibition to see in many of our variants. Yet its real area of dissemination are fairytales whose introductions follow those known from King Lindworm or the Frog King: The newly wed must not tell anyone about the nocturnal figure of the animal bridegroom nor speak further about him: the human part should not speak at home: Where it has been / what it has heard and seen / where the precious things come from / what kind of man she has / "tell nothing" / be patient and silent / never reveal his figure and wait three years for him / do not recognize him when he appears at the feast / do not laugh on the first journey home, do not speak on the second journey / do not speak of his beauty and do not say how she is / speak only three words at home / the prohibition to speak also applies on the journey to the land of the elves / do not speak of his beauty / what is prohibited regarding the animal skin: that it suffers no harm through water and fire / do not show the fur to anyone /. In other verses, a certain time limit is imposed on the human part; once this period expires, that part must return, one hour / one day / in the evening / two days / 3" / 8"/ 9"/ 16 days / 31"/ at St. Joseph's / quite soon / as soon as possible / at the right time / tomorrow at the same time / at the third shot / until she has children / as soon as he steps on her foot / as soon as he whistles / as soon as she hears his voice / as soon as the ring turns black / indefinitely /. As a fourth prohibition, the motif of the forbidden door is taken from tales like Bluebeard and Mary's Child. In addition, there is a series of nonessential prohibitions: the prohibition refers to the use of the magic mirror: She shall not fall asleep / shall not move / a ball of yarn shall not tear / she shall not cry / shall not eat / shall not let herself be embraced. /[161]

---

[161] Tegethoff, "Amor und Psyche," pp. 33–34.—Trans.

189 In the ancient fairytale "Cupid and Psyche," and in most other variants, the heroine is enticed by her envious profane sisters to use a candle to behold her bridegroom. When she spills a drop of wax on him, he awakens and disappears. This process is also recounted in "The Lame Dog" (Sweden, no. 13) and in "The White Bear King Valemon" (Norway, no. 29). In the latter tale, however, disaster is instigated by the mother, whereas in "East of the Sun and West of the Moon" (Norway, no. 31) and in "Worry and Sorrow" (Norway, no. 25), the heroine initiates the calamitous events. In each case, profane figures or tendencies suddenly intervene. The taboo-breaking intrusion of the profane world of concepts and ideas during the intermediate stage of the magical marriage disrupts the initiated development, whose basic condition is that the mystery must be safeguarded against the collective. Like all symbols, the magical marriage as a psychic reality eludes human comprehension. "For the conscious mind knows nothing beyond the opposites, and, as a result, has no knowledge of the thing that unites them."[162] This applies even less here, because the archetype of the *coniunctio*, upon which the magical marriage is based, represents the union of the most extreme opposites and encompasses the entire scale from the instinctual realm to the spiritual one. In the sphere of this symbol, however, profane, limited human consciousness can only cause destruction in a discriminatory manner.[163]

---

[162] Jung, "The Special Phenomenology of the Child Archetype," CW 9/I, § 285.

[163] See also an Indian tale discussed by Heinrich Zimmer in "The 'King of the Dark Chamber': In drei Verwandlungen von Rgveda to Tagore," *Zeitschr. d. Deutsche Morgenländische Gesellschaft*, ed. G. Steindorff (Leipzig: Brockhaus, 1929). The tale (heavily abridged here) goes like this: A King, whose subjects had never seen him, ruled his country most happily. His invisibility, however, fueled speculation that he was unsightly. He approached his beautiful wife Sudarśanā only in a "secret dark chamber" because she would not be able to bear the sight of him. She, however, desired to set eyes on him so very much that he challenged her up to pick him out in the crowd at a festival. She believed that he was identical with a charming apparition and sent this figure flowers. Influenced by the King of Kâncî, who was attending the festival as a guest and wanted to gain the woman's favor, the beautiful impostor set fire to the women's chambers in the palace. When the Queen, rescued from the blaze, realized her mistake, she threw herself back into the fire full of shame. And yet, in the dark chamber, which neither noise nor fire could reach, she encountered the "incomprehensible king of her heart," who tamed the fire: "He was black and ugly, mighty and horrible, yet not beautiful at all." She shuddered at his cold inhumanity, "his dispassionate inertia," which, however, resonated more strongly in her than "the impostor's empty loveliness." Her father, to whom she fled, denied the runaway her royal rank, and the mysterious husband sent her no sign. On the other hand, six foreign kings and, in addition, the King of Kâncî, wooed her, assisted by the beautiful impostor. They stormed her father's kingdom and took him prisoner. Resolved to die, the daughter approached the hated wooers, when the invisible king summoned the suitors. They fled, the King of Kâncî succumbed, and Sudarśanā awaited the King of the Dark Chamber most humbly. He, however, did not reveal himself. "It is futile to wait for him: Those

190 Most fairytales represent this destruction as premature illumination. The so-called Orpheus motif is also related to this illumination: Although returning to the magical sphere wreaks havoc, this "retrospective view" (i.e., "spatial" error) is aggravated by the "temporal" error of looking too soon. Light is a metaphor of consciousness.[164] (This is evident from everyday phrases and expressions such as "seen in this and that light," "now I see the light," or "as clear as daylight"; or conversely, "we are in the dark," "we are groping in the dark"). Yet just as the sun's light is identical with its fire, its heat and the danger of burning, so psychogically inner enlightenment is inconceivable without emotion; the jumping spark both illumines and scorches. In myths, the symbolism of light is therefore closely related to symbols of fire and instinct.[165] However, as Bachofen's interpretation of the tale of Cupid and Psyche shows, the light that the heroine shines on the sleeping god symbolizes the purifying of erotic desire:

191 In the restlessly flickering flame, in the glowing oil, which strives to connect with Eros, Psyche is prefigured. The noctural dark mixture with the dragon forms the content of a new stage of sexual life ... grasping the burning lamp

---

who wish to find him, must seek him." The Queen, just as she had fled from him in the past, now wandered through the dusty streets. She met the King of Kâncî, who was also searching for the King of the Dark Chamber, who had set him free. Only when she realized that it was her King who had sent her on her journey did she find him in the dark chamber; and only then did she realize that his being and his love were unrivalled and part of herself.—Trans.

[164] See Jung, *Symbols of Transformation*, CW 5, § 428, fn. 63, for a discussion of the Japanese myth in which the god Izanagi follows his dead wife into the underworld to bring her back. She forbids him to look at her, but he lights a fire (light) and thus loses his wife. See further "Parthonopeus and Meliur" (France, vol. 1, no. 4, Ernst Tegethoff, trans., *Französische Volksmärchen 1: Aus älteren Quellen*, [MdW], ed. v. d. Leyen and Zaunert, 1923): The hero, lured ever deeper into the forest by a boar, reached the sea and landed with a miraculous ship at the foot of a mountain castle. "The high walls of the fortress were built of red and white marble, alternating like a checkerboard." In the sumptuously furnished palace, the castle's beautiful fairy lay down with the hero every night; yet he was not permitted to catch sight of his beloved until that day on which she would publicly chose him as her husband. Despite his happiness, he was very homesick. On two visits home, his mother and the archbishop urged him to illumine his beloved, behind whom they suspected an ugly devil. Immediately, the fairy's magical power was extinguished, and knights and women streamed into the chamber pointing fingers at the pair. The hero was banished from the land of fairies and longed to die. (As the plot unfolds, a powerful fairy later helps the hero to betroth Meliur). For a general discussion of the motif of Germanic sagas, according to which dwarves and elves hide in the daylight, see Ninck, *Wodan*, p. 164, fn. 2; see further Maria Führer, *Nordgermanische Götterüberlieferung und deutsches Volksmärchen. 80 Märchen der Brüder Grimm vom Mythus her beleuchtet* (Munich: Neuer Filser-Verlag, 1938), p. 68.

[165] Silberer, *Probleme der Mystik*, p. 199; Jung, *Symbols of Transformation*, CW 5, § 149 fn. 46, § 230ff.

signifies the dawning of a new day, the transition to a new state, the beginning of new sufferings, which lead to eventual redemption.[166]

192 Dark passion also contains the powerful urge toward higher consciousness that enables Eros to become the creative principle.

193 The germinating or entering light of consciousness leads to a separation from the preconscious, primordial unity. This separation is painful because the original state of perfect harmony appears as a beautiful paradise, even if humankind has always sought to distance itself from that unconscious state. Prometheus steals the fire from the gods and suffers greatly as a result of becoming conscious because he has assailed distant sacred orders and powers on his own authority. He knows that the act to which he is driven is sacrilegious. This knowledge leads Prometheus to believe that the assaulted deity is wounded: After all, the human being has dragged the numinous into the world of matter, where it becomes opaque, like all living things. In "Cupid and Psyche," therefore, Cupid is wounded by the drop of oil, while in the present tale, blood seeps from the dove. However, once the precious soul-image has dissipated, the human being, whose awakening ego-consciousness was so presumptuous as to reach out prematurely (and without making any effort) for the secrets of the unconscious, is left feeling miserable and isolated.[167]

194 In the present fairytale, the "profane sisters" are to blame for this catastrophe: The light of their profane wedding drives away the lion-prince; that is, his magical aspect, and thus the *coniunctio*, is devalued by the light of the profane world. The destructive tendency of the profane attitude stems from the fact that in some variants the envious sisters or the mother coax the heroine into shining a light on the bridegroom.[168] Their ulterior motive is that she will be

---

[166] Bachofen, *Versuch über die Gräbersymbolik der Alten* (1859), p. 96.—Trans.

[167] Carus, *Psyche* (1931), p. 409: "First of all, we should remember the insight ... which taught us that the morbid and the defective, the purposeless, the embarrassing and the deficient, which bring nothing but misery into life, and constrain, pester, and torment the free, higher spirit, is *not grounded in the unconscious of the world*, but only arises with the light of our consciousness" (original emphasis).—Trans.

[168] See also the Hanoverian variant collected in Bolte and Polívka, *Anmerkungen*, vol. 2, p. 230, where the guilt of premature illumination is replaced by the following motif: "In the bedchamber of the King's daughter hung a mirror, in which she could see everything that happened in the castle; all she needed

disappointed and that her fascination with the animal prince will wane. Yet the nocturnal union of opposites, one that occurs on an unconscious level, has a natural duration in the developmental process that must not be interrupted. On the other hand, the unification of consciousness and the unconscious, almost inevitably sparks a violent conflict (hence, in a Russian variant,[169] everything is burned by igniting the light): Ego-consciousness cannot accept the inner alter ego at first, because it means negating the previous personality.

195    Consciousness mostly only expects to process sensory data and therefore often struggles to tolerate the autonomy of the unconscious.[170] Accordingly, time plays an obvious role in this regard: Unconscious contents cannot be made conscious and recognized arbitrarily, but only when the time is "ripe." This irrational circumstance arises from the peculiar relationship of the unconscious to time.[171] In this sense, time is creative.[172] It can only manifest in the psychic process because "for the unconscious time and creative life are one and the same. Creative life cannot be expressed other than through a symbol of time."[173] Therefore, the clock (mandala) is a symbol of the self, for which Jung has gathered ample evidence.[174] The self can realize itself through the human

---

to ensure was that the chambermaid could not look into the room. The King's daughter therefore always carried the key to that room with her. One day, however, she left it in the lock, and the chambermaid entered the room and looked into the mirror. The raven tore her to pieces and told the king's daughter: 'Now you must leave, serve for seven years, and do the work of seven maids.'"—Trans. The chambermaid represents the profane sisters, while the mirror is the central mystery, as is evident from a Spanish variant ("The Washerwoman," no. 37). Thus, guilt is represented here as the intrusion of a profane part of consciousness.

[169] Bolte and Polívka, *Anmerkungen*, vol. 2, p. 258.

[170] On the "devastating effect of the sensible world on the deeper psychic processes when it breaks into them," see Jung, *Psychology and Alchemy*, CW 12, § 186.

[171] On the relationship of the unconscious to time, and on time as a psychic function that is identical with life, see Jung, *Kindertraumseminar 1936/1937* (Zurich, 1937), p. 63.

[172] See the androgynous demiurges and deities of antiquity. As Jean Przyluski points out in "Die Mutter-Göttin als Verbinding zwischen den Lokal-Göttern und dem Universal-Gott" (*Eranos-Jahrbuch 1938: Gestalt und Kult der "Grossen Mutter,"* ed. Olga Fröbe-Kapteyn, 1939, pp. 42–43), they are "Creator, Time, and Fate." See also *ibid.*, p. 51ff. On the originally "magical" meaning of time, see v. d. Leeuw, *Phänomenologie der Religion* (1933), p. 364ff., esp. the chapter on festivals. On the symbolism of time in India, see Güntert, *Weltkönig* (1923), p. 231 (Atharvaveda 19, 53).

[173] Jung, *Bericht über das Deutsche Seminar von Dr. C.G. Jung. 5.–10. Oktober 1931 in Küsnacht-Zurich*, compiled by Olga von Koenig-Fachsenfeld, privately printed (Stuttgart 1932), p. 150.

[174] Jung, *Psychology and Alchemy*, CW 12, § 314: "We have at our disposal, firstly, the whole mandala symbolism of three continents, and secondly, the specific *time symbolism of the mandala* as this developed under the influence of astrology, particularly in the West. The horoscope is itself a mandala (a clock) with a dark center, and a leftward circumambulatio with 'houses' and planetary phases. The

being solely in time and space. This is quite likely the origin of this strange relation of the symbols of the self to time. For the same reason, in fairytales time is often indicated in years or days, during which redemption, for instance, can occur.[175]

196     In addition to the motif of time, Tegethoff[176] (as observed) mentions all kinds of variants, according to which another of the heroine's errors thwarts the redemption of the animal prince: Here we find the typical motif of betrayal, as discussed in the section on the "magical marriage" with the animal's anima, and where divulging the secret resulted in the irreparable separation from the beloved. Often, as in "The Jaguar Woman" (South America, no. 21), the hero's or the heroine's mother is the disrupting factor. She (and sometimes

---

mandalas of ecclesiastical art, particularly those on the floor before the high altar or beneath the transept, make frequent use of the zodiacal beasts or the yearly seasons. A related idea is the identity of Christ with the Church calendar, of which he is the fixed pole and the life" (von Franz's emphasis). See also *ibid.*, § 281ff. and 310ff.

[175] See "Little Briar Rose" (i.e., Sleeping Beauty) (*The Complete Grimm's Fairy Tales*, pp. 237–241) ) and the variants on the present fairytale, in which the animal prince reproaches the heroine that he would have been redeemed in so-and-so much time if she had not performed a certain action: "The White Bear King Valemon" (Norway, no. 29), "East of the Sun and West of the Moon" (Norway, no. 31), and "Worry and Sorrow" (Norway, no. 25). One condition of redemption, in particular regarding its point in time, is also discussed by Laistner, *Das Rätsel* (1889), vol. 1, p. 83ff.: The cursed woman can be redeemed only when the tree that she has planted has grown old, when a cradle has been made from its wood, and when the child nursed in that cradle has grown up and is summoned by the woman, who has meanwhile become a demon, to bring about redemption. With this motif, the choice of the redeemer (i.e., the calling) also plays a part: For if the one who is called fails, everything begins anew for the next one who is called. Only a child of the *magna mater* as Mother Nature (tree-wood-cradle) can be considered to perform this act—presumably because of its natural relationship, which is not inhibited by reason. In turn, the fact that the tree is planted by the woman who must be redeemed indicates her intimate relationship with the Great Mother. It is as if nature as a whole needs to be redeemed. Laistner cites the following legend in evidence: A lad from Pfullingen accompanied his parents to a field at Mount Urschelberg and found a new horse collar (part of a harness), which he placed on his shoulders according to the local custom by sticking his head through it. All of a sudden, Urschel appeared before him wearing a green skirt and red stockings. She was glad that he had come at long last. "We have been waiting for centuries for the redemption you can help us achieve." She had listened anxiously and longingly to the germination and growth of the tree, from which they had made his cradle. She had counted the minutes, days, years, and centuries until the tree was finally felled. Thereafter, she nursed and protected the child, for "now the time had come when he could express his gratitude and redeem her, which of all men he alone could achieve." She promised him immeasurable treasures and wanted to show him the castle that stood sunken into the mountain. A terrible serpent would assail him there, but he should embrace it with his heart and it would become the most beautiful woman. The ancient curse would be broken and the castle would once again see the light of day. Terrified, the young man said his prayers and, while he was saying the Lord's Prayer, Urschel disappeared. She appeared to him on several other occasions, yet he resisted her advances, in particular as he was not supposed to bring his parents with him. When Urschel threatened him with death unless he redeemed her, he promised that he would but first asked his confessor for advice. The latter said that this was the devil's work, and that a cursed soul should not be redeemed. After a year and a day, when the young man and his parents again came to the same place, Urschel appeared to him (only he could see and hear her). Scolding him, she lamented that "unless he redeemed her, she would have to suffer for centuries." He cursed her, and all of a sudden, his parents watched with horror as he dropped dead. The horse collar that one of the horses was wearing had disappeared. See *ibid.* for similar examples.

[176] Tegethoff, "Amor und Psyche" (1922), p. 33.

also the entire family) represents the connection with the profane world, by which psychic life is damaged. Evidently, the psyche sometimes needs to be isolated from profane reality to enable human beings to engage entirely and uncompromisingly with their inner experience.

197    One of the most interesting variants on the motif of the wounding and expulsion of the animal prince is an abridged Spanish tale, which is reproduced in the notes (page 325) to "The Dragon of the Rosebush" (no. 19) in Espinosa's collection of Spanish fairytales[177]: In the animal prince's castle, whom she does not get to see, the maiden hears

198    a constant wailing, but dared not go and look where the noise was coming from. One evening, when she could no longer bear the uncertainty and fear and therefore went to investigate, she found a bear, who was dying next to the plant from which her father had cut a flower; she felt so sorry for the animal that she stroked it. She cured it by placing the flower back on its stem. No sooner did she do this than the bear turned into a beautiful young man, and they married.

199    Thus, the animal prince is not wounded by the subsequent betrayal but already by the cutting of the miraculous flower. As the flower is a symbol of the self, the abrupt and forceful attempt to become conscious of the self, which, as a plant, is at first deeply unconscious, is fraught with guilt, and implies violating nature or the unconscious. It amounts to a human intrusion into a psychic realm, which until then did not belong to humankind but to the deity. Conscious realization resembles plundering that realm. The Spanish fairytale describes not only this tragic event but also how, in turn, a human being can heal the wound that they have inflicted on the hitherto extrahuman soul-image. At the end of the Spanish fairytale, nothing

---

[177] See Spain, p. 336 (sources of the works used and cited): "(Espinosa) = Aurelio M. Espinosa, *Cuentos populares españoles recogidos de la tradición oral de España* (Stanford University Publications. University Series, Language and Literature, vol. III.) 3 vols. Stanford University 1923–1926 (Note: Vol. IV not yet published)."

has changed. Well, except that now both spheres, which previously were separated and oblivious of each other, are united. Quite likely, this is the meaning of the initial distress and suffering.

200    In other accounts of the animal prince's banishment, the heroine is forbidden to inquire about the magical bridegroom's name or nature,[178] which is the actual Lohengrin motif.[179] In primitive belief, a name expresses a person's or an object's essence (we will consider this aspect in more detail in Section 2 of the next volume). Inquiring about a name is therefore an attempt to grasp the essence of one's counterpart and thereby to assimilate them to one's own sphere of consciousness. Assimilating the man's and the woman's soul-image, however, demands exceptional subtlety: It demands protracted, conflict-ridden confrontation, during which consciousness, at first "profane," is profoundly transformed; insofar as consciousness, as yet naive and undeveloped, is unable to assimilate the essence of the unconscious realities, attempting to conceptualize and name those realities prematurely offends the unconscious realm, or rather, makes it even less attainable for consciousness.

201    One fairytale, "The Soul of the Whale and the Burning Heart,"[180] which describes the raven-cum-hero's night sea journey in terms of the well-known theme of Jonah, aptly illustrates the motif of destruction by profane consciousness: The raven is swallowed by a whale and finds itself in the whale's belly:

202    For a moment, it remained dark around him, things rushed and splashed, and when he thought he was going to die, he staggered straight into a house, a beautiful and charming house, where it was bright and warm. A young woman was sitting on the bed, fiddling with a burning lamp. She got up and approached the raven in a friendly manner and said: "You are welcome as my guest if you fulfill me one wish: You must never touch my lamp.

---

[178] For an Indian variant, see Bolte and Polívka, *Anmerkungen*, vol. 2, pp. 259–260.

[179] See, e.g., "Do Not Entrust a Secret to a Woman" (Johannes Hertel, ed., *Indische Märchen*, [MdW], ed. v. d. Leyen and Zaunert, 1925, no. 72), esp. p. 307.

[180] Knud Rasmussen, *Die Gabe des Adlers, Eskimoische Märchen aus Alaska*, trans. and ed. Aenne Schmücker (Frankfurt a. M: Societäts-Verlag, 1937), p. 199.—Trans.

203 Although the raven is saved, the woman grows restless and keeps rushing out of the room. He inquires what is making her so restless, to which she replies: "Life, [...] life and my breath." Her answer eludes him, and the tale continues as follows:

204 The raven, who had now calmed down and forgotten his fear, became curious. "Why should I not touch the lamp?" he thought; and every time the woman slipped out and he remained alone, he felt more and more inclined to break his promise and go and touch the lamp just a little. At last he could no longer restrain his curiosity, and when the woman slipped out of the door again, he jumped up and touched the wick of the lamp. At that moment, the woman staggered headlong into the room, fell onto the floor, and remained there while the lamp went out.

205 Too late, the raven regretted what he had done; he staggered around in black darkness, and the beautiful, bright house was no longer there. He was close to suffocating. He wandered among the bacon and the blood, and it became so hot that his feathers fell off. Almost suffocating, he staggered around in the whale's belly, and only now did he realize what had happened.

206 The young woman was the whale's soul, and she slipped out of the door into the fresh air every time the whale needed to catch its breath, and her heart was a lamp with a large and steady flame. The raven had touched the young woman's heart out of sheer curiosity, and that was why she had died. He did not know that what is fine and beautiful is also fragile, perishable and easily destroyed, for he himself was stupid and tenacious; and now he was fighting for his life amid darkness and blood. Everything that was beautiful and pure before had now grown ugly and smelled foul.

207 The raven saves himself and returns to the human world. "He did not speak at all about the fact that out of sheer curiosity

he had touched a heart and destroyed something fine and beautiful; he only boasted arrogantly: 'I killed the whale! I killed the whale!' And he became a great man among men." This tale speaks for itself: The woman is a soul-image and therefore corresponds to the animal prince. She contains a living secret or also the secret of life. This must not be touched by blatant curiosity, which naive consciousness likes to do.

208 If consciousness in its high-handedness fails to consider the laws of the unconscious, this violates the latter's precepts and amounts to "disobedience," as our discussion of "The Golden Bird" has shown.[181] As Carus points out, the *possibility of being mistaken ... is the first step toward recognizing the truth.*[182] Higher consciousness can be attained only by rebelling against the unconscious realities. If we assess the heroine's behavior along these lines, then the animal prince, according to most versions, would have gradually been redeemed by living together affectionately with the heroine. Yet no final struggle would have taken place with the negative magical powers, the witch, or the false bride. Insofar as these figures represent the unconscious as that which inhibits the individual from conscious realization, the connection between the self, symbolized by the animal prince, and the obstructing unconscious forces, would never have been completely severed, so to speak; only the painful conflict caused by the error of consciousness reveals what lies behind the enchantment.

209 In most fairytales, however, the separation is caused by a scene familiar from the classical version of "Cupid and Psyche": A drop of tallow or oil drips from the heroine's lamp onto the sleeping Cupid and scorches him, causing him to awaken. In one variant, Psyche

---

[181] On "Cupid and Psyche," see Bachofen, *Gräbersymbolik* (1859), p. 100: "The sexual embrace with the dragon occurs without pleasure, yet also without suffering, in the unillumined spaces of the earth. If the woman had never renounced this embrace, and if she had never lifted the lamp shade, the lower creation would never have lost any of its equanimity. But Psyche is tempted to look; she desires light instead of darkness. The forbidden act causes unspeakable suffering, yet also marks the beginning of a higher existence in which the lower creation has no part."—Trans.
[182] Carus, *Psyche* (1931), p. 143 (Translator's note: von Franz's emphasis).

also wounds him with a knife.[183] Precisely this motif suggests that it is not only a question of passionate desire, but just as much of a passionate desire to recognize the ghostly lover—moreover, in a primitive form, in which instinct and spirit are still unified psychic activities.

210    Thus confronted, the figure of the animal bridegroom dissipates, that is, contact with the unconscious is once again lost. In some variants,[184] the partner not only disappears, but almost or actually dies, which represents an even more radical splitting off. In other variants,[185] the enchanted falls ill. In the above fairytale about the summer and winter garden, the heroine finds "her beloved animal" lying dead under some rotten cabbages on one side of the garden, which is now "all winter and covered with snow." Turning over the cabbages and dousing the animal with water both revives and redeems it. This intrusion of death, and in particular of coldness, indicates that the emotional participation in the unconscious event has "gone cold" because of the untimely and devaluing intrusion of consciousness. In some variants, the prince's enchantment even amounts to a sleeplike or seemingly deathlike state or having to die periodically. These motifs can all be interpreted similarly.[186] In "The White Bear King Valemon" (Norway, no. 29), the heroine must even tend the fire in the bear's castle to ensure it never extinguishes. The underlying rationale is that the unconscious values must be cherished if they are to remain effective. Thus, the heroine's guilt also involves growing tired[187] of her beloved or lacking confidence in him.

211    In one of these variants, the heroine is detained by her profane sisters, returns too late from her parents' home to the animal prince, and thus ruins their relationship.[188] Psychologically, such tardiness can be explained by unconscious resistance or by a lack of interest.

---

[183] Tegethoff, "Amor und Psyche" (1922), p. 39.
[184] See *ibid.*, p. 40.
[185] Bolte and Polívka, *Anmerkungen*, vol. 2, pp. 231–234, 243–245.
[186] See "The Story of the Beauty Who Achieved What She Wanted" (Turkey, no. 5) and "The Rose of Paradise" (Caucasus, no. 7).
[187] Tegethoff, "Amor und Psyche," p. 33.
[188] See, e.g., "The Scarlet Flower" (Loepfe, *Russische*, Olten 1941, p. 86); see further Bolte and Polívka, *Anmerkungen*, vol. 2, pp. 243ff. and 250.

As a result, however, the living inner relationship, and thus the process of development, perishes immediately. Once again, consciousness finds itself alone in its sterile arrogance. In several versions,[189] redemption is bound to the condition that the heroine agrees to marry the fiend. This decision is sufficient to redeem the ogre from its curse. Thus, love is described here as the only basic condition of redemption.

212    Matters are similar in "The Maiden and the Serpent" (Sweden, no. 8): A maiden who went out to fetch the cattle lost her way. After a while, she reached a large mountain with gates and doors. When she entered, she found a table set for supper and a bed in which lay a large snake that said: "Sit down if you want. Come and lie down in bed if you want! But if you don't want to, then don't!" The girl rejected the snake's advances and eventually was warned by the snake not to dance with anyone who entered the room. She heeded the warning and returned home. The next day, she once again failed to find her flock and came to the same mountain. Everything took the same course as on the previous day. On the third day, however, after she had entered the mountain again, she ate from the table and then lay down next to the snake. The serpent invited her to embrace and kiss it. No sooner did the girl do so than the serpent was transformed into a beautiful prince who had been bewitched and was now redeemed.[190]

213    Love enables people to accept the wholly other or the out-landish.[191] Presumably, this creative essence of love, which becomes

---

[189] See, e.g., "The Dragon of the Rosebush" (Spain, no. 19) and "Beauty and the Beast" (France, vol. 1, no. 33).

[190] See also "The Merchant's Three Daughters" (Zaunert, *Märchen aus dem Donaulande*, p. 188): in that tale, the kiss is the condition of redemption. See also Bolte and Polívka, *Anmerkungen*, vol. 2, pp. 242–245 and "The Bull" (collected in Friedrich Salomon Krauss, *Sagen und Märchen der Südslaven, in ihrem Verhältnis zu den Sagen und Märchen der übrigen indogermanischen Völkergruppen*, vol. 2, Leipzig: Verlag von Wilhelm Friedrich, 1884, no. 89): An old man only owned a bull, which he loved more than anything else, and for which, when the animal grew wild, he courted a girl. Her mother agreed, because the bull was also "created by the good Lord, as well as the other creatures." When the old man led the girl in front of the bull, it began to roar. The girl screamed, "Silence, you shall die!" Whereupon she dropped dead. The same happened to the second girl. But the third girl stroked the bull and said, "My dear little ox!" Whereupon the bull was transformed into a beautiful boy, "shining like the bright sun." And whereupon they married.

[191] Rainer Maria Rilke, *Letters to a Young Poet*, ed. Ray Soulard (Portland, Oregon: Scriptor, 2001); see the letter of August 12, 1904: "Perhaps everything that frightens us is, in its deepest essence, something helpless that wants our love," p. 31.

evident in the transforming union of opposites, exists in all acts of redemption in these fairytales, even when only the archetypal event is communicated. Yet, as observed, some fairytales emphasize love as an essential aspect of the archetypal events. One particularly dramatic and poetic example is "The Scarlet Flower," a Russian fairytale recorded by the novelist Aksakov.[192] There, the heroine lives in the monster's castle, visits her beloved ones, and returns home late, although the fiend, whose attentive and melancholy nature she had grown accustomed to despite its frightening appearance, had warned her. Out in the garden, she discovers the dead monster, which had died of grief. Embracing it, in despair, she exclaims: "Arise, awaken, my dear friend, for I love thee as my chosen bridegroom!"—whereupon, with a clap of thunder, the monster and its realm are transformed, and disenchanted, into a king and his kingdom.[193]

214    Hence, while the error committed by consciousness perhaps results from opposite tendencies, it may nevertheless have the same alienating effect: It involves either too much profane curiosity, a will to know, and desire (in the form of illumination); or vice versa, disinterestedness, due to a profane attachment or lack of love. Both attitudes are equally detrimental to assimilating the unconscious, as this process requires the consistent, patient, and loving attention of human consciousness.

215    The separation can longer be atoned for in most fairytales whose principal motif is the magical marriage (nor, for that matter, in several variants[194]). However, in the fairytale about the singing, soaring lark (*Löweneckerchen*), and in most of its parallels, including "Rakian" (Malaysia, no. 33), the heroine embarks on a quest, a Great Journey, to once again find her partner.

216    The beloved, who until now had appeared as a lion, escapes as a dove, leaving behind only a few drops of blood, which indicate the

---

[192] Loepfe, *Russische*, p. 197, and his note on "The Scarlet Flower" (p. 86).

[193] See Jakob Grimm's heartfelt observations on "Amor und Psyche" (*Kleine Schriften*, vol. 1, p. 351, cited in Bolte and Polívka, *Anmerkungen*, vol. 2, p. 266, fn. 1): "This tale points to the power of the earthly spell and to redemption through love. One step after another, purity emerges; if this development is disturbed, the misery and heaviness of the world come rushing in, and it is only when souls touch each other, and when knowledge is gained through love, that earthly life wanes."—Trans.

[194] Bolte and Polívka, *Anmerkungen*, vol. 2, pp. 243 and 244: According to a Portuguese variant, the animal curses the heroine and then dies.

direction of his flight. While the lion—as a mammal—was more closely related to humankind and symbolized the instinctual-spiritual power of the animus, the psychic force, represented by the dove, has become weaker, more fleeting, and more incomprehensible.

217 The dove, as Aphrodite's bird, represents the principle of Eros and is considered a symbol of sensual pleasure in the East. Both animus and anima often appear as doves in fairytales; the lover often visits the heroine first as a dove and becomes a human being at night (see, e.g., "The Wounded Bird"; Spain, no. 20).[195] Injured and driven away, ultimately the dove prince can be healed only if his wounds are sprinkled with a powder made from three doves. A Siberian fairytale, "Three Brothers and a Sister" (no. 6), whose structure resembles tales about the singing, soaring lark, begins by recounting how a woman living with her three brothers and seeking a husband marries a young gander (in a hut at midday) who has turned into a man. Here, however, the marriage with the animal prince is disturbed not by *her* profane siblings, but by *his* youngest brother, who cuts off the bird-bridegroom's legs, whereupon he disappears. Thus, *his* shadow aspect intrudes, a problem that we will explore in more detail below. In this fairytale, the encounter with the bird-animus is represented somewhat tersely:

218 Once upon a time, three brothers lived together with their sister. One day, they went hunting elk and reindeer, and when they returned home late in the evening, neither was a fire lit nor was the kettle boiling. The eldest brother said, "We have a sister, but have neither a fire nor a boiling kettle." The youngest brother replied, "Our sister is very angry, she would like to have a husband." He entered the house, put the sister on a shovel, and tossed her out of the house. She flew over the grass and landed amidst a grove of tall, upright trees. She

---

[195] See also "The Story of the Weeping Pomegranate and the Laughing Quince" (Turkey, no. 4), "Yonec" (France vol. 1, p. 144) ("Aus den Lais der Marie de France," no. 15), "Loving Doves" (Balkans, no. 54), "The Old Woman in the Wood" (*The Complete Grimm's Fairy Tales*, pp. 558–560). On the figure of the bird in general, see "The Feather of Finist, The Bright Falcon" (Afanas'ev, *Russian Fairy Tales*, pp. 580–588) and the French literary tale "The Blue Bird" (France, vol. 1, no. 30), where the prince visits the captive heroine as a blue bird.

started walking. When she had wandered for a while, she saw a house hanging from the end of an iron chain, whose lower gold radiated downward while the upper gold radiated upward. She walked around the house three times but could not find a door. Thereupon, she noticed the edge of an iron cramp. She picked up the cramp, opened a door, and stepped into the house. On one table stood beer, on another mead [a fermented beverage made of water and honey, malt, and yeast], and she began to eat and drink. Thereupon, Pairachta[196] came flying from the midday region in the form of a young man. He cast off his feathers and stood before her in his natural size and stature. He entered the house, and they embraced and kissed.

219 Vice versa, the woman's soul-image sometimes appears as a dove at the beginning of a story (i.e., the motif of the swan maiden) or later disappears as a dove. In "The Crab" (Modern Greece, no. 5),[197] a variant of the fairytale about the singing, soaring lark, the animal prince (who appears as a crab) possesses a magic lantern, from which, when he rubs it, girls rush to his aid. When he disappears after the heroine's betrayal, these girls become doves. Thus, the doves are female figures that belong to the animal prince. They are his female half. Referring to the fairytale about the singing, soaring lark, this would mean that also there the animal prince is a hermaphroditic being, whose male aspect is represented by the lion and whose female aspect is represented by the dove. His female aspect emerges as a consequence of the undesired illumination, as a reaction, as it were, to the overly male activity of consciousness. In the modern Greek variant, the animal prince becomes a stone column: that is, the unconscious hardens and dissipates at the same time as a result of the undesired contact with consciousness.

---

[196] See Kunike, Sibirien (Jena, 1940), p. 305, fn.: "Pairachta is the cultural hero, the goose a sacred bird of the Ostyaks."—Trans.
[197] See Paul Kretschmer, ed., Neugriechische Märchen, [MdW], ed. v. d. Leyen and Zaunert (1919).

220     As van der Leeuw has pointed out, the dove (like other birds) represents a "soul outside."[198] It is a "soul-bird," an archetypal image discussed by Weicker in *Der Seelenvogel*. This is the idea of the soul as pure and as fleeting, and which, if it is wounded, suffers. In the present fairytale, the soul-image is thus transformed into something light and floating, after the frightening encounter with the dangerous animal, which symbolizes the emotional sphere, has been lived through. Yet whereas that figure oppressed and threatened human-kind, the present figure is inaccessible and incomprehensible.

221     Regarding the anima's dual, hermaphroditic nature, the present fairytale resembles "The Washerwoman" (no. 37), a Spanish tale where the psyche is represented by two figures: the prince and a dark-skinned servant. Prematurely illumining the prince means that the servant should kill the girl. He spares her, however, because she is expecting a child. Following the prince, she finds him again as a dove and pulls a needle out of his head, which turns out to be the drop of wax that had fallen on his head during illumination; she thus redeems him. This very subtle variation requires some explanation: The splitting of the animal prince into a prince and a dark-skinned servant represents the double aspect of this peculiar archetype. As a rule, Negroes (or Moors) play the role of the "shadow" in Spanish fairytales. In "The Rose of Paradise" (no. 7), a Caucasian variant on the fairytale about the singing, soaring lark, the man's soul-image is also represented twice: first, as a man-eating *div* (desert demon) that guards the rose, whom the heroine cannot redeem and from whom she can only escape; and second, as a prince who is cursed by the sun and who is dead during the day and alive only at night.[199] His mother is later able to redeem him by appealing to the sun after the heroine has restored the connection with his parents' home by giving birth to a child there. Once more, the *div* represents a demonic shadow-figure that cannot be redeemed but from which the heroine

---

[198] See v. d. Leeuw, *Phänomenologie der Religion* (1933), pp. 129 and 273. On the "soul outside," see the last section of this volume. On the soul-bird, see also Otto Tobler, "Die Epiphanie der Seele in deutscher Volkssage," PhD Dissertation, Christian-Albrechts-Universität zu Kiel (Kiel, 1911); see Bächtold- Stäubli under *Seelenvogel* (soul-bird).

[199] The same motif (i.e., the splitting into an evil *div* and a prince) appears in "Green Cap" (Christensen, *Iran*, Jena 1939, p. 31).

can only knowingly differentiate herself. The prince, on the other hand, symbolizes a part of the unconscious psyche that can be assimilated into conscious life. In most fairytales, however, the two figures mentioned above are united in the animal prince.

222    We find a similar division in "Snow-White and Rose-Red"[200]: In that tale, the animal prince appears as a bear and is cursed by an evil dwarf, so that he must remain a bear for as long as he lives. Out of ignorant pity, the girls save the evil dwarf three times and thus defer the bear's redemption until it can, at long last, slay the dwarf. Once again, we need to understand the dwarf as the shadow component of the animal prince. While the latter can only be redeemed by love, meekly pitying the "shadow" is inappropriate. This touches on the difficult psychological question of whether human beings should approach their own darkness with relentless severity or forbearance. Animal nature, which is not evil in itself, yet often unadapted to human nature, deserves, according to fairytales, loving indulgence. The actual "shadow," however, which is not harmless, yet acts as a destructive force, should be rejected. Essentially, the dangerousness and ambiguity of the inner animal man, however, lies in his blending with the "shadow": This fusion removes his previous innocence, as a purely natural creature, which befits the animal.

223    Not only the figure of the enchanted one, but also his illumination is presented in a more differentiated manner in "The Washerwoman" (Spain, no. 37) than in the tale about the singing, soaring lark: The heroine ignites a light to see whether the Moor or the prince is sleeping with her at night. Thus, she seeks to consciously divide the dark psychic power that visits her at night into its different aspects and to distinguish them. According to that tale, she detects a mirror on the prince's chest, in which she beholds six women who are sewing a small child's clothes. In reality, she is already pregnant, and what she sees in the mirror proves to be true in the tale's happy ending.

224    Thus, the prince "mirrors" her fate, the birth of the child, that is, the self. Potentially, the self is already present in him (and, as he is

---

[200] *The Complete Grimm's Fairy Tales*, pp. 664–671.

her soul-image, also in her). By differentiating itself from the unconscious, consciousness on the one hand recognizes the darkness of this inner world, yet at the same time also reflects the heroine's own self and thus enables her to glimpse the meaning that will arise from this experience. The heroine was meant to be killed by the Moor because she violated the ban. And yet, the Moor spares her for her child's sake and tells her to look for the escaped prince. The great danger that she faces, at least temporarily, points to the potentially catastrophic effect of encountering the shadow. In this moment, however, the child becomes the saving and helping force.

225　　In some fairytales, the hero or the heroine is transformed into a bird by an evil force that sticks a needle into his or her head. Sometimes, the needle is also a hawthorn and thus induces rapture, a flight into the unconscious. In the aforementioned Spanish fairytale, the magic needle is said to have originated from the drops of wax that fell on the prince during the nocturnal illumination, and which thus are deemed to have a paralyzing effect.

226　　Dripping wax and tallow stains play an important role in some variants.[201] They are also related to the drops of blood that are left behind by the dove in the Grimm's version as a means of pointing the way forward. Although these drops indicate suffering and wounding (like that of a sacrificial animal), and are paralleled by the injury inflicted on the falcon prince by the heroine's profane sisters in "The Feather of Finist, the Bright Falcon,"[202] we can also relate them to the blood stains that in some variants must be washed out of the hero's shirt. This happens, for example, in the Irish parallel "The White Hound of the Mountain" (no. 38), where the heroine lets four drops of blood fall on the prince's shirt when she bids him farewell. Later she can prove her identity by the fact that only she can wash away these drops. Likewise, in "East of the Sun and West of the Moon" (Norway, no. 31), only the heroine's "Christian hands" can wash away the tallow stains that dropped from her illuminating

---

[201] Bolte and Polívka, *Anmerkungen*, vol. 2, p. 250.
[202] Afanas'ev, *Russian Fairy Tales*, pp. 580–588.

candle onto the hero's shirt, while the shirt only grows ever blacker when it is washed by the pagan "false bride," who is a troll.

227      These different versions contain an array of meaningful connections. Often, drops of blood point to an enraptured being: As a part of the whole, they represent its psychic substance.[203] Thus, the drops that must be washed out also symbolize a psychic encounter, yet on a level that needs to be overcome. As Bachofen explains,[204] the drops of oil that fall on the sleeping animal prince also "prefigure Psyche": The hot oil (or wax or tallow) originating in the light symbolizes the beginning transformation of her loving desire from dull instinct to spiritual experience by recognizing the partner; as knowledge obliterates the purity of the soul-image, these events denote something illicit, indeed forbidden, thus also giving the union a sacrilegious nuance; the desecration caused by the intruding artificial light (sometimes the lamp or candle has a profane origin), that is, of profane, irreverent, and avid consciousness, into the natural, innocent psychic sphere, confers upon reason, which views things in terms of opposition, a double aspect, and projects onto what is beheld a "defiled" (i.e., stained) character.

228      In "East of the Sun and West of the Moon" (Norway, no. 31), where this motif is most strongly developed, the contrast between Christianity and paganism is also included, in that Christianity—as in several Norse fairytales—is identified with the profane mind. Nevertheless, only the heroine's Christian hands can erase the stain—according to the principle that only that power that wreaked havoc can eliminate it again.[205] Thus, if the conflict has only been caused by the interference of consciousness, it can no longer be solved by constantly descending into unconscious psychic layers (the realm of trolls), yet solely by further progressing on the path to higher consciousness. "It is," as Przyluski observes,

[203] See, among others, v. d. Leeuw, *Phänomenologie der Religion*, pp. 258-261. On the significance of drops of blood, see "The Goose Girl" (*The Complete Grimm's Fairy Tales*, pp. 404–411), "Muhammäd the Shepherd and the Päri Princesses" (Christensen, *Iran*, Jena, 1939, p. 58), "The Master Maiden" (Norway, no. 21). The feather, which the dove drops in the above fairytale, is, as part of a whole, part of its psychic substance and thus a guiding intuition. In fairytales, new life can spring from the drops of blood of a slain creature. See, e.g., "The Three Cracked Oranges" (Spain, no. 4) and "The Shepherd's Son and the King's Magical Daughter" (Zaunert, *Deutsche Märchen seit Grimm*, 1922, p. 196).
[204] Editor's note: The source of this idea is unknown.
[205] See Wagner's "Parzival": "... the wound is healed only by the spear that smote it."

229     a very common idea that defilement causes both physical and moral evil. For example, among the Herero people the word *húhura* just as much means "to cleanse, to disenchant" as "to heal." ... Rasmussen tells the story of an Eskimo woman who fainted one day and, when she came to herself again, possessed the abilities of a shaman. "Nothing was hidden from her any longer and she began to reveal all the wrong that the inhabitants of the house had committed. In this way, she purified everyone."[206]

230     This example illustrates the importance of "knowledge" (i.e., "conscience") in the magical removal of evil, or "defilement."[207]

231     The variant motif, according to which the hero is transformed by a magical thorn, complements this interpretation in that it symbolizes, as it were, the "piercing gaze" of profane reasoning, which imposes on the soul-image the bird-form disdained by the profane sphere, yet whose fleetingness drives the heroine to great inner endeavor. In one variant, she must dig the pig-headed prince out of the dunghill and wash him. This motif recalls the washing of the old man in "The Stepdaughter's and the Maid's Reward" (Finland, no. 53). This endeavor involves removing the seemingly "defiled" or tarnished aspect of the man's soul-image.

232     Also in "The Stag Prince" (Denmark, no. 2), the heroine must wipe the dirt off the animal prince with some straw to redeem him. She finds him in the rearmost of three forbidden chambers, the first of which is locked with an iron door, the second with a copper door,

---

[206] Jean Przyluski, "Der Lebendig-Erlöste in dem entwickelten Buddhismus," *Eranos-Jahrbuch 1937: Gestaltung der Erlösungsidee in Ost und West II*, ed. Olga Fröbe-Kapteyn, (1938), pp. 120–121.—Trans.
[207] See *ibid.*, p. 118: "... by magic or by sacrifice man redeems himself for a time from evil, that is, from the impurity which is the cause of misfortune, disease, and premature death. This contagious defilement to which man is exposed in his family, among his cattle, and among his crops, constitutes the great obstacle to the welfare of the group ... In all peoples, one observes corresponding ideas. Everywhere, man frets over purifying himself and thereby escaping the consequences of his wrongdoing."—Trans. On the ancient ablutions in the mysteries, see Cumont, *Orientalische Religionen* (Leipzig and Berlin, 1931, pp. 36–37); Güntert, *Weltkönig* (1923), p. 202: "There is yet another image: Sin and guilt, as barely needs to be proven, are for the Indian what for other peoples are a kind of dirt, a staining, sullying substance that can be washed off with water like real dirt: The naive means of atonement rites are based on this fairly external conception of sin as defilement and impurity, and where neither repentance nor conscience are an issue: our word *Makel* [Translator's note: blemish or even mackle] still contains this old image in various phrases and expressions (*stain, our honor has been defiled, his shield is pure or bright*, etc.)."—Trans.

and the third with a wooden door. Behind the first door, the heroine finds two men stirring tar with their bare hands, "until a Christian gives them something to stir it with." She gives them a spoon. Behind the second door, two girls are stirring fire with their bare hands, "until a Christian gives them something to stir it with," which she does. Behind the third door, she finds the stag prince lying in the dirt.[208] Thus, the work of redemption means that consciousness, which provides clarity, must turn toward chaos—because the conscious person gives the unconscious the "tools" that enable it to contend with the dark and emotional elements (tar and fire).

233    Another remarkable form of redemption occurs in "The Lame Dog" (Sweden, no. 13): While searching for the vanished animal prince, the heroine encounters various animals that demand that she befriend them; yet she refuses, out of loyalty to her "lame dog." Eventually, she meets a terrifying lion. Chained, the animal is dragging itself about. It, too, demands that she befriend it and sever its fetters. A nightingale sings to the heroine: "Maiden, loosen the chain, loosen the chain!" She takes heart and does so.

234    But something wonderful happened: When the last shackle opened, the lion turned into a handsome young prince; and when the princess looked at him, it was none other than her beloved, who had previously been a dog. She sank to the ground, embraced the young man's knees, and begged him not to leave her. But the prince gave her fresh courage with his great love, took her in his arms, and said: "No, now we shall never part again, for I am redeemed and have experienced your eternal loyalty."

235    Severing fetters as a redemptive act also occurs in "The Female Giant in the Stone Boat" (Iceland, no. 24), where the anima-figure is freed from the clutches of a sea giant when her husband manages to break the iron chain.[209] (In some variants of the tale about the singing,

---

[208] See the similar motif of sweeping dirt out of the dragon's castle as a redemptive act in the modern Greek variant "The Crab" (no. 5).

[209] See also the Eskimo tale "The Fireball" (Paul Sock, trans., *Eskimomärchen*, Berlin: Axel Juncker Verlag, 1921, p. 81): A fisherman who was assailed by a ghost at the same time heard a voice from above

soaring lark, the animal prince is redeemed by beheading or by the brandishing of a sword, as happens to the fox in "The Golden Bird"). The fetters symbolize being bound to the unconscious. As long as the soul-image and the symbol of the self are tied to the unconscious sphere and its demonic spell, the development of personality remains inhibited, just as a person's adherence to the unconscious amounts to guilt (i.e., stifles conscious realization).[210] For consciousness, the fetters are thus both reproach and demand: They reproach reason for being a merely passive onlooker while demanding redemption and progression to a higher level of consciousness. Thus, the motif of the fetters parallels that of the tallow stains.

236 The seven years that the heroine must spend wandering in the fairytale about the singing, soaring lark, and which in some variants are expressed by an infinitely long time (she must, for example, wear down iron shoes[211]), indicate that consciousness assimilating the animal soul touches on a problem that dominates a large part of life (as the seven planets, the number seven points to the fate-determining powers of the soul). During this time, what is sought is merely intuited (bird). Eventually, this intuition is also lost. Now the heroine must grope along meaningless paths to those archetypes that symbolize the guiding principles of her soul: She reaches the sun (which symbolizes light and the masculine spirit), the moon (which symbolizes unconscious enlightenment and the feminine being), and the winds (which symbolize the spirit in terms of movement and impetus). Each of these archetypes gives her precious things with which she can forge a path to the prince and subsequently back to her home.

237 In "East of the Sun and West of the Moon" (Norway, no. 31), three old women and the winds show the heroine the way. Each of the women is playing with an object: one with a golden apple, one with a golden reel, and one with a golden skirt. Each woman gives the heroine her object. In "Worry and Sorrow" (Norway, no. 25),

---

telling him to untie the string around the ghost's feet. The fisherman, however, was afraid to do this, and the end of the tale confirms that he had no calling.

[210] Jung, "The Significance of the Father in the Destiny of the Individual," *CW* 4, esp. § 727. According to Güntert, *Weltkönig*, pp. 120–123, fetters are related to guilt, mythologically and etymologically.

[211] Bolte and Polívka, *Anmerkungen*, vol. 2, pp. 234ff.

these figures are giants: The husband is a man-eater whose wife must be won over by gifts. In this latter variant, the journey is particularly torturous: The heroine, accompanied by her maid, is forbidden from sleeping or even from bending her legs. She sleeps on trees in the forest, where bears, lions, and wolves howl and dance at night. She must seek shelter with disgruntled female giants and eat their dirty food and even thank them for taking her in.

238      In "The Lame Dog" (Sweden, no. 13), a toad, a wolf, and a lion attempt to gain the heroine's favor. Yet she remains faithful to the lame dog and thus passes the test. In "The White Bear King Valemon" (Norway, no. 29), the heroine first attempts to ride Valemon the bear, who is scurrying away, to avoid separation; exhausted, she falls off the bear in the middle of a large forest and must follow him on foot. She comes to various huts whose inhabitants are poor, but where in each case a little girl (looked after by a foster mother) is playing with a pair of golden scissors that produces silk and velvet, or with a bottle from which one can pour what the heart desires, or with a wishing cloth; each child gives its object to the heroine. At the fourth hut, the heroine learns that Valemon has scaled the inaccessible mountain. Yet by making the poor children living at the foot of the mountain happy with the miraculous objects, she convinces their father to forge claws on her hands and feet, so that she, too, can climb the mountain. Or she manages to undertake the last, most tiring part of the journey riding atop the wind (in "East of the Sun and West of the Moon," even the wind is exhausted by the long journey).

239      The heroine's quest exhibits the characteristic features of the "Great Journey": the familiar division into stations (as a rule, there are three stations, with the fourth one being the destination) and the appearance of threatening and helping figures along the way.[212] The

---

[212] Let me highlight the important work of Johannes Siuts, *Jenseitsmotive im deutschen Volksmärchen*, Ph.D. Dissertation Christian-Albrechts-Universität zu Kiel (Greifswald, 1911), which unfortunately came to my attention only after the printing of Volume 1 and after the completion of Volume 2 at the suggestion of Professor Otto Huth (Tübingen). These findings should have been considered in *Archetypal Symbols in Fairytales* (Volume I, Book 1, Section A). The same applies to Howard Rollin Patch's *The Other World: According to Descriptions in Medieval Literature* (Cambridge, Massachusetts: Harvard University Press, 1950).

giants, the wild animals, and the old women, who originally were presumably considered to be witches, symbolize the chthonic realm, that of the Great Mother, that is, the natural world of the unconscious with its threatening and tempting urges and instincts. Remaining in this sphere requires unflagging, conscious exertion. This explains why, in "Worry and Sorrow," the heroine may neither sleep nor bend her legs: If she does, the unconscious will overwhelm her. Encountering the self, however, means nothing less than returning to the bosom of the unconscious. Paradoxically, this means becoming conscious, as willed and guided by the unconscious. This guidance by the unconscious is represented by the assistance that the heroine receives from the figures that she meets at the various stations; in the fairytale about the singing, soaring lark, these are the sun, the moon, and the winds.

240    As symbols, the sun and the moon have various meanings: some identical, others contrasting. In the present context, in which the two celestial bodies appear in parallel, their identity is more strongly pronounced, while their opposition recedes into the background. Psychologically, this means that the unconscious tendencies symbolized by these stars take effect in the same direction and support the heroine's path. The heroine, who represents consciousness, adopts an attitude that is "free of opposites." While the sun embodies, as it were, the psyche's active forces and the energies whose concentration forms consciousness, the moon is rather an image of the luminous unconscious. In ancient belief, both stars receive the souls of the dead.[213] In India, the path to the afterlife is understood as follows[214]:

241    Truly, when man (*purusha*) passes from this world, he reaches the wind; this opens up to him as far as the opening of a chariot wheel; through this he ascends and reaches the sun; this opens up to him as far as the opening (covered with

[213] Cumont, *Orientalische Religionen* (Leipzig and Berlin, 1931), pp. 114–115.
[214] Paul Deussen, *Sechzig Upanishad's des Veda*, trans. from Sanskrit (Leipzig: Brockhaus, 1921), p. 494 (Brihadâranyaka-Up. 5, 10). See also *ibid.*, pp. 24–25 from the Rigveda (Kaushîtaki-Up. 1, 2). On the path of the soul after death according to Indian teachings, see Walter Ruben, *Die Philosophen der Upanishaden* (Bern: Francke, 1947), pp. 240 and 244ff.

leather) of a drum; through this he ascends and reaches the moon; this opens up to him as widely as the opening of a kettledrum; through this he ascends and reaches the world which is without heat and without cold; there he dwells unceasingly for many years.[215]

242 The dead person's soul travels a similar path in Manichaeism:

> ... on the fourth night after death the soul arrives from the world at the Chinvat Bridge; first it arrives at the abode of fire; thereafter suffices one step to the station of the stars, the second to that of the moon, the third to that of the sun; with the fourth it reaches the bridge itself, and one brings it to its destination.[216] ... Soon the soul has a long and difficult way to travel ... soon it ascends on ladders or is lifted up; the shining cloud or the soul-ship carries it to the homeland, or winds and storms lead it there; it flies with wings that have grown by themselves, or appears, like the divine messenger, as a mighty bird; indeed, the multitude of souls becomes a flock of birds.[217]

243 Elsewhere, wind is related also mythologically to the sun: According to a vision in the Mithras Liturgy, it originates in a tube that emerges from the sun.[218] The path of the fairytale heroine to the end of the world, via the sun, the moon, and the wind, is thus a great journey into the realm of the dead or beyond. Thus, this journey leads the

---

[215] On the teaching of the Kaushítaki Upanishad, according to which the dead journey to the moon and from there are reborn on earth, see also Heinrich Zimmer, "Tod und Wiedergeburt im indischen Licht," *Eranos- Jahrbuch 1939: Die Symbolik der Wiedergeburt in der religiösen Vorstellung der Zeiten und Völker*, ed. Olga Fröbe-Kapteyn (1940), p. 258, esp. p. 274. At the same time, the moon is "the gateway to the heavenly world: Whoever is able to answer its questions, it lets go beyond itself." On the sun as a place of the blessed, see *ibid.*, pp. 268 and 270f. See further Heinrich Zimmer, "Der 'König der dunklen Kammer,'" (1929), pp. 208–209. On the sun as a guide to the dead, see Géza Róheim, *Spiegelzauber*, Internat. Psychoanalytische Bibliothek, vol. 6 (Leipzig and Vienna: Internationaler Psychoanalytischer Verlag, 1919), pp. 223–226.
[216] Reitzenstein, *Iranische* (1921), p. 63.
[217] *Ibid.*, p. 66.—Trans.
[218] Albrecht Dieterich, *Eine Mithrasliturgie*, ed. Otto Weinreich (Leipzig and Berlin: Teubner, 1923), pp. 62–64; see also Jung, *Symbols of Transformation*, CW 5, § 486 fn. 19, and "The Structure of the Psyche," CW 8, § 317f.

heroine into the depths of the unconscious and at the same time into her innermost essence, not least because it involves the sun, the moon, and the entire intrapsychic cosmos. This conception is expressed as follows in the Chândogya Upanishad[219]:

244

> Truly, as great as this space is, so great is this space in the heart; in it both heaven and earth are resolved; both fire and wind, both sun and moon, the lightning and the stars, and what someone possesses here and what they do not possess, all that is contained therein.

245 The peculiar connection of highly meaningful symbols such as the sun, the moon, and the wind, and later also the griffin (sun-bird), is similarly evident in late ancient syncretistic mystery cults, which were almost all also sun cults. Psychologically, these symbols should likely be regarded as images of the self, of inner psychic wholeness. In the present fairytale, this is further affirmed by the fact that four winds appear after the sun and the moon. In the fairytale about the singing, soaring lark, these winds are, although less obviously, the night wind and "the three other winds." They are more clearly apparent in the Norwegian variant "East of the Sun and West of the Moon": The heroine lets herself be borne first by the east wind to the west wind, from there to the south wind, and onward to the north wind, which is able to transport her across the sea to the castle "east of the sun and west of the moon" by expending all its remaining energy. Wholeness is now clearly expressed by the four winds and the four points of the compass; the journey proceeds via opposites, with the directions of flight forming a cross, a large, cosmos-encompassing mandala. This also explains the mysterious title of this version: "East of the Sun and West of the Moon" implies the search for an irrational center, which unites the primordial opposites of the soul (i.e., polarity), while the four points of the compass point to the four functions as the constituents of the conscious personality.

---

[219] Deussen, *Sechzig Upanishad's* (Leipzig, 1921), p. 189 (Chândogya-Up. 8, 1, 3).—Trans.

It is no coincidence that the north wind is the actual savior: It is the dark and meaningful fourth wind (and corresponds to the "night wind" in the Grimm's fairytale). According to the schema of the ancient-medieval compass rose (see Hildegard von Bingen's worldview, mentioned above on p. 73[220]), the east wind blows

246    from a leopard's head from the sphere of the pure ether, the west wind from a wolf's head in the sphere of the *ruach*, the south wind from a lion's head in the outermost circle of fire. But the north wind blows from a bear's head, which is situated on the right side in the dark circle of fire ... Each wind or pneuma is at the same time an impulse, a desire or a lust which acts upon the human being. Like Aristotle's spirits, they also act on the planets and cause their movements. The role played by the north wind, the "bear," is important in this respect: It blows out of the dark circle of fire. This dark circle of fire is the "circle of judgment" or the "circle of hell." The north wind arising there is the "enemy of the sun and despises any light," the "devil who reveals his wickedness in his opposition to God." He is the fallen Lucifer whom Christ hurled into the northern corner of the universe and banished into the dark circle of fire.

247    These amplifications connect the psychopomps in the Grimm's version and the seemingly very different psychopomps in variant fairytales, where giants, trolls, and wild, menacing beasts take the place of the winds, the sun, and the moon.[221] In a Spanish fairytale, "Three Cracked Oranges," the sun, the moon, and the east wind appear as psychopomps on the Great Journey and are depicted as man-eaters. Once more, the fourth function leads to the experience of wholeness by touching, all at once, what is feared, darkness, the nonhuman sphere, God and the devil, the highest light, and the greatest darkness.

---

[220] Leisegang, *Die Gnosis* (1941), pp. 22–23.
[221] Conversely, see "The Three Dogs" (Spain, no. 27): Called "Sun," "Moon," and "Morning Star," three dogs acting as psychopomps turn out to be angels.

248    It makes sense that the four functions are represented by winds: Wind has symbolized the creative, fertilizing spirit since time immemorial. In ancient Chinese thought, wind is the all-pervading principle that enables "realization."[222] Etymologically, Indian *asu* (the principle of life) is related to Latin *animus, anima,* Greek *anemos* (wind). Wind also symbolizes breath and strength.[223] When the heroine is borne by the wind to the end of the world and later returns on a miraculous bird, this means that the processes occurring there take place in a spiritual reality so far removed from consciousness that the human being can barely grasp them with ordinary, daytime consciousness and can experience them only in a visionary way.

249    However, matters are different in those variants where the heroine must summon her remaining strength to reach the enraptured animal bridegroom. She must stay awake, that is, remain focused on the goal with all her might. She must overcome her fear of wild animals, giants, and trolls: that is, of the incalculable superiority of the emotional and instinctual sphere. She must scale an unscalable mountain with claws forged to her hands and feet; she must concentrate, also assisted by her animal nature, to support conscious realization. Presumably, both ways of approaching those symbols and the psychic center complement each other: Attaining the goal requires both the intuitive flight of the mind and the patient work of consciousness.

250    Almost all variants contain the motif of the heroine receiving gifts at the individual stations of her journey. The gifts enable her to purchase three nights with the bridegroom or to appease the demons that she encounters at the subsequent stations. The gifts vary: In "The Springing, Soaring Lark," the sun gives the heroine a small box containing a resplendent robe; the moon gives her an egg containing a golden hen with 12 chicks; and the wind gives her a nut from which she can later make the rescuing tree on her flight home. In "East of the Sun and West of the Moon," the gifts are a golden apple,

---

[222] Richard Wilhelm, *The Secret of the Golden Flower: A Chinese Book of Life,* trans. Cary F. Baynes (Brattleboro, Vermont: Echo Point Books, 2022; originally published 1931).

[223] See Zimmer, "Tod und Wiedergeburt," (1940), p. 270; Jung, "Basic Postulates of Analytical Psychology," *CW* 8, § 664f.: Leisegang, "Schlange" (1940), p. 192f.

a reel and a skirt, and a horse, which she must send back after she has completed her journey. In "Worry and Sorrow," the girl gives away what she took from her home to appease the demons: a cubit of canvas, a cubit of strong linen, and a cubit of fine linen. In return, she receives a doublet measuring seven miles, which bears her forth through the air. In "King Valemon, the White Bear," she receives a pair of golden scissors, around which pieces of silk and velvet fly when one rattles the scissors; a bottle from which one can pour whatever suits one; and a tablecloth. In "The White Hound of the Mountain," a woman gives the heroine a little comb to neatly brush her hair; a pair of scissors that turns everything into silk and brocade; and a needle that covers every fabric with gold and silver stars.

251    Of all these gifts, the golden apple, the nut, and the egg indicate familiar symbolic connections. They represent "roundness," the most precious seed and fruit, the nondescript and tiniest of things, which contains the tree of life, and thus symbolizes the self. They point to the peculiar nucleus of the human soul, the inner center to which all soul-images seem to lead, whose comprehension, however, surpasses human consciousness.[224] It is both the embryonic (egg)[225] and the outcome of long-term endeavor (fruit). The nut contains the means of rescue on the homeward journey, because when the pair, having found each another again, flies home, the griffin languishes and risks falling into the sea. As instructed, the heroine throws the nut into the sea, and from it grows a tree on which the griffin can recover. The tree, which grows from the nut at the bottom of the sea, is, as a tree of life, an image of inner development, which springs from the self. Here, the symbol of inner growth is a station on the homebound journey. Inasmuch as the griffin, according to Bächtold-Stäubli, has the body of a lion, it symbolizes a partial aspect of the animal prince. Thus, its demonic-passionate side provides the impetus to reach the sphere of consciousness. Related to the

---

[224] Deussen, *Sechzig Upanishad's* (1921), p. 189 (Chândogya-Up. 8, 1, 1): "Here, in this Brahman city (the body) is a house, a small lotus flower (the heart); in it is a small room; what lies therein, one should explore, that one should truly seek to know."—Trans.

[225] On the egg in connection with the alternation of death and life, see Bachofen, *Gräbersymbolik* (1859), pp. 39–40.

phoenix, the griffin is also the sun-bird[226]; that is, both aspects of the self come together (and are united) in this figure as a "foundational" principle; the fact that it rests (and recovers) on the tree of life recalls the mythological image of the birth of the sun in a tree or of the sun as the fruit of a tree. Thus, the inner "sunrise" is anticipated even before the successful completion of the journey.

252  Like the nut, the egg, which is given to the heroine by the moon, contains a miracle. The mother hen with her 12 chicks, which were hidden in the egg, indicates the paradox of both the hen, which exists first, *and* of the egg,[227] while the number of chicks (12) points to similar connections. In Manichaeism, for example, the 12 signs of the zodiac, as the components of the annual path of the sun, constituted time. The soul passes through the 12 hours of light into which the day is divided, and which are both its "successive transformations" and its 12 robes.[228] We find similar motifs involving the number 12 also in other late-ancient mystery cults. In Manichaean texts, however, the 12 images are often supplemented by an image that signifies their wholeness: The 13th aeon summarizes the 12 aeons that together form time in its entirety as the great aeon.[229]

253  If we consider this symbolism an amplification of the 12 chicks with the hen, then the egg, as an embryonic totality, indicates its complete development over time: The self as what exists beyond time, and what, however, must also be realized in time, as what is identical with the creative function of time.

254  The egg, like the hen or the chick, belongs to the symbolic language of alchemy, from where this motif may have entered certain fairytales: The golden hen with her chicks is often described in fairytales as having the highest value.[230] In alchemy, the chick or egg

---

[226] Bachofen, *Mutterrecht* (1861), p. 24. The phoenix is the mount of the hyperborean Apollo (winter sun). See also Leisegang, "Schlange" (1940), p. 243f., and Peter Lum, *Fabulous Beasts* (New York: Pantheon Books, 1951), pp. 46ff.

[227] See [Johann Scheffler] Angelus Silesius, *Cherubinischer Wandersmann. Nach der Ausgabe letzter Hand von 1675 vollst. hrsg. und mit einer Studie "Über den Wert der Mystik für unsere Zeit"* [On the value of mysticism for our time], ed. Wilhelm Bölsche (Jena and Leipzig: Eugen Diederichs, 1905), p. 143, no. 162, "One in the Other": "The egg is in the hen, the hen is in the egg / Two in one, and also one in two."

[228] See Reitzenstein, *Iranische* (1921), p. 15, fn. 1, pp. 95ff.

[229] *Ibid.*, p. 156f.

[230] For example, in "The Tsar's Daughter and the Dragon" (Balkans, no. 22) and "The King and His Three Sons" (Balkans, no. 36).

yolk is called the *punctum solis* (point of the sun), which is brought to life and quickened by incubation. The chick is also called the "bird of Hermes" and is a synonym for the spirit Mercurius.[231] From this emerges the meaning of the egg, the hen, and the chick when the heroine once again finds the animal husband in the present fairytale.

255 The sunlike garment, which the heroine finds in the box given to her by the sun, is an aspect of the self, as is probably evident from the previous explanations[232] of the "garment of light" in Hellenistic speculations. This image symbolizes the heavenly and immortal *doppelgänger* of earthly humans and thus of their self, which is not intertwined with the world. By countering evil with her true inner essence, the heroine receives the power to overcome the darkness of the north.

256 All the gifts in the aforementioned variants are somehow connected to the garment of light in that they stem from the sphere of spinning, weaving, and tailoring. In another parallel tale, "The Silk Spinner,"[233] the animal prince is a worm, presumably a silkworm, whose court the heroine later visits as a spinner. Spinning symbolizes the autonomy of the unconscious psyche. As in "King Thrushbeard," spinning machines therefore fascinate the animal prince's witch-bride, in particular because they are made of gold. The garment that must be made from the spun fabric will not correspond to the essence of the false bride; yet insofar as the self takes effect in the interpersonal relationship of individuals, the garment, which symbolizes a person's attitude toward their environment, becomes a desirable symbol of the self for the false bride. Even the scissors, which serve to cut and divide things, and thus symbolize a destructive force, assume a productive character as a means of producing the "garment." The bottle and the wishing cloth symbolize the unconscious as a source of inexhaustible nourishment, of permanent spiritual quickening.[234]

---

[231] Jung, "Paracelsus as a Spiritual Phenomenon," *CW* 13, § 188. On the hen as a soul-animal, see also Tobler, *Epiphanie* (1911), p. 33.
[232] See above, pp. 60–62.
[233] Zaunert, *Deutsche Märchen seit Grimm*, p. 211.
[234] See "The White Hound of the Mountain" (Ireland, no. 38) and "King Valemon, the White Bear" (Norway, no. 29). See Paulus Cassel, *Aus Literatur und Symbolik, Abhandlungen* (Leipzig: Wilh.

257     In some versions, the gifts are not given by the sun, the moon, or female giants, but by children whom the heroine encounters at the various stations of her journey. This motif is most evident in the Norwegian variant "King Valemon, the White Bear," where these children are identical with the three children once borne by the heroine and whom the bear took away from her. And so the tale ends as follows: "... and then the King's daughter saw why he had taken the children away from her and abandoned them: so that they could help her reach him."

258     This motif is more complicated, yet still as meaningful in "The White Hound of the Mountain" (Ireland, no. 38): The pregnant heroine begs the animal bridegroom to allow her to return home, which he does, albeit reluctantly. At home, she gives birth to a beautiful daughter who wears a headband, which is golden on her forehead and silver on the back of her head. Then, however, two hands reach down into the house through the chimney and steal the child. The following day, the white hound fetches the heroine back. These events recur with the birth of another girl and boy, who also wear the same headband. With the third child, however, the white hound tells the heroine that she can return to give birth to the child but that he will not fetch her. When her profane sisters, envious of her prosperity, attempt to mistreat the heroine in the forest, the white hound appears with a clap of thunder and beats the sisters, without speaking to the heroine. When she follows him nevertheless, he orders her to spend the night in a hut by the wayside and that he will wait for her in the morning. In the hut, she meets her eldest girl, without recognizing her, and receives the comb from the girl's foster mother; in the next hut, she receives the scissors; and in the third one the needle. In this hut, she finds her boy, who is missing an eye. Only when the heroine asks the foster mother does the latter return the missing eye.

---

Friedrich, 1884, pp. 272–276) for a discussion of scissors as a symbol of death (in the hands of the Parcae, i.e., fates) and as an attribute of witches, which means they belong to the magical realm.

259    The next day the White Dog told her that she was the cause of his misfortune. The curses that rested on him would have been lifted if she had given birth to the children in his house. From now on he would never look at her again. He stepped into a mound of earth. She grabbed the front of his shirt and dropped four drops of blood on it. Then the mound closed behind him, and she was turned into a large stone.

260    After nine years, the heroine awakens and learns from one of the white hound's former servants that he has married a witch. She erases the four drops of blood on the dog's shirt with her hand, yet deceives the witch that she is coming and uses the miraculous gifts to purchase three nights with the animal prince.

261    In "King Valemon, the White Bear," the helping children are intermediaries: They assist the heroine on her way to the animal prince with their gifts; they are able to do so because they descend from both these figures and thus unite in themselves the separated parents. Therefore, they represent in human form the union of opposites, the self. By leading the heroine to the animal prince, they fulfill the same function as the miraculous gifts. Like these, the children are also symbols of the self, an element that connects the opposites (just as, mythologically, the self is often represented by a child). In the Irish tale, this is vividly expressed by the golden and silver headband. Gold and silver, like the sun and the moon, symbolize primordial opposites. In another version, "The Bristle Child,"[235] the child unites all the characteristics of the stations in itself: the sun, the moon, and the stars; in other words, it encapsulates all the previously scattered individual components of the unconscious sphere.

262    In the Schwelm version of "The Singing, Soaring Lark,"[236] in which the heroine wishes to have three acorns on a stem, the child plays an essential role. The animal prince can be disenchanted only when "a little boy was aged three years, three months, three days,

---

[235] Zaunert, *Deutsche Märchen seit Grimm*, p. 286.
[236] Bolte and Polívka, *Anmerkungen*, vol. 2, p. 241.

three hours, and three minutes." "She (i.e., the heroine) put one of the acorns in the sleeping bear's mouth, ate the second one herself, and stuck the third into the ground; as soon as this germinated, the magic ceased." Insofar as the three acorns correspond to the miracle flower in other versions, we probably ought to understand them as a symbol of the self. While the stem embodies the united trinity of heroine, bear, and child, the latter needs to be understood as the third element, as that which unites the opposites. The motif that the sprouting acorn breaks the spell indicates that this unification involves natural growth and thus constitutes a time-bound process. The same idea also underlies the exact indication of the time at which redemption occurs: The child's age that this requires, the three-step rhythm, which should lead to the fourth part of time, is plainly evident.

263    Significantly, the motif of the child is depicted in "Trandafíru," a Romanian variant mentioned by Bolte and Polívka.[237] This tale ends with a wife begging her husband to embrace her, "so that the iron ring may spring from my body and that I may give birth to the son of your blood, whom I carry beneath my heart!" These words refer to the hitherto inhibited birth of the self at the very moment when the couple unites.

264    The motif of the child assumes an even more peculiar form in "The Washerwoman," the Spanish variant mentioned previously: For when the heroine illicitly illumines the prince with a candle at night,

265    she noticed that he was wearing a mirror on his chest, and so she bent over him to look into it. In it, she saw a large room in which six women were sewing and embroidering clothes for a small child. She looked at this picture with delight, yet did not notice that a drop of wax ran along the candle and fell onto the young man's chest, who awoke from the heat and exclaimed: "Alas, you misfortunate creature, now you have renewed my bewitchment!"

---

[237] *Ibid.*, p. 255.

266 Later, when the heroine once again finds the vanished prince, the tale continues:

267 The Moor entered and brought some baskets containing the child's outfit, which the girl had already beheld in the mirror that the prince had worn on his chest that night, and on which six embroiders had worked; all of this was intended for her son. Thereafter, they married and lived very happily with their child and the other children that were born to them later.

268 In the mirror, the heroine thus sees the future, more specifically that part of the future in which the couple will finally be united. In fairytales and folklore, the "truth" or the future is often beheld in a mirror. It reflects, as it were, not the beholder's superficial image, but their unconscious, which potentially contains the future. The animus-figure, as the psychic image that emerges from the indeterminacy of the unconscious on the threshold of consciousness, thus acts on human consciousness like a mirror in which a person can perceive and thus become aware of themselves.

269 In understanding herself, however, the heroine does not behold her outer appearance, but her future child, who represents her self.[238] The child also symbolizes a new sense of life, which flows from the unconscious and constitutes a renewal of life.[239] According to Jung,[240]

270 the child is potential future. Hence the occurrence of the child motif in the psychology of the individual signifies as a rule an anticipation of future developments, even though at first sight it may seem like a retrospective configuration. Life is a flux, a flowing into the future, and not a stoppage or a backwash. It is therefore not surprising that so many of the mythological saviours are child gods. This agrees exactly with

---

[238] See also the mirror as the central secret of the animal prince in the Hanoverian variant mentioned above and discussed in Bolte and Polívka, *Anmerkungen*, vol. 2, p. 230.

[239] Jung, *Psychological Types*, CW 6, § 465.

[240] Jung, "The Psychology of the Child Archetype," CW 9/I, § 278; on the child as "both beginning and end, as an initial and a terminal creature," see *ibid.*, § 299.

our experience of the psychology of the individual, which shows that the "child" paves the way for a future change of personality. In the individuation process, it anticipates the figure that comes from the synthesis of conscious and unconscious elements in the personality. It is therefore a symbol which unites the opposites; a mediator, bringer of healing, that is, one who makes whole.

271 He adds:

272 The "child" is born out of the womb of the unconscious, begotten out of the depths of human nature, or rather out of living Nature herself. It is a personification of vital forces quite outside the limited range of our conscious mind; of ways and possibilities of which our one-sided conscious mind knows nothing; a wholeness which embraces the very depths of Nature. It represents the strongest, the most ineluctable urge in every being, namely the urge to realize itself. It is, as it were, an incarnation of the inability to do otherwise, equipped with all the powers of nature and instinct, whereas the conscious mind is always getting caught up in its supposed ability to do otherwise.[241]

273 If the "child" appears as a multitude, as in "King Valemon, the White Bear" and in "The White Hound of the Mountain" (no. 38), it represents, as Jung says,

274 an as yet incomplete synthesis of personality. The personality (viz., the "self") is still in the plural stage, i.e., an ego may be present, but it cannot experience its wholeness within the framework of its own personality, only within the community of the family, tribe, or nation; it is still in the stage of unconscious identification with the plurality of the group.[242]

---

[241] Jung, CW 9/I, § 289.
[242] Ibid., § 279.

275    Thus, by the end of the two fairytales mentioned above, the personality has not fully matured. While these tales describe, through their images, that this developmental process, which resides in the unconscious, is possible, its completion is not described.

276    Strikingly, in one case the children are abducted by the animal father, while in the other the fact that the heroine gives birth at home (i.e., in the profane realm) is considered to violate acceptable conduct. The fairytale seems to suggest that it does not befit the conscious half of the personality to assign the self to its sphere because this separates it unjustly from its dark roots. Only when the heroine realizes that the self is as much a dark and demonic force that is alien to consciousness as it is a luminous, meaningful, and inner core can she free it from the "false wrappings of the persona on the one hand (the profane realm in fairytales) and from "the suggestive power of primordial images on the other" (the witch's spell in fairytales).[243]

277    Whether the children or the nature demons give the heroine the helping gifts at the stations, she always purchases three nights with her former husband from the false bride.[244] In the various versions, the "false bride," an archetypal figure that we have already considered in connection with the maiden's quest, is either the enchanting witch or her daughter, who desires the animal prince as her husband. As an image of the negative anima, which occupies the role of the persona, and thus is the inauthentic personality, the "false bride" sometimes also merges more or less clearly with the archetype of the negative mother.

278    In the Grimm's tale, the heroine first comes to the end of the world, where she finds the animal prince, a lion, wrestling with the "false bride," a dragon. The opposition between the lion and the dragon, or between the lion and the snake (which, mythologically, is familiar, among others, from the stone tablets of the cult of Mithras), symbolizes the juxtaposition of the two solstices (summer and winter); as explained, the lion represents emotionality, and

---

[243] See Jung, "The Relations between the Ego and the Unconscious," CW 7 § 269.
[244] The same motif occurs, among other fairytales, in "The Drummer" (The Complete Grimm's Fairy Tales, pp. 781–791).

mythologically the sun. The lindworm or snake, on the other hand, represents the more unconscious physical reactions of the psyche, mythologically the chthonic world.[245] In the ancient world, the lion and the snake are connected in an image of Aion as the god of the sun, time, and fire.[246] He could be interpreted as the archetype of creative life, which springs from the connection of the primordial opposites. In the present fairytale, however, this connection is ill-omened and therefore must be severed to be recognized,[247] because consciousness is only able to grasp opposites.

279     Fairytales often contain images that represent a symbol that unifies the opposites. Still, we should not interpret these images progressively, as representing the goal to which the path of individuation strives, but regressively, as a regression that must be overcome. The psychic process of life depends on opposites, which form the necessary gradient for that process to unfold. At the same time, however, it always strives to balance the opposites, as expressed figuratively in a symbol that unites the opposites. Therefore, what was a goal at a certain moment—like the first union of the heroine and the animal prince prior to illumination—must once again be torn asunder for the sake of development, so that it reunites on a higher level; or else the union—like that of the lion prince with the dragon bride—is evaluated negatively from the outset rather than considered to be a solution. This happens when both partners have

---

[245] In some variants, the animal prince is not a warm-blooded animal but a dragon or snake; see, e.g., "Ode und de Slang'" (Zaunert, *Deutsche Märchen seit Grimm*, p. 113) and "King Lindworm" (Denmark, no. 1). These fairytales describe "redemption," i.e., the assimilation of the psyche's deepest unconscious into consciousness, or—mythologically speaking—the transformation of chthonic beings into human beings.

[246] See Dieterich, *Mithrasliturgie* (1923), pp. 66–67: "But I need only recall the well-known images of Aion or Kronos: The lion's head sits on the human body, which is completely enveloped by the serpent; often the keys, the thunderbolts, are attached to the chest ... After all, the lion's head symbolized fire: The lion-headed one was the god of fire. Particularly instructive is a Roman *bas relief*, which depicts how Chronos kindles the fire, which engulfs an altar, and holds burning torches in his outstretched arms. Let us examine the individual expressions of that prayer: The god of fire shall open the fiery locks of heaven with his *pneuma*: This is precisely that god who possesses the keys of heaven. He has two bodies: that of a lion and that of a human being."—Trans. See further Reitzenstein, *Iranische* (1921), p. 168 f.: "The representation in the celestial robe corresponds to that other representation of a lion-headed god, around whose body the celestial serpent winds itself, and where the signs of the zodiac or at least the signs of the solstices and equinoxes often appear between the spirals. The sun lion points to Helios, yet the sun-god is represented differently in the cult of Mithras. This idea is related to him, but has become independent."—Trans.

[247] This is the same image as a familiar alchemical symbol: The dragon that eats its own tail. See also the conflict of opposites in the unconscious, as represented by the struggle between the magic horse and the *div* (desert demon) in "The Magic Horse" (Turkestan, no. 9).

a demonic nature and thus represent the opposites *within* the unconscious.

280     The heroine strikes the fighting animals with the 11th rod growing on the shore of the Red Sea, whereupon both become human beings. Yet the "false bride" immediately abducts the prince on the griffin. We have already interpreted the beating with rods as a means of redemption in our discussion of "King Lindworm." Strangely, however, the Red Sea is mentioned. Like the appearance of a lion, this geographical designation suggests that the tale has an Oriental origin. In Greek mythology, the Red Sea represents the East, the land of the rising sun.[248] In the present fairytale, it denotes a magical place, psychologically the depth of the unconscious.

281     Here, the heroine's rod not only has the same function as the rods in "King Lindworm." It also serves as a magic wand, in that the animals thus struck are transformed back into human beings; as such, it has the opposite effect of Circe's magic wand. The wand as a sign of the judge or leader, as well as of the shepherd, is a symbol of the Logos, of guiding reason, and of conscious decision.[249] Consciousness separates the unconscious pair of opposites and thus enables becoming conscious of them as individuals. Immediately, however, a contrary effect occurs: They evaporate and disappear on the griffin. Once more, the animal prince thus eludes the heroine, that is, the unconscious content remains inaccessible to consciousness.[250]

---

[248] Dieterich, *Nekyia: Beiträge zur Erklärung der neuentdeckten Petrusapokalypse*, 2nd ed. (Leipzig: Teubner, 1893), p. 25f.

[249] See *Archetypal Symbolism in Fairytales*, vol. 3, p. 91f.

[250] The incomprehensible nature of the animal prince is vividly depicted in the archetypal images of "The Little Bird-Man and the Raven-Man" (Siberia, no. 60): The bird-man, the rival of the raven-man, received the daughter of the Siberian creator-god, the Great Raven; when they came to a river, he ordered her to sit on him and let herself be carried across the water. "She replied, 'But you are too small, I will crush you.'—'No,' he replied, 'I can easily carry you across, you won't crush me.' As soon as Yingeangeut sat on the little bird-man's shoulders, he was completely crushed and lay dead on the ground. Yingeangeut took her husband's corpse onto her palm and sat down in the shade of a pine growing from a rock; she sat there for quite a while. In the end, she began to wail and said: 'I will starve, my husband is dead.' Immediately, she heard a voice behind her: 'What are you wailing about? I am here, your husband.' She turned around and before her stood a strong young man. Nearby there was also a tent and a herd of reindeer. The reindeer had silver antlers and hooves. She said to the man: 'You are lying. Here is my husband, he is dead.' He replied: 'I merely assumed this form to woo your father. Now you behold me in my true form, and here are my relatives. I had myself killed on purpose to appear in my true form and to bring my reindeer here.' She believed him and followed him into his tent."— Trans. (The following episode does not address the same theme but describes a struggle with the raven-man who devoured the sun). This part of the tale describes the ultimate revelation of the bird-man's splendid nature. His disenchantment necessitates "killing" his previous form, which corresponds to a "shell" or an "animal skin." The transformations do not result from a curse, but from his intention

282    The previously mentioned "The Three Brothers and Their Sister" (Siberia, no. 6) describes the reunion of the separated couple with some original variations: Via several stations where she must make different sacrifices, the heroine reaches the land beyond the holy sea, which never freezes and where her former bridegroom lives in an inaccessible house whose foundation and roof are made of gold. He is sick. She cures him without revealing herself and hides in his house as an unsightly goblin. He wants to free the sun's daughter and then the moon's, yet in both cases the goblin kills the bride with magic. When he begins to play music in despair and remembers her in his song, she reveals herself to him, and he decides to keep her with him forever.

283    The healing of the bridegroom corresponds to the redemption from the animal form in the versions discussed above. The heroine's transformation, however, is momentous. Presumably, it should be interpreted as an adaptation to the unconscious, in whose deepest layers she now finds herself. Another, new aspect is that the bridegroom desires to free the daughters of the sun and the moon, while in other versions, the sun and the moon are stations on the journey. Here, the daughters of the sun and the moon are figures of the "false bride." As archetypal images in the unconscious, they correspond to the witch's daughters in European versions. Corresponding to primitive thinking, the two stars are perceived as deeply fascinating, as potentially overwhelming, and even as threatening individual conscious realization.

284    In order to free the hero from the power of the "false bride" or—from the woman's point of view—the shadow, in most variants the heroine sacrifices the magical objects given to her shortly beforehand, as these make the "false bride" desirous. The sacrifice is considerable: Unless the heroine does not win back the prince in the three nights at her disposal, she, too, will lose everything, including any future possibility of binding him to her. Moreover, she has decisively increased her enemy's power. Thus, by sacrificing the

---

and power. No opposition between the conscious and the unconscious is portrayed, but instead the unbridled yet characteristic workings of a demonic figure.

objects, she plays a game of life and death. The egoistic ego cannot make such a great sacrifice unless the self forces it to. Jung explains the meaning of this kind of action as follows:

285     As the self can only be comprehended by us in particular acts, but remains concealed from us as a whole because it is more comprehensive than we are, all we can do is to draw conclusions from the little of the self that we can experience. We have seen that a sacrifice only takes place when we feel the self actually carrying it out on ourselves. We may also venture to surmise that in so far as the self stands to us in the relation of father to son, the self in some sort feels our sacrifice as a sacrifice of itself. From that sacrifice *we* gain ourselves—*our* "self"—for we have only what we give. But what does the self gain? We see it entering into manifestation, freeing itself from unconscious projection, and, as it grips us, entering into our lives and so passing from unconsciousness into consciousness, from potentiality into actuality. What it is in the diffuse unconscious state we do not know; we only know that *in becoming ourself it has become man.*[251]

286     Thus, we are dealing with the self becoming human. This explains the liberation of the animal prince from the witch's spell, which is achieved indirectly by sacrifice. For this symbolizes the "dissolute state of unconsciousness" in which the prince, that is, the future self destined to become human, still finds itself and from which it can be freed only by conscious human action.[252]

287     In most variants on this theme, the animal prince is not redeemed solely by the sacrifice of valuable objects. Rather, the heroine must also struggle during the purchased nights to rouse the

---

[251] Jung, "Transformation Symbolism in the Mass," *CW* 11, § 398 [Translator's note: The emphases are Marie-Louise von Franz's].

[252] In a Piedmontese variant reported by De Gubernatis, *Thiere i. d. indog. Mythologie* (Leipzig, 1874, p. 630f.), the youngest sister, in order to save her father from death, marries a frog that becomes human at night. Despite the frog's warning, the sisters make her talk, so that he falls ill and disappears. Even the magic ring, which he gave to the heroine and which provides everything, does not bring him back. The heroine throws the ring, which has become useless, into a pond, whereupon the young man emerges, redeemed.

prince from the oblivion into which the "false bride" has immersed him by means of a sleeping potion and to lead him back to her.[253] The spell cast by the witch's daughter also captures the effect and the nature of the witch's spell as a profound unconsciousness. Significantly, when the prince in the tale about the singing, soaring lark awakens, he, too, says: "Now I really am released! I have been as it were in a dream, for the strange princess has bewitched me so that I have been compelled to forget you, but God has delivered me from the spell at the right time."[254] Sometimes, the motif of awakening and recalling is intertwined with that of washing out stains. For stains, like sleep and being enveloped by the false bride or by an animal skin that must be burned, are signs of bewitchment and bondage.

288    In several fairytales, the animal prince is redeemed in the final episode of several tales: the Grimm's "Ferdinand the Faithful and Ferdinand the Unfaithful" and "The Golden Bird," as well as "The Golden Castle That Hung in the Air" (Norway, no. 35). In these tales, the animal prince is disenchanted by the hero, whose shadow he complements and whose self he represents. In "The Golden Bird," the anima-figure is his sister, not his redeemer. While the figure of the animal prince is secondary in these tales, in those about the singing, soaring lark it becomes the principal motif. In these tales, moreover, one aspect of the plot is illumined that remains unclear in the other tales: the cause of bewitchment. As in those tales, while the witch curses others, she is also described as a lover and as a false bride. Her curse is sometimes justified by her rejection by the animal prince, and so forth. This connection is expanded on, comprehensively and extensively, in "First Born, First Married" (Sweden, no. 12):

289    In a wild storm at sea, a King vowed, in order to save himself, to sacrifice to the mermaid the first male being that he

[253] On the motif of forgetting the real bride, see, e.g., "Palermo, the Sorcerer" (Spain, no. 11), "Hans Wunderlich" (Zaunert, *Deutsche Märchen seit Grimm*, p. 37), "Gold Marie and Gold Feather" (*ibid.*, p. 303), "The Drummer" (*The Complete Grimm's Fairy Tales*), "Three Brothers and Their Sister" (Siberia, no. 6), and "Ememqut and the White Whale Woman" (Siberia, no. 54).
[254] *The Complete Grimm's Fairy Tales*, p. 404.

encountered on his return; this, however, happened to be his five-year-old son. The King, however, thought that the prince was only a child and, therefore, that the next male could be sacrificed. But henceforth, no sea voyage was successful, and the people grumbled about the King breaking his word. At first, the prince was attended to very closely, but as time passed the mermaid was forgotten; when he was ten years old, the Queen gave birth to another boy. Soon thereafter, when the eldest prince was walking along the beach with his tutor, a cloud descended and engulfed them; when it had receded, the prince had disappeared. Thus the younger prince became the heir to the crown. When he was sixteen years old, a bride was sought for him. During this time, however, the seashore was haunted in a life-threatening way, and the frightened people heard the call in the evening after the clock had struck eleven: "First born, first married!" A wise woman, whose counsel the King sought, said that "this is the prince who has been taken into the sea and who is calling out in this way, and that a wife must be found for him; she must be young, beautiful, and from the most distinguished family in the country; and she should not be under the age fifteen nor over seventeen years old. ... they should first build a small house by the sea, and the disturbance might cease. In any case, said the wise woman, as long as they built a house, no ghost would haunt them. Four people should be assigned to this task. They should first prepare the site, build the foundation walls, and thereafter the house, which should consist only of two congenial rooms, one situated behind the other, and a nice hallway." As long as they worked on the house, everything remained silent on the beach; yet when they rested for a day, and when they had completed their work, the shouting resumed. In the living room of the newly erected cottage, so the wise woman, a large mirror should be hung in such a way that one could see whoever entered the room from the bed in the bedroom, even if one were facing the wall. The door between the two rooms should always be left open. As the unrest on the beach increased again, following the advice of the wise woman, the three beautiful maidens chosen for the sea prince were led one after the other to the beach cottage, so that if one of the girls pleased the prince, peace might return. The girls and their parents were distraught about their fate.

290 At ten o'clock in the evening, the eldest girl was to sleep in the sea castle, and the wise woman advised her "to lie down in the beautiful bed, but with her face to the wall; on no account should she turn around, let curiosity get the better of her, and watch what was going on. She should only see what she could see with her face against the wall in the mirror in the living room." Nor should she speak. Before eleven o'clock, after a tearful farewell, the house was locked from the outside. Around twelve o'clock, all of a sudden the hall and parlor doors opened, and the young woman saw a tall and handsome youth enter, with water dripping from his clothes. He seemed to be cold. He placed a large, beautiful apple by the window and hung a bottle on the window handle. Thereafter, he looked at the sleeping girl, undressed, lay down beside her, and fell asleep. However, the poor timid girl had only just closed her eyes, was seized by curiosity and quietly turned over. At that very moment, however, he grabbed her right hand, chopped it off, and threw it under the bed. He went back to sleep until daybreak, dressed, took the bottle and apple, and without glancing at the bed, hurried out, shutting the door behind him. The wise woman said that the maiden should not have turned round and was not allowed anywhere near the cottage for fear of her life.

291 The second girl, who was already more despondent, and much needed the wise woman's comfort, suffered the same fate.

292     Now it was the turn of the youngest and loveliest of the girls. She overcame her inhibitions, almost scared to death, fought her curiosity until she fell asleep and only awoke when the prince was getting dressed. "Thereupon he stepped over to the bed, bent over it for a while, left the room, turned round beneath the door and took the bottle and the apple, before closing the door behind him." The parents, the royal court, and the wise woman wanted to fetch the girl, like her predecessors, but she went to meet them, crying, and was led triumphantly to the castle.

293     Now the damsel slept every night in the cottage by the sea, and every night took the same course as the first one. "And yet, it seemed as if he looked at her longer every evening and every morning; she, however, always remained silent, fearful, with her face turned toward the wall, not daring to look at him than what the mirror showed her as he came and went." The two older girls grew envious and threatened to kill the youngest if she did not give them back their hands. The wise woman advised the girl that "when the prince has lain down as usual, she should—always with her face turned to the wall —say:

294     "The two damsels want to slay me,
Or have their hands back!"

295     Under no circumstances should she say anything else. When the prince, sighing, bent over the bed for longer than usual, she uttered the words in a trembling voice. Immediately, the prince answered: "Take the hands—they are under the bed— and the bottle hanging at the window, and pour from the bottle onto the arms and hands, put them together, rub them and bandage them, and after three days you can remove the bandage, and the hands will be whole." The girl fell asleep without uttering a word. "In the morning ... (the prince) approached the bed several times and looked at her from its end; she, however, did not dare to look up and kept her eyes

closed. He sighed, took his apple, but left the bottle and went out." The girl healed the hands.—In the meantime, the younger son's bride had arrived for the forthcoming wedding. The foreign princess would not be adorned more delightfully than the sea prince's bride. Both would be honored in equal measure. Once again, the other two girls grew envious and threatened to have the youngest sister murdered if they were not allowed to taste the prince's apple. On the advice of the wise woman, the youngest therefore said to the prince in the evening:

296   "The two young ladies want to kill me.
Or have your apple!"

297   The prince replied: "Take the apple lying by the window, and when you go out, put it on the ground, and follow it wherever it rolls. When it stops rolling, pick as many apples as you wish, and return the same way." "The following morning, the prince found it harder than ever to leave. He seemed agitated and restless, sighed a lot, walked around the bed several times, bent over the girl, went out into the living room, and returned to look at her again. Finally, when the sun rose, he hurried out and closed the door behind him. When the girl awoke, she had to cry, for she too had begun to love the prince ..."

298   She followed the rolling apple into a distant land to a garden wall, over which trees were hanging with the most beautiful fruits. The apple rolled through the golden gate, which opened by itself, to a low tree bearing the largest, most magnificent apples. There it stopped and the girl filled her apron with apples. Yet she didn't remember the prince's words, bumped into the apple, which began rolling again; all of a sudden, the door slammed shut with a loud bang. Startled, yet repenting in vain, the girl followed the apple, which stopped at a small fireplace; upon it stood two kettles, one large, the other small, both filled with water. "Under the

large kettle a mighty fire was ablaze, but under the small kettle only a very weak one. When the apple stopped, the girl did not know what to do. She had the idea to scrape apart the fire under the large kettle and to push it under the small one. The small kettle began to boil and the large one gradually came to rest. But the girl could not stay there; as she had violated the instructions before, she expected nothing but death, which she did not care about, because she had lost any hope of getting the prince. So she bumped the apple again, and it rolled onto a meadow in the middle of the garden, where two little children were sleeping in the bright sunshine. She felt sorry for them, took her apron, and draped it over them to protect them from the sun, and only took as many apples as she could put in her basket." She bumped the apple again and arrived unawares at the seashore where the prince lay asleep under a tree next to a beautiful mermaid. They jumped up, startled, and the prince looked at the girl, concerned and fondly. Thereupon, he jumped into the sea. But the mermaid grabbed the girl angrily and asked her (she had dropped to the ground fearing for her life) who had permitted her to advance further than the apple tree. The girl confessed her disobedience, which was not due to any evil intent. Still, the mermaid wanted to punish her. Therefore, she pushed the apple, which rolled back through the gate to the apple tree. As the apple tree was whole, the mermaid pushed the apple again and they reached the fireplace. "When the mermaid discovered that the small cauldron was boiling, but that the large one was almost stagnant, she grew terribly angry, grabbed the girl by the arm, and asked in a shrill voice: 'What have you subdued here! How could you take the fire from under my kettle and put it under yours?' The girl had no idea what evil she had committed and said she was not aware of anything. The mermaid said: 'The large kettle means the love between the prince and me, the small one means the love between the prince and you. Now you have removed the

fire from under my kettle and put it under yours, and the prince now loves you most fervently and me almost not at all.'— 'Look,' she cried angrily, 'my cauldron has ceased boiling and yours is brimming. But I will see what other evil you have done onto me, and punish you accordingly.'"
Following the apple, they reached the children sleeping under the apron. Again, the girl confessed her deed, and that she had left the other apples for the children. The mermaid said: "This act and your truthfulness will save you. I see that you have a good heart. These children belong to me and the prince. But now that he loves you more than me, I will give him to you. Go to the castle and tell what I have told you, and that your marriage to my prince should be celebrated at the same time as that of the younger brother. Also, all your jewels and ornaments and the wedding dress and the bridal chair should be like those of the other princess. From that moment when the priest blesses you and the prince, I will no longer have power over him. But since I have made sure that he possesses all the qualities befitting a regent, I demand that he inherit his father's kingdom as the eldest child. The younger prince can then rule over the kingdom that his consort will give him. You must say all this, and only on this condition will I let the prince leave me. Then, when you are in the bridal state, come here to me without anyone's knowledge, so that I may see how they have adorned my successor. Here is the apple that will show you the way without anyone knowing where you are going." With these words, she gave the apple a push. It took the girl to the castle, where the king had given instructions to prepare the two weddings.

299   When the girl was adorned, she followed the apple to the same place on the beach where the mermaid told her that the slightest disobedience would have spelled her death. However, she did not find the clothes precious enough, tore them off, and took all the jewels out of the bride's hair. The girl was to receive the mermaid's bridal attire, which she took from a

lavish shrine after picking up some grass from under the great tree. The bridal attire was studded with precious stones, and the crown beamed with the brightest emeralds. "So," said the mermaid, "go to the castle and show everyone how I was dressed on my wedding day with him.—All this I give to you and your descendants. But you must behave toward the prince in such a way that I will always be pleased with you. Let his happiness and satisfaction be your highest goal all your life." At the castle, the girl was dressed much more sumptuously than the other princesses, and not even all the treasures of the kingdom would have matched her bridal attire.

300 In the church, people were waiting impatiently for the prince, until the King at last ordered one of the most distinguished gentlemen to sit in the bridal chair in the prince's place. "But when the priest began to pray, the double doors flew open, and a tall, handsome, and strong man, with flashing eyes and dressed in royal attire, entered, strode to the bridal chair, pushed the other man away so that he almost fell over, and exclaimed: 'This is my place. Priest, say the blessing!' During the blessing, the prince again grew calm, and thereafter joyfully greeted his parents and the whole court, and for the first time embraced his spouse, who only now dared look at him. ..." He inherited the kingdom, and they lived a long and happy life. His descendants own the land to this day.

301 The composition of this poetic fairytale is unusually consistent, almost novelistic. It is a subtle love story, suspended between the dreamlike world of fairytales and reality; it seems to be a true story, which, however, lets the magical background shine through. At the same time, it is also a pure fairytale, whose secret relations to human reality become tangible. The result is an adeptly crafted narrative, which culminates dramatically in the heroine's encounter with the mermaid; however, a more succinct and simpler form would better correspond to the common fairytale style, which suggests that this tale was reworked poetically.

303     While the plot of the Grimm's "The Nixie of the Mill-Pond" parallels that of the Swedish variant considered above, its narrative style more closely resembles that of a pure, unadulterated fairytale:

302     There was once a miller who lived with his wife in great contentment … But as their wealth increased so did it again decrease … One morning he rose and went out into the open air … As he was stepping over the mill-dam … he heard a rippling sound in the pond. He turned round and perceived a beautiful woman, rising slowly out of the water … and asked him why he was so sad … "I will make you richer and happier than you have ever been before, only you must promise to give me the young thing which has just been borne in your house." "What else can that be," thought the miller, "but a puppy or a kitten?" and he promised her what she desired … He had not yet reached his house, when the maid-servant came out … and cried to him to rejoice, for his wife had given birth to a little boy. The miller stood as if struck by lightning; he saw well that the cunning nixie had been aware of it, and had cheated him.

304     In the meantime prosperity again returned to the miller's house … The miller never let the boy himself go near the water … But as year after year went by and the nixie did not show herself again, the miller began to feel at ease. The boy grew up to a youth, and was apprenticed to a huntsman. When he had learnt everything … he married a beautiful and true-hearted maiden … and they lived peacefully and happily, and loved each other …

305     One day the huntsman … shot a roe … He did not notice that he was in the neighborhood of the dangerous mill-pond, and went, after he had disembowelled the roe, to the water, in order to wash his blood-stained hands. Scarcely, however, had he dipped them in than the nixie ascended, smilingly wound her dripping arms around him, and drew him quickly

down under the waves, which closed over him. When it was evening, and the huntsman did not return home, his wife became alarmed … She hastened to the water … At last her strength came to an end, she sank down … and fell into a heavy sleep. Presently a dream took possession of her:

306 She was anxiously climbing upwards between great masses of rock; thorns and briars caught her feet, the rain beat her in the face, and the wind tossed her long hair about. When she had reached the summit, quite a different sight presented itself to her; the sky was blue, the air soft, the ground sloped gently downwards, and on a green meadow, gay with flowers of every color, stood a pretty cottage. She went up to it and opened the door; there sat an old woman with white hair, who beckoned to her kindly. At that very moment, the poor woman awoke … and at once she resolved to act in accordance with her dream. She laboriously climbed the mountain; everything was exactly as she had seen it in the night. The old woman received her kindly … "I will help you," she said. "Here is a golden comb … Tarry till the full moon has risen, then go to the mill-pond, seat yourself on the shore, and comb your … hair with this comb … and you will see what will happen." … It was not long before there was a movement in the depths, a wave rose, rolled to the shore, and bore the comb away with it. In not more than the time necessary for the comb to sink to the bottom, the surface of the water parted, and the head of the huntsman arose. He did not speak, but looked at his wife with sorrowful glances. At the same instant, a second wave came rushing up, and covered the man's head. All had vanished, the mill-pond lay peaceful as before, and nothing but the face of the full moon shone on it.

307 Full of sorrow, the woman went back, but again the dream showed her the cottage of the old woman. Next morning she again set out … and the old woman gave her a golden flute and said: "Tarry till the full moon comes again, then take this flute; play a beautiful air on it, and when you have finished,

lay it on the sand, … and you will see what will happen." The wife did as the old woman told her … When the waters parted this time, not only the head of the man, but half of his body also arose. He stretched out his arms longingly towards her, but a second wave came up, covered him, and drew him under again.

308 The dream led the wife a third time to the house of the old woman … This time she received a spinning-wheel … went to the shore as the old woman had told her … and span industriously until the flax came to an end … No sooner was the wheel standing on the shore than there was a more violent movement than before in the depths of the pond, a mighty wave rushed up, and bore the wheel away with it. Immediately the head and the whole body of the man rose into the air … he quickly sprang to the shore, caught his wife by the hand and fled. But they had scarcely gone a very little distance, when the whole pond rose with a frightened roar, and streamed out over the open country. The fugitives already saw death before their eyes, when the woman in terror implored the help of the old woman, and in an instant they were transformed, she into a toad, he into a frog. The flood which had overtaken them could not destroy them, but it tore them apart and carried them far away.

309 When the water had dispersed and they both touched dry land again, they regained their human form, but neither knew where the other was; they found themselves among strange people, who did not know their native land. High mountains and deep valleys lay between them.

310 In order to keep themselves alive, they were both obliged to tend sheep. For many years they drove their flocks … and were full of sorrow and longing … and as chance would have it they drew near each other. They met in a valley, but did not recognize each other … One evening … the shepherd pulled the flute out of his pocket, and played the tune his wife had played on the shore of the mill-pond … he recognized his

dear wife, ... and she knew him also. They embraced and kissed each other, and no one need ask if they were happy.[255]

311    This fairytale can be interpreted in light of "First Born, First Married," and we therefore focus on it below.

312    It begins with the motif of Jephthah, which recalls the Grimm's "The King of the Golden Mountain." [256] The previous dominant of consciousness (the father as a merchant or king), which experiences a crisis (poverty, storm), defies the unconscious, which approaches it as a demon and unlawfully extends its life by sacrificing its own new form (child). Steadfastly clinging to obsolete forms of consciousness amounts to betraying the self. True to the paradoxical nature of all psychic processes, becoming increasingly set on something makes the demonic side of the unconscious ever more prevalent. The self, which, disregarded as the most powerful psychic content, disappeared completely in the unconscious, bestows on it a quite extraordinary energy, which manifests as a ghost or spectre. The king's second, later-born son seems to be a weak substitute and presumably has a corresponding psychological meaning: He symbolizes a kind of pseudofuture and pseudolife, a shadowy imitation to which the previous dominant of consciousness clings in place of the lost one. When the sunken prince cries "First born, first married!" at night, we hear the voice of conscience, through which the true personality demands its right to exist and does not renounce its realization in earthly, human life.

313    The old woman, who contributes to banishing the spectre and whose instructions guide the action, is a benevolent mother-figure. She is portrayed more clearly as such in the Grimm's tale, where she provides the helpful magical objects (comb, flute, spinning wheel) that lure the husband, who has gone missing, out of the water again.

---

[255] Abridged and adapted from *The Complete Grimm's Fairy Tales*, pp. 736–742. See also "The Siren of the Sea" (Italy, no. 21).

[256] See the Book of Judges 11:30–40: The unsuspecting Jephthah promises to sacrifice what first confronts him when he returns home. This happens to be his daughter, his only child. In fairytales, this condition sometimes varies. In some cases, a demon demands the father to make a sacrifice: either the first male being that he encounters or the newly born, still unknown child. For the Grimm's tale, see *The Complete Grimm's Fairy Tales*, pp. 425–430.

In the Swedish fairytale, the king's and the mermaid's behavior at first points to a conflict between the ruling consciousness and the feminine side of the soul. Consequently, only the mother (i.e., the unconscious whose instinctive wisdom helps attain the goal also on twisted paths) can help. This explains why this well-disposed witch advises that a *woman* should perform the act of redemption. Only the woman who reacts in a purely feminine way—or the man's anima—can find a solution amid the unconscious entanglements.

314    The little house built on the beach symbolizes a first attempt (and an initial endeavor) of consciousness to lure what has vanished forever back into a sphere formed by human hands, to disentangle that psychic content that has become unconscious from its fusion with the unconscious, thus rendering it accessible to humankind. The two rooms indicate that no uniform centering can be achieved as yet, and that, at least at this stage, consciousness and the unconscious can only be brought closer. The prohibition to look directly at the prince has a similar meaning; he may be beheld only in a mirror. Looking in a mirror means looking at things indirectly: Perseus, for example, used his shield as a mirror, so he could kill Medusa without looking at her directly; if he had, he would have turned to stone. The prince, then, is treated like a dead person or like a ghost, because he has drowned (i.e., emerges freezing and drenched from the waters); thus, he is as uncanny as the sea people in "The Servant and the Sea People" (Iceland, no. 56), which is populated with drowned souls. Being submerged in water corresponds to the unredeemed prince's animal form in the fairytales examined previously. For instance, in a Dutch variant of "The Singing, Soaring Lark," the animal prince is redeemed by the heroine, who saves him from drowning.[257]

315    Common to these motifs is the symbolically represented supremacy of the unconscious. The sea prince also behaves like an evil demon toward the curious princesses. The less understood, that is, respected, the self or—from the woman's perspective—the animus

---

[257] Bolte and Polívka, *Anmerkungen*, vol. 2, p. 242. On the alchemical parable of the king's son in the depths of the sea, see Jung, *Psychology and Alchemy*, CW 12, § 434–441 and 496ff.

is, the more it seems to resemble a frightening phantom. Mirrors are often believed to protect humans against ghosts[258]; because psychologically, they mean consciousness, in that mirroring symbolizes contemplative knowledge, which drives demons out of the world; and because mirrors denote such a thoughtful, conscious attitude, they show, according to widespread superstition, not only the face that we turn toward the world, but also our dark, often demonic side; psychologically, that is, our shadow.

316  Strikingly, the Old-High German word for mirror (*scucor*) means "container of shadows." Old-Icelandic *skuggja* ("seeing shadows") denotes that the shadow and the mirror-image (i.e., reflection) were designated by the same word, because both were identified. Similarly, in Middle-High German *Schatten* ("shadow") was occasionally used to mean *Spiegelbild* ("mirror-image, reflection").[259] Although at first this refers only to the concrete shadow, this connection is nevertheless psychologically significant: As devils, witches, and so on are also beheld in mirrors, this suggests that the psychological "shadow" is also meant.[260] In popular belief, the magical mirror tends to show the lover or the beloved, that is, the animus or anima, just as often as the shadow does.[261]

317  In sum, the mirror thus symbolizes the knowledge of one's own unconscious that arises from a contemplative, conscious attitude. In the present fairytale, intellectual passivity is still quite prominent: The sea prince cuts off the right hand of those girls who violate the precept to not turn around.[262] The hand, in particular the right hand, signifies conscious action or intervention.[263] For this, however, the

---

[258] See Róheim, *Spiegelzauber* (1919), pp. 167 and 175ff.

[259] Bächtold-Stäubli under *Spiegel* (mirror).

[260] Róheim, *Spiegelzauber*, passim.

[261] Bächtold-Stäubli under *Spiegel* (mirror); see further Róheim, *Spiegelzauber*, pp. 91–93, 142, 146–147: "In Scotland, on the night of All Souls' Day, the girl sits down alone with a candle in front of the mirror, eats an apple, and combs her hair, whereupon she sees the face of her future husband in the mirror, as he watches her over her shoulder. In northern Scotland, the girl impales each apple slice on the tip of a knife and, looking in the mirror, combs her hair while holding the apple slice backwards over her left shoulder. The image of the future husband appears and reaches for the apple. Whoever eats an apple in England at midnight on All Souls' Day and looks in the mirror, *without looking over their shoulder*, sees their future husband or wife" (author's emphasis).—Trans.

[262] Ultimately, this is the Orphic motif: The soul-image, which has been devoured by the unconscious, can only be made conscious again if consciousness consistently maintains *its* point of view, *its* line of vision, or it will sooner or later be devoured itself (in the end, Orpheus was torn asunder by the Maenads).

[263] Among other tales, the heroine's activities are stifled in "The Girl Without Hands" (*The Complete*

magically appropriate moment has not yet arrived. For the time being, human consciousness must accept that the events occurring on the threshold of the unconscious (i.e., seashore) are psychic and metaphorical, without making any rational intervention, because the course of these events must not be disturbed by unrestrained instinctuality (curiosity, impatience).

318    The conditions and processes of redemption described in this fairytale are so subtle that any action diverging from the dark natural wisdom of sheer instinct (the old woman's advice) is mistaken. The world of profane thought and action, represented by the heroine's "sisters," at first proves to be nothing other than inappropriate and incapable. Then, however, driven even further into opposition by failure, it becomes quite disruptive: The girls threaten the heroine and thus endanger the whole work of redemption. Because the heroine, who represents the feminine consciousness, finds the right "mirroring" attitude toward the ambivalent unconscious content, that is, the man's soul-image represented by the sea prince, its positive effects now also emerge. These are symbolized by the healing water in its possession and by the apple, which later serves as a mystical guide. The healing water springs from psychic vitality, which now begins to emanate from the sea prince, who until then had been a cold shade, and corresponds to his burgeoning love for the heroine. The apple, however, represents that principle in the unconscious that provides meaning and direction. We have already explained its meaning as a symbol of the self.[264]

319    The image of the fruit suggests that the self is the final outcome of a natural development, and at the same time the nucleus of new life. Next, the "profane sisters," healed by the water of life, wish to taste the sea prince's apple. Just as the profane tendency of consciousness tends to reject the arduous confrontation with the unconscious, so it greedily thirsts to receive its living values and attempts to lure these over into *its* sphere. Insofar as the apple

---

Grimm's Fairy Tales, pp. 160–166) and its variants.

[264] See "Connla's Sea-Journey" (Ireland, no. 2), "Thomas the Rhymer" (Ehrentreich, *English Folktales*, Jena 1938, p. 193), "The Princess on the Glass Mountain" (Sweden, no. 16), "The Story of the Little Silver Plate and the Little Red Apple" (Loepfe, *Russische*, p. 152), "The Earth Wants Its Share" (Caucasus, no. 6), "Three Brothers" (Balkans, no. 7), "Samovilas Graze a Millet Field" (Balkans, no. 43).

symbolizes the nonhuman aspect of that psychic force also represented by the prince, it is, as it were, its double. The profane sisters thus strive to "devour," that is, assimilate him completely. In this way, the sea prince is caught between two worlds, both of which seek to overwhelm him: The abysmal, mysterious depths of the sea with their enchanting mistress; and the sphere of earthly splendor at the royal court. However, only that woman who dares to walk the labyrinthine path through the unconscious with delicate selflessness and patience—at times guided, at others taking the initiative herself—can truly free and lead the (sea) prince to his destiny.

320     The prince does not give away his apple for the "sisters" because he knows that the profane world is unable to grasp the unity (i.e., wholeness) of the self; only large amounts of fruit, that is, the beneficial effects of the self, become it. Therefore, he lets the apple lead the heroine to an apple tree in a magic garden. Being a clearly delimited part of nature cultivated by humans, this garden in some respects corresponds to the little seaside cottage, whereas the latter, however, was closer to humankind and represented a psychic sphere also accessible to the profane world, the garden is, so to speak, farther removed from the world, a psychic space inhabited by magical beings. As a feminine symbol often associated with the anima, this garden is, as it were, the psychic being that envelops the sea prince and in which he is enclosed. It is the mermaid's sphere of influence, a paradisiacal prison. There stands the apple tree, the origin of the prince's magical apple, which recalls the immortalizing apples of the Hesperides or the rejuvenating apples of the goddess Idun. Thus, fertility originates in this garden: Despite its beautiful, magical appearance, it is dangerous and should be considered a land beyond.

321     The heroine's mission is completed once she picks the apples, at least as far as the prince has given her permission. This explains why the apple guiding her does not roll any further. Somewhat arrogantly, the heroine dares to reach for her higher self and thus breaks into a forbidden or as yet forbidden realm. Her action resembles both the intrusion into the forbidden chamber in the Bluebeard type of

fairytale,[265] as well as the premature illumination in "The Singing, Soaring Lark" and its variants. It has the same psychological backgrounds: desire and impatience. Here, the heroine's instinct breaks through and interrupts her delicate probing into the magical world.

322 As in the previous fairytales, the consequences are horror and suffering. It is a question of life and death. Therefore, the courage that the heroine subsequently summons is based, as is stated explicitly, on a sense of desperation that is prepared to accept death. Acting on her own authority, yet taking instinctive and simple action uninfluenced by profane forces (which in the singing, soaring lark type of fairytale merely kindle the heroine's desire), she disobeys the magical precept, similar to the hero in "The Golden Bird," who disobeyed the fox's advice. In both cases, this disobedience leads into great dangers, yet eventually proves to be beneficial by heightening and deepening the experience of the unconscious sphere. As "The Golden Bird," the princess would have remained in the magical realm had the prince thoughtlessly obeyed the fox. Once more, the prince would thus have continued to live under the mermaid's spell and would never have been redeemed, or not for a long time. Discussing this course of events, Zimmer writes[266]:

323 What a wonderful purpose may our transgressions and shortcomings serve: By plunging us into distress and turmoil, they take us further, to ourselves in a richer form, and prepare us for a power and glory we had never suspected ... our guilt and imperfections are wings that can bear us upward to the encounter with the supreme powers of the world and to the assignments they give us.

324 When the heroine violates the precept, the garden gate closes. Like the prince, she, too, is trapped. Her way back is cut off, and the unconscious has engulfed her. There is no way back. She can only

---

[265] See *Archetypal Symbolism in Fairytales*, vol. 3, ch. 1.
[266] Zimmer, *Weisheit Indiens* (Darmstadt, 1938), p. 93.—Trans.

keep following the apple, into the unknown, unadvised and unguided. By prodding the apple, the heroine renounces her passive attitude, which until then had proven to be the only correct one. She gropes forward as if in a dream. Yet the spontaneous action with which the heroine disobeys the precept, tragically and salubriously, at the crucial moment, also saves her: because it occurs to her, just as abruptly and seemingly irrationally, that she can exchange the fire beneath the two kettles. This, as we see later, kindles the prince's love for her and lets his love for the mermaid grow cold. Here, the relationship of fire, simmering water, and passion, familiar from many figures of speech, is captured in a single image.

325     This peculiar motif, of redemption being caused by a "shift in emphasis," through which the close relationship passes from one symbolic figure to another, becomes evident in a different way in the Grimm's "The Old Woman in the Wood":

326     A poor servant-girl was traveling with the family whose service she had entered through a great forest, and … robbers came out of the thicket, murdered all they found … except the girl. When the robbers had gone away … she seated herself under a tree. After a while, a white dove came flying … and put a little golden key in her hand and said that she could use the key to open a great tree where she would find food … When she was satisfied … the dove flew to her again, and brought another golden key … and said she could open another tree with a beautiful white bed inside … In the morning the dove came a third time, and again brought a little key, and said: "Open that tree there, and you will find clothes."

327     Then one day the dove came and asked the girl to do something for its sake … The dove said: "I will guide you to a small house; enter it, and inside it, an old woman will be sitting by the fire and will say: 'Good-day.' But on your life give her no answer … but pass by her on the right side … you will enter into a room where a quantity of rings of all kind are lying … seek out a plain one, which must likewise

be amongst them, and bring it here to me as quickly as you can." The girl did as she was told … did not answer the old woman, who seized her by the gown, and wanted to hold her fast … As instructed she went into the room with the rings .. but could not find the plain one. While she was seeking, she saw the old woman … stealing away, and wanting to go off with a bird-cage … a bird was inside which had a plain ring in its bill. The girl followed the old woman, took the ring, and ran joyously home with it, and thought the little white dove would come and get the ring, but it did not. The girl leant against the tree, determined to wait for the dove … it seemed as if the tree was soft and pliant, and was letting its branches down. And suddenly the branches twined around her, and were two arms, and when she looked around, the tree was a handsome man, who embraced and kissed her heartily, and said: "You have delivered me from the power of the old woman, who is a wicked witch. She had changed me into a tree, and every day for two hours I was a white dove, and so long as she possessed the ring I could not regain my human form." Then his servants and his horses, who had likewise been changed into trees, were freed from the enchantment also, and stood beside him. And he led them forth to his kingdom, for he was a King's son, and they married, and lively happily.[267]

328 Here, the enchanted prince appears as a tree, aligning him with the primordial image of the mother and preserving a positive, living aspect. The dove, as which he sometimes appears, is the opposite of the tree: It is not the static or rooting psychic principle, but the fleeting, agile one. The dominance of the devouring mother thus not only deprives the hero of his humanity but also divides him: One half of him is earthly and vegetative, the other is sublimated into the spiritual realm. The caged bird, which holds the ring, might represent the prince's soul, because it is also held captive by the

---

[267] Adapted and abridged from *The Complete Grimm's Fairy Tales*, pp. 558–560.

mother. The central symbol, however, is the simple ring, in which lies the secret of the connection. Neither richly studded rings, that is, outwardly dazzling values, bind the hero to the mother, nor external conveniences conveying worldly pleasures, but a stoneless, simple ring represents their bond. His "plain" inner being succumbed to the terrible mother so that, psychologically speaking, the hero became fettered to the unconscious. Representing "roundness," the ring symbolizes the young man's self. This can only be freed from the spell by a woman who, as an anima-figure, replaces the image of the mother and thus becomes the image of the self. The fact that this partly reaches the human realm means that the prince again becomes human. The primordial opposition between the tree and the dove dissolves. A new and more comprehensive opposition arises in the shape of a man and a woman, which is eliminated by their union on the human level.

329    Here, too, the central symbol shifts from the demonic mother-figure to the anima assuming human form. The bond is not dissolved but transformed. In the present Swedish fairytale, the key scene in the apple orchard has the same meaning—even if it is presented in a simpler image.

330    On the other hand, the subsequent episode is more differentiated: The children are protected from the sun, which balances out events. This "kindheartedness" makes the mermaid forgive the wrong done to her (the extinguishing of the fire beneath her kettle). The action is thus compensatory, not just on the face of things, but also in terms of its symbolic meaning: Exchanging the fire under the kettles energizes spiritual life in the human realm and weakens the demonic unconscious. And yet, humankind may not enrich itself without making an appeasing sacrifice of its own. Therefore, the heroine can also only save the drowned man in the Grimm's "The Nixie of the Mill-Pond" by sacrificing the golden comb, the flute, and the spinning wheel (which later returns the flute to the heroine). In "First Born, First Married" (Sweden, no. 12), the countersacrifice consists, besides the apron, primarily in a service

to which the heroine is prompted by her maternal instinct.[268] The sun is the image of consciousness, and sunlight can also be scorching. New life, as yet undeveloped—and represented by the children—and resting in the unconscious, is harmed by the discerning function of consciousness, which strives for unequivocal clarity—similar to how lighting the lamp ruined the animal prince's peaceful existence. The heroine therefore instinctively protects these children and thus behaves unlike those heroines who expose magical figures to light. Thus, the unconscious (i.e., the mermaid) can ensure that a part of nature remains undisturbed and, in turn, sets free a part of the matter-bound spirit.

331    Thereafter, the heroine reaches her beloved, whom she finds beside the mermaid. Although she knew about his enchantment, she had no idea what was happening in the depths of the pond. Now, however, she confronts the power that banished the prince. As the heroine resorts to a life-preserving subplot to compensate for robbing the mermaid, the struggle takes a favorable turn. As so often in fairytales, the seemingly hostile and demonic unconscious suddenly becomes a helper. The mermaid not only releases the prince but also adorns the heroine with her jewels. This gift merges the two figures into a richer, more experienced pair,[269] which inherits the kingdom. The younger pair, on the other hand, which we interpreted as a surrogate- or pseudo-attitude of the old king, is cast aside.

332    Compared to the examples discussed above, in this fairytale the heroine's magical rival is depicted in much greater detail and much more vividly. In the previous fairytales, what caused the prince's enchantment is mostly only hinted at somewhat vaguely. It was

---

[268] Comparing this motif with that in "The Stolen Daughters" (Finland, no. 28) reveals how closely related fairytale motifs are, so that they readily merge: In the Finnish tale, the hero covers the young eagles with his coat because they are "so naked." In return, the grateful eagle transports the hero to the upper world. Thus, his deed is judged in the same way as in "Djulek-Batür" (Turkestan, no. 7), where the dragon threatening Simurg's children is slain. In both cases, it is about protecting emerging life from harm in the magical sphere, about consciousness intervening in the struggle between the unconscious opposites. In the Swedish fairytale discussed above, the symbol of the sun lends the motif of protective covering a slightly different meaning as that tale seems to originate in more conscious thinking than most "folk tales."

[269] In terms of the old king and the prince, this fusion means becoming aware of the anima, i.e., clarifying the relationship to the unconscious, whose "treasures" are thus salvaged.

either caused by the curse of an evil mother-figure, often combined with the motif of this witch at first striving to free the prince and, because she is rejected, becoming very evil[270]; or she had intended the prince for her daughter. This daughter-figure appears more clearly only in "The Singing, Soaring Lark" (albeit as the daughter of a "sorcerer"), where she fights the lion prince as a dragon and abducts him. In that tale, the dragon symbol means that this "false bride" represents the woman's soul-image on the psycho-physical level of the unconscious. The mermaid possesses the same characteristics as the nonhuman dragon; in her, as it were, the devouring mother (who appears to the father and later steals the boy) and the demonic "false bride" are united in one figure, as both of them are aspects of the man's anima.[271] According to ancient mythology, the sea (Oceanus) is a great dragon or serpent that bites its own tail. In some myths, the sea is embodied in a monster,[272] as an image of the devouring darkness of the unconscious and its animal and demonic powers.

333     In the Swedish tale "First Born, First Married," however, this element only appears as the mermaid's dark background and has already assumed more human traits. Rather than this being merely about struggle and repression, here confrontation and reconciliation become possible. This also explains why this fairytale also seems closer to reality in purely formal terms. The mermaid is a perfect anima-image: She is both mother and lover, eternally young and old, natural and elfish, demonic and violent, yet also human and benevolent. She personifies the sea, just as the infinitely expanding

---

[270] See Laistner, *Das Rätsel* (1889), vol. 1, p. 129, who discusses a Sicilian tale where the demonic anima-figure need not be a rejected "false bride," as in "The White Cat" (Zaunert, *Märchen aus dem Donaulande*, p. 37). Rather, every slight (like the initial deception in "First Born, First Married"; Sweden, no. 12) brings her negative powers into play: A young man bathing in the sea is pursued by a mermaid. He grabs her by the hair and drags her home. She gives birth to a son and remains silent. Friends accuse him of living with a ghost, so he threatens her: unless she reveals who she is, he will kill the child. She replies that by forcing her to speak, he has lost a good woman, and disappears. A few years later, she drags the boy, who is playing on the shore, into the sea, where he drowns. Here, the offended partner in the magical marriage causes the child's death.

[271] See "Three Brothers and Their Sister" (Siberia, no. 6): The anti-bride, as the daughter of the sun and the moon, stands opposed to the human heroine. See also the Spanish fairytale "Queen Rose or Little Thomas" (no. 45), where the same contrast is described between the hero's two mother-figures: Queen Rose, the father's demonic anima, and the human mother.

[272] Leo Frobenius, *Das Zeitalter des Sonnengottes*, vol. 1 (Berlin: Georg Reimer, 1904); see also Jung, *Symbols of Transformation*, CW 5, § 307f.

unconscious is condensed, as it were, in the anima as a tangible content. This archetypal image of the anima—the mermaid, however, is not meant to become the prince's bride—is also contrasted with the "false bride" in the profane sense, as embodied in the heroine's older companions in fate. They play a role similar to Cinderella's sisters in the eponymous fairytale.[273] In other fairytales, they are conflated into one figure: See, for instance, the profane stepsister in "The White Bride and the Black Bride" or the chambermaid in "The Goose-Girl."[274] However, insofar as the stepsister in "The White Bride and the Black Bride" is a rivaling *witch's daughter*, she resembles the demonic parallel figures in fairytales (such as ones about the singing, soaring lark), and thus also the mermaid.

334      Thus, the connections are manifold and subtle. The rivals' different characters indicate that their archetype has two aspects, one of which coincides with the mermaid. The "false bride" thus belongs to two worlds: In the unconscious, she is a demonic being; in profane reality, on the other hand, she is dazzling, represents something uncertain and hostile, and appears half-demonic and half-profane (because the effects of the profane and negative are similar to those of the magical and negative). The tale's actual heroine, who passes through between these figures, seems to be a real woman of exemplary character, whose nature is unadulterated, feminine, devoted, and sincere. In terms of the woman's psyche, she embodies the actual inner personality, which serves the self in the form of her own spiritual being.

335      However, in fairytales where an enchanted prince is redeemed, events are also illumined in terms of the man's psyche, who is freed from his unconscious attachment to the false anima-image by a genuine psychic figure.[275] In "First Born, First Married," all magical power is transferred to the heroine. This development is described quite tersely in three stages: first quietly, when the prince beholds

---

[273] The *Complete Grimm's Fairy Tales*, pp. 121–128.
[274] *Ibid.*, pp. 608–612 and pp. 404–411.
[275] On the contrast between the magical anima-figure and the real woman, see the opposition between Brunhild and Krimhild (Gudrun) in the *Nibelungenlied*; see further the saga of Undine (Fouqué), where the real woman is portrayed in negative terms.

the girl in the seaside cottage; then more forcefully, when the fire is exchanged beneath the kettles; and finally, in terms of a climax, when the girl receives the magical jewelry. Whereas in fairytales in which the animal skin is burned, thus destroying every trace of the curse, in "The Singing, Soaring Lark," for instance, the snake-witch is excluded from redemption. Nor is she transformed by "death." In "First Born, First Married," the magical realm, although "deprived," remains a factor. Whereas in the fairytale about the singing, soaring lark the partial problem remains unresolved, in the Swedish fairytale, the conscious and the unconscious worlds are radically severed by the former being assigned to a higher standpoint, namely Christianity, which protects it from further encroachment by the magical world. Nevertheless, the mermaid's renunciation is described so magnificently that it is touching, creating a sense of regret that seems to be missing in simpler fairytales. While this might be due to the almost literary form of this tale, it might also express the fact that the detachment of the anima's natural character feels like a loss. In this respect, the views of fairytales are conditioned by time and often compensate for the culturally determined and prevailing views of the world of consciousness.

336    One fairytale that illumines a man's enchantment and redemption in terms of his relationship with the anima in yet another way is "Clever Finna" (Iceland, no. 8.—Trans):

337    Finna was the beautiful and clever daughter of Thrand, a widowed judge. Rumor had it that she knew more than other people. Once, when her father went to Thing, she made him promise that he would not give her to any suitor, unless his life depended on it. He kept his word, but one evening, while riding out on his own, he encountered a scary looking man on a black horse. He called himself Geir, demanded Finna as his wife and, when Thrand refused, put a sword to the latter's chest. Now Thrand promised his daughter, who was to be taken away after half a month. At home, Finna already suspected what had happened and said that she did not expect to have much joy.

338  When Geir fetched her, she took nothing with her except for her brother Sigurd. For three days, they rode through the Alps with cattle, sheep and horses, all belonging to Geir, and finally reached his homestead. Finna, who immediately busied herself with the house, and her brother Sigurd were doing well there, although Geir cared little for his wife. But she did not pay much attention. On the night before Christmas, Geir was nowhere to be found; his foster mother said, crying, that he had not been home for Christmas for a long time.

339  When everyone had gone to sleep, Finna and her brother Sigurd took a boat to a nearby island. She went ashore alone and walked to a small beautiful house, through whose half-open door she saw a bed by a burning light, in which Geir was lying with a strange woman in his arms. Finna sat down next to the bed, spoke some words, and then returned home with her brother. When she went to her marital chamber one morning after Christmas, she found Geir pacing the room, and there was a child in the bed. Geir asked whose child this was, and she answered: "It belongs to no one other than us."

340  After a year, the same events took place at Christmas, except that Finna spoke while sitting on a stool in front of the bed. At the third Christmas, Sigurd asked to go ashore with his sister, which she permitted provided that he did not utter a word. He waited outside the house while she, sitting on the bedpost, said:

341  "Here I sit alone,
 Joy has departed me.
 The clever husband has killed
 My joy throughout the summer.
 Another has gained the one I love.
 Often the sea crashes onto the ship's crew."

342  Geir rose and said: "This shall not last any longer." But the woman lying in bed with him fainted, so Finna dabbed wine

onto her lips, and when she awoke, she was a beautiful girl. Then Geir said to Finna, "You have delivered me from great distress; for this was the last year in which I could be redeemed. ..." His father, the King of Gardareich, had married a stranger in his second marriage, who soon poisoned him. She cursed Geir and his sister to have three children together. Should he not receive a wife who knew about all of this and remained silent about it, he would become a snake and his sister an untamed filly. Now that he was redeemed, he wanted to give his sister to Sigurd as a wife and also his father's kingdom. And so it happened. Geir's stepmother was torn asunder by horses, Sigurd and Ingibjörg ruled in the Kingdom of Garda, Geir became Thrand's successor as a judge and had sons and daughters with Finna.

343 Once more, a man stands between two women and is delivered from an inherited curse by a clever and devoted heroine. Although seemingly different, almost all the motifs in this tale are familiar. Fearing for his life, the father promises his daughter to a demonic suitor, recalling the initial motif in "The Singing, Soaring Lark" and "The Scarlet Flower."[276] In comparison, however, the union is not so much the daughter's wish than her dreaded fate; on the other hand, she indirectly contributes to the fateful events by making her father promise that he will reject all other suitors. Being magical (her name means "having knowledge of magic"[277]), Finna intuits what will become her life's task. Her intimate relationship with her brother Sigurd, whom she even (although quite unusually) takes along to her new home, and who plays a peculiar, shadowy, albeit not unimportant role, seems strange. Just as the unknown suitor is cursed to commit incest, so a similar psychic tendency seems to exist between Finna and Sigurd.

[276] Loepfe, *Russische*, p. 86.
[277] Hans and Ida Naumann, *Isländische Volksmärchen* (Jena, 1923), p. 309, note. See also Adeline Rittershaus, *Die Neuisländischen Volksmärchen. Ein Beitrag zur vergleichenden Märchenforschung* (Halle a. S.: Max Niemeyer, 1902), no. XXII "Finna, the Prescient"; see also *ibid.*, p. 87: "The name Finna, which we do not encounter in any other Icelandic fairytale or legend, is probably meant to indicate this girl's extraordinary cleverness, which includes being able to foresee the future." Finnur, the masculine form of the name, is very common in Iceland and in this source is used only for a wizard and an elf. Thus, Finna's name indicates her relationship with the magical realm.

344      The unknown suitor's black horse indicates that he belongs to the dark world. In most mythologies, black is the color of the realm of the dead, of night, of demons, that is, of the unconscious in its unknown, sinister aspect. The rider of the black horse owns large cattle and sheep herds, which he shows the heroine. When the suitor points to his property (often without acknowledging his ownership or, if he does, then usurpingly[278]), he emphasizes his wealth, which in most fairytales expresses his magical power.

345      Cursed by his stepmother, Geir is bound to the unconscious world and therefore is indifferent to his real wife; this becomes plainly evident at Christmas. This Christian festival falls on the winter solstice, which was already celebrated before the introduction of Christianity in Nordic countries, because darkness culminates at this time. Consequently, Christmas, in particular in Nordic countries, where winter is long and dark, is that time of year that is haunted most by demons.[279] In these months of inactivity, imposed by nature, people are more exposed than usual to the manifestations of the unconscious.

346      Christmas is also the magical time when Geir's cursedness becomes truly apparent. His beautiful sister lives alone on an island and, also because Geir is bound to her, recalls the mermaid in "First Born, First Married," even if she possesses more human traits. When Finna discovers her husband's secret, not only does she control her jealousy, but she even recognizes, thanks to her knowledge of magic, the cursed background of these events, whose demonic compulsion can only be overcome by patiently applying a counterspell. While the heroine of the previous fairytale also redeemed the sea prince through her knowledge of magic, which she received from a wise old woman, Finna, as it were, unites both figures in herself: She is the devoted lover and possesses superior knowledge. Just as the heroine protected the mermaid's children in the other tale, here Finna even takes those who have been born from the curse back to her home

---

[278] See "King Thrushbeard" (*The Complete Grimm's Fairy Tales*, pp. 244–248) and "Puss in Boots" (France, vol. 1, no. 26).
[279] See, e.g., "Una, the Elf Maiden" (Iceland, no. 10) and "Hild, The Queen of Elves" (Iceland, no. 57). See esp. Bächtold-Stäubli under *Weihnacht* (Christmas).

and raises them. She, too, protects life, which comes from the land of spirits and attends to it in her human home, knowing that in detaching herself from unconscious ties, she needs to affiliate the future-oriented aspect of this connection with human consciousness. Gradually, year after year, she addresses her sayings to the enchanted couple, because separating oneself from the unconscious is a protracted and subtle process (similar to the heroine in "First Born, First Married," who was long forbidden to look at the prince, and only established deeper contact with him over time).

347     Finna's lament seeks to rekindle Geir's love for her. In particular, the last verse is highly meaningful, suggesting that the misfortune is an overflowing of the sea, that is, being flooded and dominated by the unconscious. The following part is unclear: We are told, quite abruptly, that once she has overcome her powerlessness, the stranger will become a beautiful girl. We might therefore assume that she was unsightly, perhaps even witchlike.[280] She would thus resemble the rival witches in the tales about the redemption of animal princes considered previously. Another trait also links this tale to this type of fairytale: The stepmother's curse associates Geir and his sister only temporarily with incest; afterward, they are supposed to become animals for good: He becomes a snake, she a wild filly.

348     The final episode, where a double union occurs, is not very common in fairytales: Not only do Geir and Finna find each other, but Sigurd marries Ingibjörg, Geir's redeemed sister, and becomes the ruler of her kingdom. Since Ingibjörg plays a role similar to that of the mermaid in "First Born, First Married," she might be considered the demonic aspect of Geir's anima. Sigurd, on the other hand, is a youthful form of Finna's animus, just as in real life the brother can be the first projection of the spouse's image besides the father.[281] Considering this psychological interpretation and also the

---

[280] On being cursed, see Lincke, "Stiefmutter" (Berlin, 1933), p. 149f.

[281] Emma Jung, "Ein Beitrag zum Problem des Animus," in *Wirklichkeit der Seele: Anwendungen und Fortschritte der neueren Psychologie*, ed. C.G. Jung (Zurich: Rascher, 1934), pp. 336f. and 348f. On the brother as the sister's helpful companion, see Benjamin Albert Botkin, ed., *The Pocket Treasury of American Folklore* (New York: Pocket Books, 1950,) pp. 328ff.; see esp. "The Devil Marriage": A girl only wanted to marry a man who wore clothes made of gold. When such a man came along, she married him despite his clubbed feet and his crippled hand. When they went to his home, she took her little brother with her. The latter drew his sister's attention to her husband's sinister behavior. He said that

specific narrative,[282] we probably ought to see Geir and Finna as real people. In that case, the four figures who unite *crosswise* represent a process by which in every true union and love of two people, not only do they come together in their concrete, daily life, but at the same time, a mystical marriage of souls, of animus and anima, occurs as a mirror-image.[283]

349  The tragic entanglements in this fairytale and in the previous ones raise the question of what causes an evil spell that requires such laborious redemption. Strangely, most fairytales are quite vague in this respect. In almost all cases, an evil mother or stepmother curses the hero—transforming him into an animal or a ghostly creature—and separates him from the human sphere.[284]

350  The fairytale about clever Finna introduces an intermediate motif, by placing sibling incest *before* the animal stage. The witch's desire for the prince in the previously discussed fairytales also somehow implies the incest motif: The witch takes the place of the mother, and the prince's union with her would thus constitute a union with the mother. Being rejected, incest therefore either causes the curse or is its content and thus is closely associated with the curse. In his comprehensive "Das Inzest-Motiv in Dichtung und

the man goaded the horse and called him the devil. The brother's counterspell made the horse run back to the girl's father's house. There, the devil asked tricky questions, which were answered by an old woman who had been fetched by the boy. Nevertheless, the devil claimed to have won the girl's soul. The old woman threw a shoe sole at him, which he caught and took with him. (Note that the figure of Conrad in "The Goose-Girl" [*The Complete Grimm's Fairy Tales*, pp. 404–411] also belongs to this group of "helpful brothers," who represent the animus-image as youthful and lively).

[282] For the father's exact name and profession, see Rittershaus, *Neuisländischen* (Halle a. S. 1902), p. 87, who observes that such specific designations of persons are uncommon.

[283] For a detailed discussion of this motif of the four figures and their relation to each other in the above fairytale in connection with an alchemical text, see Jung, "The Psychology of the Transference," *CW* 16, § 430f. (cited below, pp. 306–307). See also "Asmund and Signy" (Iceland, no. 66), "Tschuinis" (Latvia, no. 7), "Ring, the King's Son, and Snati-Snati, the Dog" (Iceland, no. 27). A more frequent fairytale motif is that two male figures, a hero and a shadow-figure (or two female figures, a heroine and a shadow-figure), marry a female (or male) couple, but not vice versa; see, e.g., "The Bird Wehmus" (Zaunert, *Märchen aus dem Donaulande*, p. 315), a parallel to "The Golden Bird" (*The Complete Grimm's Fairy Tales*, pp. 272–279), where the fox, after being redeemed, receives the sister of the princess, who has been won by the hero. This motif also appears in "The Two Sisters" (Siberia, no. 3), and most evidently in "The Princess in the Tree" (Zaunert, *Deutsche Märchen seit Grimm*, p. 1): The princess's mare and the hero's stallion are redeemed at the end and marry as prince and princess, so that the wedding takes place not only on the human level, but also in the shadow (i.e., demonic) realm.

[284] See the numerous examples in Lincke, "Stiefmutter" (1933). See also the mythological motif of the mother-goddess who transforms her lovers into animals (Circe, Artemis, Dea Syria); see further Jean Przyluski, "Ursprünge und Entwicklung des Kultes der Mutter-Göttin," *Eranos-Jahrbuch 1938: Gestalt und Kult der "Grossen Mutter,"* ed. Olga Fröbe-Kapteyn (1939), pp. 28ff. On medieval tales about witches, see Wesselski, "Versuch" (1931), p. 22f., who observes that women versed in magic transformed young boys into animals out of jealousy or put them up for sale.

Sage,"[285] Otto Rank discusses the numerous incest motifs in fairytales, myths, legends, and poetry from a Freudian perspective. Correspondingly, all mythical and poetic forms of the motif are ultimately based on an individual's concrete, instinctual longing for incest with their real mother or sister, or with their father or brother.

351    According to Jung, this is a psychological archetype, which influences individual relationships. The primary type is *archetypal incest*,[286] whose meaning is elusive and can at best be interpreted psychologically by means of amplification.[287] The image of incest symbolizes the tendency toward the self (i.e., its desired assimilation), albeit on a preconscious or unconscious level. In the present fairytale, the curse implies that, corresponding to the creative force of nature, children, as the seeds of life, are meant to emerge in the unconscious. If this germinating life is to become fruitful for human beings, they must raise it from its dark, subliminal, and aimless emergence and withering through the participation of their consciousness.[288]

352    Incest symbolism is particularly rich in alchemical literature.[289] There, according to Jung, the brother-sister pair represents the idea of opposites in general: "These have a wide range of variation: dry-moist, hot-cold, male-female, sun-moon, gold-silver, mercury-sulphur, round-square, water-fire, volatile-solid, physical-spiritual, and so on." The union of the siblings describes how "the masculine, spiritual principle of light and Logos ... like the Gnostic νοῦς (Nous), sinks into the embrace of physical nature (Physis)."[290] This mythological image expresses an unconscious process: the unconscious projection of the archetype of the god-man or self into

[285] Otto Rank, "Das Inzest-Motiv in Dichtung und Sage," in *Grundzüge einer Psycholoie des dichterischen Schaffens* (Leipzig and Vienna: Deuticke, 1912), esp. 2. sec. XIII–XX.
[286] The symbolic nature of the incest motif is also evident in an Estonian fairytale mentioned by De Gubernatis, *Thiere i. d. indog. Mythologie* (Leipzig, 1874), p. 583, fn. 1, where a prince falls in love with his sister, who comes from an egg.
[287] For a general discussion, see Jung, *Symbols of Transformation*, CW 5; "Psychological Aspects of the Mother Archetype," CW 9/I; *Psychology and Alchemy*, CW 12, § 433.
[288] On the meaning of the incest taboo, see Jung, "The Psychology of the Transference," CW 16, § 433–437 and 438, where he refers to Layar's "The Incest Taboo and the Virgin Archetype," *Eranos-Jahrbuch*, vol. XII: *Studien zum Problem des Archetypischen*, ed. Olga Fröbe-Kapteyn (1945), pp. 270–307.
[289] See "The Glass Coffin" (*The Complete Grimm's Fairy Tales*, pp. 672–678). On the sources of this alchemical literary tale, see Bolte and Polívka, *Anmerkungen*, vol. 3, p. 261.
[290] See Jung, *Psychology and Alchemy*, CW 12, § 436.

nature.[291] Thus, the pair that is united in incest represents, as a totality, an unconscious content that unites the opposites,[292] albeit in a potential state, one not animated by consciousness. This is significant for the fairytale about Finna. Geir and his sister are such a pair. However, just as alchemical siblings are destined to *separatio* (divorce) after union, so must this pair also be separated. For this union of opposites, although in itself an ideal state, resides purely in the unconscious and therefore means stagnation, which explains why the opposites must be separated and activated. "When an unconscious content" (here that of the mystical wedding) "is replaced by a projected image ... it is cut off," according to Jung,[293]

353  from all participation in and influence on the conscious mind. Hence it largely forfeits its own life, because prevented from exerting the formative influence on consciousness natural to it; what is more, it remains in its original form— unchanged, for nothing changes in the unconscious. At a certain point it even develops a tendency to regress to lower and more archaic levels. [The pair threatens to become animals.]

354 The peculiar motif of *two* pairs can also be illumined from another perspective: Finna and her brother are the children of a judge. His profession means that he represents to a considerable extent the world of reason, intellectual discernment, and moral responsibility. Geir and his sister, on the other hand, stand in the shadow of an evil stepmother who, as the negative "Great Mother," embodies the unconscious world in its irrational, amoral, and chthonic-material aspect.

355  The "Kingdom of Garda" (*Gardariki*) lies on the Baltic Sea, south of the Gulf of Finland,[294] which was conquered by the Swedes during

---

[291] *Ibid.*, § 405ff.
[292] *Ibid.*, § 496.
[293] *Ibid.*, § 12. Translator's note: The bracketed comment is von Franz's.
[294] See Felix Niedner, "Islands Kultur zur Wikingerzeit," in: *Thule: Altnordische Dichtung und Prosa, Einleitungsband* (Jena: Eugen Diederichs, 1920), pp. 23–24; see also the map of the Viking campaigns (at the end of that book).

the Viking campaigns. In the language of fairytales, it denotes a distant realm in the east and beyond the sea. Both worlds, however, also contain their opposite: In the judge's case, this is Finna, who possesses a *knowledge of magic*, which would not be possible without a secret relationship with the other world. In the stepmother's case, it is Geir, who woos Finna with the *sword*. The sword, as explained, is an image of the discerning and decision-making function of the mind and, in concrete terms, an attribute of judges. If the two worlds, hitherto separated, come into contact, their antagonistic aspects attract each other crosswise. They become completely intertwined and are no longer threatened by disintegration, in which the *enantiodromia* of the opposites comes to a standstill.[295] The mandala formed by four persons indicates that the archetypal image of the self has in the broadest sense become reality at the human level.

356    Thus, the unfortunate initial state is caused by a seemingly archetypal power (i.e., mother) striving to prevent the opposites, originally united in the unconscious (incest motif), from falling apart. This dissolution, however, is necessary for life and self-development to unfold, as we observed in the opening episode of "King Lindworm" (Denmark, no.1): The mother ate both the red and the white flower instead of only one of them. She neither wanted to nor was she able to allow the separation that is needed to become human to take place. Ultimately, the guilt for the misfortune described in other fairytales (e.g., the arrogance with which the parents or the hero/heroine even reject suitors determined by fate[296]) arises from an "incestuous desire" (e.g., the father desires the daughter, whom he is reluctant to part with[297]); that is, from refusing to confront an "Other," a stranger, or an opposite. This confrontation,

---

[295] Translator's note: In *Psychological Types*, Jung defines *enantiodromia* as "the emergence of the unconscious opposite in the course of time" (CW 6, § 709).

[296] See "The Young Wolf" (Zaunert, *Märchen aus dem Donaulande*, p. 1), "King Thrushbeard" (*The Complete Grimm's Fairy Tales*, pp. 244–248 ), "The Magic Horse" (Turkestan, no. 9), "The Little Red Man" (Zaunert, *Märchen aus dem Donaulande*, p. 10). Exhibiting a haughty attitude toward an inferior or seemingly gruesome adversary is a familiar motif: see, e.g., "The Devil's Castle" (Finland, no. 36) and "Green Cap" (Christensen, *Iran*, p. 31).

[297] See, e.g., "Allerleirauh" (*The Complete Grimm's Fairy Tales*, pp. 326–331) and "The Magic Horse" (Turkestan, no. 9).

however, is vital. Thus, both curse and enchantment seem to arise from a regressive, unconscious tendency, a tendency toward inertia, which is characteristic of matter[298] and makes people hold onto and keep things. Its image is that of the wicked and foolish mother or the obstinate, wayward father; on the other hand, resisting this tendency causes great distress, so that the human being faces a difficult decision.[299]

357    In numerous fairytales, the temporality and the exact circumstances of the curse suggest that consciousness is able to engage with it or is even meant to. The unconscious sphere is prepared to do so to a certain extent, so that consciousness not intervening when it needs to also amounts to guilt. The fact that the enchanted entreat those they desire quite so forcefully supports this idea. In "Clever Finna" (Iceland, no. 8), for instance, the three children are meant to be cursed as they make their way into the profane sphere. It is as if nature itself wants to be freed from its entanglement in the eternally embattled opposites (represented in alchemical writings as an *uroboros*, a snake that devours its own tail).[300]

358    In "The Talking Tree" (Finland, no. 23), a lost huntsman comes to a forest lake, from which emerges a large dragon. It asks to be spared as it is being pursued by another dragon, which wants to devour it. The huntsman, says the first dragon, should shoot its pursuer, by aiming at the white spot on its chest. The other dragon comes thundering along, and the huntsman shoots it, whereupon the first dragon devours the dead one and breathes into the man's mouth, making him "very wise." He understands the rustling of the trees and therefore is able to point his brothers toward a golden bowl filled with gold nuggets and concealed beneath the roots of a large tree. When the tree advises the men to use it as a doorpost, they do so and have lived prosperously ever since.

---

[298] On Plato's idea that matter inflicts evil on the spirit, see Erwin Rohde, *"Psyche": Seelencult und Unsterblichkeitsglaube der Griechen*, vols. 1 and 2 (Tübingen: Mohr, 1910), vol. 2, p. 281, fn. 3.

[299] On the unhappiness caused by accepting the witch's incestuous desire, see "The Blue Bird" (France, vol. 1, no. 30) and "Queen Rose or Little Thomas" (Spain, no. 45).

[300] On this Gnostic idea, see Wilhelm Bousset, *Hauptprobleme der Gnosis* (Göttingen: Vandenhoeck & Ruprecht, 1907), p. 353.

359    Following his conscious action, the hero receives the treasures of the "tree," as if the "Great Mother" were grateful.[301] Although such fairytales show that remaining unconscious is a curse and a source of guilt, as this cancels out psychic development, and although conscious intervention in the cycle is demanded, and even rewarded, in numerous fairytales, resisting attachment may also become guilt-ridden due to the resulting misfortune. According to Jung,[302] this happens because higher consciousness denotes guilt toward nature, tradition, and the past (and therefore is often represented by the parent-imagos). Thus, it is difficult to determine metaphysical guilt in fairytales. In some fairytales, the "summons" (or command) contained in the curse, that consciousness intervene, is also expressed in the mother's peculiar role as the personification of both aspects of the unconscious. It is as if being cursed—that is, becoming attached—often incestuously—to the magical figure (the witch as a mother or her daughter as a false bride or one's own sister), amounts to an appeal to confront the magical sphere, which, in turn, however, wishes to keep the enchanted one as the self.

360    One fairytale that subtly, yet also strangely blends a devouring greed for the treasure and for a mother's fostering love is "The Padlock" (Italy, no. 35). Overall, its plot resembles that of "Cupid and Psyche." Here, however, the heroine's guilt consists not only in illumining the prince, but also in opening, although he forbids this, a padlock given by the profane sisters, from which emerge some females wearing flax on their heads. One of them drops the flax, and the young man awakens when the heroine exclaims: "Pick up the yarn, maiden!" This symbolizes the intrusion of mundane distraction into psychic occlusion. The crucial moment of this fairytale, however, is the peculiar spell that the witch casts on the prince: "He should wander far from his father's house, until he is

---

[301] On the opposites fighting each other as hostile animals, see Jung, *Psychology and Alchemy*, CW 12, passim. See also a Lapland fairytale reported in Frobenius, *Zeitalter* (Berlin, 1904), p. 245ff.: A giant boy is pursued by a large magic cat (i.e., both are magical figures). They both ask a young huntsman (who represents consciousness) to shoot their adversary. He shoots the cat. The giant boy takes the huntsman to his father and advises him to choose the more inconspicuous of the offered gifts. Thus, as a reward for saving the son, the huntsman receives magical gifts, which help him gain the favor of a princess.
[302] Jung, "The Spiritual Problem of Modern Man," *CW* 10, § 152.

embraced by his mother and no cock crows any more." The cock (or rooster), as a sun-bird, and as the herald of the new day, embodies consciousness and conscience. Here, then, redemption means that the prince must commit to the night, unconsciousness, and the incestuous love of the mother-imago, in order to be freed from the mother's dark aspect.[303] This also explains why as a rule the animal prince can be redeemed only by a woman, as well as why, for example, in "First Born, First Married" and "Clever Finna," the heroine is characterized by loving motherliness. Only the mother can free the hero or heroine from the mother. Thus, there is neither struggle nor escape, but only transformation, through which the life-enhancing love contained in the mother's devouring greed takes powerful effect. For only in this way is the unconscious, despite its menacing aspect, acknowledged as the basis of life.[304]

361     The peculiar greed of the unconscious is also described quite succinctly in "The Sun Child."[305] In this South Sea fairytale, the sun's son visits his unknown father, who instructs him to ask the moon's aunt to give him the first of two unknown things ("Melaja" and "Monuja"). Yet he asks for the latter and the moon's aunt forbids him to unpack it as long as he is out on the water. Stubbornly, he unpacks it anyway and finds a treasure, a beautiful pearl bowl. Thereupon, he hears a tremendous roar, and a large school of fish hastens toward him to catch the treasure. The overloaded ship sinks into the depths, and the sun's boy is devoured by sharks.

362     The characterization of the hero as the sun's son and the intimated journey into the otherworld, beyond the sun and the moon, indicate that this tale is about the quest for precious, yet barely attainable objects. Yet the boy's disobedience to the sun betrays the principle of consciousness, which brings him closer, in fact ruinously, to the power of the unconscious. The pearl bowl

---

[303] In this fairytale, both aspects of the mother are personified.
[304] The transformation of the mother is plainly evident in "The Story of Batim" (Roma, no. 9): A terrible man-eater furiously pursued the redeeming heroine and her lover until her hatred turned to love for the son and, because he could not live without the maiden, she dismissed the pair with her blessing. In "The Blind Man Who Recovered His Sight" (North America, no. 9), the son's fate is negative because he avenges himself too brutally on the evil mother.
[305] See Hambruch, ed., *Südseemärchen aus Australien / Neu-Guinea / Fidji / Karolinen / Samoa / Tonga / Hawaii / Neu-Seeland u. a.*, [MdW], ed. v. d. Leyen and Zaunert (1921).

represents the feminine aspect of the precious object and thus strengthens the unconscious side, so that the unconscious contents eventually engulf everything—amounting, psychologically, to madness. Quite dramatically, the tale describes how a precious object attracts the fish, which also seem to want the treasure. A strange *horror vacui* (fear of emptiness) seemingly inheres in the unconscious, which is reluctant to release what it bears and even attempts to devour it time and again. This also explains why the animal prince is threatened from the outset by the devouring love of a terrible mother-figure: He represents the elusive precious object in animal-human form.[306]

363     The previous deliberations suggest that the so-called "animal prince" needs to be understood as the self, which appears in several aspects and relations: He is both the heroine's masculine-spiritual soul-image and the hero's animal-demonic *doppelgänger* and could be described as his own self, which is still merged with the shadow. These two meanings aside, he symbolizes an archetypal psychic reality in which man and woman participate. The suprapersonal aspect of this archetypal being is proven by its animal form or otherworldly origin.[307] Likewise, ancient representations of the motif do not depict this creature as a man, but as a god, or even as Eros. Some variants of this type of fairytale give the animal prince names that emphasize his nonhuman nature. For example, in one version

---

[306] See Hermann Usener, *Die Sintfluthsagen, Religionsgeschichtliche Untersuchungen*, Part III (Bonn: Friedrich Cohen, 1899).

[307] See "Green Cap" (Christensen, *Iran*, p. 31), "The Story of Batim" (Roma, no. 9) and especially the Japanese fairytale "Amewakahiko Monogatari" (Rumpf, *Japanische Volksmärchen*, Jena, 1938, p. 69), where the prince appears as a snake but is actually a son of heaven. See also "The Tale of the Heavenly Prince and the Earthly Princess" (Malay, no. 32): When the King's son descended from heaven to earth, he became a goat. He wooed the two eldest daughters of the duke's two eldest daughters, who replied: "Since when does one marry a goat?" The youngest, however, agreed, whereupon the duke's house became as bright as it did during daytime. At night, the woman saw how the goat washed its face clean and white, and turned into a human being. When he returned from fishing in the form of a goat, she poured hot water over him on the advice of her elder sisters; on another occasion, she dropped a sword on him, explaining to them that she did this so that he would love her even more. Saddened by this treatment, he decided to return home to his parents in heaven. But she followed him and took it upon herself to be passed off by him in heaven as his servant because his parents would not agree to his earthly marriage. The Queen instructed her son's maid to pick mustard seeds from the ground and to fetch water in a basket. But at the prince's command, ants collected the mustard seed, and eels surrounded the basket. When the prince married a woman chosen for him by his parents, the maid had to hold the torches, and the dripping resin burned her hands. After the prince had twice healed the weeping woman's hands by stroking them, he took her by the hand when searching for her a third time and returned to earth with her.

he is called "The Ruby Prince" because he was born from a ruby[308]; in the Tuscan variant cited by De Gubernatis,[309] he is the king of "Pietraverde" (green = nature, life; the hermetic "Tabula Smaragdina"[310] contains the basic wisdoms) and shines at the end "like a diamond, like the sun." In another version (also collected by De Gubernatis),[311] after his redemption the enchanted one is called "Sor Fioranto, with red and white stockings." In "The Golden Root" (Italy, no. 41), he is called "Thunder and lightning"; in "A Head" (Finland, no. 39), he consists merely of a head, yet appears as a complete being at night; the heroine describes him as follows:

364    His legs are made of silver to his knees,
       his arms are made of gold to the elbows,
       he wears a star on the crown of his head,
       a sun on his forehead
       and a moon on the back of his head;
       when he speaks, golden flowers grow from his mouth and nose.

365    In a Greek version, he is called "the enchanted head." He (i.e., the one to be redeemed) also appears as a round object in the Romanian fairytale "Trandafíru," where he is called "Pumpkin Child."[312] The round shape, the relation to the red gemstone (see the philosopher's stone in alchemy), the partly golden and silver shape, or even the function of the "bristle child" in the eponymous tale,[313] and the yellow fruit, which recalls gold and the sun, demonstrate that this prince is an image of the self, which is represented by a precious stone, a round object, and a sought-after treasure.

---

[308] Bolte and Polívka, *Anmerkungen*, vol. 2 (1915), p. 260. The Philosopher's Stone is also referred to as a "ruby." See Jung, *Psychologische Interpretation von Kinderträumen und älterer Literatur über Träume*. Seminar given at ETH Zurich, ed. Liliane Frey and Aniela Jaffé, (Zurich: privately printed, 1939/40), p. 18.

[309] De Gubernatis, *Thiere i. d. indog. Mythologie* (Leipzig, 1874), pp. 631ff.

[310] Julius Ruska, *Tabula Smaragdina: Ein Beitrag zur Geschichte der Hermetischen Literatur*. Heidelberger Akten der von-Portheim-Stiftung 16. Arbeiten aus dem Institut für Geschichte der Naturwissenschaft IV (Heidelberg: Carl Winter's Universitätsbuchhandlung, 1926).

[311] De Gubernatis, *Thiere i. d. indog. Mythologie*, p. 658.

[312] Bolte and Polívka, *Anmerkungen*, vol. 2, p. 255. In "The Snake Child," a Walachian fairytale, the prince is a pumpkin by day and a handsome man by night; see Johann Georg von Hahn, *Griechische und albanesische Märchen*, vol. 2 (Leipzig: Verlag v. Wilhelm Engelmann, 1864), p. 312.

[313] Zaunert, *Deutsche Märchen seit Grimm*, p. 286: The bristle child transforms a castle into a silver edifice, builds a golden castle opposite, and connects both with a bridge made of diamonds and crystal.

366    Yet these images reflect merely one aspect of this complex being. Although animals possess faculties that surpass those of human beings, the animal form assumed by the prince in numerous versions emphasizes a very different side of his nature: his entrapment in the instinctive regions of the psyche, whose powers cannot be consciously directed.[314] This includes, for instance, that, as "The Stag Prince" (Denmark, no. 2) suggests, as a stag prince he must lie in the dirt, in a forbidden chamber in which, according to some variants, one would expect to find a devilish figure.[315] On the other hand, in the variant "Worry and Sorrow" (Norway, no. 25), for example, in which he appears as a squalid old man, he is approximated to the archetype of the chthonic father-god.[316] He also appears as a dark figure in "The Enchanted Giant" (Iceland, no. 50), as a bewitched giant whose curse is that he must commit murder. In "The Rose of Paradise" (Caucasus, no. 7), he is a cursed man who must perish during the day and can only live at night because he once shot at the sun. Hence, he is cursed and has been displaced into the dark magical world. In one Greek tale, he is therefore also called "the lord of the underworld."[317] In Christian terms, this means that he has been equated with the devil or—more generally—with the archetype of the underworld deity. In the Siberian tale "The One-Sided Man" (no. 24), the same figure is described as a one-sided creature: "When he breathed, his heart and lungs came out of his side." This, however, is merely a mask or covering, similar to the animal attire that we have encountered in other fairytales.

367    One day he went out as usual to look for game. When he was out of his wife's sight, he took off the skin that hid his true figure and hung it on the top of a tall larch. He became a handsome young man, as beautiful as the sunrise.

---

[314] Gerardus van der Leeuw, *Der Mensch und die Religion. Anthropologischer Versuch* (Basel: Verlag Haus zum Falken, 1941), p. 174.

[315] For variants of "Our Lady's Child" (*The Complete Grimm's Fairy Tales*, pp. 23–29) where the devil sits in the forbidden chamber, see the last section of this volume.

[316] On the relation of animals to gods, see Bächtold-Stäubli under *Tiergestalt* (animal form); see further under *Tierkönige* (animal kings) for a discussion of divine rulers of animals.

[317] Bolte and Polívka, *Anmerkungen*, vol. 2, p. 255.

368 A related idea is that of the scalp, which makes the golden one appear either scab-headed or bald.[318] The higher human being is always concealed in a contemptible shroud or covering. (Besides this motif, that of being chained or fettered also appears from time to time, as in "The Lame Dog"; Sweden, no. 13). This concerns the self that is concealed from everyday glances, and which lies unrecognized in the darkness of human aberrations (i.e., in the unconscious); and which, if it remains undiscovered, urges and torments a person until, embroiled in worldly affairs, they turn toward it. This self corresponds (according to Indian teachings) to that part of the Âtman that has descended into the world.[319]

369 Similar ideas emerged first in Iranian and later in Manichaean conceptions of the divine primordial man who has descended into dark matter and who must later be redeemed by a second "Sotēr" (i.e., savior, deliverer).[320] Sometimes the sunken and imprisoned part of God is called the luminous force[321] or luminous substance, which corresponds to the world-soul and as such is a female figure.[322] According to Manichaean myth, this figure is redeemed by the divine *nous*, which descends to it, awakens it from its deadly slumber in matter, and leads it up again to its home.[323] The same cosmic process also takes place in human beings: Within them, too, sleeps a divine spark of the soul (*Spinther*), which is awakened by the *nous* or the pneuma and is guided home again.[324] The magical demon that enchants the divine spark or the "primordial human" (the archetype

---

[318] For a more detailed discussion of the motif of golden hair, see *Archetypal Symbols in Fairytales*, vol. II, book 2.

[319] On the Indian conception of that part of the Âtman that has entered the world, see Deussen, *Sechzig Upanishad's* (1921), pp. 322ff. (Maitrâyana-Up. 3, 1–3).

[320] It seems feasible to examine these conceptions in more detail to explain fairytale plots. On the theme of redemption by a second male figure, see the discussion of mythical twins in *Archetypal Symbols in Fairytales*, vol. 5 ("The Divine Twins," forthcoming).

[321] Reitzenstein, *Iranische*, p. 102f.

[322] Henri-Charles Puech, "Der Begriff der Erlösung im Manichäismus," *Eranos-Jahrbuch 1936: Gestaltung der Erlösungsidee in Ost und West I*, ed. Olga Fröbe-Kapteyn, (1937), pp. 220, 235f., and 246.

[323] *Ibid.*, pp. 247ff.: "If we are to perceive what makes our present situation ambiguous and thus divergent from the norm, we must become conscious of the Manichaean ideal ... Consciousness is indeed the illuminating presence of the spirit, of the Nous—of the redeeming element in the soul, which represents the element to be redeemed."—Trans.

[324] *Ibid.*, pp. 192–193: "The second revelation contains a soteriological myth, which stands opposed to the cosmological one, yet is closely connected to it. This myth of redemption has the task of assuring us that, even if we find ourselves in a state of apostasy, we nevertheless come from a world beyond, that we remain connected with it by our inner being, or are connected with the fallen being who will finally be redeemed, and whose fate is therefore also ours."—Trans.

of humankind) is portrayed as Az, a female demon. She makes primordial humans

370     blind and deaf, unconscious and confused, so that at first they recognize neither their primal ground nor their origin (lit. family). She has created the body and the prison; she has bound the soul, which has lost its knowledge ... She (Āz) has bound the soul firmly in the cursed body; she has made it ugly (?), as well as evil, angry and vengeful.[325]

371     This female demon is the same archetypal figure that appears in fairytales as the enchanting witch or "false bride." Sometimes, as in fairytales, she is also juxtaposed with a helpful female figure, the "Mother of Life," who sends forth the redeemer, who frees the sunken primordial human being. Redemption by becoming conscious, so-called "gnosis," is both rebirth and resurrection.[326]

372     In Manichaeism, both the redeemer and the redeemed are sometimes characterized as female, sometimes as male; thus, in the older hymns, the redeemer is referred to as *daëna* or *Fravaši*, a female figure or a multitude of female figures who represent the heavenly or living self of the person who is to be redeemed and who awaken him or her.[327] They are a person's demon, genius, or perfect nature, which unites with the pious person striving for "gnosis": in this world, in an ecstatic spectacle; in the hereafter, utterly and completely.[328] This duality is also characterized as follows:

---

[325] Translator's note: The question mark is von Franz's. Theodor bar Kōnai, Turfan fragment, p. 9, cited in Puech, "Erlösung im Manichäismus," p. 230. See also Güntert, *Weltkönig* (1923), pp. 376–377: "Gayomārt, the doublet of Yima, succumbed to the lure of a fornicating, lewd witch; Yima's fall from grace also continues this motif, that the God-man is pulled down into matter by guilt ... ."—Trans. According to Güntert, other sources suggest that Gayomart probably committed incest with his sister, recalling "Clever Finna."

[326] Puech, "Erlösung im Manichäismus," pp. 218ff., 234–235. See also Reitzenstein, *Iranische*, pp. 9–10.

[327] Reitzenstein, *Hellenistischen Mysterien*, pp. 58–59.

[328] *Ibid.*, pp. 405–406. Similar ideas are also evident among the Mandaeans. See *ibid.*, pp. 72–73, esp. p. 178 (Lidzbarski Genza, I. III 3 1, p. 559, 29):
"I go to meet my image,
and my image comes to meet me;
It caresses and embraces me,
as if I were returning from captivity."

373    ... the *Nous*, the redeeming element, and the Psyche, the element that must be redeemed. The "Old Person" ... is, in fact, above all the body (soma) ... the body endowed with all the natural impulses of matter and enlived by its connection with the soul, and thus what the Manichaeans sometimes call "demonic ego," "dull consciousness," and "dark insight." The Old Person, then, represents the soul in its suffering and doomed condition. In contrast, the New Person ... is the soul, is seen as active and redeemed, having renewed and regained its original purity ... [329]

374    In one Chinese text, this perfect nature is also called the "living self"; it is our original, luminous nature, which is our father and our mother—that is, a hermaphroditic being, which sometimes is also represented by the sun and the moon[330] (see the role of the sun and the moon in the fairytales considered above). The variant in which the prince is called "pumpkin child" seems to be almost Manichaean,[331] because Manichaeism assumed that cucumbers, melons and roots, leeks and certain vegetables contained to a significant extent the divine luminous substance.[332] Although archetypal reemergence should never be ruled out, Manichaean ideas, which survived in Oriental tales, may have influenced some of the fairytales mentioned here.[333]

375    The Iranian notion of the primordial human continued to exist not only in Manichaeism and among the Mandaeans but also entered other Gnostic systems in late antiquity. Throughout, human beings must redeem and lead home the spiritual power living within

[329] Puech, "Erlösung im Manichäismus," pp. 240ff.—Trans.
[330] Reitzenstein, *Hellenistischen Mysterien*, p. 179f. As mentioned, this self also appears in the Acts of Thomas, in the story of the King's son who went missing in Egypt and reappeared as a *doppelgänger* dressed in a celestial robe, which is significant in light of the clothing symbolism in fairytales. See *ibid.*, pp. 53ff.; Reitzenstein, *Iranische*, p. 73f.
[331] Bolte and Polívka, *Anmerkungen*, vol. 2, p. 255.
[332] Charles R. C. Allberry, "Symbole von Tod und Wiedergeburt im Manichäismus," *Eranos-Jahrbuch 1939: Die Symbolik der Wiedergeburt in der religiösen Vorstellung der Zeiten und Völker*, ed. Olga Fröbe-Kapteyn (1940), p. 140.
[333] The lion, which is not native to northern Europe, also points to Oriental influences on fairytales about animal princes. According to Bächtold-Stäubli (under *Tierkönige*, "animal kings"), the bear was regarded as an animal king by the ancient Teutons, until foreign influence ousted the "exotic lion."

them.[334] In late-ancient syncretism, this force is called Attis, thereafter Adonis, Osiris, Adamas, Corybas, Hermes, and so on. It represents the Logos, which arose from the connection of spirit and matter and forms the hermaphroditic mediator between these two realms. It is also the world-soul, which is found in everything, and is of two kinds: on the one hand, otherworldly and pure, existing in all its might; on the other, entangled in the world and involved in its suffering. The Ophites and Perates worshipped this Logos as an all-embracing serpent,[335] which we probably ought to understand in relation to the Egyptian conception of the *Agathos Daimon* ("noble spirit") as the world-ordering spirit. This, in turn, is related to the dragon or serpentlike god Eros, and even to "Cupid and Psyche."[336]

376    The lion-shaped prince in "The Singing, Soaring Lark" is related to such Gnostic and ancient traditions, as that world-spirit was also worshipped as Aion, who was depicted as a half-snake, yet bearing a lion's head.[337] Insofar as this figure was interpreted in some systems as the world-soul, we might also understand it as a female figure and as Sophia, who descended into matter, where she lamented her fate.[338] Heinrici also compares this Gnostic figure to Psyche in "Cupid and Psyche." In this case, the united pair forms a divine *syzygy*. In other Gnostic systems, the primordial human who descended into matter was also depicted as hermaphroditic. According to the Ophites, when that figure plunged into matter, he or she fell apart, into a male and a female part.[339] Redemption consists in the reunion of these two figures.

377    From the same root as the Gnostic imagery stem the basic ideas of alchemy, which sought to liberate and redeem the spark of light

---

[334] See, e.g., Leisegang, *Die Gnosis*, pp. 154ff., 222, 231–234; on the divine spark in creation and in humankind, see also Bousset, *Hauptprobleme der Gnosis*, pp. 50–58, 121, 321f.; on being bound to matter, see *ibid.*, p. 324f.; on the redemption of primordial humans, p. 180f. Adam Kadmon, who is also the soul, also appears in the Kabbalah; see Bischoff, *Elemente der Kabbalah*, p. 37; Jung, "Paracelsus as a Spiritual Phenomenon," *CW* 13, § 168.

[335] Leisegang, *Die Gnosis*, pp. 142 and 145; Leisegang, "Schlange," p. 205f.

[336] Georg Heinrici, "Zur Geschichte der Psyche. Eine religionsgeschichtliche Skizze," *Preussische Jahrbücher*, vol. 90, ed. Hans Delbrück (Berlin: Verlag von Georg Stilke, 1897), passim, esp. pp. 410ff.; see also Reitzenstein, *Amor und Psyche*, pp. 19 and 23.

[337] Dieterich, *Mithrasliturgie*, p. 66f.; on the lion-headed Jaldabaoth, see also Bousset, *Hauptprobleme der Gnosis*, pp. 18 and 324f.

[338] Leisegang, *Die Gnosis*, pp. 114, 118f., 138, 166f., 310ff., 378–382.

[339] *Ibid.*, p. 134.

or the divine spirit that had sunk into matter and thus also descended into the natural human being. The myth reflects, as Jung has explained,[340] the unconscious process of projection; the projected content is characterized as a "god-man." Insofar as it surpasses the ordinary human personality, it can hardly be attributed to that personality, which explains why Jung called it the self. This content was described, among others, as the king's son sunken in the sea, whose name recalls the Swedish fairytale "First Born, First Married." Thus, this king's son exclaims[341]:

378    Whoever frees me from the waters and transfers me into a dry state, I will make him happy with everlasting (*perpetuis*) riches. Even though this call is heard by many, none will be moved by pity and take it upon themselves to seek the King ... most ... think the voice they hear is the roar and bellow of Scylla and Charybdis ... .

379  Jung offers the following psychological explanation of this passage:

380    When we are told that the King is *exanimis*, inanimate, or that his land is unfruitful, it is equivalent to saying that the hidden state is one of latency and potentiality. The darkness and depths of the sea symbolize the unconscious state of an invisible content that is projected. Inasmuch as such a content belongs to the total personality and is only apparently severed from its context by projection, there is always an attraction between conscious mind and projected content. Generally it takes the form of a fascination. This, in the alchemical allegory, is expressed by the King's cry for help from the depths of his unconscious, dissociated state. The conscious mind should respond to this call: One should *operari regi*, render service to the King, for this would be not only wisdom

---

[340] Jung, *Psychology and Alchemy*, CW 12, § 342–356 and § 405–413.
[341] Cited from "Erlösungsvorstellung in der Alchemie," *Eranos-Jahrbuch 1936: Gestaltung der Erlösungsidee in Ost und West I*, ed. Olga Fröbe-Kapteyn (1937), pp. 62–63, as the quotation in Jung, *Psychology and Alchemy*, CW 12, § 434 is less complete. See Jung, "Paracelsus as a Spiritual Phenomenon," CW 13, § 181.

but salvation as well. Yet this brings with it the necessity of a descent into the dark world of the unconscious ...[342]

381  The Grimm's "The Iron Stove" provides evidence both for the identity of the alchemical *filius macrocosmi*, which derives from Gnostic thinking, and for the prince who must be redeemed:

382  In the days when wishing was still of some use, a King's son was bewitched by an old witch, and shut up in an iron stove in a forest. There he passed many years, and no one could rescue him. Then a King's daughter came into the forest, who has lost herself, and could not find her father's kingdom again. After she had wandered about for nine days, she at length came to the iron stove. Then a voice came forth from it, and asked her: "Whence do you come, and whither are you going?" She answered: "I have lost my father's kingdom, and cannot get home again." Then a voice inside the stove said: "I will help you to get home again, and that indeed most swiftly, if you will promise to do what I desire of you. I am the son of a far greater King than your father, and I will marry you."

383  Then she was afraid, and thought: "Good Heavens! What can I do with an iron stove?" But as she much wished to get home to her father, she promised to do as he desired. But he said: "You shall return here, and bring a knife with you, and scrape a hole in the iron." Then he gave her a companion who walked near her, but did not speak, and in two hours he took her home; there was great joy in the castle when the King's daughter came home, and the old King fell on her neck, and kissed her.

384  ... Out of fear for his daughter, the King resolved that he would send, in her place, the miller's daughter ... then the swine-herd's daughter, who was even prettier ... she, however, was no better at scaping at the iron stove ... The voice inside the iron stove said: "Go away at once, and tell the

---

[342] See Jung, *Psychology and Alchemy*, CW 12, § 436.

King's daughter to come, and tell her all must be done as was promised, and if she does not come, everything in the kingdom shall be ruined and destroyed. So the King's daughter took leave of her father, put a knife in her pocket, and went forth to the iron stove in the forest … When she had scraped a small hole and peeped in, she saw a youth so handsome, and so brilliant with gold and with precious jewels, that her very soul was delighted … He wanted to take her away with him to his kingdom, but she entreated him to let her go once again to her father … he allowed her to do so, but she was not to say more to her father than three words and return.

385  So she went home, but she spoke more than three words, and instantly the iron stove disappeared, and was taken far away over the glass mountains and piercing swords. But the King's son was set free, and no longer shut up in the iron stove … For nine days she sought it, and then her hunger grew so great … When midnight drew near she saw … a small light, and thought: "Ah, there I should be saved!"… There she came to a little old house, and much grass had grown all about it … she peeped in through the window … and saw a table well covered with wine and roast meat, and the plates and glasses were of silver … she knocked … and a small toad … opened the door … she related all that had befallen her … they gave her meat and drink, and took her to a well-made bed … When morning came … she was given three needles … that she would need to cross a high glass mountain, and go over three piercing swords and a great lake … She was also given a plough-wheel and three nuts … She stuck the needles into the mountain, first behind her feet and then before them, and she got over it … after this she came to the three piercing swords, and she seated herself on her plough-wheel, and rolled over them … When she had crossed a great lake, she came to a large and beautiful castle … she went in and asked for a place; she was a poor girl, she

said, and would like to be hired. She knew, however, that the King's son ... was in the castle ... who had another maiden by his side whom he wanted to marry, for he thought that she had long been dead.

386 In the first nut which the old toad had given her ... she found a stately, regal garment ... which she sold to the bride for one night to gain permission to sleep one night in her bridegroom's chamber ... The bride ... gave him a sleeping-draught ... and he slept so soundly that he did not hear the poor girl's tale about setting him free when he was in the iron stove and how she had walked over a glass mountain, three sharp swords, and a great lake to find him.

387 The next day the servants ... told their lord what they had heard ... the next evening, she opened the second nut, and a far more beautiful dress was within it ... and the bride wished to buy that also ...And on the third evening, she opened the third nut, and within it was a still more beautiful dress which was stiff with pure gold. When she also sold this to the bride ... This time, however, the King's son was on his guard, and threw the sleeping-draught away. She began to weep and to cry: "Dearest love, I set you free ..." and the King's son leapt up and said: "You are the true one, you are mine, and I am yours." Thereupon, he got into a carriage with her, and they took away the false bride's clothes so that she could not get up. When they came to the great lake, they sailed across it, and overcame the piercing swords with the plough-wheel, the mountain with the needles and at length they got to the little old house ... it had become a great castle, and the toads were all disenchanted. Then the wedding was celebrated, and the King's son and the princess remained in the castle, which was much larger than the castles of their fathers ... they fetched the old King, who had been grieving at being left alone, and brought him to live with them, and they had two kingdoms, and lived in happy wedlock.[343]

---

[343] Adapted and abridged from *The Complete Grimm's Fairy Tales*, pp. 571–577.

388 In this fairytale, the psychic process is described almost entirely in terms of the curse, which is unusual. According to Bolte and Polívka,[344] Wilhelm Grimm associated the stove with "hell, the underworld, where dark death dwells, but also where the forge stands. He also found the term 'iron stove' obsolete; for him, it did not refer to iron and Old High German *eitofan* but rather to Middle High German *eitoven* (fire furnace, from *eit* = chimney, fire)." But the stove, in which the shining prince is hidden, is easily recognizable as the alchemist's furnace. According to Jung, the hermetic vessel is

389 typified by the retorts or melting-furnaces that contained the substances to be transformed ... For the alchemists the vessel is something truly marvellous: a *vas mirabile* ... It is a kind of matrix or uterus from which the filius philosophorum, the miraculous stone, is to be born.[345]

390 The vessel is not a retort or something similar, but a "mystical idea," a symbol.[346] In light of the previous reflections, the further interpretation of this fairytale seems almost self-evident. The princess has abandoned, and lost, the hitherto conscious realm, although she remains connected to the father-animus to a certain extent, which at first makes her uncertain about her decisions. In the mystical language of an oracle, it is revealed to her that in the deepest unconscious lies concealed a "King's son," whose power is greater than hers and who thus includes the conscious world. He can therefore direct her homeward. The motif of signing recalls pacts with the devil and illumines the prince's demonic, evil side, which also manifests in his threat to destroy the kingdom (e.g., "King Lindworm"), when the old king, who represents ruling consciousness, wants to deceive him. Scraping is a task at which only those succeed whose calling is true. However, the princess's uncertainty

---

[344] Bolte and Polívka, *Anmerkungen*, vol. 3, p. 43.
[345] Jung, *Psychology and Alchemy*, CW 12, § 338.
[346] See *ibid.*, fig. 2, fig. 119, fig. 184; see esp. the reference in § 449 to "The Three Youths in the Fiery Furnace" (Daniel 3); see also Jung, *Symbols of Transformation*, CW 5, § 245f.

leads to the prince's rapture. Here, the fairytale emphasizes, as it does again later during the purchased nights, the redemption from the stove. The rapture constitutes such a psychic loss that the heroine decides to search for the stove and thus takes a first step toward complete redemption: The constricting spell is broken. One variant collected by Bolte and Polívka[347] contains some images that emphasize the prince's significance and the importance of being "connected" with him:

391     A girl found herself (all alone) in the middle of a large forest, and a swan approached her with a ball of yarn and said: "I am not a swan, but a dumb prince; you can redeem me if you unwind the ball of yarn by which I will fly away. Yet beware that you do not break the thread, or I will not reach my kingdom and will not be redeemed. But if you unwind the knot completely, then you will become my bride. The girl took the knot, and the swan rose into the air, and the yarn unwound itself easily. It unwound and unwound all day, and in the evening the end of the thread was already visible, when unfortunately it got caught on a thorny bush and broke off.

392     (Hereafter follows the quest via the sun, the moon and the stars, and the redemption of King Swan by three nights purchased with the gifts of the stars).

393     As a symbol of the spirit, the swan requires no detailed explanation.[348] Here, however, the swan is a consequence of the enchantment. The enchanted one can no longer reach "his kingdom" unless someone "unwinds the thread." Uninterrupted "development" is needed. Redemption and returning to a spiritual kingdom must be guided by consciousness. The fairytale about the iron stove also emphasizes the greatness of the prince's kingdom and that he attains initial liberation by returning to "his kingdom." Yet he is enraptured *alone* or, as in the case of King Swan, the thread breaks. His ruptured

---

[347] Bolte and Polívka, *Anmerkungen*, vol. 3, pp. 37ff.
[348] See *Archetypal Symbolism in Fairytales*, vol. 3, pp. 281–283.

connection with the conscious psyche binds him to a "false bride" (i.e., a negative power). "His kingdom," therefore, is a demonic one, that of the spirit in matter. And even if he is "free" in that realm and active, that is, no longer constrained (i.e., psychologically, free of inhibitions), he still needs the connection or even union with consciousness to become human.

394    In the Grimm's "The Iron Stove," the heroine's path leads into nature, in fact her own nature. The house of toads is surrounded by *green* grass, and from the house resounds the same verse as in "The Three Feathers" about the "little green maiden."[349] From the large box of the motherly being, who counterbalances the enchanting witch, the maiden receives the aids with which she can reach the animus, the self belonging to the soul, and regain it. The aids symbolize antithesis: She scales the steep mountain with the help of needles, which symbolize the application of the intellect to overcome difficulty and hardening; she "rolls over" the piercing, dividing swords assisted by the plough-wheel, which symbolizes connection and wholeness. (No details are given about the crossing of the water.) The false bride seeks to effortlessly and deceitfully appropriate the essence of the anima symbolized by her regal clothing. Her deceptive appearance is punished: Her clothes are removed, and thus she is obliterated. The psychic sphere, banished into the amphibious realm, that is, into distant (old!) unconscious precincts, is now introduced, in all its richness, to the conscious human sphere. In this great castle, the old king, divorced from real life, also finds his place; the pair, united and forming a spiritual-psychic totality, and psychologically representing the self that is connected to the anima, rules over the kingdom and extends its rule across the profane and the magical realm.

395    Insofar as the king's daughter reached the house of toads first, it lies closer to the profane realm than the distant castle situated behind the glass mountain and the swords. It corresponds roughly to the very large and redeemed castle in "The Great Fool from Cuasan" (Ireland, no. 23). Clearly designated as an inert sphere close

---

[349] *The Complete Grimm's Fairy Tales*, pp. 319–322; esp. p. 320.

to the soil, psychologically the house of toads corresponds to that part of the soul that belongs to physical nature. Redeemed, it assumes all of nature's traits, including its animatedness, in that the king's liberated children point even more specifically to blossoming. Thus, in this fairytale, a disenchanted magical realm results from redemption or from becoming conscious of the natural aspects of the soul. Also in this sense, the present fairytale is suffused with alchemical thinking: After all, the alchemist endeavors to redeem nature.[350]

396    The animal prince is a real parallel to the *alchemical filius macrocosmi or filius philosophorum*. He represents the same psychic content by being intimately related to both the dark chthonic world and evil. This is the case because the self includes darkness, contains its own negation, and casts a shadow because it is not only "spiritual" but also bound to matter. This connection to matter—in fairytales, this is the desiring and cursing mother-figure—explains why the figure of the spirit sunken into matter, which thus symbolizes the wholeness of matter and spirit, is hermaphroditic.[351] Still, fairytales do not include the hermaphrodite, which is an essential image of alchemical speculation, despite sibling incest, as depicted in "Clever Finna," being a variation of this idea.

397    Ultimately, therefore, fairytales seem to express a dualistic worldview. They presuppose a dark, evil, or suffering side of the world, in which dwells a demonic, dominating power. Moreover, they sometimes assign masculine, sometimes feminine portents to that power, according to the archetypal opposition of *yin* and *yang*, spirit and matter, bright daylight (i.e., the world of the sun) and the dark, nocturnal world of the moon. In fairytales, the animal prince's suffering is contingent on this tension between opposites. Insofar as he corresponds to the archetypal, primordial human, the animal prince also represents the suffering of humankind, which is conditioned by the demon's suffering.[352] Such fairytales contain

---

[350] Jung, *Psychology and Alchemy*, CW 12, § 26f.
[351] On Ātman and puruṣa, see, e.g., Güntert, *Weltkönig*, pp. 322ff. and 344. Other hermaphrodites include Gayomard (Iranian) and Yima (Avestian); see *ibid.*, p. 345ff. On similar thinking in the Zohar, see Bischoff, *Elemente der Kabbalah* (1913), p. 109.
[352] See the last section in this volume.

spontaneously produced, generally uninfluenced statements about this primordial image of the spark in matter. Thus, they have an essential mythological function.

◊

# B.
# The Redemption of the Enchanted Princess

398 The fact that fairytales recount the same events, sometimes about a male figure, others about a female one, enables us to deduce their secret identity, even if this is not mentioned at all. Thus, alongside the numerous fairytales about an enchanted prince, just as many deal with a female figure who suffers the same fate, is enchanted into a spirit being or animal, and redeemed by a lover. The man thus participates in this mystical hermaphroditic archetype through the feminine component of his soul, the woman through the masculine component of hers.

399 Some minor differences aside, one fairytale whose plot follows the same structure as "The Singing, Soaring Lark"[353] and its variants, yet deals with an enchanted female figure, is "The Most Beautiful Bride":

400 A farmer with three sons wanted to bequeath his farm to that son who brought home the most beautiful and richest bride. Gottschalk, the youngest and dullest son, came out from behind the stove and ventured into the world, mocked by his brothers. When he came to a forest, he shared his food with a little gray man, who turned him into a handsome young man and showed him his way. This led Gottschalk to a beautiful garden, where he fell in love with a beautiful girl. Her mother, a powerful fairy, consented to the wedding. "All acquaintances were invited, and even Death, male and female, was present."

---

[353] *The Complete Grimm's Fairy Tales*, pp. 399–403.

Gottschalk realized that every eight days his wife would lock herself in a dark room. When he kept pestering her to tell him what she was doing there, she replied that her happiness would cease if he found out. He did not remain calm for long, but on one occasion sneaked after her and peered through the keyhole. Low and behold! His wife was covered with hair from waist to toe and had scrawny goat feet instead of legs. He shuddered, realizing that this ogre was his wife. But he soon consoled himself and thought: It won't take long and she will be as beautiful as before. This time, however, Gottschalk had miscalculated. The hour when his wife usually came out of the chamber had long passed. He went to listen at the door and heard a sobbing and wailing that could have softened a stone. When he opened the door, she exclaimed: "Look what you have done. I must now remain in this form, and our happiness is over for good; and all this only because you have seen me in this form. Now you must leave, and only through true love and loyalty can you make up for what you have done to me." When he wanted to embrace her once more, the castle and garden had disappeared, and before the helplessly wailing Gottschalk suddenly stood the little gray man, who reproached him, but promised to help. Gottschalk had to find his wife's castle again, but he could not show him the way, so he should ask the sun. After wandering for a year without food or drink and now very desperate, Gottschalk finally reached the sun, who was sitting in a glass house, dressed in dark shoes and weaving golden threads. However, she did not know where the castle with the golden roof was and directed Gottschalk to her cousin, the moon. After much hardship, he arrived at the glass house, where the moon was sitting in the form of an old man with silver-white hair and a beard. But he, too, knew nothing about the castle and directed the boy to the wind. "At last he came to a mountain that had four large holes, one above, one below, one to the right, and one to the left; and inside was the wind, which blew sometimes out of this hole, sometimes out of that." The wind itself had no advice; only one of its assistants, a hunchback, had any knowledge. He took Gottschalk on his back, carried him for two days between heaven and earth, and set him down on the third day. "Gottschalk wanted to thank his bearer, because he realized that he had reached the right place; but when he went to look for him, instead of the wind's assistant, he saw his wife standing before him with tearful eyes." Her goat's feet had disappeared, and they rode happily to his father in a golden chariot drawn by six white horses. Although he had brought the most beautiful bride, he renounced the farm in favor of his brothers and returned home with his wife and father to the castle with the golden roof.[354]

402   This fairytale requires merely brief interpretation, as we have already encountered its individual phases in other contexts. Its charming images speak for themselves. As in other fairytales, the youngest and fourth member of the initial group is again summoned to be the hero because he represents the living function of the whole personality, which is closest to the unconscious; just as this fourth figure was assisted by the fox in "The Golden Bird,"[355] so is the little gray man in this tale: Like the fox, he represents the shadow, the self still hidden in its unassuming aspect. It represents a helpful, quiet voice of the unconscious, which guides the shortsighted and helpless ego according to transpersonal laws. Whereas the fourth one remained inconspicuous in the hitherto mundane life of consciousness, he is a beautiful hero in the unconscious, transfigured by the little man's magic, that is, by the radiance of the self.

403   As in several versions of "The Singing, Soaring Lark," the animal prince originates in the magical realm, as does the hero's bride in this variant; the fairy clan, which also includes the chthonic-primordial parents, emphasizes this world's otherworldly and

---

[354] See Zaunert, *Deutsche Märchen seit Grimm*, p. 343.—Trans.
[355] *The Complete Grimm's Fairy Tales*, pp. 272–280.

uncanny nature. We have already touched on the anima's relationship with the realm of the dead and spirits in our discussion of the magical marriage.[356] Yet she is connected not only to the realm of the dead but also to the underworld in its—in Christian terms—devilish—in pagan ones—Dionysian aspect. In the Christian imagination, the goat is one of the devil's animals[357]; in pagan prehistory, it represents both a god of earth fertility, vegetation, and the instinctual force awakening in spring; in Greek antiquity, it is sacred to Pan.[358] (The animal prince is also closely related to the realm of Priapus,[359] in that he appeared as an ass or as a pig, or was accompanied by these animals). The chthonic aspect is banished into the forbidden chamber, just as illumining the animal prince was prohibited, for the gaze of differentiating consciousness reveals the double aspect of the soul-image. However, a psychic factor separated from the psychic sphere lying closer to consciousness is profoundly fascinating. As confronting matters as they are is necessary for development, the forbidden chamber might be said to exist in order to be forced open. Just like the "premature illumination" of the animal prince, so the intervention of consciousness initially leads to disaster. Once more, the anima's relationship to the magical world is called into question by the fact that consciousness expresses fear and aversion, a reaction that is mirrored by the unconscious.

404    There is, however, *one* striking difference to the fairytale about "Cupid and Psyche": There the *human* side of the animal prince was not permitted to be illumined prematurely, whereas here it is the *animal* side. Like all opposites, however, these are also very closely

---

[356] See *Archetypal Symbolism in Fairytales*, vol. 1, pp. 392–394; see also "Help When in Need" (China, no. 54).

[357] On the goat as a devil or bewitched animal, see August Wünsche, *Der Sagenkreis vom geprellten Teufel* (Leipzig and Vienna: Akademischer Verlag, 1905); see Bächtold-Stäubli under *Ziegenbock* (billy goat, he-goat); on the above motif, see *ibid.*, esp. under *Ziegenfüsse, Bocksfüsse* (goat's feet): "Goat's feet play an important role in superstition and legend. In particular the devil, upon whom most characteristics of the highly esteemed god of thunder were bestowed, appears with the feet of the sacrificial animal once sacred to Donar. According to Swiss belief, the goat is created by the devil: Its feet are considered devilish and are not eaten, because evil persons have goat's feet or their goat's feet appear when they take off their boots; such persons also bear the name 'Master Goat's Feet' ... The goat's foot is the devil's seal."—Trans.

[358] On the goat as a vegetation demon, see Bächtold-Stäubli under *Ziegenbock* (goat) and Mannhardt, *Wald- und Feldkulte*, vol. 2 (1877), ch. 3. On the goat-footed anima-figure, see *ibid.*, vol. 1, p. 95, fn. 1; vol. 2, p. 79.

[359] Translator's note: In Greek mythology, Priapus was a minor fertility god.

related: for what is ultimately unbearable for human consciousness is the paradoxical double aspect of the unconscious, which manifests as animus and anima. As it strives for unequivocalness, consciousness struggles to accept that the animal and the demon are illumined at the same time. Moreover, both aspects are "numinous" and therefore frightening. The extent to which this holds true is evident in Josef Haltrich's description of a demonic anima-figure[360]:

405   She wears twelve masks, one uglier than the other; the twelfth bears the face of death; most of the suitors drop dead when she removes the third or fourth mask. The last one, however, does not, not even when she removes the twelfth mask. To him, she reveals all her beauty.[361]

406   As in "The Singing, Soaring Lark," in the present fairytale the abandoned partner wanders across the sun, the moon, and the wind in pursuit of the vanished soul-image. Here, the sun is described in more detail, while in other fairytales (e.g., "The Earth Wants to Have Its Share"; Caucasus, no. 6) the image of the woman in the glass house is an image of the anima, who is often a sun maiden (e.g., "The Son of Kimanaueze and the Daughter of Sun and Moon"; Africa, no. 34; see also "The Maiden Tsar"; Russia, no. 41).[362] The dark shoes of the sun's mother, who is dressed in red, indicate her nocturnal counteraspect.

407   In the variant of "The Iron Stove" mentioned by Bolte and Polívka,[363] the dark aspect of the sun, the moon, and the star is expressed by the fact that the husband of the old woman (Mrs Sun, Mrs Moon, Mrs Star) is a man-eater, from whose grasp the old woman only succeeds in protecting the girl with utmost difficulty.

---

[360] For fairytales about a maiden whose gaze was fatal, see Josef Haltrich, *Deutsche Volksmärchen aus dem Sachsenlande in Siebenbürgen* (Vienna: Verlag von Carl Graeser, 1882), preface to the 2nd edition, annex, p. VII.
[361] On the animal-figure deterring the redeemer, see Laistner, *Das Rätsel* (Berlin, 1889), vol. 1, p. 83f. and 88f. The unsuccessful attempt at redemption does not correspond to the recklessly destroyed "magical marriage," but rather to an intolerable intrusion of the unconscious into consciousness. Such narratives are "legends" rather than "fairytales."
[362] Carl Meinhof, ed., *Afrikanische Märchen* (MdW), ed. v. d. Leyen and Zaunert (1921), and Afanas'ev (ed.), *Russian Fairy Tales*, pp. 229–234.
[363] Bolte and Polívka, *Anmerkungen*, vol. 3, p. 37ff.

While this sun-figure may be said to extend the sought-after anima-image, we can see the moon, the green-clad wind demon, and in particular the hunchbacked wind-spirit carrying the girl as variants of the little gray man appearing at the beginning of such tales. These figures also amplify his deeper meaning as *lumen naturae* and as an inspiring pneuma and spirit transporting her toward her goal (see also the nocturnal wind in "The Singing, Soaring Lark.)

408      We have already interpreted the little gray man by equating him with the fox in "The Golden Bird." The fox prince turned out to be the anima's brother. Such a magical helper is thus so closely related and connected to her that he can be regarded as the masculine component of the anima-figure, as a spirit working inside her. The opposite sexual component, which thus also inheres in the soul-image, is reflected in fairytales in very different and reasonably clear images and motifs, as we will see in the course of this study.

409      A male ghostly figure belonging to the anima, which, as it were, is part of her, appears, for instance, in "Tapairu, the Beautiful Maiden from the Land of Fairies" (Polynesia, no. 21)[364] and in "Ititaujang, Who Married the Wild Goose" (North America, no. 7). As the masculine complement of her feminine essence in the unconscious, this is replaced by the hero advancing from consciousness into the unconscious and winning over the anima. To achieve this goal of the unconscious, this embodiment of the anima's unconscious masculine component serves in a number of fairytales as the hero's helper and as a psychopomp[365] (in the above examples from the South Seas and North America, however, he is depicted as more passive and negative, as is often the case elsewhere). As soon as the hero becomes the anima's masculine complement, the helper can disappear. Until then, however, the two figures of the unconscious—the anima and her male companion—form a unity, so to speak, and therefore are interchangeable. This conception of

[364] Hedwig Danzel and Theodor-Wilhelm Danzel, eds., *Sagen und Legenden der Südsee-Insulaner* [Polynesia] (Hagen i. W. and Darmstadt: Folkwang-Verlag, 1923).
[365] Characters like Lasse in "Lasse, My Servant!" (Sweden, no. 2) might thus also be understood as masculine components of the anima, even if this tale provides no tangible evidence for this idea. Psychologically, however, the man's "shadow" and the anima's "animus" are identical.

the helper is confirmed by a scene in "The Most Beautiful Bride,"[366] where the hero turns around to thank the hunchback, in whose place he unexpectedly finds the sought-after wife.

410   On the whole, the sun, the moon, and the wind belong to the anima, as in "The Singing, Soaring Lark," where she appears as the heroine. They reveal her cosmic aspect, either as a divine spirit immersed in matter or as the *anima mundi*.[367] As the hero was unable to accept the anima as an animal, it is crucial that he experiences her sublime background. Having at the same time demonstrated his courage and loyalty through his wandering, he has evidently become mature enough to grasp the soul-image in its entirety. The golden chariot that takes the couple on its short visits to profane regions yet also to the most distant magical ones corresponds to the griffin in "The Singing, Soaring Lark." However, the glittering vehicle and the concluding episode in the gold-roofed castle indicate that the mystery of the unconscious was only perceived during an ecstatic experience (the father is taken away without further ado, and consciousness disappears, without mention of any further confrontation, into the unconscious). Like many other fairytales, this one also contents itself with this account.

411   The central problem of this tale concerns the assimilation of the anima's animal, nonhuman side. In many primitive fairytales about the magical marriage, the anima also appears as an animal, yet without this form being the result of a curse. It was not until a European fairytale, "The Mermaid or the Great Dubhdach" (Ireland, no. 29), that, as is the case here, the animal form is seen as a curse. The primitives did not feel separated from the animal side of their psyche and therefore had no difficulty in accepting that humans could appear as animals, and animals as humans.[368] After all, the fact that the profane figure suggested that the magical spouse was affiliated with the animal kingdom was considered a slight that was difficult or impossible to make amends for. Thus, despite all the

---

[366] Zaunert, *Deutsche Märchen seit Grimm*, p. 343.
[367] See also the three dresses worn by the heroine in "Allerleirauh": "One as golden as the sun, one as silvery as the moon, and one as bright as the stars" (*The Complete Grimm's Fairy Tales*, pp. 326–331; esp. p. 327).
[368] See the numerous examples in Lévy-Bruhl, (*The "Soul" of the Primitive,* trans. Lilian A. Care 1928).

original psychic unity, a certain distinction between animal beings and human beings is evident. However, it is only when conscious differentiation occurs that human beings feel fundamentally different from animals and, unlike them, clash with themselves. The existence of such an animal soul, which is not adapted to the human world, is considered a curse, and thus raises the problem of redeeming this figure. Psychologically, however, this concerns redeeming not only the animal-figure but also the human being, who is "animalized" (i.e., wholly unconscious): because the animal prince symbolizes not only the woman's animallike, masculine-spiritual soul-image but also the man governed by the unconscious; likewise, the female animal demon represents both the man's feminine soul-image and the woman condemned to unconsciousness.

412   Like the animal prince, sometimes the animal maiden is also said to be cursed by an evil mother. A simple example is the Icelandic tale "Märdöll" (no. 7): Similar to "Sleeping Beauty," a girl who was conceived late and magically is cursed by a neglected godmother (i.e., three tall women who call themselves "blackcoats") to become a sparrow on the bridal night; the maiden is only permitted to remove the sparrow's plumage for an hour on each of the following three nights. (The other two fairies had previously conferred beauty on the girl, as well as the ability to shed golden tears). To escape the spell, Märdöll, the cursed heroine, urges Helga, her milk-sister, to take her place on the bridal night. As Helga is unable to cry gold, the deceit is discovered: Realizing what has happened, the king's son burns his real bride's plumage and thus redeems her.

413   In a similar Icelandic tale, "The Rolling Bull's Stomach" (no. 6), the heroine is bewitched by a demonic stepmother, not into an animal but into a rolling bull's stomach. When the heroine casts a counterspell, the stepmother softens her own curse so that the daughter can be redeemed by marrying a king's son, who accepts her as she is. Through spells and threats, the stomach forces a king to take it to his bridal bed. There the bewitched woman removes her terrible attire and becomes a woman. The king's mother, however, quickly has the stomach burned, thus redeeming the heroine forever.

In particular, the image of the rolling bull's stomach is peculiar[369]: On the one hand, the theme of roundness is again emphasized; on the other, the epitome of the devouring, all-absorbing organic being is depicted. From this we can derive the psychologically correct formula that those who are devoured by the unconscious themselves become devourers. (In fact, some people's tormenting, vampirish effect stems from their addiction to the unconscious and subsequent inability to behave otherwise).

414    As in "Hans the Hedgehog," in these two Icelandic fairytales burning the animal's skin is once again depicted as a redemptive act,[370] whereas in other versions it represents a catastrophe on par with the motif of premature illumination.[371] These fairytales reflect different psychological possibilities. Consciously intervening in a person's psyche that, in the language of fairytales, is cursed or, psychologically speaking, governed by a complex, may have incalculable consequences. Unleashing the tremendous emotional energies adhering to this complex may induce a healing crisis (where burning the animal skin brings redemption). Yet it may also lead to disaster and madness (i.e., the destruction of the whole personality). Here, this process corresponds to the tragic, unredeemable killing of the animal demon by burning its skin. A third possibility is that the shock of conscious intervention seems to worsen the psychological situation, which, however, initiates a lengthy process of conscious realization. In this case, the apparent catastrophe destroys the old personality (i.e., a new personality begins to be formed) and thus can become a healing crisis. Fairytales do not tell us why this sometimes happens in one way and sometimes in another. Obviously, we are dealing with what eludes human knowledge, so that these matters even defy symbolic reasoning. It is therefore never possible to derive generally valid "rules of life" from fairytales, even though they contain so much wisdom. At best, we can only ever discover the paradoxical meaning of one fairytale at a

---

[369] In contrast, the motif of the bird, as representing "evanescence" or "volatileness" (as in "Märdöll"; Iceland, no. 7), is more common (see Yonec, i.e., the motif of a lover who visits his beloved as a bird).
[370] The same motif occurs in "The Hermit and His Dog" (South America, no. 15).
[371] Bolte and Polívka, *Anmerkungen*, vol. 2, pp. 239, 245ff., 257, 258, 261.

time. Any specific conceptual formulation, however, not only contradicts the archetypal indeterminacy of fairytales but also proves to be downright misguided.

415   One fairytale that places the burning of the animal skin in a richer and more subtle context, and which follows the basic pattern of many similar tales, is "The Frog Princess" (Russia, no. 5):

416   LONG AGO, in ancient times, a King had three adult sons. The King said: "My children, let each of you make a bow for himself and shoot an arrow. She who brings back your arrow will be your bride; he whose arrow is not returned will not marry." The eldest son shot his arrow, and a prince's daughter brought it back to him. The middle son shot his arrow, and a general's daughter brought it back to him. But little Prince Ivan's arrow was brought back from the marsh by a frog who held it between her teeth. His brothers were joyous and happy, but Prince Ivan became thoughtful and wept: "How will I live with a frog? After all, this is a life's task, not like wading across a river or walking across a field!" He wept and wept, but there was no way out of his predicament, and so he took the frog as his wife. All three sons and their brides were wed in accordance with the customs of their country.

417   One day the King asked all three brides to make him a gift, so that he could see which of them was the most skillful. Prince Ivan again grew thoughtful and wept: "What can my frog make? Everyone will laugh at me!" The frog only hopped about on the floor and croaked. When Prince Ivan fell asleep, she went out into the street, cast off her skin, turned into a lovely maiden, and cried: "Nurses, nurses! Make something!" The nurses at once brought a finely woven shirt. She took it, folded it, and placed it beside Prince Ivan, and again turned herself into a frog, as though she had never been anything else! Prince Ivan awoke, was overjoyed at the sight of the shirt, and brought it to the King. The King examined it and said: "Well, this is indeed a shirt to wear on holidays!" Then

the second brother brought a shirt. The King said: "This one is good only to wear in the bathhouse!" And about the eldest brother's shirt he said: "This one is fit to be worn solely in a peasant's hut!" The King's sons left, and the two elder ones decided: "We were wrong to make fun of Prince Ivan's wife; she is not a frog, but a cunning witch!"

418 The King issued another command to his daughters-in-law: This time they should bake bread, and show it to him, so that he might see which of them baked the best bread. Before the first contest, the brides of the two elder sons had made fun of the frog; but now they sent a chambermaid to spy on her and see how she would bake her loaf. The frog was aware of this, so she mixed her dough, rolled it, hollowed out the oven from above, and poured her dough right there. The chambermaid saw this and ran to tell her mistresses, who did the same. But the cunning frog had deceived them; the moment the chambermaid left, she dug the dough out of the oven, cleaned and plastered up everything as if nothing had happened, then went out onto the porch, took off her frog's skin, and cried: "Nurses, nurses! Bake me such a loaf of bread that my dear father will eat only on Sundays and holidays!" The nurses brought the bread at once. She took it, placed it beside sleeping Prince Ivan, and turned into a frog again. Prince Ivan awoke, found the bread, and took it to his father. The King was examining the loaves brought by his elder sons. Their wives had dropped the dough into the oven just as the frog had, and had pulled out nothing but formless lumps. The King first took the eldest son's loaf, looked at it, and sent it back to the kitchen; thereafter, he took the second son's loaf and sent it back too. Then, Prince Ivan's presented his loaf. The father examined it and said: "Now this bread is good enough for a holiday! It is not slack, like that baked by my elder daughters-in-law!"

419 Next, the King decided to hold a ball to see which of his daughters-in-law danced best … The time for dancing came;

the tsar summoned his elder daughters-in-law, but they deferred to the frog. She straightaway took Prince Ivan's arm … and danced and danced away … a marvel to behold! … Thereupon, the other daughters-in-law came forward to dance. They wanted to do as the frog had done: … the King was displeased and cried: "Enough, enough!" The daughters-in-law stopped dancing.

420    The ball was over. Prince Ivan went home first, found his wife's skin, took it, and burned it. She arrived, looked for the skin, but it was gone, burned. She lay down to sleep with Prince Ivan, but before daybreak she said to him: "If you had waited a little, I would have been yours; now only God knows when we will be together again. Farewell! Seek me beyond the thrice ninth land, in the thrice tenth kingdom!" Then she vanished.

421    A year passed, and Prince Ivan longed for his wife. In the second year, he made ready for his journey, obtained his father's and mother's blessing, and left. He walked a very long time and, all of a sudden, he saw a little hut standing with its front to the woods and its back to him. He said: "Little hut, little hut, stand the old way, as thy mother stood thee, with thy back to the woods and thy front to me!" The hut turned around. He entered. An old woman was sitting there, who said: "Fie, fie! Of a Russian bone not a sound was heard, not a glimpse was caught, and now a Russian bone has come to my house of its own free will. Whither goest thou, Prince Ivan?" "First of all, old woman, give me to eat and to drink, and then ask me your questions." The old woman gave him to eat and to drink and put him to bed. Prince Ivan said to her: "Little grandmother, I have set out to find Elena the Fair One." "Oh, my child, how long you have been away! At the beginning, she often remembered thee, but now she no longer remembers thee, and has not come to see me for a long time. Go now to my middle sister, she knows more than I do."

422 In the morning, Prince Ivan set out, came to a hut, and said: "Little hut, little hut, stand the old way, as thy mother stood thee, with thy back to the woods and thy front to me." The hut turned around. He entered, and saw an old woman sitting there, who said: "Fie, fie! Of a Russian bone not a sound was heard, not a glimpse was caught, and now a Russian bone has come to my house of its own free will. Whither goest thou, Prince Ivan?" "To find Elena the Fair One, little grandmother." "Oh, Prince Ivan," said the old woman, "thou hast been long a-coming! She has begun to forget thee, and is marrying someone else; the wedding will soon be held! She is living with my eldest sister. Go there, but be careful. When thou approachest their house, they will sense it; Elena will turn into a spindle, and her dress will turn into a golden thread. My sister will wind the golden thread; when she has wound it around the spindle, and put it into a box and locked the box, thou must find the key, open the box, break the spindle, throw its top behind thee, and its bottom in front of thee. Then she will appear before thee."

423 Prince Ivan went, came to the third old woman's house, and entered. The old woman was winding the golden thread; she wound it around the spindle and put it in a box, locked the box, and put the key somewhere. He took the key, opened the box, took out the spindle, broke it just as he had been told, cast the top behind himself and the bottom in front of himself. All of a sudden, Elena the Fair One stood before him and greeted him: "Oh, you have been a long time coming, Prince Ivan! I almost married someone else." And she told him that the other bridegroom was expected soon. Elena the Fair One took a magic carpet from the old woman, sat on it with Prince Ivan, and they took off and flew like birds. The other bridegroom arrived and learned that they had left. Yet he, too, was cunning! He began to pursue them, and chased and chased them, and came within ten yards of overtaking them: But on their carpet they flew into Russia, and for some

reason he could not enter Russia, and so he turned back. The happy bride and groom reached home; everyone rejoiced, and soon Ivan and Elena began to live and prosper, for the glory of all the people.

424    The opening episode, and partly also what follows, is identical with the course of events in "The Three Feathers."[372] Its interpretation is therefore clear: Both tales concern the assimilation of the fourth, "despised" function, which is connected to the anima and the unconscious, and therefore conditions the process of development. This symbolism is further underlined by the silver bow and the copper arrows: Alchemically, silver is assigned to the moon, and copper to Venus, implying the erotic nature of the adventure.[373] The more developed functions "aim" for worldly heights, yet the fourth one strives for the human lowlands (ordinary cottages) and even for the realm of lower animal life, the swamp,[374] from which a frog responds. In a parallel Spanish version, "The Princess as a Monkey" (no. 48), the anima-figure is, as the title indicates, a monkey, which further emphasizes, albeit on a higher level, the anima's half-human nature. Whereas in "The Frog-King, or Iron Henry" and other examples[375] this animal soul demands loving acceptance from human beings and then reveals itself in its higher form, in the present fairytale the frog also demands to be married yet continues to conceal its secret.

425    Her splendid bridal gifts correspond roughly to the carpet that the youngest daughter receives from the toad in "The Three Feathers." The gifts symbolize renewal and new life, which arises from the deepest, natural layers of the soul and from a hitherto

---

[372] *The Complete Grimm's Fairy Tales*, pp. 319–322.

[373] Silberer, *Probleme der Mystik*, pp. 77, 79, 102f.

[374] This diverges from the more common type of fairytale: Here the main character, represented by the father, does not object to but approves of the magical marriage (as in "King Thrushbeard" and "The Frog-King, or Iron Henry"). Accordingly, the hesitation and "profane" shuddering is transferred onto the inferior function. Obviously, people are always somewhat shy toward the unconscious, and unless consciousness objects (which otherwise is "normal"), they reveal themselves to its inferior function.

[375] For the variant on "The Three Feathers" reported in Bolte and Polívka, *Anmerkungen*, vol. 2, p. 30f., see *Archetypal Symbolism in Fairytales*, vol. 1, p. 414.

undiscovered reality.[376] Finally, the anima appears for the first time in her human manifestation: Transformed into rain, lightning, and thunder, she arrives in a carriage drawn by six horses. In many fairytales, transformation is often accompanied by thunderstorms.[377] Loud crashing has a similar meaning.[378] In the Chinese imagination, thunder (*dschen*) is associated with excitement and enthusiasm, with the power that bursts forth from the earth in spring.[379] In some religions, lightning and thunder accompany the epiphany of the highest deity.[380] They belong to the archetype of the demonic father, who embodies a dynamic principle. Therefore, lightning and thunder symbolize creative power, intuitive knowledge, action, and emotion.

426 Related to this fairytale, the appearance of rain, lightning, and thunder indicates that the transformation of the anima is a psychic process that involves tremendous tensions through which creative energies are released to the utmost degree, as is also symbolized by the six horses drawing the carriage.[381] This new creative power is

---

[376] On the meaning of hand towels, see our interpretation of fabric in *Archetypal Symbolism in Fairytales*, vol. 2, p. 16 and 21f.; on the meaning of the cake, see our interpretation of bread in *ibid.*, vol. 3, pp. 187ff.

[377] Thus, in "The Scarlet Flower" (Loepfe, *Russische*, p. 86), when the heroine finds the dead beast, we are told: "... she fell to her knees and with her white arms embraced the head of her good lord, the ugly, hideous skull, and with a heartrending voice she implored him: 'Arise, awaken, my dear friend, for I love you as my chosen bridegroom! Yet no sooner had she uttered these words than lightning flashed everywhere, the earth shook violently from the crashing thunder, and a beam of lightning struck the colorful hill. The beautiful merchant's daughter fainted. How long she lay there unconscious, I do not know. But when she regained consciousness, she found herself in a magnificent marble hall; she was sitting on a golden, gem-studded throne, and a handsome young prince was holding her in his arms, wearing a royal crown on his head and wrapped in a golden mantle."—Trans. See also "The Female Giant in the Stone Boat" (Iceland, no. 24).

[378] On lightning and thunder accompanying the appearance of the spirit world, see "Help in Need" (China, no. 54).

[379] Richard Wilhelm, ed. *The I Ching: The Book of Changes*, trans. Richard Wilhelm (London: Penquin, 2003; originally published 1950), no. 16; see also Wilhelm, *The Secret of the Golden Flower* (1931/2022).

[380] See Psalm 97, 1–7. On the phenomena accompanying Ezekiel's vision, see 1, 4, and 5. See also the highest deity of the Gunaikurnai [an Aboriginal Australian people—trans.], which reveals itself amid the thundering sound of bullroarers [an ancient ritual instrument and device used for communicating over great distances—trans.]. See further Josef Winthuis, *Das Zweigeschlechterwesen bei den Zentralaustraliern und anderen Völkern. Lösungsversuch der ethnologischen Hauptprobleme auf Grund primitiven Denkens, vol. 5, Forschungen zur Völkerpsychologie und Soziologie* (Leipzig: Hirschfeld, 1928), pp. 98ff. On "Bajamee" (Central Australia), see v. d. Leeuw, *Phänomenologie der Religion* (1933), p. 146f. Other examples include Zeus, the Greek god of thunder and lightning, Jupiter Tonans ("the thundering Jove"), and the Germanic Donar.

[381] On this motif, see the concluding episode in "The Frog-King, or Iron-Henry"; on the relation between lightning and horses, see Jung, *Symbols of Transformation*, CW 5, § 421: "Loki propagates in the form of a horse, and so does the devil, as an ancient god of fire. Lightning, too, is represented theriomorphically as a horse."

revealed later in a magical festival, when the tomcat sings and recounts fairytales in the miracle garden.

427  The frog princess performs her magic through morsels of food that she has saved and later shakes out of her sleeve. This enables her to transform physical nourishment into fantasy figures; she creates a realm of childlike fantasies,[382] the adult's lost paradise, a psychic sphere from which all creative force emerges. This inspiring vitality nurtures spiritual life. The anima is the mysterious psychic being that produces this very immaterial nourishment (which, however, stems from physical nourishment). In her, physical life is transformed into spiritual life. Archetypally, the garden featuring a column or pillar is identical to the Garden of Paradise, at whose center stands the tree of life.[383] In India and the Near East, the *Magna Mater* (Great Mother) is equated with the great cosmic column, which bears the firmament and signifies the axis of the universe.[384] Thus, the anima—who appears first as an animal, and subsequently as a human being—also reveals her superhuman aspect. In parallel versions, the image of the garden with the column varies with that of water and swans,[385] and recalls Oriental descriptions of the *hortus conclusus* (walled garden).

428  As explained in Volume 2 of *Archetypal Symbols in Fairytales*, the swan often represents the anima (the motif of the swan maiden) or the world-spirit (like the *hamsa* in India). Thus, this image of the frog princess also depicts her higher spiritual aspect, her otherworldly being as a world-ensouling principle. Insofar as the swan also has a masculine meaning and, as a bird, represents a spiritual principle (as observed, the eagles embroidered on the cloth indicate the anima's relationship with the masculine-spiritual principle), it personifies not only the anima but also the anima's

---

[382] This motif, which recurs in Russian fairytales, amounts to a self-contained description of Paradise.
[383] On the *Irmensäule* (great pillar), see Mannhardt, *Wald- und Feldkulte*, vol. 1, chapter 3, § 10 (pp. 303ff.); see esp. Bächtold-Stäubli under *Pfahl* (stake, post).
[384] Przyluski, "Ursprünge," pp. 27–31, esp. p. 27, fn. 2 and p. 28, fn. 3; see further *ibid.*, "Mutter-Göttin," p. 44: "The all-being of the Goddess is symbolized by the gnomon or the cosmic tree, which in both cases means that the Great Mother is brought into relation with the axis of the universe. She appears as the pillar that supports the firmament, or as the vast entablature that connects the three worlds, heaven, air and earth."—Trans.
[385] See "The Frog Princess" (Afanas'ev, *Russian Fairy Tales*, pp. 119–123).

animus, and thus signifies the spirit at work in the anima (see above, p. 168 f.). The tomcat is considered a dark, demonic being.[386] He sometimes appears as a demonic anima-figure of the female protagonist, for instance, in "The Girl Soldier" (Russia, no. 31). Even then, however, he appears partly in a positive sense. In "Puss in Boots" (France, vol. 1, no. 26), he even defeats an ogre, just as in Egypt Atum, in the guise of a tomcat, fights Apophis, the sun-devouring serpent.[387]

429     According to one psychological law, however, adversaries resemble each other. Thus, we may attribute the dark-chthonic features of his enemies partly to the tomcat himself. In the present fairytale, the tomcat is part of the woman's soul-image; strikingly, he scales the column singing songs and telling fairytales, since folk songs and fairytales are produced mostly by unconscious fantasizing, which is particularly characteristic of women. Thus, this fairytale tells us something about the essence of fairytales: The anima and the dark spirit governing her, or the woman's animus, are the source of that creative imaginative activity that manifests in fairytales. This activity is described here as paradisiacal happiness.

430     This anima's creative force also expresses itself in her enticing song (the classic example is the beguiling song of the Sirens in Greek myth, yet this aspect is also mentioned frequently in fairytales). In "The Frog Maiden" (Spain, no. 68), whose content corresponds to the first half of the present tale, three brothers come across a female frog that is singing atop a high poplar. Enthralled, they promise her marriage. Yet when she skips down, they are horrified, and only the youngest brother keeps his promise. We would, of course, expect a bird rather than a frog to be singing so splendidly in a treetop. In this fairytale, the anima resembles a bird despite her froggish appearance. Quite appropriately, she thus represents a strange mixture of high and low, spirit and instinct, fascination and repulsion. We have already encountered the motif of the anima

---

[386] Bächtold-Stäubli under *Katze* (cat).
[387] Jung, *Symbols of Transformation*, CW 5, § 425.

perched in a treetop in "The Princess in the Tree."[388] Discussing this fairytale, Jung[389] explicitly mentions that the soul is bewitched at such heights. This motif is also expressed by the title of a Norwegian fairytale, "The Golden Castle That Hung in the Air" (no. 35), where the anima-figure finds herself in an air-castle. This suspension emphasizes her superhuman and unreal side, whose chthonic opposite is represented by a dragon.

431     In "Three Sisters, Of Which the Youngest Becomes a Tsarina" (Balkans, no. 17), the hero first finds the anima sitting on a poplar.[390] While the anima's "high" or spiritual side seems acceptable to consciousness, it is unable to accept the closely related chthonic side because it misjudges the figure's double aspect: Also in our principal fairytale, the hero must take unfortunate action against the frog aspect, although both parts are inseparably connected. It is significant that in "The Frog Maiden" (see above), the anima brings her magnificent gift, a golden cloak, from the sea, from where she is only able to retrieve it as a frog. "Do not worry," she says, "throw me far out into the sea." The same action must be performed to transform her into a princess. This motif recalls "Palermo, the Sorcerer" (Spain, no. 11), where the hero must cast the wizard's dismembered daughter into the sea to make her whole again. In a variant of "The Three Feathers" reproduced by Bolte and Polívka,[391] the hero himself must enter the water, and the frog calls out to him:

432     "Embrace me and immerse yourself!" Yet he refused, so the frog called out a second time and a third one: "Embrace me and immerse yourself!" The fool seized the frog and carried it up to a pond and jumped into the water with it; but no sooner had the water touched them than he held the most beautiful maiden in his arms.

---

[388] Zaunert, *Deutsche Märchen seit Grimm*, p. 1.

[389] Jung, "The Phenomenology of the Spirit in Fairy Tales," CW 9/I, § 433ff.

[390] On the golden-haired girl sitting in a tree, see "The Three Sons of Padishah" (Turkey, no. 18). In "Three Lemons" (Norway, no. 4) and its variants, the anima is temporarily "displaced" onto a tree, thus causing havoc.

[391] Bolte and Polívka, *Anmerkungen*, vol. 2, p. 31.

433 As a symbol of the unconscious, water or the sea contains the secret of vitalization, transformation, and making whole. The frog anima, however, is the mediator in this mystery because she unites both spheres.[392]

434 One fairytale that contains some of the motifs of this group, yet adds even more profound ones, is "The Frog Maiden" (Balkans, no. 31):

435 A childless couple asked God to give them a child, "even if it were a frog." After nine months, the woman gave birth to a frog, which satisfied the parents. The frog's daughter stayed in the vineyard where the father worked; she let him lift her onto a cherry tree, where she began to sing as beautifully as a *vila*.[393] The singing attracted a King's son, who asked the old man who was singing the fine tune. At first, the old man was ashamed to tell him, but when the King's son insisted that he answer his question, he confessed that it was his frog daughter. He called her down from the tree, and the King's son said to her: "Be my sweetheart! Tomorrow my two brothers' sweathearts will come to the court, and whichever of them brings the most beautiful rose, the King has promised to leave the kingdom to her and her fiancé. Go there as my sweetheart and bring a rose that you have chosen." The frog answered: "I will do as you wish, but you must send me a white rooster from the court, and I will ride on it." Thereupon, he sent her a white rooster from the court. But she went to the sun and asked for its clothes. The next morning, the frog mounted the rooster and took the sun's clothes with it... No sooner had she entered the town than her rooster turned into a white *vila*, and the frog became the most beautiful girl in the world. She put on the sun's clothes.

[392] On the anima as a toad in the pond, see the close parallel "The Strange Marriage" (Zaunert, *Deutsche Märchen seit Grimm*, p. 263). On the anima as Melusine (i.e., nixie, a female spirit of fresh water), see Peuckert, *Deutscher Volksglaube des Spätmittelalters*, Sammlung Voelkerglaube, ed. Claus Schrempf (Stuttgart: Spemann Verlag, 1942), pp. 156ff.
[393] Translator's note: A *vila* is a Slavic fairy that resembles a nymph. See von Franz's interpretation of this tale after the quoted passage.

Yet instead of a rose she carried an ear of wheat and entered the King's palace." The King looked at the rose of his eldest daughter-in-law, the carnation of the second and finally the ear of wheat of the third. He acknowledged her for "bringing the most beautiful and useful rose." And so the youngest son inherited the kingdom and the frog's daughter became his queen.

436    The initial episode, which recounts the birth of the frog maiden, relates this fairytale and the parallels mentioned above to ones like "Hans the Hedgehog"; it also reveals the close parallelism between the animal prince and the animal princess. Most significantly, however, the frog in the cherry tree sings so beautifully that one believes one is listening to *vilas*. Her mount, a white rooster, also turns into a *vila*. *Vilas* or *samovilas* are spirit-beings. Common in Balkan fairytales, they are beautiful, nymphlike women who dwell in forests, mountains, and lakes and often appear as flying creatures, just as swan maidens do.[394] In this tale, when the female frog sings magically in the tree like a *vila*, her nature plainly resembles that of a bird, retrospectively confirming our assumption about the horror experienced by the brothers in "The Frog Maiden" (Spain, no. 68). This idea is further supported by the fact that the anima-figure later rides a white rooster to her lover's court. Thus, she often seems to have been associated with a bird.

437    In the present Russian fairytale, the frog princess conjures up swans on a lake, later becomes a cuckoo or a swan, and flies away. Presumably, the tree in the Spanish and Balkan versions, like the column (scaled by the cat) in the present Russian version, has the archetypal background of the world-tree. In "The Frog Maiden" (Balkans, no. 31), it is also significant that the female frog, who rides to her lover's court on a rooster, wraps herself in clothes she has borrowed from the sun. We have already pointed out the relation-ship between the rooster, the tree, and the sun, and between the

---

[394] Leskien, *Balkanmärchen* (Jena, 1919), p. 324, esp. the note on "The Maiden and the Vampire" (Balkans, no. 12); see further "The Shepherd and the Three *Vila*" (Balkans, no. 15), esp. p. 324, and "The Twelve Morsels" (Balkans, no. 38), esp. p. 326.

anima, the swan, and the sun.[395] All these significant mythological connections are alluded to here. Only one further motif needs to be mentioned: The frog-maiden's most beautiful rose is an ear of corn. The ear epitomizes corn, which symbolizes the corn spirit, and embodies the vegetation demon. It is an attribute of the goddesses Isis (whose brother-husband Osiris was the god of corn) and Demeter (whose daughter Persephone suffers the ear's fate and thus becomes its symbol). The idea of the corn mother exists in many countries, where it manifests in harvesting customs. In northern Europe, it is supplemented by the image of a "corn maiden," who also represents the corn spirit. The latter is killed symbolically in harvesting customs. This spirit is sometimes understood as an animal, as a rooster whose head, like corn, is severed with a scythe in autumn, in anticipation of its resurrection in spring, when its feathers become scattered with the seed.[396]

438    If the anima-figure carrying an ear of corn and riding atop a rooster in the Balkan tale represents a fertility goddess, then we can also draw a line to the ability to bake bread and cakes, as depicted in the Russian version (the motif of the frog princess) and in similar tales (the motif of the anima-figure). Although the somewhat naive narrative style suggests an almost humorous approach to this motif, its meaning runs deeper, from the anima-figure back to the mother-goddess as the goddess of crops.[397] It also leads back to her cult, to which belongs the mystery of death and resurrection, just as it does to the symbolism of harvesting customs. In Eleusis, the appearance of the ear of corn marked the culmination of the mysteries. It was subsequently equated symbolically with Adonis, Attis, Hermes, and finally with the Logos by the Hellenistic Gnostics.[398] Thus, the anima is represented vividly here (in the simple and succinct manner

---

[395] See *Archetypal Symbolism in Fairytales*, vol. 1, pp. 353–355.

[396] On Osiris as the god of corn and grain, see James Frazer, *The Golden Bough: A Study of Magic and Religion*, abridged edition (London: MacMillan: 1925), chapter XL; on Isis, see chapter XLI; on Demeter and Persephone, see chapter XLIV, on corn mothers and corn maidens, see chapters XLV and XLVI–XLVIII, which also discuss the corn spirit. On the latter as a rooster, see *ibid*. See further Mannhardt, *Wald- und Feldkulte*, vol. 1 (1875) and vol. 2 (1877).

[397] In "The Frog Maiden," the Balkan version of this tale (no. 31), the following episode is omitted: The frog daughter carries her on her back to the vineyard after the mother has become too old to perform this task.

[398] Leisegang, *Die Gnosis*, pp. 129 and 132.

characteristic of fairytales) as the psychic force that conveys nourishment in the broadest sense, both natural and mystical, which only the self is capable of doing. The anima's mysterious power, which fairytales emphasize so explicitly, also arises from this capacity to give.

439    Thus, in the Russian fairytale "The Frog Princess,"[399] the anima reveals herself on three levels: as a despised yet fatefully powerful animal soul; as a beloved woman; and as a mysterious, magical goddess who transcends the human sphere. Ivan, the hero of this fairytale, is evidently unable to accept the latter aspect at first.[400] Driven by curiosity, and presumably also by the desire to be allowed to preserve the woman permanently in human form, he sneaks home and burns the animal skin that he finds there. Not higher knowledge makes him do this, but contempt for the animal form, a cheeky or clumsy need to fathom the secret of possible transformation, and the desire to make the incomprehensible magical being his own for good. These motives contrast, at least to some extent, with the naive and successful burning of the animal skin in other versions. Moreover, they probably stamp the same action—similar to the premature illumination observed in some of the previous fairytales—as a failed intervention of consciousness, which leads to detours and complicates inner development[401] (in other versions, by contrast, this motif already brings about a definite solution; see, for example, "The Shepherd and the Three Samovila" [Balkans, no. 15] and "Lubi and the Earthly Beauty" [Balkans, no. 49]).

440    Just as the animal prince disappears as a bird after his premature illumination in "The Singing, Soaring Lark," and just as the bride whom it is forbidden to behold simply vanishes in "The Most

---

[399] Afanas'ev, *Russian Fairy Tales*, pp. 119–123.

[400] In other variants, e.g., "The Princess as a Monkey" (Spain, no. 48), the divine aspect, and thus a fundamental complication, is missing. Consequently, that tale ends in the same way as the Grimm's "The Three Feathers."

[401] For a parallel to "The Poor Miller's Boy and the Cat" (*The Complete Grimm's Fairy Tales*, pp. 482–485), see Bolte and Polívka, *Anmerkungen*, vol. 2, pp. 466–467: The simpleton, after living happily for a while with the king's daughter, meanwhile liberated from her toadish existence, throws the animal clothing she has carefully stowed away into the fire. Angered by this, she spits in his face. Saddened, he buries himself 25 fathoms underground in a cave until the princess's father finds him, brings him up again, and reconciles him with his daughter.

Beautiful Bride,"[402] so the burning of the animal skin makes the bride disappear here: She becomes a cuckoo or, as in other versions (see, e.g., "Tsarevna the Frog"), a swan. The cuckoo is a shy bird that, despite its coquettish call, does not like to be seen. It is thus suited to representing a content that is perceptible to consciousness, yet remains elusive. In myth and folklore, the cuckoo possesses demonic traits: It represents the devil[403]; in other versions, it is a demon that accrues money and gives bread.[404] The swan is easier to recognize: We have already defined it as the image of the swan maiden's anima on the one hand and of the spirit-being governing her on the other. However, the latter meaning—the swan as a symbol of the spirit— also clarifies the meaning of the cuckoo. It, too, is a demonic spirit, which now rules the anima so completely that we may speak of identity. The anima's demonic nature, hinted at by the tomcat and the swan (i.e., her aspect of a chthonic, creative-demonic spirit-being), has now become dominant and reveals itself in this new form to consciousness as something completely foreign and incomprehensible. This compels the hero to make yet another great effort to reach the deeper layers of the unconscious and to regain the lost human, female being, the actual anima. The old gray man, who shows Ivan the way, is clearly the archetype of the ancient sage, a manifestation of the chthonic spirit. His color emphasizes his ghostly nature on the one hand and his positive nature on the other.

441       Ivan is also helped by a bear, a falcon, and a pike, which he spares. In essence, these three animals symbolize further aspects of the helping old man whose character is rather extrahuman: The bear represents instinctual force, the falcon farsightedness and swiftness, and the pike primitive aggressiveness (it is called "sharp-toothed"!), ravenousness, and skillful orientation in the sea, the unconscious realm. All of these traits are specific to the Lord of the Underworld and here reveal his double aspect: The luminous human helper is

[402] Zaunert, *Deutsche Märchen seit Grimm*, p. 343.
[403] See the exclamation *Hol dich der Kuckuck!* (lit. "May the cuckoo get you," i.e., "Get lost!"—Trans.) rather than the more common *Hol Dich der Teufel!* (lit. "May the devil get you?" i.e., "To hell with you!"—Trans).
[404] Bächtold-Stäubli under *Kuckuck* (cuckoo). The Indian god Indra can also appear as a cuckoo. See Güntert, *Weltkönig*, p. 308, fn. 1.

joined by a dangerous group of animals, which adumbrates his primordial and ambivalent power. On the whole, the old man and the three animal-helpers form a group of four. This lends them a special meaning because together they obviously represent the self. However, the self remains predominantly extrahuman. Only one of the four functions, which together constitute the conscious personality originating in the self, has a human character of sorts. Thus, only one of these functions can be assimilated by consciousness, while the other three functions are still archaic. The fourth, the pike, is still completely submerged in the unconscious (the sea). Yet, as so often, precisely the forces belonging to the personality's shadow and opposed in kind to the conscious being are best suited to attaining the goal: the connection with the vanished image of the soul.

442     Just as the heroine is often supported by helping mother-figures against the evil primordial mother who banishes the animal prince, here a father-figure provides support against the frog princess's dark father, who is later said to have enchanted her. Yet not only the image of the "father" supports the hero on his journey into the unconscious. The "mother" must also stand by him. Her double aspect does not appear in two different figures, but in the primitive figure of the evil witch, who—if properly addressed—also helps. This correct form of address consists, on the one hand, in the hero's confident appearance and determination (note how he snaps at the old woman); and, on the other, however, in his conscious restraint and indecisiveness (he replies that he may or may not be willing to come), as well as in his neither-nor attitude: He is driven and at the same time also consciously wishes to venture into the unconscious. This paradoxical behavior corresponds to an awareness that is not based on profane cleverness and one-sided purposefulness, but instead means actual wisdom, which Ivan has probably gained from his encounter with the old man; just as another Ivan, the hero of "The Maiden Tsar," was initiated in his grandfather's cellar before his dangerous encounter with the primordial mother.[405]

---

[405] Afanas'ev, ed., *Russian Fairy Tales*, pp. 229–234. Note the parallelism between these parts of these tales.

443     The witch reveals to the hero that his vanished wife must serve with her brother on an island in the sea. This island, an isolated land mass, symbolizes a conscious center in the unconscious, a mandalalike centering of the undefined unconscious space, and as such may be said to symbolize the self. This center in the unconscious behaves toward consciousness like a mirror-image: Both provide the human spirit with solid ground relative to the sea of the unconscious. Nevertheless, this center is not directly accessible to consciousness because it is a mirror-image and because consciousness, being determinate, is unable to grasp its own counterimage. Therefore, only psychic forces that belong partly to the unconscious and partly to consciousness, and which we might call phantasies, can bring the hero to the island. Most expressive is the image of the fairytale bridge built by the pike out of the most precious material. As we have seen, the animal prince erected a similar bridge—between the golden and the silver castle—in "The Bristle Child."[406] A bridge connects separate objects, in this case two pieces of land, between which lies impassable water or an abyss, which psychologically both symbolize the unconscious. Within what must be bridged often dwells—mythologically—a demon, so that crossing a bridge even becomes dangerous. Due to this apparent impossibility of crossing the space in between, as the demonic sphere might attack the conscious personality, the unknown "other shore" also becomes an image of the unconscious, for all unfamiliar and detached psychic realities.

444     Thus, the anima-figure once more feels strange to Ivan and has become a seemingly unattainable opposite (theme of antithesis). Although building bridges is an achievement of human consciousness, the bridge in this fairytale is conjured up by a fish. For when a person's conscious mind fails, an unconscious spirit often takes its place, creating inspirations and achievements that are unaccomplishable without that spirit. As mentioned, the pike is the fourth and unconscious part of the helping spirit that appears as part of a group of four. Like the island, it symbolizes the self. Here, too,

---

[406] Zaunert, *Deutsche Märchen seit Grimm*, p. 286.

we encounter the paradox that only the self can enable a person to find the self (in this case, the anima). The self, however, is also the source of all the resistance encountered on this path. Therefore, the chthonic spirit appears not only in the figure of an old man and animals, but also as an evil father who curses the anima, and moreover as a dragon whom she must serve. These two figures parallel the witch mother and her daughter. In several fairytales, they curse and enchant the animal prince, as well as represent the evil spirit or, as it were, the animus that governs the frog princess. The dragon, as an amphibious fiend, is related to the frog; it reveals the demonic background and thus the secret of the anima's froggishness: She is governed by a spirit-being, which is dragon-shaped and thus belongs to deeply submerged, prehistoric layers of the unconscious.

445     This spirit has imprisoned the maiden in a glass palace, where she is separated from the world outside by three doors: an iron, a silver, and a golden one. These metals, whose value increases the further one enters the palace, indicate that the psychic image hidden behind the last door is even more valuable than gold. The glass palace on the island symbolizes the self because it corresponds roughly to the maiden tsar's castle (Russia, no. 41), the moon fairy's crystal palace (China no. 19), or "The Golden Castle that Hung in the Air" (Norway, no. 35).[407] While the clarity and transparency of glass symbolize the purity of the self, which is uncorrupted by anything earthly and opaque, and instead is suffused with light, its smoothness, hardness, and brittleness also make glass represent the anima's corresponding properties. These envelop or banish the anima and impede her relationship with the surrounding world.[408] Therefore, the glass house may assume a negative meaning, that of a prison. This aspect prevails as long as fear, alienation, and rejection still exist in consciousness.[409]

---

[407] On the glass vessel in occidental alchemy, see Jung, *Psychology and Alchemy*, CW 12, § 243, and in Chinese alchemy, see Wilhelm, *The Secret of the Golden Flower*.

[408] On the meaning of the glass coffin in this respect, see "Snow White." See also Jung, "The Spirit Mercurius," *CW* 13, § 245.

[409] Like all "magical places" or symbols of the unconscious, the glass mountain also refers to the realm of the dead and the hereafter. See Dieterich, *Mithrasliturgie*, pp. 183–185, and Bolte and Mackensen, *Handwörterbuch* (under *Glasberg*, glass mountain); see also "The Wife of Death" (France, vol. 2, no. 32) and Tegethoff, *Französische Volksmärchen*, vol. 2, p. 333f.

446    The princess who is banished to (i.e., held captive in) an inaccessible glass palace, or on an unscalable glass mountain, is a common fairytale image.[410] Even the animal prince is sometimes banished to a glass mountain instead of a distant realm, which the claw-fingered heroine must scale to redeem him.[411] The opposite motif is more common: The hero must redeem the king's daughter either from or out of the glass mountain. Related to this is the idea that the anima-figure is "too elevated": She is located either in an "air-castle," an infinitely high tree, or in an inaccessible tower or castle, which the hero can reach only on a miraculous horse (capable of scaling great heights) or by flying to its top.[412] This motif, which we have discussed above in connection with "The Golden Castle that Hung in the Air" (Norway, no. 35), expresses the fact that the anima is literally "too elevated:" She is glimpsed in a divine, otherworldly realm rather than in the human sphere,[413] meaning that human

---

[410] In one variant of "Snow White," she is not borne away to the mountains, but to the glass mountain. See Bolte and Polívka, *Anmerkungen*, vol.1, p. 452 and vol. 2, p. 247; for a more general discussion, see also Bolte and Mackensen, *Handwörterbuch* (under *Glasberg*, glass mountain).

[411] See "The Spinner" (Zaunert, *Deutsche Märchen seit Grimm*, p. 211): A girl promised to carry a little worm, in which lay concealed an enchanted prince, around for three years in order to redeem him. Every year, she was allowed to visit her parents if she returned in time. The third time she arrived late, so that the worm prince was transported (enraptured!) to his kingdom. She set forth to look for him and reached a glass mountain, which was so smooth that she could not climb up it. After a smith had shoed her hands and knees, she managed to scale the mountain. When she reached the King's castle, she offered her services as a spinner and purchased three nights in the King's chamber with the three golden spindles that she had received from an old woman on her travels and which the Queen desired to possess. In the end, the prince recognized the maiden, was redeemed, and married her. See also "The Iron Stove" (*The Complete Grimm's Fairy Tales*, pp. 571–577).

[412] See, e.g., "The Winged Prince" (Roma, no. 50): An emperor's son purchased a pair of wings from an artist and flew nine worlds away to a city where an old woman took him in. "When he set off, he caught sight of the emperor's castle, which had three floors of stone and one of crystal. He asked the old woman: 'Who lives in the castle, and who inhabits the fourth, crystal floor?' 'The emperor's daughter lives there, but is never permitted to leave the castle; her food is brought to her with a rope.'" The prince's son flew to the crystal floor and into the chamber through the window. "The princess was lying on her bed as if she were dead. He touched her, but she uttered no sound. But when he took down the candle that stood by her head, she rose, clasped him around the neck, and said: 'Because you have come to me, you are mine, and I am yours.' They made love until daybreak. Then he put the candle back in its place, and the princess again lay on the bed as if she were dead; he left the chamber, closed the window, and flew back to the old woman. For half a year, he visited the princess, who became pregnant." The emperor was informed and, to find the intruder, he ordered the garret to be covered with dough to record any traces. On his next visit, the winged emperor's son left traces in the dough, was found out, and was about to be burned together with the princess. However, they took flight from the pyre and, after several adventures, returned to his parents with their newborn son. For a weaker version, see "The King's Son Who Learned to Fly" (Zaunert, *Deutsche Märchen seit Grimm*, Jena 1922, p. 281).

[413] On such an anima-image lying beyond human reach, see "The Earth Wants Its Share" (Caucasus, no. 6): On his long quest for the "place of immortality," the hero finds far away in the sea a glass house, where the immortal beauty lives. She says: "... I was created on the first day of creation and am still as I was then. I am called Beauty; I will forever remain as I am. You could have stayed with me eternally, but are not worthy of immortality; eternal life will disgust you."

effort is needed to bring her within reach. As a rule, the great height at which the anima dwells for as long as she hovers in the extrahuman realm of spirits is compensated for by an equal depth or darkness, which is embodied in a ruling demonic figure or dragon. Sometimes, the spell of the glass mountain has been cast by a witch[414]; that is, by the mother-archetype, which dominates the anima or the real woman so strongly that she cannot participate in life. More often, however, the spell of the glass mountain is cast by a male figure that corresponds to the father-archetype, that is, the earliest image of the husband.

447    In the Grimm's "Old Rinkrank,"[415] for instance, a father was prepared to give his daughter only to that person who could walk across a specially erected glass mountain; when one man attempted to perform this feat, the daughter fell and was devoured by the gaping mountain. Inside lived Old Rinkrank, an old, bearded giant, who was 17 legs long and had a golden foot. He wooed the girl, who, through her cunning and aided by the hero, managed to save herself.[416] The girl was enchanted by the father, and moreover by the demon in the mountain, who apparently represented the father's

---

[414] See, e.g., "The Raven" (*The Complete Grimm's Fairy Tales*, pp. 431–436): Opening the window, a Queen said impatiently to her disobedient child: "I wish you were a raven and flew away, so I would have peace." Transformed into a raven, the child flew off through the window and out into a dark forest. The girl told a man who was passing by how she might be redeemed: "Go further into the forest and you will find a house; in it sits an old woman, who will give you food and drink, but you must not take anything; if you eat or drink anything, you will fall asleep and you will not be able to redeem me. In the garden behind the house stands a large pile of wood; stand there and wait for me. For three days, I will visit you every midday in a chariot, first drawn by four white stallions, then by four red ones, and finally by four black ones. But if you are not awake, I will not be redeemed." The man promised to fulfill these conditions, but on each occasion he was enticed by the old woman to at least take a sip from the glass, so that the princess found him asleep. On the third occasion, she placed a loaf of bread beside him, a piece of meat, and a bottle of wine; the food and wine did not grow less. "Thereupon, she took a gold ring bearing her name from her finger and put it on him. Finally, she placed a letter beside him wherein was written what she had given him, and that none of those things would ever grow less. The letter also said: "I see right well that you will never be able to set me free for as long as you are here; but if you are still willing to redeem me, come to the golden castle of Stromberg; it lies in your power, of that I am certain." — The man set out in search of that castle, which he reached with the help of a giant whose favor he had gained with the princess's magic food. But the castle stood on a glass mountain, and the cursed maiden drove around the castle in her chariot and then went in. He rejoiced when he saw her and wanted to climb up to her; but no matter how hard he tried, he kept slipping on the glass." Deeply perturbed, he built a hut at the foot of the mountain to wait for the princess. After a year, he succeeded in tricking three robbers out of a horse that could even climb up the glass mountain, as well as out of an invisible mantle, and a stick that could open the castle's doors. With these implements, he reached the princess and threw the ring she had given him into a goblet so that it rang. And thus, he set her free, and they celebrated their wedding. For a discussion, see Führer, *Nordgermanische* (Munich, 1938), pp. 12 and 23; see further "The Drummer" (*The Complete Grimm's Fairy Tales*, pp. 781–791).
[415] *The Complete Grimm's Fairy Tales*, pp. 796–798.
[416] Bolte and Polívka, *Anmerkungen*, vol. 3, p. 423f.

magical background. In the present fairytale about the frog princess, we should also understand the dragon as a part of Clever Vasilissa's father. The father, who keeps his daughter out of reach (and thus for himself) also appears in "The Story of the Crystal Palace and the Diamond Ship" (Turkey, no. 1), where the king buries his daughter in an underground pit whose roof is made of glass. Later, she asks him to build her a glass palace out at sea, where she finds a prince who conquers her after many adventures.

448

One tale whose motif corresponds to "Old Rinkrank" is "The Lost Golden Shoe" (Iceland, no. 17), whose heroine is banished by a giant into a submarine glass house that he holds by a chain and from which she is later freed by the chain being severed. In "The Devil as a Teacher" (Spain, no. 42), the devil builds a glass coffin for the heroine, who had rejected his advances (Old Rinkrank and the giant in "The Lost Golden Shoe" also desire the princess[417]). Corresponding to the double aspect of all the characters, however, giants, dwarfs, or a "wild man" often assist those endeavoring to ascend a glass mountain.[418] Sometimes, the swan maiden disappears

---

[417] This motif is particularly evident in "Prince Shaadot" (Turkestan, no. 10): An old man who is guarding the princess's image in a magical garden claims to be her rejected lover. Father-daughter incest is also hinted at in Loepfe's variant of "The Frog Princess" (*Russische*, p. 34). When the tsar demanded that the most beautiful carpet be brought, the frog princess exclaimed: "Wild winds, bring me that carpet upon which I once sat with my father." On the other hand, the old man's words point to a competition with her father: "O woe, Prince Ivan, why did you have to burn the frog's skin! You neither gave it to her nor were you permitted to take it. Clever Vasilissa is cleverer and wiser than her father. This angered him, so he ordered her to live as a frog for three years. Here is a ball. Follow it wherever it rolls." In "The Magic Garden" (Italy, no. 14), the motif of the enchanting old man, who is half-father, half-husband, is related to the problem of time: The hero enters a magic garden belonging to a witch who becomes a beautiful girl at night. Her jealous husband, meanwhile deceased, had banished the maiden to this place for four years (!). If she saw a youth who appeared as a girl, she would become a snake forever. The hero illumined her at night, whereupon she escaped, making a hissing noise, and leaving him to mourn her ever since. Laistner observes that if the magical wife, after becoming human again, escapes nevertheless and even harms her human family, legend has it that this happens because she rejects a powerful sorcerer, who avenges himself by turning her into a ravenous snake (*Das Rätsel*, vol. 1, p. 121).

[418] See "The Raven" and "The Drummer" (*The Complete Grimm's Fairy Tales*). See also "The Princess on the Glass Mountain" (Sweden, no. 16): One day, while out hunting, a King encountered a "dwarf or wild man"; because this fellow refused to answer him, the King had him arrested. Whoever set free the prisoner would be condemned to death. When the King left home to fight a war, he gave the Queen the key to the wild man's cage. One day, the little prince was playing with his golden apple, but it flew into the cage. After returning the apple several times, the wild man said that he would only continue playing if the prince stole the keys from his mother and freed him. The prince did as instructed but was condemned to death by the angry father on his return from his military campaign. But the servants spared the prince, who left his native land and offered his services as a shepherd at a court in a distant land. There ruled a King whose beautiful daughter would be given to that man who could ride up to the glass mountain, upon whose summit she sat "with a golden crown on her head and a golden apple in her hand ... But the mountain was so very high, slippery, and steep" that most of the suitors almost

up or into the glass mountain after recovering her feathers; her human husband, who had forced her into marriage by stealing her plumage, must pass many tests on his long quest to redeem her.[419] Thus, the state of rapture on the glass mountain, as an image of the anima's detachment and inaccessibility, resembles her swan-maiden aspect, which in turn symbolizes her elusive, ghostly nature. Birdishness and the glass mountain, or glass house, also belong together in the Russian fairytale about the frog princess. The elusiveness of the swan-anima is related to the motif of the "magical contest," in which the hero must prevail, either with the magical bride's father or with her, to free the maiden from the demon ruling over her.

449    We will consider this motif in more detail in the last section of this volume. It also appears in "Tsarevna the Frog," a Russian variant of the present fairytale about the frog princess. The frog princess, who is called Clever Vasilissa in that variant, flees to the so-called "Immortal Koshchei," a demonic sorcerer very familiar in Russian fairytales. The hero must either overcome the magician or (as in another version) snatch Vasilissa, who, like Proteus, transforms into different shapes. When she becomes a spindle, the hero breaks the instrument on the advice of Baba Yaga. He throws one part behind him, the other in front of him. Behind him grows a birch tree, and before him stands Vasilissa. She surrenders because he knows how to separate the chthonic part from the human one. What makes the anima appear so "miraculously clever," so knowledgeable of magic, and capable of transformation, is her relationship to the magical spirit, with which she is either identical, or which appears as an independent archetype. Next, a mysterious fusion occurs between her and the primordial image of the chthonic spirit or the primordial

---

immediately fell down. Meanwhile, the prince, who was herding oxen in a deep forest, was complaining that he could not take part in the tournament. Whereupon, the wild man came to his aid out of gratitude. He gave the prince a horse and a suit of steel armor, with which the latter stormed halfway up the glass mountain and, turning his horse around, disappeared before the eyes of the astonished crowd. On the second day of the tournament, the prince, clad in silver armor, rode up to the summit on a white horse to receive the apple from the princess. Once again, he vanished. He hid in the crowd as a shepherd but was recognized by the princess. In return, she became his wife, and he received one half of the kingdom. But nothing more was ever heard again of the wild man. See also "A Boy Sets Free Twelve Enchanted Girls" (Balkans, no. 46), where we also find the motif of animals and the devil as helpers.
[419] See, e.g., "The Huntsman and the Swan Maiden" (Zaunert, *Deutsche Märchen seit Grimm*, p. 133).

father, who in many fairytales occupies this strange role of the anima's animus. (In almost all fairytales, the bride must eventually be freed from another being or creature, for instance, a dragon, a dwarf, a giant, or a jealous father; often, however, this figure is merely hinted at, while in some fairytales, like the present one, it is more prominent).

450     Golden-footed Old Rinkrank (in the eponymous fairytale), and the devil in the Grimm's "The Devil with the Three Golden Hairs,"[420] are saturnine demons. They symbolize the nocturnal sun,[421] which stands opposed to the daytime sun, which symbolizes an enlightening ruling spirit. The psychic image appears in an almost ridiculous, yet harmless manner in "The Tale of Sänämâ," where the animal princess is a bee.[422] She is redeemed by making Princess Peri, who has a swordfish stuck in her throat, laugh. This deed redeems her and, out of gratitude, also the bee (from its animal form). The swordfish stuck in her throat means that Princess Peri is a *doppelgänger* of the bee princess, while the swordfish (like the bee's stinger) represents her hidden "sharpness," which is one of the animus's qualities. The swordfish might also illumine the meaning of the pike in the Russian fairytale about the frog princess. Although similar, she seems less closely connected with the anima and acts benevolently toward the hero. Nevertheless, this "animus of the anima" or this "shadow of the hero," who builds the bridge to the anima's island and appears with the chthonic spirit (old gray man), has an ambivalent character due to his predatory nature.[423]

---

[420] *The Complete Grimm's Fairy Tales*, pp. 151–158.

[421] On Saturn as the nocturnal antithesis of the sun, see Paul Schmitt, "Sol Invictus," *Eranos- Jahrbuch 1943: Alte Sonnenkulte und die Lichtsymbolik in der Gnosis und im frühen Christentum*, ed. Olga Fröbe-Kapteyn (1944), p. 171f., who refers to Boll-Bezold, *Sternglaube und Sterndeutung* (1926) and Alfred Fankhauser, *Horoskopie* (1939).

[422] Christensen, *Iran*, p. 107.

[423] On the spirit dominating the anima, see the 12 black men in "The King of the Golden Mountain" (*The Complete Grimm's Fairy Tales*, pp. 425–430): Although they torment the hero at night, his steadfastness cancels out their power. In "The Three Black Princesses" (*The Complete Grimm's*, pp. 620–621), redemption fails: The hero, a fisherman's son, is warned by his mother about three black princesses. Following her advice, he pours the wax of consecrated candles onto their faces. Turning half-white, they curse him, because now no one can redeem them. "Our three brothers, who are bound by seven chains, will tear you to pieces." A loud shrieking could be heard all over the castle, whereupon the hero leapt out of the window and broke his leg. Following this commotion, the castle once again sank into the earth and the mountain closed. Caused by forcefully applying blessed candles, the sudden partial redemption in this tale is a Christian form of "premature illumination." For a discussion of this somewhat distorted tale, see Bolte and Polívka, *Anmerkungen*, who argue that its "ancient core" is

451     The anima is mysteriously connected not only with the dark and often devilish father-figure and its animal-helpers but also with the demonic mother-figure. In "The Most Beautiful Bride," the hero encounters the sun on his journey.

452     In a see-through little house that was made of bright glass sat the mother sun, turning a wheel with which she spun the most beautiful golden threads. Her head glittered and burned like the greatest oven fire, and yet she did nothing of the kind. She wore a crimson silk skirt, which grew ever darker toward the bottom, and pitch-black shoes.[424]

453     On the one hand, this description recalls that of the frog princess, who also sits in a glass house and counts (flax) threads; on the other, it recalls Baba Yaga's hut.[425] These nocturnal mother-figures may be said to represent a dark background that belongs to the woman's soul-image, just as we can relate Baba Yaga to the heroine in "The Maiden Tsar" (Russia, no. 41); on the other hand, this tale also emphasizes the anima's relationship with the sun. Further evidence of this idea appears in "A King's Son and an Enchanted Maiden" (no. 25), a Lithuanian variant of the tale about the frog princess: A king instructs his three sons to look for a bride wherever the shots he fires strike the ground. The youngest son finds a female frog, who at night turns into a beautiful woman. To prevent her from transforming back into a frog during daytime, the king's son burns her animal skin, whereupon she says: "Now you have destroyed me." She gives

---

nevertheless evident (vol. 3, p. 114). See also Siuts, *Jenseitsmotive* (1911), who calls "'The Three Black Princesses' ... a mutilated fairytale that is interspersed with saga elements" (p. 5, fn. 1). In discussing this tale, Bolte and Polívka also refer to Wilhelm Grimm: "As magic unfolds or dissolves due to overpowering interventions, it entails ruin or complete annihilation. It wishes to remain secret and therefore shuns light; this explains why the three princesses are black and gradually turn white. It also shuns speech and it remains unaltered if, when the treasure is lifted up, the first word forces it to sink seven times deeper" (*Anmerkungen*, vol. 3, p. 114, fn. 2). Insofar as Christianity is the religion of a highly developed consciousness, it can be easily related to the motif of "premature illumination"; the fisherman's son is not mature enough to contend with the forms of the Christian religion. When he recognizes the anima's dangerous animus, his inner world (castle) and his point of view are shattered (broken leg), so that the tragic consequences of "premature illumination" can no longer be amended for.

[424] Zaunert, *Deutsche Märchen seit Grimm*, p. 343.

[425] See, e.g., "The Maiden Tsar" (Russia, no. 41) and "Beautiful Vasilissa" (Loepfe, *Russische*, p. 5); in the latter, three horsemen underscore the relationship with the sun.

him a letter for her eldest sister that contains instructions for the blacksmith: He should make the youth a pair of iron shoes and give him a piece of iron measuring the size of a piece of bread. Thus equipped, the young man should go to the eldest sister and lie in her bed with the letter around his neck. Only if he endures these trials will they be reunited. "You have subjected me to the greatest torment." Saying this, she flies out the window. The king's son acts as instructed.

454     It was not long before the sister came flying with a thunderous roar, spitting and shouting: "Who smells of human flesh here? Oh, you brother-in-law, you are here, you are a good bird, I should tear you asunder." But she took the letter from his neck and read it: "Well," she said, "get up! Come here, I will give you food! For you have traveled far and are tired."

455  Thereafter, they eat from the iron loaf of bread.

Immediately afterward, someone else came rushing toward them with a roar of thunder. She asked: "Where shall I hide thee!" She hid the young man beneath the stove. Whereupon someone entered the room and wailed: "What has the villain done to me? What torment have I suffered?" She replied: "If you saw your husband, what would you do to him?" "I would tear him into little pieces." Thereupon, she flew off again.

456  Next, the eldest sister gives him a letter containing the same instructions as before for another sister. He does as instructed, and events unfold as they had previously. Yet when the second sister attempts to cut the piece of iron, it turns into bread. Once more, "someone" rushes along and says: "'If only you knew how difficult this is for me!' But the sister said: 'If you saw your husband, what would you do to him?' She answered, 'I would tear him into four pieces.'" After speaking these words, she flew off, and he crawled out from underneath the bed where he had been hiding.

457　　The second sister gives him a letter for the youngest one. As before, the iron again turns into bread; to rescue him from the approaching woman, she lets him crawl under her skirt. "She entered the room cheerfully, and her sister asked: 'If you saw your husband, what would you do to him?' 'I wouldn't do anything to him, nothing at all.' She raised her skirt and said: 'Look, here is your husband.'" There follows the wedding, and the tale concludes with the words: "The queen was bewitched before she was born, and she was meant to be a frog until the wedding. If he had not burned her skin, however, she would have become a woman at the wedding." Here, the anima plainly reveals her demonic character and resembles her witchlike sisters (so that her desirable side is complemented by the negative one, revealing her double aspect). In retrospect, behind the anima stands a chthonic primordial couple, which corresponds roughly to the devil and his grandmother, as well as similar archetypal pairs.

458　　Besides combining several fairytale forms and motifs explained in this study, "The Cat" (Roma, no. 41) illustrates how the anima image depends on the parental imagos:

459　　An emperor forbid his wife to return home from a sea voyage unless she was in good spirits and hopeful. After a long journey, she got caught in thick fog and a fierce storm, but the next day she saw a palace on the sea. She went ashore with her servants and learned that the palace belonged to the Mother of God. She could not restrain her desire to pick a golden apple from the apple tree standing in the courtyard. She got someone to steal an apple for her, became pregnant, and happily sailed home. When the Mother of God noticed the theft, she swore that if a girl was born by eating the apple, she would be as beautiful as the sun, but that in her seventh year she would become a cat and remain enchanted together with the whole palace until an emperor's son cut off the cat's head. Events came to pass as she had predicted.

460  An emperor living in a distant country instructed his three sons to bring a canvas so thin "that one can blow through it and thread it through a needle." The eldest son rode for two months along a barren path where he starved and only met a little dog; the second chose a path where he had food, but his horse starved. After two months, he found a piece of canvas that would need to be threaded through a needle a few times if he wanted it. The youngest got caught in torrential rain in a forest; on the third morning, as he grew increasingly desperate, he recognized a palace ahead of him in the lightning. Its gate was locked and the surrounding wall stood very tall. Above him, he saw a leg of meat (which, however, was made of precious stones), scaled the wall to reach it, became stuck, heard the sound of a bell, and let himself drop from a considerable height for fear of being found out. When a hand opened the gate, he stepped into the courtyard: not a soul was around, neither in the yard nor inside the palace. Instead, he saw a table, a candlestick, and a bed in a room. When he sat down, ten hands tore off his clothes, beat him, brought food and new clothes. The same events unfolded on the second day in another room. On the third day, he was led in golden clothes into the golden hall, where a hundred cats were playing wonderful music. He was seated on the golden throne and before him stood a golden basket with a beautiful little cat, which rose at midnight and proclaimed him the lord of cats, who then kissed his hand. After he had stayed with the cat for a year and was reluctant to return home, the cat induced him to bring his father what he had promised. Since he would have to travel for nine years, she summoned a lightning chariot by cracking her fiery whip and gave him a nut to crack open before his father. This he did. First, he found a grain of corn, and inside that a grain of wheat.

461  Disappointed, he cursed the cat. He felt a claw on his hand, which was now covered in blood. Inside the grain of wheat

he found a corncockle seed, from which he obtained a hundred yards of the desired fine linen. The father wanted to cede the kingdom to him, but the young man wanted to return to his own empire, which the father would not permit until each of the sons had brought a wife. The husband of the most beautiful maiden would become the heir. They set out. Before long, the youngest brother returned to the cat in a chariot of fire. She listened to his report in silence. After a while, she asked him to return home, which he refused to do. Instead, he asked her why she was a cat. He should not ask her "just yet," she replied, and that she abhorred living in the world. She accompanied him in the lightning chariot to his father. The emperor, seeing his son's wife, said: "Oh, now what do you want with a cat? Don't you talk to her?" Annoyed, the cat jumped out of the golden basket, slipped into another room, rolled over, and returned as a girl, as beautiful as the sun, and embraced the young emperor's son. The father and brothers were "dumbfounded," and the youngest son received the kingdom. While the young man refused yet again, the girl rolled back over, once more became a cat, and returned to the kingdom of cats. As he was disappointed by her renewed transformation, she hinted at the curse that had been cast upon her. After some time, she asked him to cut off her tail; when he had done this after some resistance, she became half a girl. After pleading with him time and again, she convinced him to also cut off her head. When he performed this feat, she was redeemed along with all the other cats and the whole town. They went to his father. Overjoyed by this transformation, he fell in love with his son's wife and tried to rid himself of his son and abduct his wife. Although the son knew that she would not let him die, and although she struck the father, they managed to escape. Strife erupted between the two kingdoms. In the end, the son defeated the father, who surrendered, and the son inherited the kingdom.

462 The story about the princess's birth recalls that of the heroine in "Rapunzel."[426] When discussing this tale (also with reference to the Low German variant "De Eddelmannsdochter in 'n Tôr'n"),[427] we observed that the father is indirectly involved in the daughter's prenatal enchantment as much as the mother is. This is also true in the present fairytale: The emperor threatens to disown his wife and thus forces her to resort to magical means. The "Mother of God" takes the place of other *magna-mater* figures.[428] Her name refers to a female demon, that is, the mother-archetype. Thus, the daughter is enchanted by the curse placed on her mother. Psychologically, the supremacy of the hitherto dominant consciousness has forced the woman to resort to the unconscious. Beholden to the curse, the rapacious, even impetuous appropriation of unconscious values thwarts the development initiated by the previous action. This stifling is expressed by the daughter's transformation into a cat. In myth, we find an image in the realm of cats that is related to "The Poor Miller's Boy and the Cat."[429] Unlike that tale, the present one mentions the cat's "sharp" claws: This animus aspect of the anima-figure is caused by her enchantment.

463 The subsequent plot resembles that of "The Three Feathers."[430] Yet the tale threatens to conclude without redemption in the "magical sphere" because the hero repeatedly refuses to leave the realm of cats, whose mistress in the golden basket (mandala!) and whose emotional splendor (cat music!) delight him. But the anima sends him back to the world of profane consciousness, most likely for the sake of her redemption. (Her lightning chariot parallels the thunderstorm amid which the frog princess appears at the tsar's court in "The Frog Princess"; Russia no. 5). In that tale, as observed, lightning guides the hero from the dark forest toward the castle in what constitutes a vivid image of the enlightening intuition that springs from the deepest possible despair).

---

[426] *The Complete Grimm's Fairy Tales*, pp. 73–77.
[427] Wisser, ed., *Plattdeutsche Volksmärchen*, [MdW], ed. Zaunert (1927), p. 208.
[428] Walther Aichele also emphasizes this point in *Zigeunermärchen* (1926), p. 328.
[429] *The Complete Grimm's Fairy Tales*, pp. 482–485.
[430] *Ibid.*, pp. 319–322.

464   Contained one within another, the symbols of the self (nut-maize-wheat-grain-corn), which, once regurgitated, eventually reveal the long-awaited canvas, are images of a mystery that opens up ever more deeply, until the fine fabric of psychic and spiritual connections appears. In the meantime, the cat baffles the profane world by displaying its double aspect. The hero's premature questions about the cat's appearance neither weigh heavily in this fairytale nor do they have consequences. On the other hand, the father-figure poses a threat because the emperor wants to possess the daughter-in-law. Although the folkloric, coarse description of this episode seems foreign compared to the rest of the tale, and is perhaps added to enable a confrontation between the son and his otherwise friendly father, it is psychologically and artistically consistent: The redeeming "dismemberment" requested by the cat has revealed the anima's nature to the son, who now knows that she belongs to his conscious being and that she is powerful. However, the son and the disenchanted one must both confront hitherto ruling conscious-ness because the son has a strong tendency to remain in that world on which he has bestowed the human aspect. Although he assimilates that world with his consciousness, he is unable to properly connect it with tradition: He consistently refuses to inherit the father's kingdom.

465   Consequently, the anima-figure is not completely categorized either. This fairytale tells us that traditional consciousness, pre-sumably because it is not connected with the son as the nucleus of the personality, strives to make the anima serve its interests without acknowledging either her actual place—as a part of the renewed personality—or her actual essence. Thus, a struggle ensues. It is not until the old emperor realizes that he has played all his cards, and that his son is entitled not only to the empire but also to the anima, that the young couple is able to rule over both realms.

466   This fairytale, whose details are not entirely logical, yet whose motifs are nevertheless manifoldly intertwined, subtly depicts how the essential characters are connected. Except for the father-figures, all other characters are both profane and magical, both conscious

and merged with the unconscious, so that a realistic picture of the human soul emerges, in particular since the father-figures, due to their rather profane nature, are causally linked to the unconscious events. Therefore, this fairytale, which at first glance resembles a patchwork of familiar fairytales, offers good insight into archetypal psychological connections.

467     Nevertheless, "Dragojlo and Dragana," a Slavic tale, is more significant on account of its more succinct narrative and unusual symbolism:

468     A poor widow, who was treated unkindly by people, humbly sheltered a very old man for one night. When he left, he blessed her and her son Dragojlo. A few days later, the two goats, the widow's only possessions, returned from the pasture with broken udders, so that the next morning Dragojlo accompanied them with his hoe. A snake entwined itself around one of the goats, and when Dragojlo wanted to kill it, it revealed itself as the daughter of the snake emperor and promised him a little golden cloth which, wrapped around the goat's horns and then shaken, would grant him all his wishes. Dragojlo wandered with the snake to the sea and across a bridge (created by its call) to the snake emperor's castle. Although the emperor would have rather given Dragojlo other things, he finally gave him the golden cloth. When he returned to his goats, Dragojlo procured delicious food and placed it under his pillow at home. The next day, he wanted to show it to his mother, but it had disappeared. Taking his hoe, and accompanied by a dog and a cat, he went out to search for the missing food. When he reached the sea, he ordered the dog to swim across with the cat on its back, to sneak unnoticed into the castle, to steal the cloth from the sleeping emperor, and to swim back with the cat and the cloth. During their escape, however, they were pursued by a snake, which Dragojlo drew to the cat's attention. When the cat meowed at the snake, the cloth fell into the sea. Catching

it, the snake shouted: "You won't get the cloth until you bring me living fire." When Dragojlo ran desperately along the shore, he saw a fish in a puddle and threw it back into the sea at its request. In return, he received a scale with which he should scrape the earth assisted by the fish. When he killed the dragon threatening young eagles with his axe, he received a feather from the old eagle, which he was told to swing above his head in bad times. After the dog and cat had followed him, he swung the feather and asked the eagle for living fire. The latter promised Dragojlo this if he gave him a pan made of diamonds. The fish retrieved the pan from the depths, the eagle flew off with it and made a living fire in it. Dragojlo sailed across the sea with the fire, with the cat riding on the dog. "The serpent laid aside her shirt (her skin) and burned it in the living fire." No sooner had she done this that she turned into the most beautiful girl, the only daughter of "this emperor's kingdom." She gave Dragojlo the little cloth and wanted to marry no one other than him and rule with him over her father's kingdom. Dragojlo asked why she was this emperor's daughter and the snake emperor's at the same time. She explained that she was the emperor's daughter Dragana, whose mother's curse had turned her into a snake with the words: "Serpent, thou art the Snake Emperor's child!" At the same time, she was abducted by the snake emperor, who told her: "Only when your snake's skin is burned in living fire will the spell be lifted and will you be transformed into a Christian soul again." After the wedding, they brought Dragojlo's mother to the empire and the emperor handed over his powers to Dragojlo.[431]

469 Once again, the parent-imagos initiate the plot: from Dragojlo's benevolent personal mother through the very old man to the helpful underworld deity, which probably takes the place of the hero's personal father (similar to the "godfather" in "Ferdinand the Faithful

---

[431] See Krauss, *Sagen der Südslaven*, vol. 2 (Leipzig, 1884), no. 84.—Trans.

and Ferdinand the Unfaithful,"[432] whose actions decisively influenced the hero's fate, while the personal father receded into the background). The hero is unable to hold onto the magic cloth, which he acquired too easily with the help of the serpent's anima and her "bridge" across the sea. The cloth disappears when the hero, who is bound to the mother, wants to give her his gifts. His brief ownership corresponds to a premonition, the episode to a prelude. The hero's departure, accompanied by the animals (i.e., instincts), is promising. Nevertheless, he fails to obtain the treasure, which provides infinite nourishment, also in the second episode, where he lets the animals (without consciousness becoming involved!) cross the sea. Once more, the snake reveals its negative aspect, probably due to the insufficient participation of consciousness. The hero makes the mistake of asking the cat to resist the snake; the contrast between the hero's two animal natures—the cat, which, as a warm-blooded domestic animal, is closer to consciousness; and the snake, which, as a reptile, is removed from consciousness—makes him lose the treasure. The snake soon demands a *quid pro quo*, namely, "living fire," which is meant to bring the light of consciousness into the darkness of the unconscious. In his despair, the hero finds several helpers: two animals whose powers complement those of his companions. If these denote the instincts at one's disposal in a quiet life, then the fish symbolizes a deeply unconscious creature, while the eagle represents the conscious spirit.

470     Obtaining fire requires finding an appropriate vessel. Here, we probably ought to interpret this as the soul, which ingests the living fire of the spirit. It is raised from the sea because it rises from the unconscious to consciousness and envelops it. The material is clear and hard (like the crystal ship in "Connla's Sea Voyage"; Ireland, no. 2). It is also precious and corresponds to the symbol of the self. In nature, the diamond is consumed by fire. Yet the spirit (i.e., "living fire") does not harm the soul but lets itself be borne by it. The image of the living fire in the pan made of diamonds symbolizes the union

[432] *The Complete Grimm's Fairy Tales*, pp. 566–571.

of male and female. As such, it is the archetypal precursor of the union of the hero and the anima, of Dragojlo and Dragana.

471    Endowed with this highest value, the hero now crosses the sea himself, whereupon the snake princess—who now possesses the "living fire"—burns her animal skin. This motif is probably unique in fairytales. Reported quite straightforwardly, as a self-evident consequence of the hero's feat, it reveals the anima's yearning and humble devotion to the "living fire." Quite naturally, the hero receives the forever nourishing little cloth once the anima has been redeemed.[433]

472    The subsequent discussion between Dragojlo and Dragana (whose names indicate their predetermined affiliation) establishes that although the mother cursed the daughter first, the snake-demon thus summoned determined the duration and the condition of redemption. Her human father represents ruling, tradition-bound consciousness, which is powerless against the demonic antagonist. Therefore, the hero, who stands up to the demon, inherits the realm: As a renewing force familiar with both spheres, he dominates the personality.

473    In a series of poetic images, the fairytale describes with astonishing clarity an inner development: For the "widow's son," the old man's visit is the first encounter with the higher personality, the masculine spirit in the form of an ancient sage. Soon after the hero awakens from his unconscious state, the demonic anima-figure attacks him and demands that he renounce his mother and confront his psychic world aided by his instincts and spiritual powers to make his personality whole. Due to his conscious endeavor, which is "blessed" by the luminous father-image and unhindered by the mother, the power of the overpowering and therefore negative parent-imagos, which dominate the unconscious, is broken, and the psychic image is freed from its opacity.

---

[433] See Mrile, the hero of "The Tale of Mrile" (Africa, no. 9), who also brought fire into the magical realm and received cattle in return, a benefit corresponding to Dragojli's "little cloth." However, his weak consciousness prevented him from recognizing further values and even made him perish after his return.

474     In the fairytales considered here, as in those where an animal prince is redeemed, the spell is cast mostly by an evil mother.[434] By contrast, in those tales where an animal princess is redeemed, it is cast mostly by the archetypal evil father. Thus, he is blamed for bewitching the heroine, among others, in the passage about the maiden's quest in "The Mermaid or the Great Dubhdach" (Ireland, no. 29), as well as in "Allerleirauh" (Brothers Grimm) and "The Cat's Fur."[435] Significant in this context are the words of the old man who escorts the heroine in "The Frog Princess"; in Loepfe's version (*Russische*, p. 34), he tells Ivan why he was not permitted to burn the animal skin: "You neither gave it to her nor were you allowed to take it. Clever Vasilissa is cleverer and wiser than her father, who was therefore angry with her and told her to live as a frog for three years." This, as well as the anima-figure knowing about the curse, points to an existing conflict with the father-archetype, to which she seems beholden. The unconscious is willing to strive for detachment, or redemption, yet this evidently requires the hero to prove himself equal to his father.[436]

475     The anima's peculiar connection with the realm of a dark primordial spirit sets the stage in numerous fairytales. In many tales informed by Christian thinking, the anima is ruled by the devil, from whose clutches the hero must free her on his "Great Journey." One example is "In Hell,"[437] a Danube tale in which the devil is a "terrible dragon" that steals a king's daughter. Advised by an old woman, and equipped with her little stick, the feather of a black

---

[434] Note, however, that the father of the "false bride" plays a weaker role in "The Singing, Soaring Lark" (*The Complete Grimm's Fairy Tales*). This tale concludes by observing that the foreign king's daughter had bewitched the prince, whereupon "they both left the castle secretly in the night, for they feared the father of the princess, who was a sorcerer" (*ibid.*, p. 404). This indicates the existence of the primordial couple.

[435] Ehrentreich, *Englische Volksmärchen* (1938), p. 71. See also the woman's brother as the creator of the animal fur in "Yingeangeut and the Cloud People" (Siberia, no. 58): Ememqut, the "son of the creator," throws a dog's fur over his sister, Yingeangeut, when he leaves her alone in the tent to protect her from the young men. The envious one, however, envies Ememqut for his beautiful dog and plays with it, teasing it until it breaks free from the post to which it was tied. The dog runs until it is exhausted, then sheds its fur and once again becomes Yingeangeut, who after many adventures finally returns home to the creator-father.

[436] However, he is not equal yet because, among other things, he prematurely burns the animal skin. This probably explains why he must so often compete with the father-archetype in a magical contest, especially in connection with redeeming the anima. For more details, see the last section of *Archetypal Symbols in Fairytales*, vol. II, book 2.

[437] Zaunert, *Märchen aus dem Donaulande*, p. 16.

rooster, and the whiskers of a black goat, which should serve him as a passport, so to speak, the poor widow's son descends into hell. The little stick, as a magic wand, embodies mysterious nature, while the feather and the hair belong to animals that symbolize the devil, so that the hero, as so often, defeats evil through a related force, psychologically through expedient mastery, and by employing his own dark impulses. He kidnaps three royal daughters, one of whom he marries, who are being held captive by the "dragon." The fact that he must redeem three women corresponds to the same number in "The Golden Castle that Hung in the Air" (Norway, no. 35).

476

Another fairytale that considers the relationship between the anima and the demonic world in Christian thought is "The King's Black Daughter":

477

> An elderly royal couple remained childless, so the Queen prayed for a child before the crucifix situated on the right side of the bridge, but to no avail; she did the same on the left side of the bridge before the statue of Lucifer and received a little girl. "The King did not know he was guilty of this, but did not say much good or bad about it." The girl was pitch-black and grew up in twenty-four hours and said: "You unfortunate father and you unfortunate mother, now comes the unfortunate hour in which I must die. And when I am dead, bury me in the church behind the high altar in a tomb. And when I am buried, a man must stand guard at the tomb every night. And if he is absent once, things will not be well; and if this happens more often, things will become worse." Then she dropped dead. She was buried according to her wishes and every night her guard was torn to pieces. The King borrowed a regiment of soldiers from his brother-in-law, and one of the three brothers, Rudolf, was the first to stand guard. On the first night, after saying his prayers, he hid in the pulpit and made crosses on the steps. "When the clock struck eleven, she (the deceased princess) rose from the tomb as a fiery woman and exclaimed: 'Rudolf!' And when she did not find

him, she threw all the chairs on top of each other and struck down all the saints." She found Rudolf too late—the clock struck twelve and there she lay "black again, and the chairs and the saints were all back where they belonged." Rudolf was to keep watch for the second night; an old zither player on the street, who promised him that he would be happy, prevented him from deserting and advised him to hide behind the Mother of God. So he escaped like the first time. The third time, the old man, whom he found deserting again in the forest against his will, advised him to stand by the tomb with his eyes closed. And when the princess escaped, he should lie down in the tomb immediately and not leave despite her threats and pleas, even when she took him by the right hand and said: "Rudolf, get up!" He did as commanded, and at midnight the princess became a snow-white, beautiful, redeemed maiden, whom he married, and he became king.[438]

478  One variant, "The Soldier and the Black Princess," reports that

> … the royal couple received a fertility potion from an old woman and, while he was drinking it, the King said: "Drink, woman, in God's name with the devil all the time!" A black child was born to the couple. "The girl neither ate nor drank, neither laughed nor cried, neither screamed nor spoke; and yet she grew so fast that at the age of one she was already as tall as a five-year-old child. On her first birthday, the girl suddenly opened her mouth at the twelfth hour of the night on which she was born and cried: "Father!"—"What do you want, my child?" replied the king, startled.—"Now I speak for the first time," said the black princess, closed her mouth, and again fell silent. In the second year, the girl grew so tall that she looked like a ten-year-old. At the midnight hour of her second birthday she again exclaimed: "Father!"—"What do you want, my child?" asked the King more anxiously than

---

[438] Zaunert, *Märchen aus dem Donaulande*, p. 150.—Trans.

the first time.—"This is the second time I've spoken," his daughter replied, "but you'll be surprised when I open my mouth for the third time." With that, she closed her lips, and spent the third year as she had spent the first two years, except that at the end of the third year she had grown as tall and strong as a manly maiden. Before her third birthday, the king was deeply horrified, and he would have preferred to have been a hundred fathoms beneath the earth than to have this child. And yet, he had to endure this torment. When the bell struck twelve, the girl opened her mouth, as she had foretold, and said: "Father!"—"What do you want, my child?" replied the king, trembling. "Have an iron coffin made for me," said the princess, "lay me inside and place the coffin before the altar in the great cathedral. Every night a soldier must keep vigil at my coffin; if this does not happen, I will bring calamity after calamity upon your kingdom." Thereupon, she fell silent again, and the fearful king obeyed her order. The soldiers keeping watch disappeared without a trace in the morning. Finally, a soldier assigned to this duty wanted to escape. But when he had crossed mountains and fields and a beautiful meadow, all of a sudden a little man with a long gray beard stood before him, "but that was our dear Lord God, who no longer wanted to see the misery that the devil was causing every night." The little man persuaded the soldier to return and hide behind the organ before eleven o'clock and not to answer the princess's call. She rose and, with a imploring wail, looked for the guard to take pity on her. But just as she was about to pounce on him, the clock struck twelve and she had to return to the coffin. The next day, the delighted King offered the soldier three hundred thalers if he stood guard in the church on the following night. This time, the little man advised the soldier to hide beneath the altar. He heard the princess complain that she was hungry and wanted to devour the guard. But matters unfolded as they had previously. Once again, the King promised three hundred thalers, and the soldier kept watch for the third night and, on the advice of the little man, placed bread, wine, and roast meat on the bench beside the altar and crawled under the coffin. When she climbed out, he should lie down in the coffin. When she wanted to lie down in the coffin again at the stroke of twelve and found her place occupied, she grew very angry and threatened to tear the guard apart if he did not get out of the coffin. As advised by the little man, the soldier did not move. And so she began pleading and finally—as the little man had predicted—she asked the soldier that he inflict Christ's three wounds on her. After these words, she became snow-white and beautiful. She proffered her hand to the soldier and said that he had redeemed and freed her from the devil's clutches and that she was now no different from any other human child. They ate and drank bread, roast meat and wine. The King fetched them from the church, they celebrated their wedding, and the soldier inherited the kingdom.[439]

479   Here, the anima-figure is a real "child of the devil" or of Lucifer, the usurped bearer of light. She appears like a spirit of the dead; that is, she is so far removed from the profane world and spellbound by the demonic sphere that she barely has contact with life. This also explains why she thirsts for life, a hunger that is satisfied after she is redeemed by eating the food brought to her by the soldier. The fact that she is characterized as "fiery" in the Danube version recalls the burning log into which the girl who fell under Frau Trude's spell in the eponymous fairytale was transformed.[440]

480   As a "traveling musician," the zither player who advises Rudolf, a soldier, in "The King's Black Daughter,"[441] is close to the world of demons and represents a helpful shadow-figure. As a musician, he

---

[439] Zaunert, *Deutsche Märchen seit Grimm*, p. 189.—Trans. For further variants, see Bolte and Polívka, *Anmerkungen*, vol. 3, pp. 531ff. On this type of tale, see also Siuts, *Jenseitsmotive*, pp. 6–7, § 6: "Here the underworld is a mausoleum." For even more variants, Siuts refers primarily to Reinhold Köhler, *Kleinere Schriften zur Märchenkunde*, vol. 1, ed. Johannes Bolte (Weimar: Emil Felber, 1898), p. 320.
[440] *The Complete Grimm's Fairy Tales*, pp. 208–209.
[441] Zaunert, *Märchen aus dem Donaulande*, p. 150.

primarily serves the expression of feeling and thus also as a mediator in the confrontation with the anima.[442] In "The Soldier and the Black Princess," his place is taken by a little man with a gray beard, who is meant to function as "our dear Lord God" and as a magical figure, as the positive aspect of the chthonic spirit, and as the counteraspect of the demon who cursed the princess. In terms of her psyche, he is a paternal animus-figure that complements the frail old king and at the same time is the soldier's genius or self.

481     We will discuss the motif of hiding from demons in more detail in the final section of this volume. Therefore, only what concerns redemption is considered here. In the two versions mentioned above, the soldier hides on the pulpit behind the Mother of God, behind the organ, and beneath the altar. On each occasion, he thus attempts—without looking the demon in the eye—to hide, generally speaking, behind Christian rites, to "protect himself in advance." Inasmuch as these are feminine symbols, they correspond, psychologically speaking, to the anima's luminous aspect. He addresses this aspect in the woman whom he must redeem, yet thereby merely defers the outbreak of her demon. As the dark powers govern the cursed woman, she does not recognize the luminous ones. It is not until he demonstrates that he can comprehend her suffering and knows about her separation from the world and its dark background—the realm of the dead, whose lord is the antagonist—that he can redeem her. He tests this knowledge— which preconditions all action—by lying in the princess's coffin. Thus, he adapts to her situation and distances himself from the world and its desires; he knows that the coffin belongs to the essence of the woman who must be redeemed and that it protects her from the world (see the heroine's glass coffin in "Snow White").

482     By entering her essence, he goes far beyond hiding behind any cults and rituals. Figuratively, he dies and thus no longer adheres

---

[442] See "The Piper and the Puca" (Ireland, no. 26) and Sigurd, the musician, in "Sigurd and the Ghost" (Iceland, no. 54). On the connection of the figures across the bridge of feeling, see the variant "The Lovers" (Krauss, *Sagen und Märchen der Südslaven, in ihrem Verhältnis zu den Sagen und Märchen der übrigen indogermanischen Völkergruppen*, vol. 1, no. 93): A princess loved a soldier and died of love when the King sent him far away to prevent the marriage. After she had devoured a regiment, the King reinstated her beloved in the royal guard, whereupon he redeemed the princess.

consciously to the luminous and safeguarding symbols of the Beyond. Nevertheless, he is not afraid to reveal his conscious position and to experience the dark unconscious. His resolute action carries consciousness into the unconscious, light into darkness, and brings about redemption. His steadfast and deliberate resistance to the demonic forces makes the cursed woman realize that light is more powerful than darkness.[443] Thus, the hero's journey through the realm of death leads to the heroine's redemption, her accursedness to his maturation.

483     Especially in the Danube version of the fairytales discussed above, the anima indirectly becomes the devil's daughter. Some fairytales, which also apply Christian imagery to depict the liberation of the soul from dark matter, depict her entirely as a devil's daughter who dwells in hell. Her affiliation with the luminous world is represented by her need for redemption and by her associated inclination toward humankind and its consciousness. One example is "The King's Son and the Devil's Daughter":

484     A King promised the devil, who appeared as an unknown person, "a new rope" if he let him win the lost battle. The devil took "an iron scourge with four tails" and struck the four winds with it. A large number of soldiers gathered, with whose help the King won the war. It later transpired that it was not a new rope (Transylvanian: *e noa Sîl*), but "a new soul," and that the King had sold his son, who had been born in the meantime, to the devil. The devil later abducted the prince to hell and showed him "the infernal fire and said ... he would be thrown into this fire in the morning if he could not execute his instructions for that night. But there was a huge pond nearby. The devil demanded that the prince drain it during the night, turn it into meadow, mow the meadow, make hay, put the hay in barns so that it could be brought in

---

[443] This interpretation relates Christian fairytales to their original psychological, as it were, natural content, independently of the Christian idea that the demonic world is subordinated to the Christian powers. True to the nature of fairytales, only few contain symbols of the Christian doctrine or cult. In such tales, Christianity is sometimes assigned a positive role, sometimes a negative one, depending on the narrator's faith and times.

first thing in the morning. The devil then locked the King's son in a lonely chamber." But the devil's daughter, who brought the young man food, took pity on him and performed the task with the devil's four-tailed magic scourge.

485  The same events took place on the second night, when the prince was ordered to clear a forest, plant a vineyard, and harvest the grapes. On the third night, he had to "build a church with a dome and a cross that stands firm and holds together." However, the devil's servants, summoned by the devil's daughter's magic scourge, were unable to perform this task; "they erected half the church several times, but it kept collapsing; when it was almost completely finished, the dome was vaulted, and only the cross was missing at the top; but when the devils wanted to place it there, the whole church collapsed again. When the devil's daughter saw that everything was in vain and that time would soon lapse, she dismissed the devils and, without further delay, went to the King's son and cried: 'Get up, get up! I can still save you if you wish to be saved! I will turn myself into a white horse, so mount me quickly and I will carry you home.' No sooner had she said this than a white horse stood before the prince, who swung himself up and galloped off." When the devil discovered what had happened, he shouted: "My daughter! ... ha, she has human feelings! Now everything is clear to me; she has clogged my ears, she has performed the business as I told her by using my power for the sake of the wretched man and has now departed with him! Ha, wait, I will bring you both back in a moment!" An army of devils pursued the fugitives like a giant black cloud. The devil's daughter transformed herself into a church, her lover into the priest, and ordered him to sing without stopping. As he kept singing, "Lord, be with us! Lord, protect us!", the devils were unable to question him about the fugitives and returned home without achieving anything. But the prince of hell "saw the church in the distance and heard the singing so softly that

it pierced his soul." He ordered the church to be destroyed. Once again, a host of devils, like a dark cloud, even larger and more terrifying than before, approached the horse and its rider. The devil's daughter turned into an alder tree and the young man into a golden bird, which sang fearlessly: "I'm not afraid! I'm not afraid!"

486 They escaped a second time, but again the devil noticed the deceit and sent out the pursuers for a third time. The couple escaped their pursuers as a rice field and a quail, which called out: "God, be with us! God, be with us!" Thereupon, the devil himself began chasing them. He "soared ... into the air and rode after them. The devil's daughter and the King's son had already fled a good distance as horse and rider. Seven miles from the earthly kingdom, they heard such a violent storm and roaring sound as they had never heard before. The white horse said to its rider: 'Look back; what do you see?'—'A black spot in the sky, even blacker than the night, with fiery lightning flashing from it'—'Woe, oh woe! That is my father; if you do not faithfully do as I tell you, we are doomed. I'll turn into a big pond of milk and you into a duck. Keep swimming around in the middle and keep your head hidden; don't let yourself be tempted to pull your head out of the milk or swim ashore!" The devil could not harm them in this state, "for devils drown in pure milk. So he had no choice but to lure the duck to him with flattering words: 'Dear duckling, why are you always wandering around in the middle, look around you; look how beautiful it is where I am!' The duck neither heard nor saw anything for a long time, but gradually the desire to look out at least once began to stir inside. When the tempter continued to lure the duck, it looked up quickly, and the Evil One immediately abducted its face, so that it was as blind as a bat. The milk pond immediately became a little cloudy and began to ferment, and a plaintive voice came to the duck: 'Woe, woe! what have you done!" The duck now vowed not to be tempted by anything; the milk was not yet

cloudy enough for the devil to swim to it although he tried to. Thereupon, the devil turned into a large goose and slurped up the pond and the duck before "slowly wobbling home."— 'Now all is well,' said a voice from the milk to the duck, and the milk began to ferment and boil. The devil became increasingly sultry and nauseous; he struggled to move. "If only I were at home!" he sighed, but to no avail; the boiling milk had already inflated him. He staggered away a little further; all of a sudden, there was a loud crash: He had burst and disintegrated, and there stood the King's son and the devil's daughter in their youthful beauty and glory." And so, the couple returned home on the seventh day since the prince's descent into hell and celebrated a magnificent wedding.[444]

487    Not only is the bride's father a devil, but she even seems to have no human mother, which underlines her spiritual nature. Still, "she has human feelings," as the devil aptly says. Her role recalls that of the "devil's grandmother," who often takes pity on the hero in fairytales (e.g., "The Devil with the Three Golden Hairs"[445]). While in "The King's Black Daughter" the heroine herself is evil and attempts to corrupt the hero (apparently a curse urges her to do so), in the present fairytale the figure of Psyche, despite being the devil's daughter, is nevertheless divorced from the evil principle and acknowledged as a psychic force able to assist humans in their struggle to liberate themselves from evil. Her connection with evil can be severed, and she strives for this separation herself, thus reviving the ancient motif of the animal- or spectre-like anima who longs to be redeemed and become human.

488    The hero's fate, to have been sold to the powers of hell by his own father, is described in "The King of the Golden Mountain."[446] The power that magically enables the king to assert himself in life turns

---

[444] See Zaunert, *Deutsche Märchen seit Grimm*, p. 155.—Trans. The images in this fairytale suggest that Christian, late-Gnostic speculation has sneaked into the plot and employed the related archetypal motifs.
[445] *The Complete Grimm's Fairy Tales*, pp. 151–158.
[446] *Ibid.*, pp. 425–430.

out to be a demon, to whom human beings owe their strength in the profane world, yet to whom they have become psychologically enslaved without realizing. This prince of hell wields a four-tailed scourge, with which he whips together servants from all points of the compass; he thus possesses the symbol of the self (i.e., psychic wholeness), which, however, is still associated entirely with the dark roots of the psychic personality. Like the rod, the scourge or whip is a phallic symbol[447]; here, it symbolizes the primordial force of the chthonic demon. The psychic energy that enables the father to emerge victorious in life proves to be a dark power, which subjugates his actual being—the son. Only a heroic psychic effort can break the devilish spell; quite unexpectedly, the anima-figure intervenes to help the son. She takes the four-tailed miraculous scourge, with which she controls all demons, and thus carries out the instructions. Using the scourge, she takes possession of the creative force of the underworld ruler, so that her nature resembles that of the Great Mother. We can understand this four-tailed scourge as the anima's animus, as the symbol of the paternal spirit dominating her, while at the same time it represents the prince's shadow and his self. Thus, this symbol, which takes effect deep inside the unconscious, passes from the realm of darkness and evil into that of the helping anima-figure; it thus becomes an intrapsychic reality that lies closer to consciousness.

489    The tasks that the demon demands the hero to perform are revealing: They are "cultural works." The demonic world demands human consciousness to transform nature into values. Because only then does it recognize its superiority. The devil's desire is demiurgic. According to ancient tradition, the evil one creates the works of culture and civilization, just as Cain built cities. Here, however, the devil instrumentalizes the adverse hero: The association of the demonic sphere and consciousness means that the required cultural works are not created by the demiurge but by human beings. Moreover, the imminent deadline reveals that the tasks do not

---

[447] Jung, *Symbols of Transformation*, CW 5, § 577, 638. According to Bächtold-Stäubli under *Peitsche, peitschen* (whip, whipping), in popular belief the crack of a whip, like all noises, is said to ward off demons and evil spirits. In the present fairytale, matters are the other way round.

involve working concretely on outer nature, but instead magical, intrapsychic transformation, in which formed and differentiated values are wrested from the unconscious and where the instincts are made to serve human consciousness. This demands summoning more strength, which in turn requires the cooperation of the anima, who personifies the soul.

490      While the hero accomplishes the first two tasks with the help of the devil's daughter, the devilish servants are unable to perform the last task, the erection of an entire church. Here, the fairytale draws on Christian concepts, according to which the devils (which inhabit hell) cannot establish the symbols of Christian salvation in hell. Psychologically, this might be explained as follows: As the tasks served to consciously transform natural conditions, this succeeded by mustering all psychic forces. Ultimately, however, the demon demands that the highest religious symbols be handed over to him. If this happens, they would become governed by the unconscious forces. A devotional building originating in demonic impulses would correspond to an anti-church. Acting as a mirror-image (e.g., certain forms of intoxication), this would signal the renunciation of a conscious location beyond the unconscious world. The fact that the hero strives to perform the devil's ambivalent and treacherous task with the help of his soul and all its devilish urges shows that he, consciousness, faces the greatest possible danger and that failure is welcome. As the demonic force can rarely be overcome as long as the individual is under its spell, in its realm, only escaping can bring salvation, which the hero most certainly senses through his anima-bride. The anima therefore transforms into a white horse that carries the hero away as swiftly as the wind. In many myths, especially Indian ones, the white horse symbolizes the savior.[448] It embodies the positive and consciousness-inducing aspect of psychic energy and instinct.

491      The fact that the hero is carried away by the anima amounts to an escape—and seems the only way of resolving the situation. Thus,

---

[448] See the white horse in "Ferdinand the Faithful and Ferdinand the Faithful" (*The Complete Grimm's*) and the comparative material cited in our discussion (*Archetypal Symbols in Fairytales*, vol. 1, pp. 346ff.).

there are moments on the path of transformation and development in which a person, trusting their instinct and the sustaining powers of their soul, must first of all avoid confronting the principle of evil, because permanently engaging in conflict is "unbearable and inimical to life."[449] In the present fairytale, it might not even be about remaining locked in a conflict between good and evil. Rather, the hero, who as yet is unable to sufficiently prove that consciousness is superior to the unconscious powers, would be destroyed by the devil. If he fails to escape, his personality risks destruction.

492    This evasion, however, means that the problem is not permanently solved and that another confrontation ensues. This occurs as a so-called "transformative escape," whose goal is ultimate liberation from the demon through manifold transformations. Evident in many fairytales,[450] this motif and its meaning will be discussed in the final section of this volume. For the moment, it suffices to say that the connection between the hero and the heroine always symbolizes the self. In their impersonal forms, their *symbolic* meaning expresses itself as intrapsychic figures rather than as concrete ones. Time and again, their connection is a union of opposites, which withstands the danger of being torn asunder by conflict, by the onslaught of instinctual impulses represented by the host of devils. It represents an inner unity, as is also evident from the hero's consistent words, which concede no power to the devils. Together, they express a single-mindedness and steadfastness that spring from inner wholeness. The first pair of images—Church and priest—is an attempt to master the demons by ritual means, yet this succeeds only temporarily. On the other hand, the second and third pair of images—a tree with a little golden bird and a rice field with quails—are attempts to protect oneself with natural forces; the tree symbolizes rootedness, the rice field the bearing of fruit, and the bird spiritual freedom and mobility. However, not even these psychic forces suffice to make inner wholeness permanently unassailable.

---

[449] Jung, *Psychology and Alchemy*, CW 12, § 24.
[450] See, e.g., "The Wizard of Palermo" (Spain, no. 11).

493 The fourth(!) image is a pond with a duckling. Like all secretions, milk belongs to those substances to which magical properties are attributed and which therefore play a significant role in superstition. It is offered to gods, demons, and snakes; in mysticism, it is a means of attaining immortality; mixed with honey, it is ingested by religious novices (i.e., those newly born into religion). It is as important as blood, a symbol of fertility, and cathartic. It is the life potion of elves and vegetation goblins.[451] In alchemical symbolism, it represents both primordial matter and the essence of life.[452] From this comprehensive meaning of milk as a psychic-spiritual symbol emerges its identity with the anima and thus its capacity to obfuscate, to ferment, and to destroy evil. Therefore, the devil must perish from it. The duckling manifests the hero as a bird, that is, as a spiritual principle, which in this form eludes the grasp of the evil, chthonic powers. However, as the duckling belongs to the pond, to the anima, that is, to the psyche connected with the world, the devil manages to entice and thus blind it—which corresponds to a "blinding" by the shadow (as in the Grimm's "The Two Travelers").[453]

494 The human spirit can also be reached and perverted by evil. Consequently, "milk," as a symbol of psychic "innocence," becomes opaque. Crucially, however, the devil cannot catch the duck *alone*—which would burst asunder the opposites united in the self—and thus is forced to devour *both*, despite the opacity. Like geese in general, pelicans belong to the Great Mother. In this animal, the devil reveals his hermaphroditic aspect; his nature also contains the essence of a maternal, devouring monster; he is the devouring unconscious *par excellence*. Yet as the hero often defeats the monster from within during the night sea journey,[454] here his psychic force (anima) explodes the devil from within, so that he disintegrates, which enables the opposites to unite in human form as king and queen. The anima acts like a fermenting agent. Thus, the devil is defeated by the devil's daughter—according to the law of self-

---

[451] Bächtold-Stäubli under *Milch* (milk) and *Milchopfer* (milk sacrifice).
[452] Silberer, *Probleme der Mystik*, pp. 81 and 88.
[453] *The Complete Grimm's Fairy Tales*, pp. 486–496.
[454] See, e.g., "Djulek-Batür" (Turkestan, no. 7).

absorbing similarity; the sorrowful human involvement means that the poisoned soul, which adheres to the demonic sphere, is transformed into a healing power that releases humankind from the bondage of evil.

495    The dark being with which the anima-figure was associated in the fairytales considered above is represented, as it were, in various guises: The figures in which it appears in some fairytales suggest that they should be understood as the hero's shadow-figures (despite their paternal character), such as the giant in "The Lost Golden Shoe" (Iceland, no. 17) or the fettered brothers alluded to in "The Three Black Princesses."[455] Most fairytales, however (such as those where the anima is cursed or where she is the devil's daughter), portray the dark being as a figure that might be the hero's shadow, yet which, moreover, is an image of the chthonic spirit, whose demonic influence far exceeds those of a person's personal shadow. Occasionally, this dark power is divided into a friendly and a helping part. As observed, the helping part (e.g., the zither player in "The King's Black Daughter") represents the personal shadow, while the little gray man (e.g., "our dear Lord" in "The Soldier and the Black Princess") rather emphasizes this figure's superhuman, divine aspect.[456] Thus, the anima problem is subtly interwoven with the man's shadow problem, and with the fact that the latter reaches deep down into religious depths.

496    One fairytale that vividly illumines these manifoldly interwoven questions is "The Comrade" (Norway, no. 7):

497    "Once upon a time, a peasant boy dreamed that he would have a princess, far, far away, and that she would be as white as milk and as red as blood and so rich that her wealth would be infinite." He sold all his possessions, set off in search of the princess and, "one winter, he finally arrived in a land where all the roads were straight and did not bend at all." In a town, he saw a lump of ice in front of a church door and a corpse

[455] *The Complete Grimm's Fairy Tales*, pp. 620–621.
[456] Zaunert, *Märchen aus dem Donaulande*, p, 150, and *ibid.*, *Deutsche Märchen seit Grimm*, p. 189.

inside, and the entire congregation spat on the dead body as it filed by. The priest told the young fellow that this wretched miscreant was being displayed in public as a sign of contempt: This man, a wine merchant, had poured water into the wine. The young man asked whether the condemned man, who had been executed, could not be given a Christian burial and thus be able to rest in peace, and that his remaining funds would pay for his burial. He had not walked far when a man came up behind him, struck up a conversation, and offered himself as his servant. The young fellow refused, but the man said: "But you need a servant, I know that better than you do ... and you need someone whom you can rely on in life and death. But if you don't want me as your servant, then at least take me as a companion; I promise that it won't be your loss, and I won't cost you a shilling. I'll travel at my own expense, and you needn't worry about food and clothes."

498    The young fellow agreed and his companion led the way. After a while, they suddenly came to a high rock. The companion knocked and the rock opened. After they had entered the mountain, a witch approached them and offered them a chair. "You sit down!" the companion said to the witch. She did as she was told and remained seated because the chair held everything in place. The companion asked the witch for a sword, which was hanging above the door, and said that he would free her from the chair. The witch screamed and at first refused to give him the "sword of the three sisters" (which belonged to her and her two sisters), but finally she obliged. But the companion abandoned her nevertheless.

499    After wandering another fair stretch of the road, the two comrades reached another rock and, once again, the witch suffered the same fate as her sister. Except that this time, it was a ball of golden thread that the comrade was looking for and eventually found in the mountain. In the third mountain,

with the third witch, the comrade found an old hat. —In the end, the wanderers came to a river. "The comrade took the ball of thread and threw it so hard at the mountain on the other side of the river that it came flying back; after it had flown back and forth several times, a bridge stood before them." After crossing the river, the young fellow had to quickly rewind the golden thread, so that the three witches could not tear it to pieces. When he managed to do this, and the witches, who were scurrying to grasp the end of the thread, drowned in the river.

500 Thereupon, the wanderers reached a castle, and the comrade said it was the home of the princess about whom the youth had dreamed, and that he should tell the King about his dream and his destination. The young fellow was well received and immediately recognized the princess at the table. But she said that although she would gladly accept him, he would first have to pass three tests. The first was to keep the princess's golden scissors, which she gave him, in his safekeeping and return them to her the following day. This test was not simple, she said smiling, but if he did not pass it, he would have to die just like so many other suitors. The young fellow believed that the test was simple but did not notice how the princess, while joking and flirting with him, secretly snatched the scissors from him. Only when his comrade asked him for the scissors that evening did he realize what had happened. The comrade comforted the despondent young fellow and attempted to retrieve the scissors. He went into the stable where the princess's mighty goat, which could fly through the air, was standing. Striking the goat twice between its horns with the sword of the three sisters, the comrade persuaded the goat to tell him that the princess would be out riding at eleven o'clock. The companion put on the three sisters' hat and became invisible. The princess rubbed the goat with ointment and exclaimed: "Up! Up! Over gable and tower, over land, over sea, over

mountain and valley, to my beloved, who is awaiting me in the mountain!" As the goat soared into the sky, the companion swung up behind it, and they journeyed as swiftly as the wind to a rock on which the princess knocked and stepped into the mountain to her beloved, a troll. She told him about the suitor and gave the scissors to the troll, who laughed and placed them in a shrine with three locks. At that moment, the companion took the scissors away. The troll carefully hid the keys to the shrine in a hollow tooth. At midnight, the princess and her companion returned home. The following afternoon, the princess pertly demanded the scissors and received them.

501　Although she was frightened, she gave the young fellow a ball of golden thread as a second test with a sweet voice. As before, the princess took off at midnight. To make it impossible for the suitor to perform his tricks, the princess and the troll decided to burn the ball of thread. But when they threw it into the fire, the companion caught it; as morning approached, they began their journey home; at noon, when the princess asked the young fellow about the ball, he threw it onto the table, and the crashing noise startled the King.

502　The princess, now as white as a corpse, announced the last test: The suitor was to procure what she had in mind by noon the next day. The comrade was barely able to calm the desperate young fellow, but he finally fell asleep. At one o'clock, the companion mounted the goat and blew the princess through the air during the ride. In the mountain, she complained about being so upset by the weather, recounted everything that had happened, and said that she was thinking about her beloved's head. It would be impossible for the suitor to obtain it. The troll "laughed and indulged his malicious glee." Towards morning, the princess wanted to return home. But she was afraid and believed that someone was persuing her and did not dare to travel home alone. The troll therefore accompanied her on his goat. The companion sat behind the troll and flogged the goat so hard that it flew lower and lower and almost fell into the sea. The troll protected the princess and accompanied her to the castle. As she was closing the door behind her, the companion cut off the troll's head and took it to the young fellow in the chamber. The following day, when the princess asked what she had been thinking about, the young fellow hurled the head across the room so that the table toppled over. Pale as death, the princess had to agree to marry the young fellow. Their wedding overjoyed everyone in the kingdom.

But the comrade warned the young fellow that if he loved his life, he should not shut an eye on his wedding night until the princess had been freed from her trollish skin. "He should whip the skin off her with nine new birch rods and rub it off in three milk baths; first, he should scrub the skin off in a tub of mature whey, then rub it off in a tub of sour milk, and finally wash it off in a tub of sweet milk. He had placed the birch rods beneath the bed and the three tubs of milk in the corner ..." That night, the young fellow pretended to be sleeping when the princess pulled out a large butcher's knife and wanted to cut off his head. He grabbed her and did exactly as his comrade had told him. In the whey bucket, he saw that her body was "pitch black." But after the trollish skin had been removed, the princess became more beautiful than ever.

The following day, they set off for the young fellow's home. During the night, the companion had brought all of the troll's treasures from the mountain to the castle, and the whole courtyard was brimming. "This dowry is worth more than all the King's land ..." To transport everything home, the companion loaded the troll's six goats, which struggled under their heavy load and could go no further. The companion loaded the entire dowry and the goats onto his back and carried everything to the vicinity of the young fellow's home.

There he insisted on bidding farewell. When the young fellow asked what his companion wanted in return for all his help, the latter said: "If I am to make a wish, I would like half of everything you gain in the next five years." He was promised this. After five years, when he returned, the young man divided all his possessions into two halves. "But," said the companion, "there's one thing you haven't divided," by which he meant the child that the man had fathered in the meantime. The man raised his sword to cut the child in two, but the companion grabbed the tip of the sword and prevented this. "Aren't you glad you didn't have to strike the child?" he asked. "Yes, I have never been happier," said the man. "I was also so happy when you freed me from the lump of ice." He revealed himself as a ghost, and the young man kept his possessions. The comrade left forever, "for now the bells of heaven were calling him."[457]

Another version of this material is "The Cursed Princess."[458] Rather than reporting that tale in detail, let us discuss some of its significant episodes. The "comrade" is not a criminal, but a poor man whose funeral is paid for by Peter, the hero. The man seems "so good and well-behaved" that the hero immediately befriends him.[459] The princess is referred to explicitly as enchanted.

"... a black flag was flying on top of the castle as a sign of mourning. Peter asked why that was. The people replied: The princess was bewitched by a mountain spirit, was quiet and introverted during the day, but sometimes so wicked that she smashed and killed everything that she encountered; those who dared to redeem her would die unless they could solve the riddle she gave him. Many a handsome prince had already perished at her hands, as had many other good fellows, so that for over a year no one had been found who

---

[457] Translator's note: I have adjusted the paragraphing to improve readability.
[458] Zaunert, *Deutsche Märchen seit Grimm*, p. 237.
[459] It is probably a formal error that he identifies himself immediately as the "grateful dead man."

would have redeemed her; and yet, she had been (and still was) so beautiful and good-natured." On the advice of his companion, Peter volunteered to solve the riddle and they discussed the forthcoming adventure. "Peter's companion fetched a jar and a pair of large wings from his knapsack and a rather slender, iron rod. The spirit told Peter to undress and spread the ointment that was in the jar on his shoulders and mounted the wings on them. Then he said, 'Now fly to the princess's chamber window and watch out when she comes out; beat her with the rod, fly wherever she flies, and sneak in wherever she enters. Thereafter, you must hide and listen to what the mountain spirit says. She will tell the spirit everything and also ask it what riddle she should give you. Listen carefully and remain silent.'" Peter did as he was told, found the princess with her wings on, flew after her, and gave her a terrible beating with his rod. "At long last, they reached a high mountain, which opened up and they both flew inside. 'Now I must be careful,' thought Peter and crept into the great hall, where a large altar stood by the door. He hid behind the altar, so that he could hear everything and escape immediately if things got bad, or when it was time to leave. The princess ran up to the mountain spirit, who embraced her. It was an old man with a white beard and whose eyes glowed like the embers of a fire. He was so fierce and dangerous that Peter was truly frightened and began to regret having followed the princess. But he could neither move nor leave. The door had disappeared and a large rock lay where there instead. Eventually, the mountain spirit said to the princess, 'You haven't been there for a long time, you haven't killed anyone for a long time, you haven't been able to rejoice in the blood of your saviors for a long time. Has another bird flown into the trap?'—'Yes,' she replied, 'there is another one, but only an ordinary man, neither a prince, nor a count nor a nobleman. But a violent hailstorm is raging outside. See, my noble spirit, how I am torn and shattered by the hailstones,' and blood flowed down her body. 'Do nothing,' said the mountain spirit, 'the more you must torment your human being, the more pleasure you must take in his blood, the more you must drink of it, the sooner you will become pure for me and mine.'—But what riddle shall I ask him, what shall I think of?' said the princess. 'Think of your father's white horse,' replied the mountain spirit. 'All right,' said the princess, and begged, 'Let me out, for it is three-quarters to twelve, I have a long way to fly, and you know that twelve o'clock is fast approaching.'" On the way home, Peter beat the princess again, and the next morning he announced himself to her; "she was sitting in a beautiful room on a little sofa, and looked quite sad, but was a very lovely girl. Her eyes were so gentle and good; she was not tall and strong, but finely and gracefully built; it was impossible to believe that she had killed anyone, and yet nine men had already lost their lives at her hands." When Peter guessed her riddle, she turned pale, but ordered him to return the following day. The second night was like the first one, except that this time Peter beat her with two rods. "But when they came to the mountain and entered the hall, the room was lit more brightly than on the previous night; at its center stood the moon, whose light suffused everything, and on the altar lay a large spiny fish. The night before, merely a few stars had appeared on the ceiling and the altar had been empty. When the princess entered the room again, and after Peter had sneaked in behind her, the door closed; the princess approached the mountain spirit, who was sitting on a sort of throne, and said: 'High spirit, the man has guessed our first riddle. What do you say to that?'"—'This is not right. A secret power is at work here that is repugnant to me and to you. But this time, it shall not guess our riddle. This time you should think of your father's battle sword.'"

507 Peter guessed the riddle again, and the final test followed. This time, on the advice of his ghostly companion, the hero took two iron rods and another double-edged sword to behead the mountain spirit. He had been warned to hide himself very well, because everything would become very bright. Once again, he beat the princess on the way. "When they entered the great hall together, the sun was shining on the ceiling and everything was as bright as during daytime; on the altar lay the spiny fish and stood a fiery wheel, yet behind the altar everything was dark, and Peter was hiding there. The princess went hastily to the mountain spirit, threw herself around his neck, and said, desperately: 'His guess was correct again!'—'That is bad,' said the spirit; 'so think of my head this time. No mortal can think of that, least of all an ordinary man.' But Peter cut off the spirit's head before it flew away. The following morning, the princess asked "in a trembling voice, as if her life or death depended on it: 'What am I thinking of?' Without answering, he untied the hand-kerchief and placed the head of the mountain spirit on the table. The princess exclaimed, 'My savior!', and fainted in his arms. He laid her on the sofa and rang the bell. Immediately, servants arrived; the King was called, and so were the doctors. When the princess regained consciousness, the King gave his daughter to Peter as his wife." On the advice of his comrade, he had to immerse the princess in a tub of water on the bridal night, from which she flew away as a raven. When he immersed her in the water, she became a dove, and the third time she emerged in her former angelic beauty and piety and was now redeemed forever. The companion, however, disappeared from the world.

508 The initial episode contains the widespread motif of the "grateful dead,"[460] which sometimes also appears in other types of fairytales.

---

[460] This motif occurs frequently in literary texts. See Bolte and Polívka, *Anmerkungen*, vol. 3, pp. 490ff., esp. the examples mentioned on p. 494, fn. 1, which refer to Köhler, *Kleinere Schriften*, vol. 1, pp. 5–39. For a similar collection of materials, see *ibid.*, pp. 5 and 21, nos. 3 and 4 ("The Grateful Dead and Good Gerhard" and "The Tale about the Grateful Dead").

As our discussion of the realm of the dead has shown, we can understand the ghost motifs in fairytales in two ways. On the one hand, they might be based on real conditions, such as those studied by parapsychological research while, on the other, most empirical reports of such phenomena plainly indicate additions, which originate in the unconscious psyche of those having such experiences: Ghosts often represent archetypal figures (e.g., the anima, shadows), which fairytales report in dreamlike sequences, unaffected by the spirits of the dead, and which therefore can only be interpreted by referring to the individual's psychic system.

509     Thus, the "grateful dead man" represents the "shadow," as evidenced by the fact that he often appears as "inferior," as a criminal, or as a sinner[461] (in addition to being a "poor soul"). Sometimes, he also appears as a helpful animal (e.g., a fox). His role as a companion of shadows is familiar from "The Golden Bird" (a classic example) and several other fairytales.[462] In one instance, he is also the hero's brother,[463] who also often plays the shadow[464]; in this case, the inner identity with the hero is indicated by kinship. Sometimes, the dead man is also characterized as "poor," suggesting that the shadow is not really evil, but rather "the poor devil inside us." It is, in other words, that part of our soul that is unable to participate in the living wealth of the world, because it has been discarded by the ego and by profanity. In most cases, the motif of the dead person's unsettled debts is added to their poverty. This, too, is psychologically revealing: "Debts" are associated with "guilt" and, for those concerned, they signify what they are due, yet are denied. Money, however, symbolizes power and life, and thus indicates that

---

[461] See, e.g., "The Sinner and the King's Son" (Finland, no. 22): On his quest for a bride, a King's son ransomed a sinner outside a church door, whom passers-by were supposed to spit on. In return, the priest demanded and received the prince's entire property and entourage. On his travels, the prince was joined by a beggar boy, who raised the funds to pay for their night's lodging. The boy also saved the prince's life by spending the first three nights with him while he courted a King's daughter whose suitors were usually slain by a goblin. After the wedding, the boy disappeared, for he was an angel of God.

[462] *The Complete Grimm's Fairy Tales*, pp. 272–279. For examples of ghosts and shades (i.e., spirits of the dead) appearing as animals, see Bolte and Polívka, *Anmerkungen*, vol. 3: as a fox (pp. 494, 502); as a bird (pp. 495–497, 500, 501, 505, 506); as a wolf (p. 503); as a fish (p. 496); as a hare (p. 500), as a black dog (p. 503); as a beetle (p. 504); but also as a stone (p. 506). See also "The Grateful Dead Man" (Zaunert, *Deutsche Märchen seit Grimm*, p. 245).

[463] Bolte and Polívka, *Anmerkungen*, vol. 3, p. 504.

[464] See, e.g., "Three Stories about the Brothers To Kabinana and To Karwuwu" (South Sea Islands, no. 16) and "Women's Words Separate Flesh and Bone" (China, no. 1).

the shadow has unjustly failed to release something of value. Unlived life preys on the dead man (and thus also on consciousness).[465] However noble the hero's gesture,[466] psychologically it is quite natural that he pays the stranger's debts: After all, they are *his* debts. *He* is responsible that the shadow has participated insufficiently in the human community and is unable to find peace. He ransoms himself from *his* inner restlessness.[467]

510    The fact that the shadow-figure is described as "dead" suggests utmost repression. This becomes plainly evident in the present Norwegian version, where this figure is also transformed into a lump of ice; any emotional contact has "died" completely. Related to the shadow motif of these fairytales is "The Story of the Indian King with the Corpse" (an Indian tale where a king must carry a corpse several times over an execution site. As the king's answers and behavior satisfy the spirit inhabiting the corpse, it helps the king overcome a demon that is secretly threatening him). Heinrich Zimmer has aptly described the meaning of this corpse:

511    ... we all carry this corpse on our shoulders: something that has been, something that is decaying, and yet is one of our egos—one of how many? A cipher and a part of our being.

---

[465] This is also the psychological background of the motif, so prevalent in folklore, of the dead man who finds no rest in the grave until certain deeds are atoned for.

[466] Rohde, *Psyche* (1910), vol. 1, pp. 216ff., on the "obligation of those who survive to the dead ... to bury their body" (in Greek antiquity): "The religious precept extends beyond the law." Whoever left a body unburied was cursed. A symbolic burial suffices to avert "abomination." Already in the *Iliad*, the soul of the unburied finds no rest in the afterlife and stalks the world as a ghost.

[467] For an intriguing inversion of the motif of the dead man who is hanged, see "The Priest's Ghost" (Spain, no. 25): After a very long time, a mother's wish to give birth to a son was granted. At the same time, however, it was prophesied that he would be hanged when he reached the age of twenty-one. When the young man ventured into the world, his anxious mother demanded that he should attend the first mass in every village he came to. He pretended to do so until finally, in one village, he went to a midnight mass that no one else ever attended. As he entered the church, he saw a skeleton rise from a grave and walk to the vestry. The young man helped this figure put on priestly robes and read the mass. When the mass was over, the dead man revealed himself as the ghost of a priest who had sinned, and who the young man had set free and would protect in return. When the day came on which the young man was supposed to be hanged, as had been prophesied, he encountered a band of thieves who were sharing stolen loot among themselves. He stole the booty from them and rode away on the white horse that had been given to him by the priest's spirit. But the thieves caught up with him and hung him. As soon as they had disappeared, the priest's spirit untied the young man, who was able to return home safely.—In most fairytales, the "grateful dead man" and the hanged man are one and the same. Here, however, the priest is the "grateful dead man" *and* the sinner, while the hero is the hanged man. The hero is a thief, even if his guilt seems mitigated by the fact that he steals from thieves. This strange variation of the motif of the "grateful dead man," according to which the hero can also be hanged, not just the dead man, is particularly well-suited to demonstrating the identity of these two figures.

And the ghost chattering from within that being —how much is that an ego of ours, behind and above the royal one we are conscious of, and which is the strongest of all: With its ghostly voice, it threatens us with a quick death and imposes conditions, chases us hither and thither to fetch its dead, just as one who is transfixed by an idea must repeat, nonsensically and infinitely, a part of the past ... It appears uncanny and disdainful, as adverse and as grotesque as much as surprising. How could it seem otherwise to us? After all, is it not the epitome of what we have neglected, never completed? Is it not the ghost of unconsciously accumulated guilt? It is also the savior that wishes us well, the only thing in the world and in the darkness of our being that can save us from its evil magic, since we were able to submit to its wilful game and patiently did what was imposed upon us as if to mock and test us. It is the most knowing of all the forms of our being, which skirts around us in so many guises and breaks out of us ... The power that forgets nothing and knows everything in advance on account of its fathomless knowledge, and which snatches us with a blink of an eye from the abyss toward which our conscious being consistently strives. It is much more capable than our royal ego, capable of everything ... The tangible king and the intangible ghost, this world and the world beyond, the royal ego of the day and the ghostly voice of our profoundest darkness, belong together. They cannot exist without each other without both withering away: They are a living whole. If they did not act in unison, they would be lost: The decisive action must be taken by the King, the self-conscious and corporeal side of our being; and yet, the decisive inspiration is whispered by the ghostly voice of our intangible sphere. And so, they both set each other free: The spectre delivers the King from death through the blindness of bare consciousness, while the King delivers the spectre from the spell of its existence as a ghost condemned to dwell in the corpse of what has been.[468]

---

[468] Zimmer, *Weisheit Indiens* (Darmstadt, 1938), p. 95f. —Trans.

512 A Latvian fairytale, "The Corpse" (no. 8), tells a similar story: A servant courts a girl, who wants to deceive him, however, and demands that he must first earn enough money in a foreign land. He leaves and spends the night in an inn, where he is repeatedly disturbed in his sleep until he discovers a dried corpse hanging from a rope behind the stove. He leaves immediately, yet is stopped by the innkeeper, who suspects him of theft and denies the existence of the corpse.

513 They both returned to the inn, turned on the light, and stepped behind the stove: The servant saw the corpse, but the innkeeper did not. How silly, thought the servant, because how could he convince the innkeeper? Finally, the servant had a good idea: He drew his sword and cut the rope. Plop! The corpse fell down and now the innkeeper also saw it. The man was well and truly dead. They buried the body the next morning.

514 After the funeral, the young fellow spends another week at the inn (at the innkeeper's request). There being no longer any sign of haunting, he can continue his journey, richly rewarded. On the way, he meets the dead man who, out of gratitude, accompanies the young fellow, saves him from the antics of the evil bride, and helps him find the right woman.[469]

515 Here, too, detaching the corpse from its suspended state proves significant: This position now also becomes visible to "profane" people, whereas before it was only visible to those with a calling. Contact with the earth means becoming concrete. Before, the repressed shadow is literally suspended and therefore incomprehensible, half-real. When the hero "strikes," that is, consciously decides to sever the shadow from the unconscious, he makes it tangible, which indicates that psychic facts can be distinguished solely in a conscious state. The figures separated in consciousness—

---

[469] In "The Merchant's Son" (Wisser, *Plattdeutsche*, vol. 1, p. 107), a Low-German fairytale whose beginning parallels that of the aforementioned Latvian one, the hanged man has debts and therefore has been hung in the smokestack.

for instance, the shadow, the anima, the Great Mother, the old man—are amalgmated in the unconscious and have a mysterious "haunting" effect—without, however, being recognized as the cause. If the shadow can be separated from the unconscious, it can be recognized as autonomous and taken into account. Consciousness, of course, remains responsible for the shadow associated with it. However, it is through differentiation, that is, by recognizing the shadow as a counterpart that it comes into its own and thus can exert a positive effect. Cutting down the hanged man with the sword in the above fairytale signifies such differentiation. If, generally speaking, the hero settles the dead man's debts, he does the right thing, because he takes responsibility for his companion, that is, for the figure that is effectively a part of him.

516     In some cases, the creditor is still alive, in others he is dead. In "'Load and Fire!'" (Finland, no. 35), the hero finds two dead men who are quarreling because one owes the other a hundred thalers. He settles the dispute by paying the debt. In this case, the dead represent an intrapsychic opposition, of which only one side has been lived so far. Thus, in terms of inner wholeness, one part of the psyche owes the other part a piece of life. Consciousness must intervene and seek to achieve a just solution through its own sacrifices.[470]

517     A Caucasian fairytale, "The Faithful Servant" (no. 17), combines this motif with that of succeeding the throne, which we have discussed as a concluding episode and as an outcome of many fairytales[471]: To test their character, a king gives each of his three sons the same sum of money, and instructs them to use it as they see fit. While the two older sons squander their money, the youngest one embarks on a journey. In a cemetery, he sees a man beating a grave with a stick[472] because the man buried there owes him seventy rubles. The king's son pays the debt and returns home. The king is

---

[470] The motif has a similar meaning to resolving fights between animals over prey. Like every instinct, every aspect of the shadow should be given its due share of the goods of life, through which that aspect becomes helpful.

[471] See *Archetypal Symbolism in Fairytales*, vol. 2 ("The Hero's Journey").

[472] See Dirr, *Kaukasische Märchen* (1922), p. 88, fn. 1: "According to Caucasian belief, this is the greatest insult that can be inflicted on a dead person."

angry with the older sons, but gives the youngest one a house and money and asks him to keep a servant. He should, however, only "take one, who, when instructed at dinner, 'Come here, eat with me,' will not obey your command."

518    Only the third servant is as modest as required and is hired for seventy rubles. When the prince leads a caravan to a neighboring country, the servant, whose service his master has come to esteem, persuades the latter to choose the shorter and more dangerous of two paths. During a nightly encampment, the prince's dog starts barking at midnight; the servant, who is standing guard, hears a voice call out to the dog: "Hey, dog, your master will probably soon kill you and smear your blood on his eye, so let me take his possessions." Yet because the servant and the dog are keeping watch, the journey continues in the morning. On their way home, they spend the night in the same place, where the same events recur. On this occasion, the servant wakes the prince and asks him to follow the voice with him. Following a man who escapes the camp and disappears into a hole in the ground, the servant comes across three girls who are surrounded by treasures. He kills seven *divs* (desert demons) and takes their ears, thus freeing the three girls. The servant returns to the upper world together with the maidens and the treasures. Back home, the prince discovers that his father has gone blind and that his sisters have lost their minds after hearing that he had chosen the more dangerous path. One day, while out hunting, the servant kills the dog and dips his handkerchief in the animal's blood. Out of love for his servant, the prince remains silent. A few days later, the servant says: "My time is coming to an end. You three brothers must now marry the three girls we have taken from the *div* pit." And precisely that is what happens. Toward the end of the agreed year of service, which the servant chooses not to extend, the prince takes him for a walk to the cemetery where the grave was once desecrated.

519    As they approached, they saw light coming out of a grave; it was a fresh, well prepared grave. Climbing in, the servant

said: "I want to see if it fits me." He lay down in the grave, and it fit him perfectly. Even the prince said: "It is as if this grave were meant for you.' 'Give me your hand and help me out,' said the servant, and when the prince proffered his hand, the servant put the seventy rubles and the blood-soaked handkerchief in it and said, 'Smear the blood on your father's eyes and boil the *divs'* ears in water and give it to your sister to drink; then your father will regain his sight and your sister will be well again. Your father should leave his throne to you.' After he had uttered these words, the grave closed. The prince felt very sorry for his servant and returned home deeply saddened. Nevertheless, he immediately carried out his servant's orders, and his father's face once again had eyes, and his sister regained her mind. The old king stepped down from the throne and his youngest son took his place and ruled for the good of his subjects.

520    This course of events suggests that the father ceding the throne to the son is related to the nature of the servant and the dead man because succession takes place precisely after he has performed his task. Once more, the old king represents prevailing consciousness, whose one-sidedness had gradually caused his "blindness," so that it needs to be "complemented" by the unconscious. The father is therefore later replaced by the hero, who at first seems to be his shadow, yet steadily develops into a new inner personality, in which the self and the ego coincide.

521    The dead man, or rather the servant, in the Caucasian fairytale corresponds somewhat to the fox in "The Golden Bird."[473] As a dead debtor, however, he is an inanimate part of the soul: that part of the soul that previous, one-sided consciousness (i.e., the old king) prevented from living and working. After the son, who represents the new union, has developed, and after he has permitted and

---

[473] *The Complete Grimm's Fairy Tales*, pp. 272–279. For example, in "The Story of the Blind King Who Dwelt in the Westlands" (Malay, no. 43), the fox is replaced by a bird that represents the soul of a grateful dead man. The fox is also replaced by a bird in numerous variants on "The Golden Bird"; see Bolte and Polívka, *Anmerkungen*, vol. 1, pp. 504, 506–507.

enabled the shadow of the old king, that is, of the total personality, which has been repressed into the unconscious, to take effect as intended, both opposites, which condition each other, are eliminated: the old king and his compensatory figure, the dead man. Both disappear, albeit not tragically this time, but peacefully. The problem of opposites, depicted differently in "'Load and Fire!'" (Finland, no. 35), namely, as a quarrel between two dead persons, and which many other fairytales describe merely as the secret suffering of an old king and an animal-helper, is resolved by the hero's development.

522    Thus, the animal-helper (e.g., the fox in "The Golden Bird") and the grateful dead man in the fairytales analyzed above are related; as are the fate of these magical helpers and the problem of the old and suffering father-king. These connections are also illustrated by "The Red Fish" (Caucasus, no. 18): Physicians tell a blind king that "a colorful fish with a horn on its head is swimming in the white sea and is called 'The Red Fish.' If one could catch it and paint the king's eyes with its blood, he would regain his sight." The king sends his son to catch the fish. When the son and some fishermen catch the fish after a tremendous effort, it is so beautiful that they throw it back into the sea without telling the king. However, when the king's son beats one of his father's Moorish servants, the poor fellow avenges himself by betraying the secret to the king. Angered by this news, the father banishes his son from the kingdom. When the young man bids his mother farewell, he tells her:

523    If a man follows you on the road, stop and pretend that you were going to piss; if he comes up to you, take him as a companion; if he gives you more than he takes at dinner, become friends; if he stands guard at night when you go to sleep, pretend you were asleep; if he stays awake, stay his friend!

524    The king's son does as he is told and befriends a stranger. Together, they come to a royal court. The friend tells a riddle and makes the king's mute daughter speak, whereupon the king gives her to the

prince as his wife. On the wedding night, the friend slays a monstrous serpent that is crawling through the window into the bridal chamber. When the young couple and the friend return home, the king gives them many servants, female slaves, camels, and treasures. When they reach the place where the friend had joined the king's son, the friend demands that the possessions be shared. After the servants and treasures have been divided, only the king's daughter remains. "We must split her in half," says the friend. Although the king's son begs the friend not to kill the young woman, but instead to take her whole, the friend ties her to a tree and threatens her with his diamond sword. Fearing for her life, she vomits snakes. The friend explains that a snake had slept with her every night and that its breath had made her pregnant and mute.

525 "Now I must leave you. I give you my share. Your father is blind; take a little earth from my horse's hoof and sprinkle it on your father's eyes, and the light will return to them. You will see me no more; I am the fish that you did not allow to be killed." No sooner had he spoken these words than he disappeared. But the King's son returned home with all his possessions, servants, slaves, camels, valuables, and his young wife. He smeared his father's eyes with a little earth from the hoof of his companion's horse, and the old king immediately regained his sight. And ... that is the end of this fairytale.

526 The fish is also spared in "The Bird Called Flower Trill,"[474] a Persian variant of "The Golden Bird": A physician prescribes a sick sultan a green fish with a golden ring in its mouth. The fish, says the physician, must be caught, and if pieces of it are placed on the sultan's heart, he will recover. The fishermen bring the fish to the king's youngest son, who is amazed at its beauty and discovers a pious saying on its forehead. Deeply moved by the words, he has the fish thrown back into the sea. Angered by his son's decision, the sultan disinherits him, and his illness grows worse. He only recovers when the youngest son,

[474] Christensen, *Iran*, p. 44.

after many adventures, brings him a bird called Flower Trill, whereupon the king declares the hero to be his heir.

527      When the old and suffering father-king realizes that only the fish can cure him, he is on the right path: The fish represents—as its identity with the "grateful dead man" indicates—the shadow, an unlived part of the soul, that part that fatefully takes effect as the self. Although his understanding is correct, the old king, somewhat remarkably, cannot find a solution because he wants to kill the fish and capture its living essence in a form that is comprehensible and familiar to the profane world because he believes that he can thus assimilate its healing power. His rigid, one-sided attitude renders him unable to deal peacefully with the opposition within himself. Only capable of either-or reasoning, and despite recognizing the shadow, the king strives to forcibly assimilate it to himself and his kin. In so doing, he refuses to transform the shadow—and thus himself—by turning toward it. This would require accepting one's counterpart and its actions as they are, without succumbing to them. Only the hero is capable of this, that is, of that core of the personality in which consciousness and unconsciousness coincide.

528      These tales also reveal a close relationship, indeed identity, between two motifs: that of the grateful and ransomed dead man, and that of the grateful animal that has been spared and becomes a helper. Both figures symbolize the shadow, that is, a natural part of the personality that is exposed to darkness, which needs tolerance and even assistance to prevent it from becoming a dangerous inner enemy.

529      After the hero has ransomed the dead man, in most cases the latter joins him unrecognized as a servant or as a traveling companion. Just as meaningfully as mysteriously, he says in "The Comrade" (Norway, no. 7):

530      But you need a servant. I know that better than you do, and you need someone you can rely on in life and in death. But if you do not want me as a servant, then take me as a companion; I promise you that this will not be to your detriment ...

531    Thus, and in particular with the words "in life *and in death*," he implies that he is also at home in the hereafter and participates in the human psyche, which outlasts worldly life. He thus resembles the semidivine escort of the dead or the heavenly *doppelgänger* in Gnostic texts.[475] The Khidr in the 18th Surah (chapter) of the Koran and in the Islamic legends also corresponds to this figure in some respects. The companion's superhuman, otherworldly quality in the present tale reveals that, despite his shadowy garb, he personifies unconscious spiritual powers that are superior to consciousness. This is confirmed by variants in which this figure, having been ransomed or buried along the way, accompanies the hero as a white or green servant or as an angel; or, as in chivalric romance, as a white knight.[476]

532    As observed, white is the color of the other- or spirit-world. Here, it also implies positivity, light, or immaculateness: It is flawless; that is, it is neither mixed with nor corrupted by inert, earthly, or worldly things. Green is the color of nature, and the Khidr is therefore called "the Verdant one ... the immortal."[477] Thus, if the color green belongs to the spirit of the dead in fairytales, it symbolizes an unconscious, invigorating spiritual effect, which evidently emanates from that companion. This luminous, pure, and spiritually animated aspect plainly compensates for the image of the guilt-ridden dead man, the first appearance of this archetype in fairytales.[478] Since the hero lovingly attends to the unconscious, rejected part of the personality, this part now reveals its other side as a superior leader.[479] It therefore

---

[475] Reitzenstein, *Hellenistischen Mysterien*, passim; Reitzenstein, *Iranische*, passim; see also Bousset, *Hauptprobleme der Gnosis*, passim.

[476] Bolte and Polívka, *Anmerkungen*, vol. 3, pp. 496f., 501, 507. This figure appears as Saint Nicholas (of Myra) in *ibid.*, p. 503 and in "Nicholas, the Miracle Worker" (Russia, no. 48), where this motif is interwoven with that of the man-eating anima-figure as in "The King's Black Daughter" (Zaunert, *Märchen aus dem Donaulande*, p. 150). See also "The Sinner and the King's Son" (Finland, no. 22).

[477] Jung, *Symbols of Transformation*, CW 5, § 285.

[478] On the dead gradually becoming divine according to Egyptian belief, see Roeder's introduction to the "Book of the Dead" in his *Urkunden* (1923), p. 225: The dead are said to assume the form of the gods, appear in their bodies, possess their power, and experience their fates. Thus, the dogma wants the dead man to become Osiris, the king of all gods, the powerful sun-god, a lotus flower like Nefertem, and a snake; "this enables him to become the sun, Horus, Uto [the goddess of Lower Egypt], and many other things in the same text (chapter 66)." See also *ibid.*, "The Book of the Dead," p. 256.

[479] In "The Man of All Colors" (France, vol. 2, no. 53), the hero buries a dead man and takes his iron rod, which weighs nine hundredweight, with him on his onward journey. As in "The King of the Mountain of Fog" (Finland, no. 69), the rod signifies guidance, leadership, etc.

seems quite logical that some fairytales refer to the miraculous wandering companion as an angel, saint, or Jesus; or even as the Lord himself,[480] because this *"doppelgänger"*[481] transcends humankind.

533     The episode with the three witches, whom the "comrade" tricks out of the magic objects that later prove helpful, occurs solely in the Norwegian version.[482] It aptly illustrates the companion's supernatural power in greater detail and characterizes the sphere toward which the two wanderers venture. The three witches recall the three stations to which the Baba Yaga sisters come on their journey in the Russian variant[483]; they also correspond to the ancient Parcae, Gorgons, or Graeae, who also mostly appear in threes. The journey thus proceeds into the realm of the *Magna Mater*, the unconscious.

534     The underworldly aspect of the three witches' psychic realm is emphasized by the motif of the chair on which those who are enticed to sit must remain seated. As is well known, this happened to Pirithous when he journeyed to the underworld with his twin brother Theseus. This process has the same meaning as the Orphic

---

[480] Bolte and Polívka, *Anmerkungen*, vol. 3, pp. 497, 501, 504, 506, and 510; see also "The Comrade" (Roma, no. 58): A poor man realized that he and his children were going to starve and went out to kill the good Lord. The latter, however, approached him as a journeyman and declared that he wanted to accompany him; they called each other "comrade." When the good Lord saw that the gypsy could barely continue because he was so hungry, he sent him a goose and a cake. The gypsy first ate one leg of the goose, brought the rest to the good Lord, and swore that the goose did not have a second leg. Thereafter, the "comrades" hired out their services to a landowner, who ordered them to complete the mowing work of 366 farmhands by the evening or they would be sentenced to death. The good Lord solved the task, but the landowner nevertheless had them thrown into the furnace. However, when he opened the furnace door the next day, the comrades were sitting on chairs and smoking pipes. Each received a bag of gold as a reward. On their onward journey, they entered the services of a count as physicians capable of healing his dying wife, which the good Lord easily managed to achieve. Once more, he demanded a bag of gold. On the way, the gypsy wanted to share the money with the good Lord, "because I can perform the same work as you." The good Lord refused and bid the gypsy farewell. The latter promised the emperor to heal his wife, or else they could hang him. He proceeded like the good Lord, but unsuccessfully, so that the rope was put around his neck. Thereupon, he exclaimed: "Comrade, comrade!" The good Lord prevented the execution by exclaiming that the empress had recovered. As a reward for healing her, he asked for another bag of gold. On the way, he divided the money into three piles. The third, he told the gypsy, was for the goose's leg. Once more, the gypsy swore that the goose only had one leg. "But the good Lord gathered up the money, rolled over three times, and, transformed into a dove, flew away. But the gypsy cried: "Comrade, comrade, come back!" The motif of division links this tale to "The Comrade" (Norway, no. 7) and proves that the hero and the companion are identical.

[481] For details on this figure, see *Archetypal Symbolism in Fairytales*, vol. 5 ("The Divine Twins"; forthcoming).

[482] In some variants mentioned in Bolte and Polívka, *Anmerkungen*, vol. 3, pp. 496 and 502, the animal-helper creates such magical devices himself; in one case (a Danish variant), the helper is replaced by an old woman.

[483] See, e.g., "The Maiden Tsar" (Russia, no. 41), as well as the three female giants in "Worry and Sorrow" (Norway, no. 25).

motif of being forbidden to look back: The great danger of coming into contact with the unconscious lies in "becoming stuck," of sinking forever into the dream world of fascinating images, from which consciousness, if it wishes to avoid being drawn away from real life, can only free itself again by exercising self-restraint and great effort.

535    These female figures, which embody the indeterminacy, the apparent meaninglessness, and the pleroma (all-fullness and all-emptiness) of unconscious archetypal images, possess three objects: a sword, a golden ball, and a hat. Contrary to the mother-archetype, these objects signify something that is spiritually determined and also belongs to the unconscious psyche. We have seen that the sword is the discriminating Logos, the ball is the guiding, fate-determining secret meaning that emanates from the self, and the hat is a mandala (i.e., that which covers the head and therefore, in generic terms, denotes a decision-making stance). In this fairytale, the hat later proves to be a magic hood, which transports its wearer into the spirit-world, where he becomes invisible to his opponents through sheer determination. In other words, a spiritual attitude is represented symbolically; knowing that the unconscious is paradoxical, this stance remains subtly determined, yet also indeterminate, and thus intangible and unassailable. Despite its clarity, this superior wisdom remains veiled.

536    The sword and the hat later serve to fight the trolls that are courting the princess. The ball, on the other hand, serves as a guiding principle, as is common in fairytales. One particularly vivid image is that of the companion "weaving" a bridge from the ball across which the wanderers pass into the otherwise inaccessible land beyond. At first, the unconscious seems impenetrable to the discerning faculty of consciousness. Fittingly, it is therefore represented first as an inhibiting rock face because consciousness perceives the unconscious as rigid and opaque: that is, as what prevents it from progressing in life and with which no living relationship can be established.

537  Another image that describes the difficulty of establishing contact with the unconscious is the impassable chasm or river; or what, in the Chinese oracles of the *I Ching*, is called the "great water." Although the unconscious suggests that it is accessible, the first step toward reaching it is extremely dangerous. We see neither a "way" nor any "sense." We must therefore, as it were, "pick up the threads"[484]; that is, we need to mentally establish meaningful connections between unconscious realities and conscious knowledge. From this follows that the supposedly "meaningless" and "fantastic" images of the unconscious have a secret—indeed symbolic—connection with everyday conflicts. Thus is formed the bridge, across which we can enter psychic reality and consciously experience its contents, through which we become familiar with our inner counterpart. Yet the present fairytale tells us that the ego is unable to accomplish this feat of its own accord. Rather, this involves gaining knowledge and maturity, which requires either being taught by a knowledgeable person or being inspired—as a sign of being guided by the unconscious. Therefore, the "comrade," as the self, builds the bridge between the two worlds. The pursuing witches, who seek to snatch the end of the thread, suggest that experiencing unconscious events and invisible guidance as meaningful remains threatened by chaos, fear, and instinct, which all strive to devour consciousness. What impeded the hero now also undoes the witches: They drown in the river; once again, as so often, they are defeated by their own kind.

538  In both versions of this fairytale, the hero reaches the princess, who is destined for him and in whom we easily recognize the anima-figure. It is significant that in "The Comrade" (Norway, no. 7), he dreams of her beforehand, which alludes to this figure's symbolic significance and her fateful affiliation with the hero. Whereas in this version the anima is unfathomable and initially dangerous, in "The Cursed Princess,"[485] she is depicted rather as a sufferer who means no harm. Her bouts of madness and depression, during which she

---

[484] On this magical connection, see Bächtold-Stäubli under *Faden* (thread).
[485] Zaunert, *Deutsche Märchen seit Grimm*, p. 237.

becomes diabolical, are followed by states in which the evil spirit departs from her and leaves her behind as an unfortunate figure. If she were a real woman, we would speak of states of possession, during which she is dominated by a terrible animus. These states seem to be caused by the mountain spirit. Her plight resembles that of mentally ill women in early 20th-century Egypt who were still called "brides of Zâr." Meaning the same as "div," "Zâr" refers to a semidivine desert demon.[486] In medieval Europe, pathological phenomena in women were also often explained by the fact that they allegedly courted the devil or other impure spirits.[487]

539     The mountain spirit or troll in the present fairytales can therefore be described as the anima's animus, just as the heroine's demonic father, the tomcat conjured up by her, and the dragon whom she was made to serve are defined thus in "The Frog Princess" (Russia, no. 5). One of their equals is the Luciferian father of the devil's daughter in "The King's Black Daughter."[488] Psychologically, this figure, as far as it reaches into the narrower human sphere, needs to be regarded as the woman's animus and as the man's shadow. Yet the composition of many fairytales reveals that, as a fully-fledged archetype, this figure is the image of a god and corresponds to the father-archetype. Ultimately, the mystery of the anima, her incomprehensible demonic nature, and her greatness derive from her affinity with this archetype. Precisely this explains why confronting the anima leads the man to fundamental questions and decisions.

540     In the present fairytale, this situation is presented in such a way that these connections are the anima-figure's personal secret. While she hides these associations from others as best as possible, their revelation determines whether the hero wins the anima's favor. What again becomes evident is the paradoxical behavior of the unconscious: Time and again, it tempts people to solve dreadful,

---

[486] Reitzenstein, *Hellenistischen Mysterien*, p. 251; see also also the role of the *div* in "The Magic Horse" (Turkestan, no. 9) and its futile courting of the heroine in "Muhammed the Shepherd und the Pärî Princesses" (Christensen, *Iran*, p. 58).

[487] See Laistner, *Das Rätsel*, vol. 1, p. 121: If his advances are rejected, the sorcerer curses the princess, who becomes a snake. Psychologically, rejecting the demonic spirit may lead to severe entanglement (and descending into a vegetative state), unless no luminous, spiritual principle can take its place.

[488] Zaunert, *Märchen aus dem Donaulande*, p. 150; see also the variants.

even hopeless tasks by offering them opportunities, yet forbidding them from seizing these.[489]

541 The mysterious connection of the female psyche with sublime and demonic, otherworldly powers, as well as her liberation from those forces, is a motif that also occurs in another, widespread type of tale, where it becomes a central, albeit simpler motif than in the present fairytales. Examples (discussed below to amplify the motifs) include "The Shoes That Were Danced to Pieces"[490] and its formally clearer Russian parallel "May the Bag Fill You" (no. 36). The latter goes as follows:

542 The tsar had a daughter who "kept running away." No one knew where, not even magicians could find out. A soldier who had spent his leave at home was heading back to his regiment and came to a swamp, which he tried to cross. He saw three woodsmen fighting over seven-league boots, a magic hood, and a small bag. The three men called on the soldier to referee their dispute. He awarded the items to that man who was quickest in finding the bullet fired from his shotgun in the swamp. While they were searching, he took the objects, continued his journey to St. Petersburg, and decided to track down the tsar's daughter. He was given three days to drink himself into a stupor before his "certain death." Thereafter, he was given a room next to the princess's. One could see the entire room through its crystal door. The princess ordered that twelve bottles of liquor be brought to the soldier. But he poured most of it into the bag and pretended to be drunk. When the tsar's daughter believed that the soldier had fallen asleep, she had twelve pairs of shoes brought to her: She put on one pair and took the others, which she tied in a cloth, under her arm, opened a trapdoor under the bed, and disappeared. The soldier, wearing a magic hood and seven-league boots, followed her. "The tsar's

---

[489] On the dual aspect of the spirit-archetype, see Jung, "The Phenomenology of the Spirit in Fairytales," CW 9/I, § 413ff.
[490] *The Complete Grimm's Fairy Tales*, pp. 596–600.

daughter wore one pair of shoes until they broke, threw them away, put on new ones, and continued running. The soldier hurried after her and ordered: 'Little bag, gather them!'

543

They reached a copper garden. The soldier thought: 'Oh, I must pick an apple.' He went to a beautiful tree and, lo and behold, he held an apple in his hand. All of a sudden, strings began to sound, drums began to beat, and there was an almighty commotion! The tsar's daughter thought: 'If I continue, they will find out where I was. And what caused this uproar? She turned back, but had worn all twelve pairs of shoes to pieces. The soldier threw himself on his bed before she did and fell asleep."

544

The following night, the soldier received twenty-five bottles of brandy, poured some into his bag, and pretended to be drunk. The princess had twenty-five pairs of shoes and, unnoticed by the soldier, went into the silver garden. He picked two apples, the strings sounded, and they both turned back. On the third night, she walked into the golden garden with forty-five pairs of shoes, the soldier picked an apple, the strings sounded, and they both turned back. On the fourth day, the journey continued with seventy-five pairs of shoes through all three gardens to the fiery sea. There stood a chariot of fire. The soldier jumped up behind the princess and shouted: "Hurry, Whitefoot! Light has not fallen yet in the courtyard!" On the other side of the sea, the astonished princess met a man who led her by the hand into his golden-roofed house. He showed her and the soldier who was following her unnoticed into a richly decorated hall, and then into a dressing room. The soldier had his sack filled with clothes, in the third room with golden crockery, and with other items in the pantry and bedroom, which the man eventually showed to his astonished "sweetheart." They arranged the wedding for the following day. On the chariot, the soldier said: "Hurry, Whitefoot! Day is breaking in the courtyard!" When the man found the bare walls in his house, he turned into a six-headed dragon and set off in pursuit, but the sea of fire scorched him. "Thereafter, he went out onto the balcony, hurled himself down, and burst into smithereens." The tsar's daughter and the soldier returned home. In the morning, the tsar sent for the soldier and asked whether he had been successful. The soldier had five rooms cleared out and all the senators assembled. Thereupon, he reported on his travels and showed the apples and the entire contents of his sack as proof. In return, he received the tsar's daughter as his wife.

545     The Grimm's version is different: One night, the 12 royal daughters go out dancing, and whoever attempts to guard them does so in vain, and no one can discover their secret. The hero is a wounded soldier whom an old woman helps by giving him a camouflage coat. The princesses descend underground in the eldest's bed. The soldier follows them, and the youngest princess suspects that someone is pursuing them yet is reassured by the others that she is mistaken. They dance with underground princes whom they wish to redeem. The soldier reveals the secret and marries the eldest princess. "But the princes were cursed again for as many days as they had danced night after night with the twelve princesses." (One similar tale is "The Night Reveller" [Balkans, no. 64], where a tsar's daughter goes dancing with the *vilenzar*'s son, as well as a weaker version, "The Tsar, His Daughter and the Tailor" [Balkans, no. 19].)[491]

546     In both tales, the hero is an ordinary soldier. Unlike the tsar or king, who symbolize the hitherto dominant consciousness, he represents the undeveloped side of the personality, which, being more original, is able to access the unconscious and its secrets. In the Grimm's version, the soldier who heals evil is wounded. Karl Kerényi has compiled the ancient material on the motif of the wounded warrior who heals others.[492] This material shows that

---

[491] See also "Soldier Hans and the Princess" (Spain, no. 8) and "The Princess with the Twelve Pairs of Golden Shoes" (Denmark, no. 18).
[492] Karl Kerényi, "Heros Iatros. Über Wandlungen und Symbole des ärztlichen Genius in Griechenland," *Eranos-Jahrbuch Band XII: Studien zum Problem des Archetypischen,* ed. Olga Fröbe-Kapteyn (1945), pp. 331f. and esp. pp. 39–43.

"being wounded" is a precondition of "being able to heal" and that inflicting wounds, sustaining injuries, and healing wounds can be subsumed under the term "war" ("Machaon," the name of the first wound care physician, means "slaughterer"). For only those who know about the death and suffering of living creatures can heal; and only those who have experienced fighting and suffering, the opposites of this world, can master them. The wound, whether Wotan's, Prometheus's, or Amfortas's, symbolizes the clash of opposites, that is, of the confrontation between spirit and matter; only those who bear such marks possess enough insight to heal others.

547    This explains why the soldier in the Grimm's version is able to reveal the underworld mystery of the mysterious tsar's daughters and thus to restore to the human realm a part of life that otherwise threatens to be lost to the demonic world.[493] Here, the soldier represents all the forces, which in other versions are divided into two figures (see "The Comrade" and "The Cursed Princess"). Their identities, however, are established as follows: In one version, the comrade accompanies the princess on her nocturnal journey, whereas in the other version the young fellow escorts her. Thus, these fairytales do not consider distinguishing these figures important and let them take each other's place. While the human and the superhuman aspect are combined in the soldier, who follows the night-reveling princesses, the same hero-archetype appears in these principal fairytales as two figures, thus better illumining the individual aspects. Yet any psychological interpretation must consider the theme of identity.

548    In the version collected by Zaunert in *Deutsche Märchen seit Grimm*, the hero undertakes the journey himself, assisted by the wings given to him by his companion, which enable him to join the winged princess. The princess magically grows her own wings. This is characteristic of witchcraft, as riding a goat in "The Comrade," the parallel version, demonstrates. In the folklore of all countries and

---

[493] In some respects, the plot is the opposite of "Clever Finna" (Iceland, no. 8), where a female character observes the man's nocturnal activites in the underworld.

almost all regions of the world, witches "ride out" at night, either on brooms, goats,[494] or other demonic mounts. If anointed, they can fly by themselves. Or, as in this tale, they fasten wings to themselves.[495] In so doing, witches or sorcerers leave their bodies, which appear to be dead, at home. Or their egos split: One part remains behind, while the other perishes and wreaks havoc.[496] This is not mentioned in the fairytales considered here. Yet because the anima-figure is described as a winged creature, mythologically it is characterized as belonging to the world-spirit. It has become a subtle body, which moves independently of the laws of space and time. Its actual nature as a "soul-bird" becomes apparent. Much parallel material could be adduced for the motif of riding a goat (as in the Norwegian tale).[497] However, its psychological meaning remains the same: As a plant and fertility demon, as an animal associated with Donar (the god of thunder) and the devil, and by serving ghosts as a mount (among others, hunters and witches),[498] the goat symbolizes instinct and thus the hero's "shadow." When the anima-figure (which sometimes rides an animal, often a horse, belonging to the demonic realm in fairytales) rides a goat, it belongs to her as an instinctual animus-figure, so that in her passion she dominates, as it were, the hero's instinctual side, by which she is borne.[499]

549     Sometimes, fairytales also suggest that the anima is identical with her mount, because in the man's unconscious she coalesces with this (i.e., his) shadow side. In "The Shepherd and the Three Samovilas" (Balkans, no. 15), the *samovila*'s evil horse becomes the pursuing demon and the hero's real antagonist.[500] Thus, this shadow, which

---

[494] See the identity of the anima and the billy goat in "The Tailor and the Treasure" (collected in Zaunert, *Deutsche Märchen seit Grimm*, p. 81, and discussed in *Archetypal Symbolism in Fairytales*, vol. 1, pp. 426–428).

[495] Laistner, *Rätsel*, vol. 2, pp. 420ff.; Hertz, *Werwolf* (1862), pp. 71–77; Bächtold-Stäubli under *Ziegenbock* (goat).

[496] See, e.g., Lévy-Bruhl, *The "Soul" of the Primitive* (1922), pp. 265–269.

[497] On the motif of a maiden riding a goat, see Mannhardt, *Wald- und Feldkulte*, vol. 2, p. 176f.; on the goat as a mount, see Bächtold-Stäubli under *Ziegenbock* (goat).

[498] Mannhardt, *Wald- und Feldkulte*, vol. 2, pp. 157ff.; Bächtold- Stäubli, *ibid*.

[499] See Jung's comments on "The Princess in the Tree" (Zaunert, *Deutsche Märchen seit Grimm*, p. 1) in "The Phenomenology of the Spirit in Fairy Tales," CW 9/I, § 39f.

[500] A shepherd watched three girls who were bathing in a pond. He stole their shirts and thus forced the girls, who said they were *samovilas* [beautiful female creatures—trans.], to let him have the youngest sister as his wife. Before the two oldest girls, whose shirts he returned, flew away, they warned him not to give her shirt to his wife or she would escape. But because he wanted the beautiful *samovila* to dance

symbolizes the hero's weak side, threatens to destroy the value of encountering the anima and enabling subterranean forces to break out instead. In that fairytale, however, the hero escapes the danger and very wisely banishes it into the future. In "The Cursed Princess,"[501] the anima's animal component is less emphasized, contrary to her state of possession: She hastens back and forth in the room before flying off to the mountain spirit; she is characterized as mentally disturbed, suffering, and restless.

550    In "The Three Fairies" (Spain, no. 56), which also depicts the sufferings of an anima-figure, an eagle pecks out one of her eyes (the eagle had raised her as a foster father; as he is jealous, he refuses to give her to the wooing prince). As she is also persecuted by her mother-in-law, she suffers greatly until she is healed and freed to marry the prince. Cyclopia (i.e., one-eyedness) impairs conscious-ness and spiritual vision.[502] (In this sense, the one-eyed heroine is a variant of the possessed and melancholic female protagonist in the principal fairytale discussed here). To understand what makes his soul suffer, and to redeem it from suffering, the hero must adapt to the circumstances and immerse himself completely therein. He must accept the uncanny aberrations of his soul and follow these paths without consciousness prematurely correcting matters. Only trusting the transpersonal spirit-guide enables him to accomplish this task. The fact that he chastises the princess with one iron rod, and later with two rods, recalls "King Lindworm" (Denmark, no. 1), where the heroine must bathe the enchanted animal prince in milk

---

at a feast, he gave her the shirt after plugging all the cracks in the room. After the dance, however, she escaped through the chimney and called out to him that he could see her again in the village of Kushkundaleo. He set off to search the maiden and met an old man in the mountains. The man directed him to his brother, from whom he received the help of some birds, who took him to the house of the three *samovilas* in the village. The older sisters tied his wife to a saddle, so that he could fly home with her: "'She will wake up during the flight and shout as loud as possible, so that her horse will hear her. It will run to free her; but if it discovers that you have crossed the three mountains, it cannot harm you; but if it finds you before them, it will tear you to pieces and abduct your wife.' After the *samovilas* had spoken these words, the shepherd mounted the horse and was borne away by a strong wind. When they had crossed the three mountains, the *samovila* awoke and cried for her horse. Immediately, it flew off to catch up with the shepherd and reached the three mountains; but it had exhausted its strength and returned." When he returned home, the shepherd burned the *samovila's* shirt, and they lived happily ever after. — On the role of horses, see also "The Girl with Roses" (Zaunert, *Märchen aus dem Donaulande*, p. 269).

[501] Zaunert, *Deutsche Märchen seit Grimm*, p. 237.
[502] Jung, "The Phenomenology of the Spirit in Fairytales," *CW* 9/I, § 413.

and at the same time beat him with rods dipped in lye.[503] From being enslaved to the unconscious sphere ensues an envelopment of sorts, being lost in dense fog, which separates one from reality and also from other people. Being freed from this envelopment by conscious guidance requires understanding everything and, under certain circumstances, standing firm. It demands tearing asunder the shroud, as it were, so that one awakens from the fantasy world and becomes conscious by abruptly confronting the concrete world.[504] When the hero treats the anima-figure in this way, he treats himself in exactly the same way: On the one hand, he participates in the aberrations of his soul; on the other, however, he also "castigates" it and thereby attests to his conscious point of view, which has remained independent.[505] He is thus highly self-critical.

551    At the end of the journey, the secret that causes the princess's peculiar conditions is revealed: She is spellbound by a secret lover. While in the Norwegian version he is a troll, a grotesque nature demon, in the version collected in *Deutsche Märchen seit Grimm* he is a mountain spirit, characterized by an uncanny loftiness, and quite explicitly as a father-figure. The father-child relationship is even more pronounced (yet similarly problematic) in other fairytales: in "No One Can Harm Those Whom God Helps" (Balkans, no. 27), for instance, the hero redeems a tsar's daughter, about whose father we learn:

552    This tsar had been very evil and depraved, had recently passed away, and only his only daughter had remained in his palace. Many had courted her, but of all the suitors who had come to the palace, none had remained alive, because the tsar had turned into a vampire that returned at night and strangled them.

---

[503] See also "The Young Wolf" (Zaunert, *Märchen aus dem Donaulande*, p. 1).

[504] One peculiar version is "The Magic Ring" (Finland, no. 10), where the hero beats the woman who deceives him to death. See also Aarne, *Vergleichende Märchenforschungen* (1908), pp. 3–38, 55: The only similarity between those fairytales and the present one is the anima's attachment to a dark lover; the hero either stops loving her or imprisons or kills her. Thus, consciousness is unable to come to terms with the anima's dark aspect and once again detaches itself completely from the unconscious.

[505] In this Norwegian version, this motif loses its meaning and almost amounts to a "trick" played by the comrade.

553    This account recalls that about Sarah in the *Book of Tobit*. Possessed by Asmodi, an evil spirit, she kills her husbands; the father's secret role is intimated insofar as he always prepares the suitor's grave in the garden in advance. Once more, the domination by the man's soul-image hinges on a father-child relationship, whose psychology we have discussed in Volume 3 ("The Maiden's Quest"). Incidentally, this type of fairytale reverses the incest motif described in "Clever Finna" (Iceland, no. 8). There, the heroine discovers the secret of her husband's nocturnal excursions and redeems him from his attachment to his sister, which resulted from the mother's curse; here, a hero performs the same feat with a female figure who has succumbed to her father. Just as the animal prince is often mesmerized by a dark mother-figure who refuses to release him, so here the princess is spellbound by a demonic father-figure. It is as if the world of darkness and evil were filled with a secret love for the human soul, whether to powerfully realize itself or to establish contact with light.

554    Unlike the primitive conception of the underworld god as a Norwegian troll, the mountain spirit in "The Cursed Princess" is amplified by the accompanying symbols, which also help to explain why the princess loves this figure. Adorned with the different symbols, the altar characterizes the inside of the mountain as a temple. Presumably, this fairytale originated in pre-Christian times, as is suggested by the temple vision and by an older version, and was later influenced by Christian ideas in other versions (e.g., the aforementioned Norwegian one). When the hero answers the first question, the princess grows pale and says (in the present German version): "... May fortune continue to be favorable to you ..." (as with the second answer). This tale seems to originate in the Harz region.[506] In the older version, which is literally identical, this passage is slightly different as the princess matter-of-factly remarks: "May the gods be gracious to you" (i.e., "assist and stand by"). The editor of the *Deutsche Märchen seit Grimm* changed the phrasing: Christianity is not hinted at, except for the expressions "angelic

---

[506] Ey, ed., *Harzmärchenbuch oder Sagen und Märchen aus dem Oberharze* (1862), p. 64.

beauty" and "piety," which describe the redeemed princess at the end of the tale. Therefore, the symbols on the altar should not be interpreted according to their Christian meaning.

555    Regarding the fish and its mythological interpretation, we refer to Dölger's comprehensive account, as this also deals with non-Christian symbolism. Concerning the psychological meaning of this archetypal image, several aspects should be noted: First, the fish is a phallic symbol.[507] According to De Gubernatis, in Sanskrit the god of love is called, among other things, "one whose emblem is a fish."[508] This meaning leads to a second one: The fish is a primordial being, a symbol of chaos, from which creatures either emerge or which devour them again (as a whale).[509] On the other hand, this symbol acquires a divine nimbus; for example, Oannes, the Babylonian teacher of wisdom, was represented as a penis fish[510]; in Egypt, the prophesying Abdufish swims beside the solar barque and announces the approaching enemies[511]; in India, the fish-shaped Vishnu once again raises Brahma's sacred knowledge "from the floods of the end of the world."[512] Such acts of salvation lend the fish the meaning of a principle that renews life and psychic energy, as well as sustains or nurtures it. It invites comparison with the sun, which dives into the water like a fish.[513] In the underworld, it becomes the midnight sun and thus represents the deity of the chthonic realm.

556    In fairytales, fish often point to this figure. For example, a Mingrelian variant of the "Myth of Polyphemus" (Caucasus, no. 65) reports that one day the fishermen's lines became entangled in the fins of a gigantic fish, so that the fish dragged the men along. It took them to a river containing the sweetest honey on which it feasted so

---

[507] Dölger, "Ichthys." Das Fischsymbol in frühchristlicher Zeit, vol. 1 (1910), pp. 109 and 429, fn. 2; see *ibid.*, vol. 2 (1922), p. 225; see also Jung, *CW* 5.

[508] De Gubernatis, *Thiere i. d. indog. Mythologie*, p. 193; see also Winthuis, *Zweigeschlechter*, p. 136f. and fn. 138.

[509] On Cipactli, the Mexican fish, from which the earth was formed, see "Primordial Time" (Aztec, no. 1), collected in Krickeberg, *Märchen der Azteken und Inkaperuaner, Maya und Muisca*, [MdW], ed. v. d. Leyen (1928), esp. p. 4f.

[510] Jung, *CW* 5, § 291. According to Dölger, he was half-man, half-fish ("Ichthys," vol. 1, p. 115).

[511] Adolf Erman, *Die Religion der Ägypter. Ihr Werden und Vergehen in vier Jahrtausenden* (Berlin and Leipzig: de Gruyter, 1934), p. 19.

[512] Zimmer, *Maya* (1936), pp. 82, 116f.

[513] Jung, *Symbols of Transformation*, *CW* 5, § 290; see also "Forms of Rebirth," *CW* 9/I, § 244ff. For a comprehensive discussion of fish symbolism, see Jung, "Aion. Researches into the Phenonomology of the Self," *CW* 9/II, ch. VIII–XI.

greedily that the river almost dried up. In the meantime, the fishermen managed to cut their lines. Yet before they were able to leave, a flock of sheep, shepherded by a one-eyed giant, approached. He hauled the ship onto the shore and drove his flock and the fishermen to a large edifice in a mighty forest. There he slaughtered one fisherman every night until only two were left. They, however, were able to poke out his eye with his roasting spit. Wrapped in sheep skins, the two men fled the giant with his flock and reached their ship, on which they eventually returned home after a lengthy odyssey.

557    We find a related episode in the "Adventures of a King's Son" (Latvia, no. 21). After his ship loses its way at sea, a king's son reaches an island, where he enters a castle:

558    He entered a room, which was empty; he entered a second room, which was full of sheep, and at whose center stood a large sheep; he entered a third room, which was filled almost entirely by a fish: Its tail was on one side of the door, its head on the other side, and its body stretched across the whole room; its eyes were as large as that of a sieve. The King's son quickly drew his sword and gouged the fish's eyes. The fish was instantly transformed into a huge iron giant, who groped aimlessly for the King's son to seize him, but the King's son slipped away among the sheep.

559    Hidden beneath the belly of the great sheep, the king's son escapes past the giant into the open.

560    These variants are instructive: In classical antiquity, Polyphemus is the son and protégé of Poseidon, Odysseus's enemy; as the god of the sea and water, Poseidon is associated with fish symbolism. While in "Kitschüw" (Caucasus, no. 27) the hero must free a princess from the clutches of a sea demon, the latter keeps its soul inside a box, which is contained inside a fish. In other mythological contexts, the fish also blends with the anima-figure: As Melusine, for instance,

this figure is half-woman, half-fish.[514] The Eastern cult of Cybele worshipped fish, and its priests were forbidden from eating them.[515] This goddess rather symbolizes the maternal and chaotic aspects of the anima-figure. As a phallic symbol, the fish might be said to represent her masculine-spiritual aspect (i.e., her animus). Thus, the fish symbol in the hall of the mountain spirit in the present fairytale connects, among other things, the princess and the demon, insofar as it represents her chaotic animus. On the other hand, in mythology the fish, as Usener's insightful compilation of figures who transport others across floods reveals,[516] can embody Apollo. They might also be dispatched by him or be Hermes's *doppelgänger*.[517] They might even be a dead person who, as a dolphin, as it were, ferries others across water. Thus, in the present fairytale, the fish also establishes a connection to the comrade or to the demonic mountain spirit as the ruler of the underworld.[518] The hero, who in this tale traces the suffering of his soul, thus finds this symbol deep inside himself, which encompasses all parts of his being, his wholeness.[519] The fish spikes indicate the aloofness and elusiveness of this symbol of the self, whose significance becomes even more obvious if we consider the circumstances in which it appears.

561     The fish lies on the altar, that is, in a mandalalike space. The altar also denotes a cube or a body. Jung has discussed the maternal meaning of the altar as the place of fertilization and creative emergence.[520] This basic idea has been extended by van der Leeuw, who compares the altar to the hearth as the place of fire-making by deriving the origin of the altar from the hearth.[521] As the place of fire,

---

[514] Peuckert, *Volksglaube* (1942), pp. 154ff., 170ff. On the meaning of this figure, see Jung, "Paracelsus as a Spiritual Phenomenon," *CW* 13, § 216ff.; on the fish as a symbol of womanhood, see Jung, *Symbols of Transformation*, CW 5. See also "The Fish Girl" (Siberia, no. 20).

[515] Jung, *Symbols of Transformation*, CW 5, § 662, fn. 59.

[516] Usener, *Sintfluthsagen* (1899), pp. 115f., 163f., 166ff., and 223–229.

[517] On Khidr as a fish, see the 18th Surah of the Koran and Jung, *CW* 5, § 282.

[518] According to Dölger, fish were sacrificed to Ninazu, the Babylonian god of the underworld, and were *donated to the dead* (see "Ichthys," vol. 2, pp. 242f.).

[519] In alchemy, the "round fish" is a divine symbol of the self. See Jung, *Psychology and Alchemy*, CW 12, § 433 and fn. 30; "The Visions of Zosimos," *CW* 13, § 101 and fn. 69; *Psychological Types*, CW 6, § 92, fn. 27.

[520] Jung, *CW* 5, § 200.

[521] On the domestic cult in ancient Rome "where the hearth was entrusted to the female members of the house (the later Vestals), whose father presided over the fire while his sons (the *flamines*) acted as kindlers," see v. d. Leeuw, *Phänomenologie der Religion*, p. 44. On fire as the principle of the world, see *ibid.*, p. 46.

the hearth becomes the sacred place in the house, where "power" is renewed.[522] Thus, in the cult, the sacred or saintly is symbolized by the altar, "the throne or table of God, because here the sacred becomes 'stately,' settles down, as it were. ... On the seat of God, God is enthroned. His image can now be placed there. ... The *image of God* is a means of holding onto God, of vouching for his presence."[523] Seen thus, the underworld altar in the hall of the mountain spirit emphasizes the symbolic importance of the fish and the wheel by bearing them, motherly and solemnly, as the beginning of new life.

562

Later, the wheel appears on the altar of the mountain spirit. It refers to symbolic contexts similar to those of the fish, because this image has been related to the sun since the earliest times and in almost all mythological spheres.[524] The wheel symbolizes the idea of the fateful cycle and of the psyche's proper (i.e., inherent) motion.[525] Seen negatively, in Eastern culture the wheel represents the sorrowful consequence of karma-induced rebirths.[526] It is the wheel of the path and therefore also symbolizes the passage of time.[527] Seen positively, however, the wheel is a symbol of the self: It depicts the

---

[522] See v. d. Leeuw, *Phänomenologie der Religion*, pp. 375ff., esp. p. 378; see also Güntert, *Weltkönig*, p. 277f.

[523] v. d. Leeuw, *Phänomenologie*, p. 426f.

[524] Güntert, *Weltkönig*, pp. 46f., 273f., 295; see also Jung, *CW* 5, § 297 f.; Mogk, *Germanische Religionsgeschichte und Mythologie* (1927), p. 36f.; Bächtold- Stäubli under *Rad* (wheel): "Wheels were frequently applied in annual fire-festivals ever since the early Middle Ages. Toward the end of the 19th century, rolling wheels around villages and cutting rounds of woods in the forest were almost extinct in Germany. These practices have recently become more common again in some places, just like Easter and Solstice fires, in the vein of a new romanticism ... Both cultic customs have always been closely related in scholarship, which has regarded them as remnants of a Germanic sun cult. In some places, they were separated, so that the wheel discs, as a symbol of the rising sun, were originally only suitable for spring fires, whereas rolling wheels, as a symbol of the descending sun, were used for midsummer fires. ... In some instances, the vernacular likens the sun or other heavenly bodies to a wheel. On the other hand, comparisons between the sun and the wheel are familiar in Indian poetry about the gods, and they also appear among the Greeks and Romans ... Sometimes, wheel dances are common. In Transylvania, for example, people dance around a wheel at Easter that has been placed at the top of a tree; in Brandenburg, wedding guests also used to dance around a burning wheel. ... The wheel was immensely popular as an ornamental symbol in pre-Christian times. ... It was certainly regarded as a sun symbol in Asia and the Mediterranean region, although connections to other cults are not uncommon. In northern Europe, the wheel first appeared in the Stone Age as a circular ornament with an inscribed cross, adopted from the Orient; in part, these signs probably had a symbolic meaning already in those times."

[525] See, e.g., Silesius, *Cherubinischer*, p. 6, no. 37: "Die Unruh kommt von Dir" [Disquiet comes from within yourself]: "Nothing moves you, you are the wheel / that rolls on its own and has no rest."

[526] On the wheel as an instrument of torture, see "One Who Cursed the Prince of Hell" (China, no. 43); on the legendary significance of the wheel, see Rhys Davids, "Zur Geschichte des Rad-Symbols," *Eranos-Jahrbuch 1934: Ostwestliche Symbolik und Seelenführung*, ed. Olga Fröbe-Kapteyn (1935), pp. 173ff. See also "John Gethin and the Candle" (Ehrentreich, *Englische Volksmärchen*, 1938, p. 179).

[527] Davids, "Rad-Symbol," p. 173f.; on the wheel as the archetypal symbol "of circulation, of the inescapable unfolding of fate," see also Ninck, *Wodan*, p. 215, esp. p. 312.

structural order of the psyche, which, in this form, compares to the sun, that wheel which travels across the sky of its own accord and thus symbolizes the essence of the human psyche. In both Chinese and Western alchemy, the "cycle of light" (*rotatio* or *circulatio*) is the process by which the so-called inner pearl or philosopher's stone is produced.[528] The wheel, as a mandala, is related not only to the sun, but also to the eye: As Jung observes, the mandala is "actually an eye that projects itself." He observed two cases,

563

> in which the series of visions began with the patient being led to a rock face into which he was supposed to crawl, but which had no opening. Eventually, he discovered a small hole where he could squeeze in; on both occasions, the rock looked like an eye from the inside. This also corresponds to the experience of entering the sun ...[529]

564 This amplification is significant in the present fairytale insofar as the unconscious again appears first as an impenetrable rock and subsequently as a mandala.

565 At the same time, the vision of the fish and the wheel is paralleled by the interior of the mountain becoming increasingly illumined in three scenes: first, by the stars; second, by the moon; and third, by the sun. Consequently, the hero can barely hide in the shadow of the altar (note its corporeal and maternal meaning[530]). While this steadily increasing illumination is rare in mythology, we find the motif of an antisolar point or midnight sun shining in the underworld in the ancient mysteries. Apuleius, for instance, describes the initiation into the Isis mysteries as follows[531]:

---

[528] See Wilhelm, *The Secret of the Golden Flower*. See Jung, "Commentary on the Secret of the Golden Flower" (*CW* 13, § 38) for a discussion of the idea of "circulation," which means "fixation and concentration." He adds: "The sun-wheel begins to turn; the sun is activated and begins its course—in other words, the Tao begins to work and takes the lead."

[529] Jung, *Bericht über das Deutsche Seminar* (Stuttgart, 1932), p. 76.—Trans.

[530] Thus, the hero hides as the ant does in the grandmother's skirt in "The Devil with the Three Golden Hairs" (*The Complete Grimm's Fairy Tales*, pp. 151–157). The altar in the temple of the mountain spirit might be said to represent the positive maternal aspect in the above fairytale, whereas the negative maternal aspect is represented by the witches.

[531] Apuleius, *The Golden Ass*, trans. E. J. Kenney (London: Penquin, 2004), p. 183. See also Dieterich, *Mithrasliturgie*, p. 87; Reitzenstein, *Iranische*, pp. 169 ff; Leisegang, "Schlange," pp. 243 f., 249f. On the role of the sun in the Egyptian realm of the dead, see v. d. Leeuw, *Phänomenologie der Religion*, p. 300f.

566    I came to the boundary of death and after treading
Proserpine's threshold I returned having traversed all the
elements; at midnight I saw the sun shining with brilliant
light; I approached the gods below and the gods above face
to face and worshipped them in their actual presence.[532]

567    Mitra and Varuna-Agni are also juxtaposed in India: as the luminous
lord of the day, and as the fire that is hidden in the earth, in the night,
and in the dark waters.[533] Significantly, the midnight sun shines

---

[532] Some of the details reported by Dölger resemble the ideas of the present fairytale so closely that we
mention them even if they come from a completely different cultural background and seem unlikely to
have migrated. Dölger writes (see *"Ichthys,"* vol. 1, pp. 427–429): "The Musée Guimet houses a similar
cylinder seal. A fish lies on an altar that is shaped like a table. On the right stands a Babylonian figure
with a long beard and seated on a chair. Its right hand is raised and its left one is touching the fish. On
the left side of the altar another Babylonian figure is making the same gesture. Above the altar stands
the crescent; in the left field stands a tree. Although somewhat different, a cylinder seal housed in the
British Museum seems identical, at least in terms of its basic idea. Here, too, the sun and the moon
appear in the central field as sacred symbols, with a fish lying on an offering table below. The figures
are related to the sacrificial act; they are priests of the 'god of the deep waters.' On page 113f., reference
was made to a notable Babylonian custom according to which the priest appears clothed in a mighty
fish skin. There, however, the priests, who are dressed as fish, were engaged in exorcising the sick. At
this juncture, I can point to a cylinder housed in the Imperial Museum of St. Petersburg: It is made of
chalcedony and connects the priest who is wearing the fish garment to the fish sacrifice. ... The priest is
conceived as the one who performs the sacrifice. ... The fish, however, seems to have been not only a
sacrifice and sacrificial food, but also a sacred symbol. As such it appears together with the sun, the
moon, the rhombus, the tree of life, and the goat. The rhombus (vulva) is the sign of female fertility
and symbolizes the goddess of life. In this context, the fish was most likely a symbol of life in Babylon."
Dölger also refers to other cylinder seals (vol. 2, pp. 215 ff), where a large fish lies on a table, and above
it hovers the winged solar disk; facing the table, a male figure dressed in a long robe sits on a chair while
the crescent moon appears in the background. "To the right of the table stands a male figure in a long
robe and a cap, with one hand raised, while the other seems to be grasping the head of the fish. In this
sacrificial scene, the figure standing beside the table is the priest, while the seated figure is the god."
Sometimes, the crescent moon and a tree also appear above the altar. In another case, "the seated god
... appears to be identified as the god Adad by a cluster of thunderbolts. Behind his throne lies the
rhombus, beneath it a goat and Ištar, a goddess of the stars." He continues: "The frequently repeated
depiction of the fish as a symbol of good fortune is even better understood through its identification as
a symbol of fertility and life. A hymn to Ištar-Tamuz has taught us that the vulva was understood as a
symbol of Ištar, the goddess of life. The vulva symbol, usually depicted as a rhombus on Assyrian-
Babylonian seals, was itself a symbol of life. It is significant that the fish was depicted so obviously beside
and together with this rhombus" (p. 225). The similarities between the images on Babylonian cylinder
seals and in the German fairytale are striking: Even the goat appears in both cases. Instead of the
rhombus, a wheel appears in the fairytale. Dölger's reference to the exorcism of the sick should be noted
with regard to the "sick" princess in the fairytale. Many other connections could be established. And
yet, it seems too daring to venture beyond a general similarity, in particular as the appearance of
archetypal images is not confined to national territories.—The strange symbols surrounding the
mountain spirit in the aforementioned fairytale and their outlined relationships raise the question of
when visions such as those depicted in fairytales were first created or recounted in a self-contained
form. In this regards, I refer to Otto Huth's "Märchen und Megalithreligion," in: *Paideuma, Mitteilungen
zur Kulturkunde*, vol. V October 1950 (Bamberg: Verlagshaus Meisenbach, 1950). This stimulating
contribution to the history of religion connects fairytales and megalithic religion. I would very much
welcome Professor Huth to provide a more detailed account of the peculiar features of fairytales from
different cultural eras and regions—which he has mostly kindly delineated in personal correspondence
with me.
[533] Güntert, *Weltkönig*, pp. 281ff.

when the *mystes* (i.e., initiate) penetrates the depths of the underworld. The light that he finds there reflects the daylight, that is, his consciousness: By extinguishing or allowing daytime consciousness to languish, and thereby letting it descend into the darkness of the psyche, the psychic world becomes ever brighter, and its paradox becomes more understandable. Integral to consciousness are concentration and unequivocalness. Together, these attributes prevent seeing things in the unconscious because the manifold meanings of the archetypal world cannot be reduced to clearly defined formulas. Therefore, human beings must dim the lamp of their intellect, as it were, to see in the twilight of the unconscious. Then, however, meaning will emerge. It will spread its own light and reveal to consciousness the independent activity of the objective psyche.

568     The motif of the subterranean sun, moon, and stars, or that of the midnight sun, also plays its part in fairytales (e.g., "May the Bag Fill You"; Russia, no. 36). Thus, the underground hall where the tsar's daughter encounters the *vila* tsar's demonic son in the aforementioned variant ("The Night Reveller"; Balkans, no. 64) is described as follows:

569     They entered a large, grand hall, surrounded by pillars made of ivory, upon which rose a vault like the sky, in the middle of which shone a sun, surrounded by the moon and stars. The flute sounded from above, as if the angels of heaven were playing the harp. The *Vila* and their consorts joined hands and began to dance.

570  A relationship with the sun, that is, with the sun's orbit, also seems evident in "May the Bag Fill You": The hero and the princess ride a chariot drawn by a horse called "Whitefoot." Their journey lasts exactly until the sun rises. When "Whitefoot" returns, light rises at the royal court. In Germanic and Mediterranean mythology, the sun chariot is drawn by white horses, which suggests that the hero journeys across the Western sea with the tsar's daughter on the sun

chariot. The gardens through which the princess drives, and where copper, silver, and golden apples grow, correspond to the mythological gardens at the limits of the earth. There, as Dieterich says,

571

> the noctural river flows and the sky opens up. The garden was always associated with the sun and the sun-god: It was located where the sun rises or, according to the most widespread conception, where it sets, in the uttermost west.[534]

572     Thus, the dragon that is courted by the tsar's daughter resembles the devil in "The Devil with the Three Golden Hairs."[535] It resembles a midnight sun-god and rules over magnificent, distant subterranean realms. These details are related to the number 12, which oddly enough recurs quite frequently in these contexts: Either the princess ruins 12 pairs of shoes in 12 dances or there are 12 princesses, and so on. The number 12 represents, as we observed when discussing the 12 dark men who at night torment the liberator of the snake princess in "The King of the Golden Mountain,"[536] the 12 hours of night or the 12 stages into which almost all mysteries of the afterlife were divided.[537]

573     Strangely enough, the dance motif also occurs in the ancient Gnostic mysteries in this context. In the *Corpus Hermeticum* XIII, 18, the 12 benevolent divine powers perform a round dance in honor of the supreme god. When the *mystes* participates in this dance, he attains gnosis, the vision of God, through the ecstasy thereby induced.[538] Dance is a means of expressing primordial religious

---

[534] Dieterich, *Nekyia* (Leipzig, 1893), p. 21. He adds: "There stood the stables of Helios... there Helios, the son of Zeus, when he reaches the depths of the dark, sacred night, goes to his mother... in the shady laurel grove. There is his palace... where his rays lie in a golden chamber."

[535] *The Complete Grimm's Fairy Tales*, pp. 151–158.

[536] *Ibid.*, pp. 425–430.

[537] Reitzenstein, *Hellenistischen Mysterien.*

[538] Max Pulver, "Jesu Reigen und Kreuzigung nach den Johannes-Akten," *Eranos-Jahrbuch 1942: Das hermetische Prinzip in Mythologie, Gnosis und Alchemie*, ed. Olga Fröbe-Kapteyn (1943), p. 170. In this context, we must also mention Jesus' mystical dance with his twelve disciples in the Acts of John (see Pulver, *ibid.*, esp. pp. 155 ff). See also the whirling dervishes of the Orient. (Unfortunately, I do not have access to van der Leeuw's posthumous *Wegen en Grenzen*, which addresses this subject and thus far has only been published in Dutch). Note also the dancing fairies in "The Piper and the Puca" (Ireland, no. 26). According to Lum, it is believed almost universally that a special magic lies in dancing and that certain steps have certain effects (see *Fabulous Beasts*, New York 1951, p. 12).

experience. The nightly dance of the tsar's daughter also has an otherworldly meaning in the present fairytale, as its amplifications reveal. It is performed for the dark sun, the ruler of the realm of the dead. Thus, the dragon, which in some versions is a troll (i.e., a *"vila tsar"* = a ruler over nature spirits), is, if we consider its relationship to the midnight sun, the *dark* aspect of the father-archetype, which is split off as an independent figure.[539]

574 In some indigenous myths, the "father" and the "sun" merge into a dangerous primitive image of God. For instance, in "The Visit to Heaven," a North American myth about twins, the boys encounter their solar father, the bearer of the sun, in the afterlife. At first, he threatens to destroy the sons before helping them at a later stage. Mythologically, the sun-god is predominantly a father-god,[540] because the sun creates life. As a sun in the underworld, however, the sun-god also rules the realm of the dead (as Osiris does in Egypt).[541] In India, Yama, the god of the dead, is a son of the sun-god.[542]

575 Notably, the demonic father-archetype in the present Norwegian fairytale is secretly related to the anima-figure's concrete father, who otherwise appears as a profane king. He, too, has a murderous side: He orders those who are unable to divine his daughter's secret to be slain. In the *Book of Tobit*, which we can treat as a parallel in this regard, the young woman's old father also quietly digs a grave in the garden for the suitors who are killed by the spirit that haunts his daughter at night, thus betraying his secret participation in their murder.[543] This secret relationship also exists between the mountain

---

[539] We find a related figure in the "The Girl with Roses" (Zaunert, *Märchen aus dem Donaulande*, p. 269): The dragon, the maiden's demonic guardian, sleeps for a whole year, which might be related to the course of the sun.

[540] Dieterich, *Mithrasliturgie*, p. 135.

[541] Cumont, *Orientalische Religionen*, p. 82f.

[542] Zimmer, "Tod und Wiedergeburt," p. 255. On the conception of Dionysus as the father of the sea and the earth, and as an all-generating sun, see Leisegang, "Schlange," p. 161f. On the sun as the lord of the dead and as a primordial ancestor, see Róheim, *Spiegelzauber*, pp. 228 and 262. On the threatening role of the sun, see "The Farmer and the Golden Sun" (Russia, no. 50); on the symbolism inside the mountain, see Bächtold-Stäubli (under *Berggeister*, "mountain spirits"), who suggests that nature spirits can appear as animals "or even as metal (gold), as a flame, or as wheel or ball of fire."

[543] For details, see Jung, "The Significance of the Father in the Destiny of the Individual," CW 4, § 742–744, esp. § 743: "The story shows father Raguel in his two roles, as the inconsolable father of the bride and the provident digger of his son-in-law's grave. Humanly speaking he seems beyond reproach, and it is highly probable that he was. But there is still the evil spirit Asmodeus and his presence needs

spirit and the king in the version collected in Zauner's *Deutsche Märchen seit Grimm*: The puzzle demanding to be solved twice revolves around the profane father-king's horse and sword, while on the third occasion, it concerns the head of the mountain spirit, suggesting a certain parallelism between the figures.

576    We have already interpreted the symbolism of the horse and the sword on several occasions in this study. Briefly put, the former symbolizes psychic instinct, the latter the discriminating function of the spirit, that is, psychic energy, in particular of the masculine type, which is predominantly spiritual.[544] This symbol attains perfection and culminates in the image of the head, which the words of the mountain spirit describe as numinous: "... this time, think of my head. No mortal can think of it, least of all a human being." We have already discussed the meaning of the head in the section about the realm of the dead, and therefore it is only reiterated briefly here. According to a widespread primitive view, the head is the seat of the individual's mysterious life and creative force.[545]

577    The head symbolizes male creativity, the paternal principle, and heaven also according to the *I Ching*, the Chinese Book of Changes.[546] According to Plato's "Timaeus," the head is round; it is thus complete and contains the divine core. This ancient view persisted among the Arabs, who therefore used human heads for prophesying[547]; the Chinese sign for Tao consists partly of a head, which probably should be interpreted as the "beginning."[548] In alchemy, the dragon's severed head, also referred to as the head of Osiris, or a crow's head, or the Ethiopian's head, plays a major role.[549]

---

explaining. If we suspect old Raguel personally of playing a double role, this malicious insinuation would apply only to his sentiments; there is no evidence that he committed murder. These wicked deeds transcend the old man's daughter-complex as well as Sara's father-complex, for which reason the legend fittingly ascribes them to a demon."

[544] The symbols have a similar meaning in the Norwegian version: The scissors, like the sword, are a symbol of the Logos, of the mind, while ball points to a secret meaning.

[545] Thurnwald, "Primitive Initiationsriten," pp. 322 and 372f.

[546] Wilhelm, ed. and trans. *The I Ching: The Book of Changes* (1950/2003), p. 3.

[547] On the role of the head in alchemy, and on the severed head of Osiris, see Jung, "Transformation Symbolism in the Mass," *CW* 11, § 365–367.

[548] Wilhelm, *The Secret of the Golden Flower* (1931/2022).

[549] Silberer, *Probleme der Mystik*, p. 84; Jung, *Psychology and Alchemy*, CW 12, § 484, including fn. 171 and fig. 219; on the head that is detached from the body as a "round" element and as the epitome of perfection in alchemical symbolism, as "detached" consciousness in the form of wholeness, see Jung, *Kindertraumseminar* (1938/1939), p. 165.

It means the *materia prima* in its spiritual aspect, or the *meaning* of the unconscious. Only those who can grasp the meaning behind the grotesque, ambiguous appearance of the unconscious are immune to being spellbound by its inferior aspect, and consequently to mastering the unconscious realm just as little as those who reject it from the outset as "meaningless."

578    One episode that resembles that about the head of the mountain spirit (or troll) occurs in "Ivan the Cow's Son and Storm Prince" (Russia, no. 22), a fairytale that otherwise is structured differently. The episode goes like this:

579    Ivan-Zarevich was courting the daughter of the Indian king. She seemed to accept his advances, yet requested that she could leave for a while to change her clothes. Ivan the Cow's Son, the suitor's brother, a magical helper, secretly watched the maiden transform into a dove and fly to the sea. He followed her as a falcon. "The King's daughter reached the sea, threw herself to the ground, transformed into a beautiful maiden, and said: 'Grandfather, grandfather, golden head, silver beard![550] Let me talk to you. The grandfather raised his head out of the blue sea: 'What do you need, my dear grandchild?'—'Ivan Tsarevich is wooing me; I did not want to become his wife, but now our whole army is slain. Give me, dear Grandfather, three golden hairs from your head, and I will show them to the tsar's son: 'Tell me, Ivan Tsarevich, from which root has this grass grown?'" The grandfather gave her three hairs; she threw herself on the ground, turned into a dove, and flew home. But then Ivan threw himself to the ground, turned into a maiden as she had, and said: 'Grandfather, Grandfather, come out again and talk to me: I forgot to say something.' No sooner had the Grandfather raised his head from the water than Ivan grabbed him and tore his head off. Then he threw himself to the ground, transformed into an eagle, and flew to the palace faster than

---

[550] Afanas'ev's variant, "Ivan the Cow's Son," has a golden head and a silver mop of hair.

the King's daughter. He called the tsarevich out into the corridor. 'Here, Ivan Tsarevich, take this head. The King's daughter will come before you, show you three hairs, and say: "Tell me, Ivan Tsarevich, from which root has this grass grown?" When she does, you must show her the head.'

580

The King's daughter approached, showed Ivan Tsarevich the three hairs, and said: "Guess, Tsarevich, from which root has this grass grown? If you recognize it, I will follow you as your wife; if I do not—do not be angry with me!" But Ivan Tsarevich pulled the head out from under his coat-tails, threw it on the table, and said: 'There's the root!' The King's daughter thought to herself: 'These are industrious fellows!' Thereupon, she made a request: "Allow me, Ivan-Zarevich, to change my clothes in the other room." She returned to the old man in the sea, yet Ivan the Cow's Son conjured the head back into place so that she found the grandfather alive again. After being been beaten with iron, copper, and tin rods on her bridal night, she was tamed and surrendered to her husband.[551]

581

The three golden hairs are nothing other than the devil's three golden hairs, which we interpreted in our discussion of the eponymous Grimm's tale.[552] As observed, this motif is related to solar mythology, which is also evident in the present tales. Hair epitomizes the "mana" personality and its thoughts, and thus confirms our deliberations on the horse, the sword, and the head. The hero must be able to grasp, as it were, the secret thoughts of the world-spirit, which shine in the dark unconscious, in order to discover the correct relationship with

[551] Only an abridged version of this tale is discussed here. See Afanas'ev's variant, "Ivan the Cow's Son," where the hero must guess three times what Elena has in her possession to provide something similar. He succeeds twice. On the third evening, Elena drives the carriage to the sea at a gallop, followed by Ivan. Elena calls her grandfather, who has silver hair and a golden beard. When he lets Elena remove the lice from him, she pulls out three of his silver hairs, but Ivan pulls out a whole tuft at the same time. "The grandfather awoke and shouted, 'Have you lost your mind! That hurts!' 'Forgive me, grandfather. I haven't combed you for so long. Your hair is all tangled.'" When the same happens to the beard, the grandfather jumps up screaming and throws himself into the sea. But in the morning Elena is outdone by the tsarevich: Instead of three hairs, he shows her a large tuft. "Chuinis" (Latvia, no. 7) contains the same episode.
[552] See "The Devil with the Three Golden Hairs" (*The Complete Grimm's Fairy Tales*, pp. 151–158).

the soul-image. He accomplishes this great task in "The Comrade" and its parallel tale because he has fearlessly confronted his personal shadow. This experience also helps him to find his way through the dark unconscious.

582 After the troll or the mountain spirit has been slain, the princess reveals that her love for this figure was a spell that also forced her to commit evil against her will.[553] In "Illuga saga Griðarfostra," a Nordic saga, the heroine is condemned to being a murdering giantess, who must reluctantly kill her half-sister's suitors until a man arrives who does not fear her sword[554] (note the role of the father's sword in the present fairytale!). Psychologically, he can withstand the animus ruling her. The assertion that the anima's destructive side corresponds to an involuntary compulsion is relatively frequent, while her demonic paramour is mostly described as intrinsically evil. More rarely, however, it is suggested that he, too, is a sufferer, a cursed one, who only commits evil involuntarily. As much is hinted at in "The Shoes That Were Danced to Pieces,"[555] where the princesses dance with 12 *cursed* princes *to redeem them.* Nevertheless, the wretches are punished for having fettered the princesses to themselves. Thus, the otherworldly ruler's love for the anima is not born merely out a desire to possess her, as in "The Comrade," and in particular in "The Cursed Princess." It has also arisen from the secret longing of this demonic world for humankind.[556]

---

[553] The same motif appears in "The Enchanted Giant" (Iceland, no. 50): The giant Kol, who corresponds to the animal prince, must kill whoever approaches him.

[554] Lincke, "Stiefmutter," p. 149f.

[555] *The Complete Grimm's Fairy Tales*, pp. 596–600.

[556] The same events take place in "The Princess in the Tree" (Zaunert, *Deutsche Märchen seit Grimm*, p. 1): A hunter, who probably corresponds to Wotan, abducts and curses the princess. Jung interprets this situation as follows: "The hunter first appears in the story as a black raven. He has stolen away the princess and holds her a prisoner. She describes him as 'the devil.' But it is exceedingly odd that he himself is locked up in the one forbidden room of the castle and fixed to the wall with three nails, as though crucified. He is imprisoned, like all jailers, in his own prison, and bound like all who curse. The prison of both is a magic castle at the top of a gigantic tree, presumably the world-tree. The princess belongs to the upper region of light near the sun. Sitting there in captivity on the world-tree, she is a kind of anima mundi who has got herself into the power of darkness. But this catch does not seem to have done the latter much good either, seeing that the captor is crucified and moreover with three nails. The crucifixion evidently betokens a state of agonizing bondage and suspension, fit punishment for one foolhardy enough to venture like a Prometheus into the orbit of the opposing principle. This was what the raven, who is identical with the hunter, did when he ravished a precious soul from the upper world of light; and so, as a punishment, he is nailed to the wall in that upper world" ("The Phenomenology of the Spirit in Fairytales," *CW* 9/I, § 427).

583    This aspect of the anima's demonic lover is also illumined by "A Soldier Redeems the Tsarina from a Curse" (Balkans, no. 35): A girl loves a young man who, however, without her knowledge, dies in a foreign land. Hearing the young woman's lament, an old woman casts a spell that will enable the bereaved to see the dead man. In fact, the young man visits her at night and asks her to turn around. Fast asleep, she is unable to satisfy his demand. He threatens her that in that case, her mother will die the following day. Consequently, the young woman loses her parents and both siblings and eventually dies herself. A rose grows on her grave, which only the young tsar manages to pick. He pins the flower to his hat, which he places in his room, and notices that the food lying there is eaten at night. Keeping himself awake the following night, he watches the rose transform into a beautiful girl who eats the food. He speaks to her, and she agrees to become his wife if he promises never to mention the church. He obliges. One day, the couple meanwhile has three sons, he utters the word "church." His wife dies instantly and is buried in the church. However, all the soldiers who are keeping vigil are mysteriously torn asunder the next morning. Advised by an old woman, an old veteran, however, manages to summon the dead woman back to life. Thanking him, she explains that he has redeemed not only her but also her children from the dead man's curse.

584    The plot of "The Vampire" (Roma, no. 13) is similar, except that the dead man's lover is a crowfooted dead demon from the outset who recalls Goldnose, a demon in "The Bridegroom with the Golden Nose" (Finland, no. 52). Instead, the final episode in the church is missing, which relates the Balkan tale to that about the black king's daughter (see above).[557] The previous comments on the "grateful dead man" also apply to the dead man in this tale. He haunts others because he thirsts for life. He needs others to realize himself and thus to be released from his sojourn in this world. On this occasion, however, he is not redeemed. On the contrary, he is split off in the end, which is obviously also regarded as a solution.

---

[557] See "The King's Black Daughter" (Zaunert, *Märchen aus dem Donaulande*, p. 150).

585    In "The Cursed Princess," the secret vampiric nature of the mountain spirit is revealed in its words: "... the more you must torment your human being, the more you must take pleasure in his blood, the more you must drink from it, the sooner you will become pure and mine." In "A Soldier Redeems the Tsarina from a Curse" (Balkans, no. 35) and in "The Vampire" (Roma, no. 13), the princess's possession (by demons) expresses itself not in malice (although she is indirectly to blame for the death of her relatives), but in the fact that she is dead and a flower; that is, she is both removed from life and nonhuman.[558]

586    It is quite obvious to compare the shades of the dead in the latter fairytales with the "grateful dead man" in "The Comrade" and similar tales.[559] The comparison suggests that that part of the "shadow" that can be redeemed as the "grateful dead man" is the personal "shadow," which transforms into a helpful instinct. Yet there is also a more general shadow, which ultimately reaches into the

---

[558] One example where the anima-figure is destroyed by a dominating demon or shadow-lover is "The Spinner and the Dead Man" (Krauss, *Sagen der Südslaven*, vol. 1, no. 70), a Southern Slavic tale in which the spirit turns the girl to dust and ashes.

[559] This is the hero's "shadow." On the identity of the man's "shadow" with the woman's animus, see "Hans Wunderlich" (Zaunert, *Deutsche Märchen seit Grimm*, p. 37). Another, humorous example is "The Bad Wife" (Afanas'ev, *Russian Fairy Tales*, pp. 56–57): An evil farmer's wife persistently defied her husband. One day, he warned her, with the intention of getting rid of her, about picking berries by a bottomless pit, whereupon she did precisely that and promptly fell into the well. After four peaceful days, he decided to find out how his wife was: He lowered a rope into the pit and pulled out a small gnome. Frightened, he wanted to drop the unsightly creature back into the hole, but the imp begged him to be left in the world, since an evil woman had come into the pit and was tormenting everyone to the death. The farmer wanted to leave, whereupon the imp promised to make the wives and daughters of merchants mad and sick, and leave them again when the farmer appeared. The farmer became a wealthy doctor. Eventually, the imp considered him to be rich enough and warned him to attend to the next patient, a *boyar*'s daughter, or the man would devour him [Translator's note: A *boyar* was the highest rank in the feudal nobility of several Eastern European states including Kievan Russia]. However, the farmer made the *boyar* gather the local people outside the house and made them shout, "The wicked woman has come!" Horrified, the imp asked the farmer, whom he was about to devour, for a hiding place, and the former advised him to return to the abyss, where the woman would not go. No sooner had the imp done this, the farmer received the *boyar*'s daughter.—In this tale, the woman's animus pursues the farmer as his shadow, until he, whose consciousness is reluctant to engage in a confrontation, succeeds in finding an acceptable solution by completely splitting off the unconscious force.—In contrast, in "Tolojäla and his Daughter" (South Sea, no. 48) the attempted separation fails. Limascheimalug, the anima-figure, is Tolojäla's magically begotten daughter. Despite his warning, she bathes in a brook rather than in a well. Through her oil, which the brook carries into the world, King Schautelur becomes aware of her and marries her. During her pregnancy, she demands to eat more fish liver than he can procure, so that following the advice of a sorcerer he kills her father and cooks his liver for her. This food makes her sing, whereupon Limascheimalug rushes home and finds her father dead in the hut. She sets the hut on fire and lets herself be burned with him. Schautelur, who has followed her, also jumps into the flames.—Schautelur's attempt to painlessly sever the connection with his father-animus by cunningly forcing his assimilation ends tragically: The unconscious wreaks havoc on everything.

divine realm and can be integrated into human life only to a limited extent. Human beings must resist its power for their own safety, to avoid being devoured or torn apart by it.

587

Chinese fairytales also report the existence of a demonic sphere: Concealed behind the ghostly bride and dominating her, this sphere merges with the man's shadow. For instance, "The Painted Skin" (China, no. 81) describes the following events:

588

> A man called Wang met a girl on the street who was traveling alone. As she was young and pretty, he spoke to her sympathetically and learned that she had run away from a hard-hearted mistress. When he asked about her destination, she replied: "Lost people have no home."—The young man took the girl home and hid her in a secluded room. One day, he met a priest who looked at him amazed and asked whom he had met. When Wang replied "Nobody," the priest said: "You are surrounded by an ominous breath. So why do you say nobody? ... It is strange that some people who are approaching their death can't be brought to their senses!" The young man, who had grown suspicious, tried to laugh off the priest's words. When he returned home, he found the gate locked. The door to his room was also locked. He peered through the window and saw "a hideous devil, whose face was blue and green, and whose teeth were sticking out of its mouth like a saw." This figure spread a human skin over the bed and began painting it. When it had finished, it picked up the skin like a piece of clothing and put it on. Thereupon, it transformed into the girl. The terrified young man fled the scene.—He went to the priest and begged him to save him. The priest said: "We want to drive her away. This creature is also in real trouble. She is about to find a substitute, but I cannot bring myself to harm her."[560] He gave the young man

---

[560] In *Chinesische Märchen*, p. 382, Wilhelm comments on this fairytale as follows: "... the spirit lures another man into disaster ... and becomes free to be reborn." See also the previous comments and "The Spirits of the Hanged" (China, no. 66). Despite the cultural differences, demonic malice is justified in Europe as well as in China as a means of achieving redemption.

a magic wand to hang on the door of his room and promised to see him again in the temple of the green lord.—During the first watch, the young man heard a clanging noise outside the door. He sent his wife to find out what was going on. She saw how the girl did not dare to enter, but remained standing, gritting her teeth, and then left. After a little while, she returned, broke the wand, smashed the door, went across to the bed, tore open the man's body and heart, and disappeared. The distraught woman sent word to the priest, who exclaimed angrily: "I took pity on her, and now the devil is so impudent!" When he arrived at the house, he realized that the devil had become an old woman in the brother's house in the southern courtyard. The priest shouted: "You, child of the devil, give me my wand!" Hearing these words, the woman turned pale and wanted to flee. After a fierce struggle, during which the demon turned into a pig and then into smoke, the priest trapped it in a bottle.—Tearfully, the woman begged the priest to bring her husband back to life. But the priest was unable to raise the dead and directed the woman to a madman lying in excrement in the marketplace. "You can try to move him with your pleas. If he insults and mistreats you, you must not grow angry." The woman went to the market and encountered the repulsive, dirty beggar, "who was singing at the top of his voice like a madman." The woman slid over to him on her knees and uttered her lament. He laughed and said: "Darling, do you like me?" When she continued her lament, he beat her with a stick and said: "When someone is dead, it is strange to ask me to bring them back to life. Am I the prince of hell?" When she put up with his antics, he cleared his throat and spit into his hand. "Holding it to her mouth, he said: 'Eat it!'" Remembering the priest, the woman overcame her disgust and swallowed it. She felt something hard slide down her throat like a round lump that remained stuck in her chest. The beggar bursted out laughing: "Darling, you *do* like me!" With these words, he disappeared into a temple.—Desperate and ashamed, the woman returned home. But when she embraced the man's corpse, the lump in her chest rose and fell into the dead man's chest, becoming a human heart that revived him. All that remained was a scar.

589 Here, the luminous aspect of the woman's soul-image is represented by the hero's wife, the dark, enchanted, and magical one by the female demon. Wang, our hero, falls completely for the female demon and, without his wife and the priest, is helpless against her. The anima's separated halves are united (by evil being assimilated in the spiritualized form of smoke), while the adherence to the dark world is overcome by Wang's wife, the luminous part of his soul, confronting the mad beggar and humiliating herself before him; before that power, that is, which seems to cause the demonic spell and make the "lost" girl suffer, and which has indirectly taken possession of Wang's heart or self, precisely because he was unable to look the dark aspect in the face. The madman is thus the man who has gone mad, who has "lost his heart" to the demonic world. By possessing this heart, the madman becomes Wang's "shadow,"[561] his demonic self: "Consciousness" lies there "dead."

590 In this tale, the priest occupies an intermediate position—between paralyzed consciousness and the demonic world—and is able to point the way that should be taken. As such, the priest counterbalances the "madman": He is a more luminous, more conscious aspect of the shadow, and functions as a psychopomp. By unmasking the girl as a devil with a green face and red hair,[562] he once again places the demonic being in the existing divine order and thus protects Wang from being assimilated completely into that world. It is strange, and attests to the existence of secret knowledge, that he (i.e., the priest) wanted to meet Wang again in the "temple

[561] In "The Ghost of Hagi" (Iceland, no. 64), the ghost attempts to drive its victim "crazy." According to Bolte and Mackensen's *Handwörterbuch*, the German word *Gespenst* (ghost) originally meant an "alluring illusion" (i.e., phantasmagoria).
[562] See also the motif of the horn-producing fruit that the hero feeds to the woman who is governed by the evil animus; see *Archetypal Symbols in Fairytales*, vol. 1, p. 473, and Aarne, *Märchenforschungen*, pp. 85–142. The horns characterize the masculine, demonic component; in most cases, this insight eliminates—albeit in a roundabout way—the anima's connection with the false bridegroom.

of the green lord." He is the lord of the woods, who dwells in the East and watches over the procreation and emergence of all creatures. He is also the god of love and the power of spring.[563] This suggests a connection between this god and the erotic, seductive green devil. The mad beggar, however, disappears "in a temple." Was he perhaps this god, the anima's demonic lord? After all, he asks so misleadingly: "Am I the prince of hell?" Moreover, he wishes to be loved to the point where the woman conquers her revulsion. In the end, he becomes inaccessible to profane eyes: Wang's only memory of his anima experience is a scar.[564]

591    In the principal fairytales considered here ("The Comrade" and "The Cursed Princess"), the princess, to whom we now return, is not yet liberated once and for all[565]—even if the demon of the underworld has been slain. Accordingly, another bathing episode ensues, which corresponds to that in "King Lindworm." Suddenly, the princess is "pitch-black," and this blackness is in fact a troll's skin: While the motif of the black princess is combined with that of the animal skin, the meaning of this combination, an overpowering by the shadow and its world, is evident from the previous deliberations. In "The Cursed Princess," the anima-figure is not only as black as a raven. She *is* a raven, which subsequently transforms into a dove and only then becomes human.

592    This raven recalls that in "The Princess in the Tree"; in that tale, however, it represents the spirit dominating the anima. Here, the secret identity of the two archetypes becomes apparent. While in the Christian imagination the raven symbolizes the ungodly spirit, the dove, by contrast, represents the celestial spirit. In pagan terms, as explained, the raven is a harbinger of wisdom, the knowing helper of gods and humans, while the dove is assigned to Venus. Insofar as the dove must also be overcome in "The Cursed Princess," this fairytale, as shown above, reflects purely pagan ideas. In "The

---

[563] Wilhelm, *Chinesische Märchen*, p. 382, and "The Incarnation of the Five Elders" (China, no. 15).

[564] Just as the prince of hell hides behind the mask of a beautiful girl, so in the Aztec legend the dark antagonist Tezcatlipocas Uemac hides behind enticing female demons (see "Quetzalcouatl's Fall from Grace and Tollan's Downfall" [Aztec, no. 12], esp. p. 69f.).

[565] On the difficulties of liberation, i.e., on the firm grip with which the dark world has taken possession of the anima, see, e.g., "Maria Morevna" (Afanas' ev, *Russian Fairy Tales*, pp. 553–562), where the demon takes possession of Maria twice before the hero is eventually able to unite with her.

Comrade," however, the Christian evaluation of manifestations ultimately prevails: The princess is supposed to lose her "trollish skin," and the comrade's departure to the kingdom of heaven, to which the bells summon him, is even a somewhat unexpected Christian formulation. This example shows that fairytales sometimes align Christian ideas with pagan ones. In such cases, fairytale images serve as a dark psychic foundation on which Christian ideas are based.

593    In the Norwegian version, the healing of the princess is first followed by the test of loyalty, by the division of property, and by the division of the child, as demanded by the comrade. In response, the hero must prove his loyalty to his companion. Even those who are familiar with this adversary, and who have thus gained him as a cooperating psychic factor, must exercise utmost moral vigilance and detach themselves completely from the egoism adhering to the opposites. They must do so because the shadow always creates conflicts that expose the human soul and the innermost personality to the danger of being torn apart. The imminent division of the child might thus once again tear asunder the self, which has gradually come into existence.

594    In several versions, on the other hand, the hero's willingness to divide the child is contingent on the dead man's liberation from his attachment to the world. Examples include "The Dead Man's Gratitude"[566] and "The Grateful Dead Man" (Spain, no. 72). After the hero has agreed to divide the child, and after the spirit has renounced its share, the dead man says: "This had to be done for my sake, so that I could behold the face of God." Accordingly, the shadow largely demands a person's willingness to sacrifice and share their life. The destiny of consciousness and the unconscious, of ego and shadow, is contingent on a balanced give-and-take. The division of the child, as accepted by the ego, and the magical helper's abstention, reveals that, ultimately, they accept their mutual dependence.

---

[566] Zaunert, *Deutsche Märchen seit Grimm*, Jena 1922, p. 245; see also p. 267, fn. 472.

595
In some respects, however, the motif of division or splitting seems to make more sense in those variants where the dead man's companion does not threaten the *child* with the sword but the apparently tamed and redeemed *princess*, whereupon snakes and poisonous worms continue to fall from her womb, which she had received from her demonic paramour and which would have killed the hero in the bridal night.[567] Instead of a real child, in which the self would be recognizable, a pseudochild has thus been conceived first. Instead of the higher entity, a hidden multiplicity of unconscious impulses is hidden in the core of the psyche; this unconscious sphere has deadly consequences.[568] The otherworldly *doppelgänger*, who "confronts" the human being, that is, his soul, in a moral conflict, brings these dark impulses to light and rids the psyche of them. They also originate in a spirit-father, who has diabolic features, however. The real child, on the other hand, is begotten by the hero as human consciousness, for the self is the conscious person's father and son: The father, because it precedes the human being and begets the ego; and the son, because it becomes visible solely through the human effort to become conscious.

596
A considerable number of fairytales belonging to the group about the "grateful dead man" also describe a complication, which intensifies toward the end. It is not caused by a demonic paramour, but by the princess's profane lover. Aided by the "grateful dead man," in each case the hero gains the king's daughter or beautiful rich wife,

---

[567] See "The Grateful Dead Man" (Roma, no. 5), "The Miserly Tsar and His Compassionate Son or: The Good Deed Is Never Lost" (Balkans, no. 2), "The Tale of Ssila Zarevich and Ivashka, White Shirt" (Russia, no. 55), "The Red Fish" (Caucasus, no. 18), and other variants mentioned in Bolte and Polívka, *Anmerkungen*, vol. 3, pp. 502ff. See also "The Hunter and the Seven-Headed Forest Devil" (Siberia, no. 5): After her forest-demon (i.e., suitor), who was out to kill the hunter, is killed by the latter, his sister puts one of the devil's teeth under the brother's mattress after his wedding feast, so that the groom is fatally pierced. But his animals save him and then kill the sister. See also "The Marriage-Shy Princess," a peculiar, albeit weak and distorted version collected in von Hahn's *Griechische Märchen*, vol. 2, no. 114. In that tale, the hero solves the tasks assigned by the princess unaided by magic, whereupon the dragon bridegroom leaves his bride to preserve her life and his, as he tells her, with a "despondent" look as he departs. The following day, however, the hero spurns the King's daughter, who is already wearing her wedding dress, and returns to his father and finds happiness with a beautiful and virtuous woman. In this case, the bond with the demonic bridegroom is only partially severed. Instead, the hero separates the unconscious sphere from his profane life. As a result of his endeavor and "insights" into the unconscious world, he at first becomes happy in the profane world. However, this solution remains unsatisfactory and seems unreliable. See *ibid.*, p. 320.
[568] On these circumstances, see the snake-daughter of the blacksmith of Pont de Pile in "Goldfoot" (France, vol. 2, no. 52). See also Wilhelm Hertz, *Gesammelte Abhandlungen*, ed. v. d. Leyen (1905), p. 156, esp. his discusssion of "The Tale of the Poison Girl."

only to be slandered by the rival or pushed from the ship into the water and deprived of his bride. The dead man, who appears as a ghost, swan, fish, wooden plank, and in various other guises, rescues the hero onto an island and later brings him to the court of the princess's father, where the hero prevents the imminent wedding with the false bridegroom, exposes the latter, and hands him over for punishment, and is invested with his rights.[569]

In some versions, this "profane" rival or "false bridegroom" is related to the bride's divine-demonic father-lover and occupies, as it were, an intermediate position. One example is "Wood collector, cat, snake and fish, or: Do good to animals, you will not regret it" (Balkans, no. 6), where the rival is a Moor,[570] while in "The Jew and

597

---

[569] See, e.g., "The King's Son Thorstein and the Grateful Dead Man" (Iceland, no. 32): His extravagance makes a King's son lose his possessions, friends, and kingdom, so that he leaves his native realm. On the road, he settles a dead man's debt. At a crossroads, and despite a farmer's warning, he takes the road to the east and arrives at a homestead where he serves giants and tricks out of a princess who they are holding captive. The couple boards a ship whose captain (Raud) desires the princess. Therefore, he abandons Thorstein on the high seas. But the latter is rescued by the dead man, who he had freed from his debt and who is brought to the home of the King's daughter, where he enlists as a stable boy, as advised by the ghost. The princess is supposed to marry Raud, her presumed savior, but she asks her father to let the stable boy first tell his story. When he does, everything comes to light: Raud is slain, and Thorstein inherits the kingdom.—This tale has the same basic motif as "The Dead Man's Gratitude" (Zaunert, *Deutsche Märchen seit Grimm*, p. 245): On a trading expedition, a merchant's son uses all his funds to settle a dead man's debts. Although his father is angry, he sacrifices his ship and its goods a second time for a girl who pirates want to sell into slavery. When he returns home, he severs ties with his father. After a while, the young couple decides to visit the woman's home by ship. She is one of three missing royal daughters, and her father's ships have been searching her for three years. They meet one of these ship and board it. The three commanders, however, seek the rescuer's reward and throw the merchant's son into the sea. The princess is meant to marry one of her purported saviors; as they have sworn her to silence, she postpones the wedding with the ruse that the bridal rooms must first be painted to her taste. But she never approves of the painters' work. The abandoned merchant's son is taken to an island, where he is fed by a white swan. After several years, a little gray man arrives in a small vessel and promises to help the young man if he shares everything that he and his wife have acquired in the first year. Thereupon, he arrives in the town, where the King asks him to paint his daughter's rooms. He obliges. In the third room, he describes how the King's daughter was freed and how he was betrayed. When the princess sees the paintings, she falls to the ground as if she were dead and confesses everything to her father. The false servants are killed, and the merchant's son receives the kingdom. After a boy is born to the young couple, the little gray man appears. The young King immediately offers him his possessions, but the man points to the child. The young King's hair stands on end. "But the little gray man quickly appeased the King and said: 'Be of good cheer, I want neither all nor half of your money, nor your child. Do you know who I am? I am the white swan who rescued you from the sea onto land. I am also the spirit of the man whose body you ransomed and buried honestly. Now I can sleep until the Last Judgment.' Thus spoke the little gray man and disappeared."—Beyond the motif of the grateful dead man, see the figure of the profane rival in various tales collected in *Deutsche Märchen seit Grimm* (1922): "Rinroth" (p. 179), "The Quick Soldier" (p. 257), "The Iron Boots" (p. 376), and "The Jew and the Padlock" (p. 397). See also "Cindarella and the Sea Dragon," Ehrentreich, *Englische Volksmärchen* (1938), p. 212; "The Golden Castle That Hung in the Air" (Norway, no. 35); "The Story about the Old Witch" (Spain, no. 65); "Born by a Fish" (Finland, no. 31); "The Tsar's Son and the Grateful Animals" (Balkans, no. 10); and "The Sprosser and the Nightingale" (Caucasus, no. 8).

[570] See "Cindarella" (Modern Greece, no. 11). For further examples, see Aarne, *Märchenforschungen*, Helsingfors 1908.

the Padlock," he is a Jew. These figures are typical shadow-figures and already possess a more "magical" aspect. Like all other archetypes, the anti-bridegroom (i.e., the shadow) has multiple aspects: a positive[571] *and* a negative one, a magical *and* a profane one, a divine *and* a human one, a high *and* a low one.

598     A peculiar circumstance makes the problem of these characters even more subtle and more exciting, even if it is more difficult to interpret: A secret connection, or identity, can be established not only between the demonic and the profane false lover, but also between the helpful shade (i.e., the spirit of the dead) or comrade and the false bridegroom.[572] This is evident, for instance, in "The Fortress of the Curaoi" (Ireland, no. 3):

599     A King's son journeyed to Asia to free a maiden who lived in a large fortress surrounded by a magical wheel. The fortress belonged to her father, the King of Asia, who wanted his daughter to marry a rich old king. When the son of the Irish King, saddened by his powerlessness and full of longing for the princess, was about to return home to look for a magician who could prevent the wheels from turning, one appeared in Curaoi. When the prince asked who he was, he replied: "That does not matter. I have known the lord of this castle since time immemorial. We learned magic together from the arch-wizard in Asia. I have always been superior to him and will overcome him now if you instruct me to do so." "Well, then, stop the magical wheels!" said the son of the Irish King, "and you shall have what you want in the castle. But I wish to know where you are from and what your name is."

600     "I am Curaoi and come from far away in Ireland." He did indeed bring the wheels to a halt, so that he could storm through the gate with the prince, to the horror of the King of Asia. When the latter summoned his daughter and when the

---

[571] In the present fairytales ("The Comrade" and "The Cursed Princess"), this can be deduced merely indirectly from the amplifications of the sun-god and from the meaning of his "round" head as the self.
[572] In "Squire Roland" (Ehrentreich, *Englische Volksmärchen*, p. 207), Merlin the wizard helps defeat the king of fairies.

prince asked Curaoi for his reward, he replied that the most precious thing he wanted from the castle was the princess. Once this arrangement had been agreed, nothing could be done to change it. Agrieved at having to marry an old druid, the princess travelled to Ireland with the prince and Curaoi. When they arrived, she made it a condition that she would only marry a man who owned a castle as big as her father's. Curaoi promised to build one and instructed people to fetch the largest boulders. Meanwhile, the prince travelled through Ireland as a harp player. The princess summoned him, and they agreed that if one day he saw milk flowing to the sea down a particular waterway, she would be waiting for him at the gate. As Curaoi's giants were collecting boulders to build the castle, and as Curaoi had gone out hunting, the maiden absconded with the prince. When Curaoi could not find her on his return, he called his men back with his magic horn; but when they arrived, they found him dead, "and no one knew how he had died." The fortress that they started building remained unfinished, while the son of the Irish King and the princess married and lived happily ever after.

601   Here, the helper unexpectedly turns into the bride's abductor. This peculiar version also underscores the fact that the comrade's demand for division, as observed in the fairytales about the "grateful dead man," was not a harmless test. Also there, the helper's spirit could have become a robber or destroyer of what had been gained. Curaoi, as the annotations suggest, is related to Balor (see "Balor"; Ireland, no. 4) and Odin; he tends to go unnoticed among the Irish heroes and is also called "graycoat."[573] He is thus a manifestation of the world-spirit. Importantly, this plot is different because the hero has neither confronted nor grappled with the helper. Accordingly, the latter has not been brought closer to the human sphere: He has not become a personal shadow, but has remained, quite archetypally, an evil primal spirit. Psychologically, discrimination, that is, detaching

---

[573] See Müller-Lisowski, *Irische Volksmärchen*, p. 320f., esp. the note.

the personal shadow from the unconscious, is necessary because only thus can human beings maintain a balance between their shadow and consciousness and avoid being possessed by a devil. Thus, while the shadow expresses itself as a personal weakness and inadequacy, it does not become a demon that poisons a person and their surroundings. In "The Fortress of Curaoi," the process of gaining knowledge through the shadow, which would have made that knowledge conscious, never occurred. Therefore, its help is problematic, and the helper once again becomes the demonic robber.

602    Another motif of this fairytale is also worth highlighting: the magic wheels. These recall the wheel standing on the altar of the mountain spirit in "The Cursed Princess." These wheels may be said to represent a negative aspect of the sun wheel, to which the wheel of eternal rebirth or the wheels of hell could be added as amplifications: as symbols of being embroiled infinitely in recurring and apparently futile psychic events. Because just as the fish, despite symbolizing fertility and the self, had a negative aspect due to its spikes in "The Cursed Princess," so the wheel also has a negative meaning besides its positive connotation. Both symbols are primitive because they still contain the double aspect in *one and the same* figure. Precisely this, however, explains why such images also point to the future: They enable reuniting aspects that have been torn apart too forcefully by reason; that is, they enable uniting one-sided perspectives in a single, comprehensive image.

603    The theme of the next section emerges from a fairytale that combines, in quite a surprising manner, three motifs: the anima-figure's demonic, ghostly husband; the animal shadow-brother who must be redeemed; and the problem of incest.

◇

## C.
## The Siblings Redeem
## Each Other

604   The fairytale that assembles and illumines the themes mentioned at the end of the last section in a very new way is "The Son-in-Law from a Foreign Land" (Balkans, no. 39):

605   In his last will, a King decreed that his two sons should give their only sister to the first stranger who asked for her. The suitor was "a man ... who looked somewhat strange and wild." The older brother did not want to give his sister to this suitor, but the younger one honored his father's wish and gave her to the stranger. After a long time, the older brother set off in search of his sister and, after an arduous journey, came to the hut of an old woman who warned him not to continue his journey. One day, he reached for the fruit of a tree near the hut, but the tree withdrew and enticed him to follow it. When he had followed the tree for a whole day, it stopped. An old man climbed down and said to the King's son as he tried to return to the hut. "My dear, you will never return to where you came from today. The region there is bewitched by an evil spirit and the old woman you were with is one of his servants. If you had stayed with her any longer, she would have handed you over to him. So praise the Lord and get some rest." The old man prepared some food for the King's son and then carried him through the air to a gateless castle, whose mistress had the sleeping man brought into the castle. He recognized his sister, who told him: "The old man is none other than my husband; he has only brought you here to kill

you." The ghost spent three days feasting with the brother-in-law. On the fourth day, they went for a walk. When the ghost returned alone, the sister knew that he had taken her brother out of the world.

606 After the younger brother had waited for his siblings at home, he also set off on a journey and first came to a city made of iron. The place was deserted. Only one house remained unlocked. Inside, the King's son met a dragon that was roasting lamb on a spit. When the dragon did not acknowledge his greeting, the King's son started a brutal fight and pursued the wounded figure into the castle, where a young girl was weeping in the corner of a room. She answered his questions with these words: "My father ruled this town, and the dragon was a magician; he asked my father to give me to him. When my father refused, the dragon ransacked the town and abducted me. A little box hangs around his neck, with a little bird inside; kill it and the whole town will come to life again." The King's son acted accordingly and brought the town back to life. Thereafter, he went to the old woman whom his brother had stayed with and was also taken by the ghost to his sister's castle. Finding the gate, he entered and learned the fate of his older brother from his sister. That evening, he hid in the ghost's bedchamber and planned to kill him. But he noticed that the ghost was wearing a small red box containing a little bird around his neck. As soon as the King's son touched the box, the ghost awoke and begged for his life. When the King's son asked him about his brother, the ghost gave him an ointment to put on the horse in the stable. The oil transformed the horse into his older brother. "When the younger brother broke the bird's neck, the ghost immediately disappeared, and suddenly a handsome young man entered the stable. He said: 'I am the ghost that has just disappeared. I was destined to commit evil until someone would slay me in the ghost's body. You have redeemed me, so now give me your sister as a wife.'" They all returned home together. The

old woman's hut had disappeared, and the younger brother married the redeemed queen of the iron city.[574]

607 Although this fairytale diverges from those considered so far, its hero must also redeem a woman who is associated with a hostile demon. Whereas in the previous examples this figure did not really seem in need of redemption, and remained unredeemed, in the above Balkan tale the hero resolves the problem posed by this demon by transforming the spirit into a human being, thus satisfying the secret longing for humanization (already latent in the mountain spirit's bloodlust).[575] Once more, however, redemption requires killing, but the spirit explains that this liberates its humanity from the *ghost's body*. Presumably, the decapitated demonic paramours suffered the same fate in the fairytales discussed previously, where the human being who took their place was the hero.[576] The destruction of the demon corresponded to consciousness completely acknowledging and assimilating the shadow. In the fairytales about the "grateful dead man," even this ousting of the demonic sphere by the human realm was twofold: The dead man also disappeared because he was gradually replaced by the hero.[577]

---

[574] One parallel is "The Story of the Raven" (Siberia, no. 17). After many years of marriage, an elderly couple received a daughter. When she had grown up, the maiden was abducted by the raven-man. Following the old woman's prayer, the couple had a son, who set out to look for his sister. When he reached the raven-man's house, the son lost a nut-cracking contest and was roasted to death in a hot bath by his brother-in-law. The sister hung his bones on a tree. The same fate befell the second son; only the third succeeded in defeating his brother-in-law in the nut-cracking contest and pushed him into the bathhouse, where he burned to death. Thereupon, he revived his brothers with the water of life, and they returned home together.

[575] For a positive evaluation of the demonic sisters-in-law, also because they help the hero, see "The Daughter of King Tsun Matsun" (Modern Greece, no. 26) and "Maria Morevna" (Afansa'ev, *Russian Fairy Tales*, p. 553). These demonic sisters-in-law are examples of the close connection between the shadow and the underworld deity, as well as of their double aspect, which is self-evident in these as yet undifferentiated conceptions.

[576] See Jung's interpretation of the parallel process in "The Princess in the Tree" (Zaunert, *Deutsche Märchen seit Grimm*, p. 1) in his "The Phenomenology of the Spirit in Fairytales," CW 9/I, § 433f.

[577] This is confirmed by a motif in "The story of the two sisters who envied their youngest sister," a fairytale collected in Littmann's *Die Erzählungen aus den Tausendundein Nächten*, complete German edition in six volumes. First published in the original Arabic text of the Calcutta edition of 1839 (Leipzig: Insel-Verlag, 1923): On the 756th night, an old man warns the young men who are searching for the talking bird, the singing tree, and the golden water of the dangers they might encounter on their journey. However, when they insist on pursuing their quest, he gives them golden balls to show them the way. They succumb and are turned into stones. After their sister has gained the treasures and redeemed the brothers, and after they take the same path to return home, the old man has disappeared. Thus, the secret identity of the helper and the guardian of the treasure, who must be slain, is revealed. The fact that the hero is related to the latter is already evident from the account of the hero's journey, and thus establishes the trinity of hero, helper, and adversary.

608    In the present fairytale, the demon becomes human because the woman is the hero's sister and therefore does not qualify as his bride. Rather, the hero later marries a woman who he has liberated from the power of a dragon under very similar circumstances to those in which he freed his sister. The difference, however, is that when the hero destroys his "outer soul," this demon has not become a human being but has died once and for all. The symbolism of this intermediate episode is significant in several ways. The demon has turned the city of the king's daughter into iron. This recalls the furnace in which the prince is held captive in "The Iron Stove."[578] As in that tale, this also means the paralysis and hardening of the psyche, which prevents it from developing and participating in life. If we see the girl in the iron city as a real woman, this inertia is caused by the animus, the demonic spirit-bridegroom, and corresponds to the sleep of death, the glass mountain, and similar symbols. The hero confronts the dragon, that diabolical spirit that has bewitched and imprisoned the anima, just as the mountain spirit and the troll do in the previous tales, in a situation that is characteristic of its nature: It is roasting a lamb on a spit. The lamb, symbolizing innocence and youth, is represented as the victim of the dragon, that demon which represents the dangerous forces of life; they drive the naïve, helpless, childlike psyche into the tormenting fire (i.e., the passions). Insofar as the hero intervenes against the lamb's tormentor, and in favor of the king's daughter, the lamb may be said to represent a parallel image to the captive maiden, in particular because in myth she is usually the innocent victim whom the dragon intends to devour. Thus, both denote the hero's soul, which is trapped in the realm of darkness and must be freed. Put differently: As long as the anima appears as the concrete sister, the hero cannot bring her deeper essence to life. Cultural history shows that some primitive social systems enact marriage laws according to which the man must marry his mother's brother's daughter and, if possible, at the same time give his sister to her brother as a wife.[579]

---

[578] *The Complete Grimm's Fairy Tales*, pp. 571–577.

609      In this way, the endogamous tendency, which strives for marriage with the sister, is satisfied at least insofar as the "foreign" woman still belongs to the immediate clan; on the other hand, the exogamous tendency, which demands "fresh blood," physically and psychologically, is also taken into account. This occurs according to a basic archetypal pattern identified by Jung as the "marriage quaternio."[580] This archetype becomes evident in the present fairytale: The sister is replaced by a figure who, however, as the story of her conquest reveals, is remarkably similar to the real sister. The latter is given away to a stranger, in whom, however, we recognize a secret relationship with the father.[581]

610      The older brother, who remains with the sister, is the "older hero"[582]; that is, he is a more archaic type of hero, whose relationship with the sister is still incestuous and who is therefore also temporarily transformed into an animal, because psychologically the animallike unconscious corresponds to the incestuous level. The younger hero, the real one, is called to higher consciousness. He gradually replaces the tragic fate into which unconsciousness has turned with a higher relationship both with the real woman and with his own soul.

611      The relationship between brother and sister is an ancient form of the connection between man and woman. It is the theme of many fairytales, in which the brother, as in the above example, is occasionally threatened by bewitchment, just as the love of these siblings is burdened by a curse (because, as explained, it is still too archaic, too unconscious). The basic form is plainly evident in the Grimm's "Brother and Sister."[583] This well-known tale goes as follows:

---

[580] Jung, "The Psychology of the Transference," CW 16, § 425.
[581] See "The Man in the Moon" (Siberia, no. 73): The man in the moon abducts the hero's older sister. The hero manages to follow them into the clouds where he marries the sister's little daughter, who takes back to earth, where he becomes powerful.
[582] On the relationship of the older to the younger hero, see below ("The Divine Twins").
[583] The Complete Grimm's Fairy Tales, pp. 67–73; slightly abridged and adapted. Other fairytales about the persecuted brother and sister include "Hänsel and Gretel" (The Complete Grimm's, pp. 86–94) and "The Water-Nixie" (ibid., pp. 364–365). For a couple who are not siblings but lovers, see "Gold Mary and Gold Feather" (Zaunert, Deutsche Märchen seit Grimm, p. 303). However, the tale unfolds like other sibling fairytales, just as the protagonists' similar names point to their secret kinship. See also "Jorinda and Joringel" (The Complete Grimm's, pp. 339–341), as well as Bolte and Polívka, Anmerkungen, vol. 2, p. 69. In these tales, the brother is threatened most by magical forces and needs his sister's help.

612 Little Brother took his little sister by the hand and said: " … our step-mother beats us every day … Come, we will go forth together into the wide world.

613 They walked the whole day … and in the evening they came to a large forest, and they were so weary … that they lay down in a hollow tree and fell asleep.

614 The next day when they awoke … the brother said: "Sister, I am thirsty." But the wicked step-mother was a witch … and had bewitched all the brooks in the forest. When they found a little brook … the brother was going to drink out of it, but the sister heard how it said as it rain: "Who drinks of me will become a tiger." The sister cried: "Pray, dear brother, do not drink, or you will become a wild beast, and tear me to pieces." The brother did not drink, although he was so thirsty, but said: "I will wait for the next spring."

615 When they came to the next brook the sister heard this also say: "Who drinks of me will become a wolf." Again the brother did not drink and said he would wait for another spring, but then "I must drink, say what you like; for my thirst is too great."

616 And when they came to the third brook the sister heard how it said as it rain: "Who drinks of me will become a roebuck." Again the sister beseeched her brother not to drink. But the brother knelt down … and drunk some of the water, and as soon as the first drops touched his lips he lay there in the form of a young roebuck.

617 The sister untied her golden garter and put it around the roebuck's neck, and she plucked rushes and wove them into a soft cord. This she tied to the little animal and led it on, and she walked deeper and deeper into the forest.

618 When they had gone a very long way they came at last to a little house; and as it was empty, she thought: "We can stay here and live."

619 For some time they were alone like this in the wilderness. But it happened that the King of the country held a great hunt in the forest. On the first day, the young roebuck sprang away and escaped back to the house and his sister. The next day when the King and his huntsmen again saw the young roebuck with the golden collar, they all chased him … and by the evening they had surrounded him, and one of them wounded him a little in the foot, so that he limped and ran slowly. Then a hunter crept after him to the cottage and saw the young roebuck enter the cottage.

620 But the wound was so slight that the roebuck, next morning, did not feel it any more … The sister could not do otherwise, but opened the door for him with a heavy heart, and the roebuck … bounded into the forest.

621 When the King saw him, he said to his huntsmen: "Chase him all day … but take care that no one does him any harm."

622 As soon as the sun had set, the King followed the roebuck to the cottage and saw the frightened maiden, who was more lovely than any he had ever seen. But the King looked kindly … and said: "Will you go with me to my palace and be my dear wife?" "Yes, indeed," answered the maiden, "but the little roe must go with me. I cannot leave him." When the King agreed, she tied the roebuck with the cord of rushes, took it in her own hand, and went away with the King from the cottage.

623 After the wedding, they lived for a long time happily together; the roebuck was tended and cherished, and ran about in the palace-garden.

624 But when the wicked step-mother … heard that they were so happy, envy and jealousy rose in her heart and she wanted her daughter, who was ugly and had only one eye, to become queen.

625 As time passed, the Queen had a pretty little boy, and it happened that the King was out hunting; so the old witch took the form of the chamber-maid, and with her daughter

went into room where the Queen lay, and they persuaded her to have a bath … they carried the weakly Queen into the bathhouse, put her into the bath, then shut the door and ran away. But in the bathhouse they had made a fire of such hellish heat that the beautiful young Queen was soon suffocated.

626 When this was done the old woman took her daughter, put a nightcap on her head, and laid her in bed in place of the Queen. She gave her too the shape and the look of the Queen, and the King did not find out that a false Queen was lying in the bed.

627 But at midnight, the nurse … saw the door open and the true Queen walk in. She took the child out of the cradle, laid it on her arm, and suckled it … and she did not forget the roebuck, but went into the corner where it lay, and stroked its back. The next morning the nurse asked the guards whether anyone had come into the palace during the night, but they answered: "No, we have seen no one."

628 She thus came many nights and never spoke a word … until one night the Queen began to speak:

629     "How fares my child, how fares my roe?
    Once will I come, then never more."

630 The nurse did not answer, but the Queen had gone, went to the King and told him all. In the evening he went into the nursery, and at midnight the Queen again appeared and said:

631     "How fares my child, how fares my roe?
    Once will I come, then never more."

632 And she nursed the child as she was wont to do before she disappeared. The King dared not speak to her, but on the next night he watched again. Then she said:

633     "How fares my child, how fares my roe?
    This time I come, then never more."

634 The King could not restrain himself; he sprang towards her, and said: "You can be none other than my dear wife." She answered: "Yes, I am your dear wife," and at the same moment she received life again, and by God's grace became fresh, rosy, and full of health.

635 She told the King the evil deed which the wicked witch and her daughter had been guilty of towards her. The King ordered both to be led before the judge, and judgment was delivered against them. The daughter was taken into the forest where she was torn to pieces by wild beasts, but the witch was cast into the fire and miserably burnt. And as soon as she was burnt to ashes, the roebuck changed his shape, and received his human form again, so the sister and brother lived happily together all their lives.[584]

636 From the outset, brother and sister are overshadowed by the hostile Great Mother, who keeps pursuing them as a wicked stepmother. They find themselves in the same situation that the animal prince or the animal princess face alone in other fairytales. In this tale, the enmity toward the male part prevails at first; accordingly, the mother is portrayed as more hostile than the father. Nevertheless, in some versions the little sister is also persecuted and bewitched into an animal. In "Nennillo and Nennella" (Italy, no. 44),[585] a shark appears,

[584] A weaker parallel is "Vanjuschka and Annuschka" (Russia, no. 34). In other versions, the mother-in-law or witch who later appears as an enemy is identical with the stepmother who appears at the beginning. On a version edited by Wilhelm Grimm, see Lincke, "Stiefmutter" p. 51f.: "Wilhelm Grimm supplements, or rather changes, this version from the point where the little brother becomes the golden stag; he also reports the great hunt and the wedding. At the very end of the supplement, we find the rather impromptu remark: 'But the girl had a stepmother who was always envious and resented the girl's happiness.' This is followed by the motif of the foisted bride and the stepmother's punishment (she is rolled down a mountain in a barrel filled with sharp knives). The late introduction of the stepmother seems unmotivated compared to the final version. Also, the depiction of the three bewitched wells is improbable. This version does not seem very coherent: Not the scheming stepmother appears in the end, but a second, newly introduced figure: the mother-in-law; in the final version, by contrast, these figures have been merged into *one* figure." See also *ibid.*, p. 56.
[585] Bolte and Polívka, *Anmerkungen*, vol. 1, p. 87: In "Mary and her Little Brother" (Gonzenbach, no. 49), "the brother is transformed into a sheep with golden horns, but the sister is thrown into a cistern and swallowed by a large fish. Thereupon, the sheep laments by the well:

Little sister, little sister, with ringed hair,
For me they sharpen the knives,
For me they bare the kettles,
To cut off my slender neck.

as an image of the dark father-god,[586] and devours the maiden; in some variants, the father is a man-eater and causes the children to flee.[587] This corresponds to the above observation that, as a rule, the animal prince is spellbound by a terrible mother-figure, whereas the enchanted princess falls under the spell of a demonic forefather.

637    These two motifs are often combined in tales about siblings. On the one hand, this makes such tales seem less differentiated than ones in which only a single male or female figure is bewitched. On the other hand, they cast new light on the interplay of all these archetypal motifs. Deeper connections appear whenever the possibility of incest is hinted at: The primordial mother or father bewitches the heroine or hero because they refuse to free them for love's sake; psychologically, enchantment thus corresponds to a paternal or maternal bond. It is perhaps worth emphasizing, however, that this concerns not only the attachment to the concrete, personal father or mother. Beyond that, it also highlights the psychic prevalence of the father- or mother-archetype and all its psychological implications.

638    In sibling tales, however, we find yet another incest motif: The siblings also seem to be bound to each other. In our present fairytale, this "bond" is expressed both subtly and vividly by the little sister leading her little brother by his golden collar and by the cord that she has woven from rushes. Bound to each other in incest, the siblings are also a motif of alchemical symbolism. According to Jung, the "brother-sister pair stands for the unconscious or for essential content." If consciousness confronts the unconscious, then an opposition, that is, a conflict, manifests on the surface. "Since the conflict is never lacking in moral complications, it is, from this point of view, appropriately expressed in the morally obnoxious form of

---

A voice answers from the depths:

    I cannot help you, my little brother.
    The evil shark clutches me between its jaws;
    I cannot bring my little child into the world.

[586] The father heeds the stepmother's request and abandons the children in the forest. When a prince who is out hunting approaches, the boy hides in a hollow tree and the girl flees to the beach. While the boy is found and raised by the prince, a pirate takes the girl. She perishes with him and his ship at sea, is swallowed by a fish and spat out again on the beach near the prince's castle. There follows recognition, the summoning of the father, and the punishment of the stepmother.
[587] Bolte and Polívka, *Anmerkungen*, vol. 1, pp. 89 and 95.

incest."[588] Jung's explanations of the so-called "Visio Arislei"[589] (in which Arisleus follows the *Rex marinus*'s call for help and descends into his dark realm, which constitutes a dangerous undertaking for consciousness, represented here by the alchemist) establish that incest is the *coniunctio oppositorum* in the unconscious: Advised by the philosophers, the king of a barren country mates his children Thabritius and Beya. Michael Maier, the 17th-century alchemist, depicted this incest as the union of mother and son.[590] "The brother-sister pair," so Jung[591]

639    stands allegorically for the whole conception of opposites. These have a wide range of variation: dry-moist, hot-cold, male-female, sun-moon, gold-silver, mercury-sulphur, round-square, water-fire, volatile-solid, physical-spiritual, and so on. ... In the *Rosarium* version of the "Visio" the death of the son is the result of his complete disappearance into the body of Beya during coitus. In another version he is eaten by his father, or the Sun is drowned in Mercurius or swallowed by the lion. Thabritius is the masculine, spiritual principle of light and Logos which, like the Gnostic Nous, sinks into the embrace of physical nature (Physis). Death therefore represents the completion of the spirit's descent into matter. ... Since all this means a diminution or extinction of consciousness, an *abaissement du niveau mental* equivalent to that "peril of the soul" which is primitive man's greatest dread (i.e., the fear of ghosts), the deliberate and indeed wanton provocation of this state is a sacrilege or breach of taboo attended by the severest punishments. Accordingly the King imprisons Arisleus and his companions in a triple glass house together with the corpse of the King's Son. The heroes are held captive in the underworld at the bottom of the sea, where, exposed to every kind of terror, they languish for

---

[588] Jung, *Psychology and Alchemy*, CW 12, § 496.
[589] On the philosopher Arisleus, see Jung, CW 12, § 435 and fn. 35.
[590] Jung, CW 12, § 435, fn. 38 and fig. 225.
[591] See *ibid.*, § 436–438.

eighty days in an intense heat. At the request of Arisleus, Beya is imprisoned with them. (The *Rosarium* version of the "Visio" interprets the prison as Beya's womb.) Clearly, they have been overpowered by the unconscious and are helplessly abandoned, which means that they have volunteered to die in order to beget a new and fruitful life in that region of the psyche which has hitherto lain fallow in darkest unconsciousness, and under the shadow of death ... Although the possibility of life is hinted at by the brother-sister pair, these unconscious opposites must be activated by the intervention of the conscious mind, otherwise they will merely remain dormant.

640   As in alchemy, incest, as an image of the too intimately related opposites in the unconscious, also represents psychic stagnation in fairytales. Representing infertility, incest is considered offensive and therefore forms the psychological background of the stepmother's curse; in "Clever Finna" (Iceland, no. 8), sibling love was even the content of the curse. In "The Son-in-Law from a Foreign Land" (Balkans, no. 39), the dying father's command to give the daughter to any stranger has a similar background: The older brother refuses to carry out the order, apparently because he does not want to give away the sister[592]; unlike the younger brother, he later falls prey to the ghostly spirit dominating the sister and is bewitched by it into an animal (a horse in the sister's stable!). The ghostly stranger is probably the deceased father, whose figure has now been extended to the father-archetype. The older brother rivals him because he, too, is bound to the sister. His enchantment into a horse corresponds to that of the little brother in the present fairytale.[593] The younger

---

[592] This motif is more clearly evident in the Modern Greek variant, "The Daughter of King Tsun Matsun" (no. 26), where the younger brother says: "We must give her to him according to our father's command and curse."

[593] Similarly, see the transformation of several siblings into animals in "The Poor Stepchildren and the Wicked Harem Women" (Turkestan, no. 13), where the smallest girl exclaims:

Oh sister, my dearest sister!
I drink this water.

The eldest sister admonishes her:

Don't drink it, don't drink it, little sister!
The water is foul and not pure,

brother, on the other hand, who on the human level obeys the father more than the older one, does not succumb to incest on the ghostly level and breaks the sister's spell. By seeing through the demon's nature, he supports and enables, as it were, the transposition of the paternal bond from the level of the concrete "family romance" to the psychic level. He thus acts in the interests of life because a psychic complex can only be solved by transformation, not by splitting off.

641    The French tale "The Nine Brothers Who Became Lambs and Their Sister" (France, vol. 2, no. 34), an otherwise not particularly interesting variant of the Grimm's "Brother and Sister," is a counterpart to the Balkan tale discussed above: A sister and nine brothers live in their father's castle after his death; the sister presides over her siblings like a mother. One day, while hunting in the woods, the brothers come to a witch's house. She gives them some water but in return demands that the eldest brother, Goulven, become her husband. Dismayed, the brothers promise to seek their sister's advice. When the old woman goes to the castle the following day to receive the answer, the sister firmly declines the request. The old woman turns the brothers into white lambs, and the environs become a wasteland.[594] Whereas in "The Son-in-Law from a Foreign Land" the father and the elder brother were united in their incestuous desire for the sister, in the French tale the witch-mother and the maternal sister are bound to Goulven and his brothers. Just as the strange father-spirit wooed the sister in the former tale and carried her away to the gateless castle, so here the witch desires and enraptures the brothers. Thus, the strange and close relationship

---

It could be your misfortune.

The same happens to another sister, and eventually the boy calls out:

Ah sister, my dearest sister!
I drink this water.

The eldest sister pleads:

Don't drink it, don't drink it, little brother!
You will become an animal like the poor little sisters!

Here, water represents the shadowy and regressive aspect of water.

[594] In the course of this tale, the sister marries a nobleman. When she is expecting a child, she is thrown into the well by the witch's daughter, who pretends to be a noblewoman. She pretends to be sick and demands to eat the meat of the largest white lamb. The astonished husband, knowing that his wife adores lambs, complies with the request and follows the animal, which runs around the well bleating miserably. From inside the well, he hears a moaning voice and manages to pull out his wife. She gives birth to a boy and makes the lamb his godfather. At the boy's baptism, the lamb, now liberated, regains human form, and the priest also lifts the curse from the brothers by putting on the stole [i.e., ecclesiastical vestment].

between the siblings is related to their cursing by the primordial father or mother. Overall, this complex of cursing and sibling bond indicates that the unconscious prevails in family ties. Hostile to life, the unconscious is so powerful that it constrains life to an unnatural extent. Based on his studies of primitive peoples, Layard[595] concludes that the incest taboo serves to prevent a negative *participation mystique*. Considering this aspect, Jung writes[596]:

642

> Incest, as an endogamous relationship, is an expression of the libido which serves to hold the family together. One could therefore define it as "kinship libido," a kind of instinct which, like a sheep-dog, keeps the family group intact.

Elsewhere, Jung writes:

643

> In the interests of the welfare and development of the tribe, the exogamous social order thrust the endogamous tendency into the background so as to prevent the danger of regression to a state of having no groups at all. It insisted on the introduction of "new blood" both physically and spiritually, and it thus proved to be a powerful instrument in the development of culture. ... Layard writes: "Its latent or spiritual purpose is to enlarge the spiritual horizon by developing the idea that there is after all a sphere in which the primary desire may be satisfied, namely the divine sphere of the gods together with that of their semidivine counterparts, the culture heroes." ... "Thus the incest taboo," says Layard, "leads in full circle out of the biological sphere into the spiritual." .... On the primitive level the feminine image, the anima, is still completely unconscious and therefore in a state of latent projection.[597]

---

[595] Layard, "Incest Taboo," p. 271. On this topic, see also Claude Lévy-Strauss, *Les structures élémentaires de la parenté* (Paris: Presses Universitaires de France, 1949), passim.
[596] Jung, "The Psychology of the Transference," *CW* 16, § 431.
[597] *Ibid.*, § 438.

644 Layard's reflections and Jung's psychological explanations suggest that, on the primitive level, the concrete figures, that is, the family members, at first form a union with what they represent psychically. Only by severing these family ties, and thus obliterating the primordial identity of the anima, the concrete sister, and the concrete wife, can the anima's psychic and independent reality be realized. Only thus, however, can a man enter into a psychic relationship with a woman that extends beyond pure biology and common interests. The same applies to the woman, who can find her own soul or her own spirit and relate to the man only by severing the bond with her brother and father.

645 One fairytale that describes the brother-sister incest problem and its first primitive solution by producing a marriage quaternio[598] is "Prince Danila Govorila":

646 A prince's son received a ring from a witch, whose magical power was bound to the condition that he marry no other girl than the one on whose finger the ring would fit. Once he had grown up, he went in search of a bride, but in vain: The ring would not fit anyone. He complained to his sister, who wanted to try on the ring. It fit like a glove. The brother wanted to marry her, but she believed this was a sin and sat outside the house weeping. Old beggars wandering by comforted her and gave her the following advice: "Make four dolls and put them in the four corners of the room. If your brother calls you to the wedding, go; if he calls you to bed, take your time! Hope for God and follow our advice!"

647 After the ceremony, the brother called the four dolls to bed. There they sang:

648 "Prince Daniel has commanded it,
Wants to take his sister as his wife,
Earth open up,
Receive her."

---

[598] Jung, "The Psychology of the Transference," CW 16, § 427ff.

649     The earth opened and swallowed the sister. The brother called out to her three times. But the third time she disappeared into the earth. She went her way underground and came to the hut of Baba Yaga, whose daughter kindly gave her shelter and hid her from the witch. But the witch soon discovered the guest and had the oven heated. The two girls put the old woman in the oven and escaped the witch. They reached the brother's principality, where the sister was recognized by her brother's servant. But he could not tell the two girls apart, they looked so alike. The servant now suggested that the prince take a test: He should take a skin filled with blood under his arm. He (the servant) would then plunge a knife into his side and the master should fall down as if he were dead, and the sister would betray herself. And so it happened: The sister threw herself over him, wailing. But he jumped up and embraced his sister. The magic ring also fit the witch's daughter's finger, as a result of which the prince married her and gave his sister to a real man as a wife.[599]

650     Based on this fairytale, Jung discusses the problem of incest as follows[600]:

651     In this tale the incest is on the point of being committed, but is prevented by the peculiar ritual with the four dolls. The four dolls in the four corners of the room form the marriage quaternio, the aim being to prevent the incest by putting four in place of two.[601] The four dolls form a magic simulacrum

---

[599] See Afanas'ev, *Russian Fairy Tales*, pp. 351–356. One tale with a similar plot is "The Tsar's Daughter in the Underworld Kingdom" (Russia, no. 9): A tsar and his wife command their son to marry his sister as soon as they, the parents, have died. They die soon afterwards. The sister "made three dolls, put them on the windows, put herself in the middle and shouted: 'Ye little dolls, cuckoo!' The first doll said, 'What do you want?' The second said: "The brother takes the sister!' The third said: 'Earth, open up, sister, descend!'" This is repeated three more times. "Thereupon, she sank and entered the other world." After much suffering, and after living a Cinderella-like existence in the otherwordly tsarish kingdom, the heroine gains the love of the tsar's son and becomes a ruler.—Incest is depicted even more explicitly in "The Journey to the Underworld to Fafá, the Whirlpool Cave" (South Seas, no. 63): A brother violates his sister in her sleep, whereupon she escapes, in utter despair, to the realm of the dead, where she is found by another of her brothers after an adventurous journey and revived.

[600] Jung, "The Psychology of the Transference," *CW* 16, § 430f.

[601] My footnote: In "The Tsar's Daughter in the Underground Kingdom" (Russia, no. 9), there are three dolls, to which the heroine adds herself as the fourth one.

which stops the incest by removing the sister to the underworld, [602] where she discovers her alter ego. Thus we can say that the witch who gave the young prince the fatal ring was his mother-in-law-to-be, for, as a witch, she must certainly have known that the ring would fit not only his sister but her own daughter ... In the Icelandic story ["Clever Finna" [603]] we have the schema[604]:

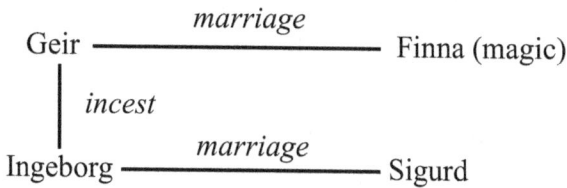

$$
\begin{array}{ccc}
& \textit{marriage} & \\
\text{Geir} & \rule{3cm}{0.4pt} & \text{Finna (magic)} \\
\mid & & \\
\textit{incest} & & \\
\mid & \textit{marriage} & \\
\text{Ingeborg} & \rule{3cm}{0.4pt} & \text{Sigurd}
\end{array}
$$

652    In the Russian[605]:

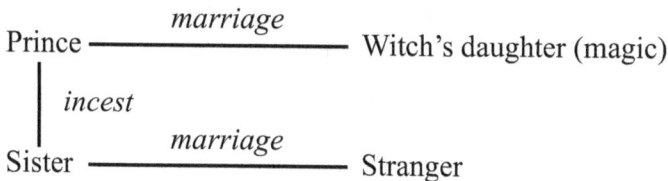

$$
\begin{array}{ccc}
& \textit{marriage} & \\
\text{Prince} & \rule{3cm}{0.4pt} & \text{Witch's daughter (magic)} \\
\mid & & \\
\textit{incest} & & \\
\mid & \textit{marriage} & \\
\text{Sister} & \rule{3cm}{0.4pt} & \text{Stranger}
\end{array}
$$

The two schemata are remarkably similar. In both cases, the hero wins a bride who has something to do with magic or the world beyond.

---

[602] My footnote: The dolls function like an inner voice or conscience, and as such they signify, as Jung suggests, "a co-operation of 'infantile' or unconscious forces" (*CW* 12, § 302). As "homunculi," they lead into the earth, i.e., into the unconscious realm, where the self is rooted in earthly reality, in the body and its chemical elements (see Jung, "The Spirit Mercurius," *CW* 13, § 241f.). On dolls in superstition, popular belief, and social customs, see Bächtold-Stäubli under *Puppe* (doll): Considered elvish spirits, dolls are "mentioned together with idols, false gods, goblins ... ." Demons are represented as dolls. At the same time, demons and spirits are said to be deceived by dolls. Thus, at Roman *compitalia* [annual festivals held to honor the *lares compitales*, household deities—Trans.], "woollen dolls were hung up for the household deities at crossroads and house doors ... to please them." See *Ibid.* for further material, especially on dolls as representations of human beings. See also the Estonian tale mentioned in *Archetypal Symbols in Fairytales*, vol. 3, p. 283 (see De Gubernatis, *Thiere i. d. indog. Mythologie*, p. 118f.), where a little girl who is pursued by her stepmother loses her way in a forest and meets a woman who is dressed in gold. The latter makes an image (i.e., doll) of the girl and sends this to the stepmother, who uses it as a scapegoat. As dolls also manifest the psyche, as Tobler has argued, using them to ward off evil means that similar things are fought with similar things or the unconscious is tackled with unconscious forces (*Epiphanie*, p. 64). Insofar as dolls correspond to the psychic "shadow," its task is to protect the personality, as happens in numerous, albeit differently structured fairytales.

[603] My footnote: Iceland, no. 8.

[604] Jung, *CW* 16, para 431.

[605] Jung, *CW* 16, para 432.

653 While this alludes to her anima-character, essentially the anima and the real wife coincide, which Jung comments on as follows[606]:

654 Marriage with the anima is the psychological equivalent of absolute identity between conscious and unconscious. But since such a condition is possible only in the complete absence of psychological self-knowledge, it must be more or less primitive, i.e., the man's relationship to the woman is essentially an anima projection. The only sign that the whole thing is unconscious is the remarkable fact that the carrier of the anima-image is distinguished by magical characteristics. These characteristics are missing from the soror-animus relationship in the stories; that is, the unconscious does not make itself felt at all as a separate experience ... Therefore we must expect that on a still more primitive level the anima too will lose her magical attributes, the result being an uncomplicated, purely matter-of-fact marriage quaternio.[607]

---

[606] Jung, "The Psychology of the Transference," CW 16, § 433.

[607] One fairytale that is worth considering here is "Remedies Against Bewitchment" (Krauss, *Sagen der Südslaven*, vol. 2, no. 130). Although it does not address the problem of siblings, it is oriented from the outset toward the marriage quaternio: Its characters are mutually dependent and cannot realize themselves without each other: "One day, an emperor's son walked over bewitchments, whereupon his hands and feet become bent and lame. In vain, the emperor promised half of his empire to whoever could cure his son. One night a girl appeared to him in a dream and said that her mother had bewitched the son; 'still, I advise you, procure the eyes of a lindworm, the heart of a dragon, and a winged serpent caught on a virgin's day. Have these objects boiled by an orphaned girl in an unused pot in untouched water at a self-igniting fire, and let your son drink this potion on three successive mornings on an empty stomach from a sacrificial cup, and he will recover and marry me." The emperor promised half of his kingdom to whoever brought him the things needed to cure his son. Finally, a youth promised to procure them if the emperor gave him his daughter as a mistress. With a magic ring that illumined the night, the youth blinded the dragon in a fierce struggle and snatched its heart. Thereafter, with the help of the ring, he scorched the wings of a lindworm at sunset and poked out its eyes; and he caught the winged serpent while it was gazing spellbound at the rising sun. Aided by the ring, he also circumambulated the fireplace at the emperor's court three times, so that the fire ignited itself. The emperor's son died, the girl in the dream came forward, and the emperor married his son to her and his daughter to that young man. Here, too, the curse that calls into question the future of the realm is cast by the Great Mother. Thereupon, the anima appears from the unconscious and indicates that the negative aspect of the magic world must be confronted and fought because it must be transformed through sacrifice, so that the power lurking in darkness can be incorporated in the form of a marriage between the emperor's son and the anima into conscious life and thus neutralized. However, because the luminous side of the nuclear personality is paralyzed, so that also the anima manifests itself only quietly, the actual action passes over to the shadow-figures. One of them, the youth, possesses the fiery-blinding ring (symbol of the self, midnight sun), with which he overcomes the dark forces (while the old consciousness [sun] descends and the new one rises spellbindingly like a mirror image of the ring). In the magic rite, he reawakens the inner flood, whose power purifies the demonic forces and through which they can be assimilated and can exert a healing effect according to the law of overcoming similarity with similarity. As an orphan, the girl who prepares the medicine appears like a doubling of the dream figure. She might be called "The girl from nowhere," analogously to the anima-figure in the

655 As Jung points out with reference to Layard,[608] at the end of these tales this marriage quaternio has its ethnological parallel in the primitive rite of so-called "cross-cousin-marriage," a custom existing in certain primitive tribes: To prevent incest, the man marries the mother's brother's daughter and gives his sister to the brother as a wife. Jung observes:

656 While marriage classes have all but disappeared among civilized peoples, they nevertheless re-emerge on a higher cultural level as spiritual ideas. In the interests of the welfare and development of the tribe, the exogamous social order thrust the endogamous tendency into the background so as to prevent the danger of regression to a state of having no groups at all. ... Whenever an instinctive force—i.e., a certain sum of psychic energy—is driven into the background through a onesided (in this case, exogamous) attitude on the part of the conscious mind, it leads to a dissociation of personality. The conscious personality with its one-track (exogamous) tendency comes up against an invisible (endogamous) opponent, and because this is unconscious it is felt to be a stranger and therefore manifests itself in projected form. At first it makes its appearance in human figures who have the power to do what others may not do— kings and princes, for example. This is probably the reason for the royal incest prerogative, as in ancient Egypt. To the extent that the magical power of royalty was derived increasingly from the gods, the incest prerogative shifted to the latter and so gave rise to the incestuous *hieros gamos*. But when the numinous aura surrounding the person of the king is taken over by the gods, it has been transferred to a spiritual authority, which results in the projection of an autonomous

Balkan fairytale (no. 30). She is actually a shadowy, sisterly helper, similar to the one in "Djulek-Batür" (Turkestan, no. 7), who also disappears after fulfilling her task. Thus, little by little, helpful male and female figures emerge alternately from the unconscious to realize redemption, until eventually a marriage quaternio, in which the profane as well as the magical spheres take part in equal measure, manifests the renewal of the personality.

[608] Layard, "Incest Taboo," passim.

psychic complex—in other words, psychic existence becomes reality. Thus Layard logically derives the anima from the numen of the goddess. In the shape of the goddess the anima is manifestly projected, but in her proper (psychological) shape she is *introjected*; she is, as Layard says, the "anima within." She is the natural *sponsa*, man's mother or sister or daughter or wife from the beginning, the companion whom the endogamous tendency vainly seeks to win in the form of mother and sister. She represents that longing which has always had to be sacrificed since the grey dawn of history ... The endogamous tendency finds an outlet in the exalted sphere of the gods and in the higher world of the spirit. Here it shows itself to be an instinctive force of a spiritual nature.[609]

657  The fairytale describes the marriage quaternio on what is still a completely unconsciously projected level as a first attempt to solve the incest problem; however, all future possibilities of development are also anticipated in this symbolic image. While the fateful power that causes incest or provides its correct solution is a witchlike mother-figure in "Prince Danila Govorila," it is described as a father-figure in the Grimm's "The Glass Coffin."[610] This tale seems to be influenced considerably by alchemical ideas and probably goes back to an alchemical parable,[611] which we will not discuss further here: One night, a poor tailor loses his way in a forest and reaches the cottage of a little gray man, whom he begs for shelter. In the morning, he is awoken by the noisy fight between a stag and a black bull. The latter is defeated and slain. The stag takes the tailor on its

---

[609] On the division of the tribe into two opposite halves, and also for the subsequent quotations, see Jung, "The Psychology of the Transference," *CW* 16, § 434–439.

[610] Afanas'ev, *Russian Fairy Tales* (pp. 351–356) and *The Complete Grimm's Fairy Tales* (pp. 672–678).

[611] According to Bolte and Polívka, *Anmerkungen*, vol. 3, p. 261, this fairytale is based on a novel: "'Das verwöhnte Mutter Söhngen oder Polidors gantz besondere und überaus lustiger Lebens-Lauff auf Schulen und Universitäten von Sylvano' (Freiberg, 1728), pp. 22–32. For a verbatim reprint, see Ullrich, "Des Schneiders Glück," *Zs. f. Volkskunde*, no. 3, p. 452; see *ibid.*, pp. 6 and 102; see also Hamann, *Die literarischen Vorlagen der KHM* (1906), p. 82. According to Wilhelm Grimm, while the content was preserved unaltered, the original plot was not; it is most certainly based on a genuine legend, even if this was revised and supplemented." For a psychological account of this tale, see Jung, "The Psychology of the Transference," *CW* 16, § 440, especially his comments on the essence of alchemy as the projection of metaphysical ideas into nature.

antlers and carries him off to a rock, which it opens with its antlers. The animal disappears into the rock amid lots of fire and steam.

658    Heeding a voice from within the rock, the tailor enters a hall of polished square stones on which unknown signs are inscribed. Following the voice, he steps onto the stone at the center of the hall, from where he descends into a similar hall with recesses in its walls in which stand glass chests filled with colored spirits or bluish smoke and in whose middle stand two large glass chests. In one is a tiny castle, in the other a beautiful girl, who is asleep and dressed in a precious robe. She awakens and orders him to open the coffin. She climbs out and kisses him and is ready to set him free. She tells him that she is a count's daughter who loved her own brother so dearly that she longed to stay with him forever and marry him. One day, however, a stranger arrives: Able to pass through closed doors, he assails and completely paralyzes the maiden. Because she rejects him, and thus incites his anger, her brother suddenly disappears. She finds him again as a stag, tied to the magician's leash, in a forest. The latter transforms the maiden into the glass coffin, her servants into the bottled spirits, and the castle into a small object in the other glass chest. Yet the maiden had dreamed previously of the young man who would set her free. Together, they lift the glass chest onto a large stone, and everything, including her brother, is transformed back into its normal shape, and the couple celebrates its wedding.

659    The violent stranger signifies that amount of exogamous unconscious energy that impedes the endogamous tendency, which strives to attain a higher level of culture. He also resembles the ghost in "The Son-in-Law from a Foreign Land" (Balkans, no. 39). Contrary to that tale, here he is neither humanized nor does he receive the sister; instead, he is eliminated in the end. The story does not begin with the brother and sister but makes the tailor (i.e., the exogamous groom) the protagonist; this does not happen by accident, but because it describes a more advanced stage of the problem. Among other figures, the tailor also corresponds to the king who goes out hunting in "Brother and Sister." Hostile to life, sibling incest must be obliterated in the interests of higher

consciousness. Thus, even the unconscious initiates the couple's separation. The "ghost," who interferes as an evil sorcerer and pursues the maiden, is both the brother's shadow-figure and the personification of the sister's animus. If, however, the sister symbolizes the (tailor's) animus-figure, the magician represents, as it were, the anima's animus (and a different aspect of it than the brother). We have already come across this archetype in "The Comrade" and its variants. This demon severs the connection between brother and sister. In other words, the originally harmonious coexistence of opposites in the unconscious disintegrates and yields to a conflict-laden, threatening aspect of the unconscious.

660     Psychologically, this disintegration is probably a result of consciousness, which questions the original situation, growing stronger. Thus, the opposites also disappear: The "evil magician" abducts the brother as a stag into the forest; he also plunges the sister into a magical sleep in the glass coffin, which he keeps underground. As a *cervus fugitivus* or *servus fugitivus* (a fugitive deer or slave), the stag symbolizes Mercurius in his manifestation as spiritus.[612] In some variations of "Brother and Sister," the brother is not transformed into a roebuck but into a golden stag.[613] Embodied in the sister, the feminine aspect in the fairytale about the glass coffin does not become an animal that takes flight but instead is held captive in the glass vessel. Thus, the sister's imprisonment (i.e., spellbound state) contrasts with the brother's disappearance.

661     Insofar as the two figures are a projection of consciousness, we can interpret this double aspect as an image of psychological experience, according to which the unconscious fascinates and at the same time captivates consciousness, which is fleeing from it. The glass vessel (which, moreover, is located deep inside a rock) points to the splitting off and inaccessibility of that psychic content that is

---

[612] Jung, "The Spirit Mercurius," *CW* 13, § 259; see also Jung, *Psychology and Alchemy*, CW 12, § 84, 187, 518, fig. 240.—On the connection between the stag and the notion of light, see Cassel, *Literatur u. Symbolik* (Leipzig, 1884), pp. 278–282. The stag is also the animal of Heracles and "fights the same enemies as the latter." As an image of light, he defeats death, which explains his role in; see also *ibid.*, p. 265f.

[613] Bolte and Polívka, *Anmerkungen*, vol. 1, pp. 82, 89f., 94, 96.

symbolized by the anima-figure. This image recalls the castle that is overgrown with thorns in "Sleeping Beauty" or the glass coffin in "Snow White": Both images represent the inaccessibility of the anima-image for consciousness.[614] The process described here, which leads to psychic stagnation, is not reported until the end of the tale, because it takes place entirely in the unconscious. From this story emerge the enchanted brother and sister. Dwelling in the forest and inside the rock, they are awaiting redemption. They also appear elsewhere, for example, in "The Golden Bird,"[615] where the princess is abducted from a distant realm by an evil father, while her brother is transformed into a fox. Alchemically, the pair represents the "spirit in matter" that must be redeemed.[616] The separation of the pair— achieved by confining the sister and by making the brother disappear—creates a difficult situation for this "spirit in matter," which requires human consciousness to intervene. This intervention results from human beings losing their bearings and being forced to heed the unconscious processes. Thus, the tailor loses his way and is soon confronted with his soul's demonic aspect.[617]

662     No sooner does the hero enter the unconscious sphere (i.e., the forest) and is even still asleep (i.e., as yet completely unaware of his future tasks) than the hitherto latent conflict erupts and manifests itself to him as a struggle between the stag and the black bull, as which the hostile magician appears in animal form. Thus, to begin with, the opposites were indistinct in the unconscious; later, however, this harmony became a latent conflict because a new creative content, which dissolved the former unity, intervened. All of a sudden, the problem of opposites existing in the unconscious is

---

[614] *The Complete Grimm's Fairy Tales*, pp. 237–241 and pp. 664–671. Unlike with the alchemical vessel, here the *pair* lies in the glass coffin or vessel after the *coniunctio*, which is represented as them being buried together in the *putrefactio* (decomposition); see Jung, *Psychology and Alchemy*, CW 12, fig. 223 and § 438.

[615] *The Complete Grimm's Fairy Tales*, pp. 272–279.

[616] The corresponding chapter in Jung's *Psychology and Alchemy* (CW 12, § 405ff.) has the same title.

[617] The little gray man recalls the psychopomp (see Zosimos), who is sacrificed and calls himself the "guardian of spirits" (see Jung, "The Visions of Zosimos," CW 13, § 86 III, I, 2 – III, V, 3). He represents the world-spirit, which in this tale appears as the lord of the forest. As Jung suggests, the little gray man also personifies the transforming substance or the arcane substance of the alchemists. Because this substance can appear, among others, as bull and stag (see Jung, CW 12, § 528f., 548), the little gray man, the magician-bull, and the stag are essentially one and the same. As the fairytale unfolds, the stag serves the hero as a psychopomp (as the fox does in "The Golden Bird")—and is the anima's brother.

perceived by the human being and presents itself as a fierce nocturnal fight between two animals, the magician, who appears as a black bull, and the stag, who eventually defeats the former.

663      We have encountered the motif of fighting animals several times, for instance, in "The Golden Castle That Hung in the Air," where a donkey helps to fight the unicorn and the dragon, as well as in "The Magic Horse," where the heroine's magic horse defeats the *div* (desert demon), which appeared underwater as a black donkey. These animal fights often have a strange characteristic: One of the animals is more domesticated, more closely related to humankind, as expressed by the head of the self-devouring snake.[618]

664      While the plot has thus far described an unconscious process, in which the hero is not involved at first, before "awakening" and participating as a spectator, he is now literally dragged into the process: Borne aloft by the victorious stag on its antlers, he is transported to a rock, which the animal opens with its antlers, whereupon the hero disappears into fire and steam. These events represent the hero's psychic enchantment and passionate involvement. The stag, which wrenches open the rock with its antlers, recalls the "perforating," all-pervasive power of the alchemists' *spiritus mercurialis*. After the stag has prized open the rock for the hero, he enters a subterranean hall that is built on square stones, in an allusion to the quaternity, which also plays a particular role in alchemy as the four elements of which the philosopher's stone is composed.[619] By standing on a stone at the center of the sub-

[618] In "The Talking Tree" (Finland, no. 23; see above, p. 153), one of the two dragons turns toward the human being, who decides the battle of opposites in the magical realm. As observed (see above, p. 157, fn. 301), Frobenius (*Zeitalter*, pp. 245ff.) mentions a tale about the opposition between a giant boy and a demonic cat. The alchemical image of the self-devouring dragon (*uroboros*) illumines the secret equality of opposites. This motif is frequent in fairytales: For example, in "The King's Son Who Feared Nothing" (*The Complete Grimm's*, pp. 545–550), a lion fights the giant, while in the Norwegian tale "Kari Woodenskirt" (no. 27) a blue bull helps the heroine battle the many-headed trolls. The bull symbolizes the unbridled creative power of nature; its black color in the fairytale about the glass coffin characterizes it even more as dark and chthonic. The stag, on the other hand, represents the more spiritual and less dangerous aspect of the same creature, whose symbolic meaning is described by Jung in terms of the archetype of the unicorn (see *Psychology and Alchemy*, CW 12, § 518ff., esp. §527f.). The latter embodies the "wild, rampant, masculine, penetrating force of the spiritus mercurialis" (*ibid.*, § 519 and § 524f.). On the unicorn as *spiritus vitae* (the spirit of life), see *ibid.*, § 518.
[619] Jung, CW 12, § 165, 173, esp. 213f., fig. 82, § 529. On the quaternity as an imploring simulacrum for warding off incest in the form of four dolls, see "Prince Danila Govorila" (Afanasyev, *Russische*, 1906, no. 21), as well as once again the motif of sinking.

terranean hall, the hero descends even deeper into a second hall. (In the visions of Zosimos,[620] a sunlike, resplendent temple that has been built out of a single slab of white marble stands above the spring. The treasure lies in the spring inside the temple). This stone is an image of the "philosopher's stone," a symbol of the self. It carries the hero into his own depths, as that invisible force whose impetus guides human beings on their path toward consciousness.[621] By entering the magical realm, the hero, through his presence and a kiss—like the prince in "Sleeping Beauty"—breaks the entire spell, because thereby these unconscious contents are connected to the human personality as a whole, and in turn become effective. The tailor celebrates his wedding with the count's daughter and thus takes the place of the brother and the magician. Thus, the anima is delivered from her attachment to the shadow-figures and is connected to the core of the personality; as such, those opposites that were separated as a brother-sister pair in the unconscious are reunited for the sake of conscious realization.

665     The corresponding process in the Grimm's "Brother and Sister" is the king's wedding (with the exception of the epilogue): A "false bride"—the daughter of the cursing stepmother-witch—interferes and must be overcome. It is not until this difficulty has been endured that the brother can also be redeemed. Obviously, the interference of the "false bride" is related to his unredeemed state. The king, the

---

[620] Jung, "The Visions of Zosimos," *CW* 13, § 86 III, I, 3.

[621] In this respect, a peculiar motif, which is probably due to the fact that this fairytale originates in medieval alchemy, is that of the two coffins that the hero finds in the depths of the earth: One contains the sleeping anima-figure, the other a miniature version of her enchanted castle. As observed, castles, palaces, cities, or vessels are feminine symbols, and thus partially identical with the anima. If these two images are explicitly separated here, while otherwise the anima mostly appears within the enchanted castle in this tale, then this splitting occurs to make the essential content conscious (similar to the separation of the siblings, which served the same purpose). Thus, the anima is distinguished as the principle of life in the man's unconscious from the unconscious as that which encompasses the whole personality in terms of a matrix. As every archetype is connected to all unconscious images, it needs to be isolated, artificially as it were, by human consciousness to make it recognizable. Thus, separating the anima and the castle makes it possible to grasp the anima on her own. The magician therefore reduces the size of the castle (i.e., diminishes its meaning), and thus also its function as that which encompasses the *coniunctio oppositorum* in the form of incest, so that the latent opposition can emerge. Thus, the magician drives, albeit demonically, conscious realization. The fact that he imprisons the servants as "spirits" in bottles has the same meaning: As Jung observes ("The Spirit Mercurius," *CW* 13, § 245), the bottle "is an artificial human product and thus signifies the intellectual purposefulness and artificiality of the procedure, whose obvious aim is to isolate the spirit from the surrounding medium." The fact that a demon rather than a figure representing human consciousness causes this isolation, which is the result of intellectual intervention, indicates that the human intellect also originates in the unconscious.

sister, the brother-cum-stag, and the false bride form a marriage quaternio. This, however, is marred by two facts: One of the masculine parts is an animal; and one of the feminine parts attempts to force its way into the sister's marriage with the king rather than attend to the unredeemed animal-brother. Consequently, this part pursues an impure goal and therefore is branded the "false bride." We have explained her archetypal meaning in Volume 3 ("The Maiden's Quest"): On the one hand, she is the heroine's shadow-figure; on the other, she is an image of the man's soul that has been secularized or otherwise distorted into a persona. If, considering the connection between this figure's fate and the brother's redemption, this "false bride" is assumed to belong to the stag-brother's unconscious psyche (according to the quaternio rule, she would have to marry him), this means that a part of his soul, his anima, wants to disrupt the sister's marriage. Of course, such behavior would solely intend to secretly regain the sister for himself. From this emerges a new definition of the "false bride": She is the unrealized endogamous tendency (and therefore is linked to the evil mother in many fairytales); deprived of its goal, this tendency unsettles the soul, yet thereby indirectly forces more subtle differentiation and greater awareness.

666     The "false bride" interferes in precisely this way in several parallels: "The Lost Golden Shoe" (Iceland, no. 17), "The Werewolf's Skin" (Finland, no. 84), "The White Bride and the Black Bride" (Grimm), "De lütt Ent" (Wisser, *Plattdeutsche*, Jena 1922, vol. 1, p. 72), and "De Köni un de Ent" (*ibid.*, p. 182). The last three tales are related in particular to the Grimm's "Brother and Sister": According to Bolte and Polívka,[622] in some versions the little sister enters the kitchen as a duck to inquire about her child or her little brother. In one version, she sings:

667                   Oh, little brother, be patient!
                         I lie in the deepest pit;
                         The earth is my lower bed,

---

[622] Bolte and Polívka, *Anmerkungen*, vol. 1, p. 84f.

668
> The water is my upper bed.
> Oh, little brother, be patient!
> I lie in the pit.

669 Afterwards, when the little sister comes into the kitchen to the cook and has made herself known to him, she asks:

670
> What are my girls doing, are they still spinning?
> What is my little bell doing, is it still ringing?
> What is my little son doing, is he still laughing?

671 He replies:

> Your girls are no longer spinning,
> Your little bell is no longer ringing,
> Your little son so much is he crying.[623]

672 The fact that the stag-brother becomes human at the end of the present fairytale is mentioned only briefly, suggesting that this event is of no particular interest. Its deeper meaning is familiar from the tales about animal princes.

673 The problem of redemption in sibling tales expresses itself in three ways: Sometimes, the siblings suffer the same plight; according to Bolte and Polívka, in variants of the Grimm's "Brother and Sister," the little brother, for example, is slaughtered as a lamb while the little sister is meant to be devoured as a fish or to be transformed into one.[624] Sometimes, however, either the sister is the most cursed, as in Grimm's "The Glass Coffin," or the brother, as in the above version of "Brother and Sister." The most heavily cursed part is particularly far removed from the human sphere.[625] The transformation into an animal or an otherworldly being always means that the *concrete* realization of an archetype is destroyed in favor of its transformation into a *psychic* reality.

---

[623] On the meaning of this episode, see *Archetypal Symbols in Fairytales*, vol. 3, pp. 399–402.

[624] See "The Lambkin and the Little Fish" (*The Complete Grimm's Fairy Tales*, pp. 625–627), and Bolte and Polívka, *Anmerkungen*, vol. 3, p. 137; see also Italian fairytale "Mary and her Little Brother," *ibid.*, vol. 1 p. 87 (cited above, p. 279f., fn. 487). See further *ibid.*, vol. 1, p. 90.

[625] On the identity of being-dead and being-enchanted-into-an-animal, see the section on the realm of the dead in *Archetypal Symbols in Fairy Tales*, vol. 1, pp. 105–113; see also Adolf Thimme, *Das Märchen. Handbücher zur Volkskunde*, vol. 2 (Leipzig: Verlag von Wilhelm Heims, 1909, pp. 42–45). On enchantment and rapture, see Ninck, *Wodan*, pp. 44–49, 133ff., 145.

674    One fairytale in which this destruction and rapture are described in the starkest terms is the Grimm's "The Juniper Tree":

675    It is now long ago, quite two thousand years, since there was a rich man who had a beautiful and pious wife, and they loved each other dearly. They had, however, no children, though they wished for them very much, and the woman prayed for them day and night, but still they had none. Now there was a court-yard in front of their house in which was a juniper-tree, and one day in winter the woman was standing beneath it, paring herself an apple, and while she was paring herself the apple she cut her finger, and the blood fell on the snow. "Ah," said the woman, and sighed right heavily, and looked at the blood before her, and was most unhappy, "ah, if I had but a child as red as blood and as white as snow!" And while she thus spake, she became quite happy in her mind, and felt just as if that were going to happen. Then she went into the house and a month went by and the snow was gone, and two months, and then everything was green, and three months, and then all the flowers came out of the earth, and four months, and then all the trees in the wood grew thicker, and the green branches were all closely entwined, and the birds sang until the wood resounded and the blossoms fell from the trees, then the fifth month passed away and she stood under the juniper-tree, which smelt so sweetly that her heart leapt, and she fell on her knees and was beside herself with joy, and when the sixth month was over the fruit was large and fine, and then she was quite still, and the seventh month she snatched at the juniper-berries and ate them greedily, then she grew sick and sorrowful, then the eighth month passed, and she called her husband to her, and wept and said, "If I die then bury me beneath the juniper-tree." Then she was quite comforted and happy until the next month was over, and then she had a child as white as snow

and as red as blood, and when she beheld it she was so delighted that she died.

676  One day the woman had gone upstairs to her room, and her little daughter went up too, and said, "Mother, give me an apple." "Yes, my child," said the woman, and gave her a fine apple out of the chest, but the chest had a great heavy lid with a great sharp iron lock. "Mother," said the little daughter, "is brother not to have one too?" This made the woman angry, but she said, "Yes, when he comes out of school." And when she saw from the window that he was coming, it was just as if the Devil entered into her, and she snatched at the apple and took it away again from her daughter, and said, "Thou shalt not have one before thy brother." Then she threw the apple into the chest, and shut it. Then the little boy came in at the door, and the Devil made her say to him kindly, "My son, wilt thou have an apple?" and she looked wickedly at him. "Mother," said the little boy, "how dreadful you look! Yes, give me an apple." Then it seemed to her as if she were forced to say to him, "Come with me," and she opened the lid of the chest and said, "Take out an apple for thyself," and while the little boy was stooping inside, the Devil prompted her, and crash! she shut the lid down, and his head flew off and fell among the red apples. Then she was overwhelmed with terror, and thought, "If I could but make them think that it was not done by me!" So she went upstairs to her room to her chest of drawers, and took a white handkerchief out of the top drawer, and set the head on the neck again, and folded the handkerchief so that nothing could be seen, and she set him on a chair in front of the door, and put the apple in his hand.

677  After this Marlinchen came into the kitchen to her mother, who was standing by the fire with a pan of hot water before her which she was constantly stirring round. "Mother," said Marlinchen, "brother is sitting at the door, and he looks quite white and has an apple in his hand. I asked him to give me

the apple, but he did not answer me, and I was quite frightened." "Go back to him," said her mother, "and if he will not answer thee, give him a box on the ear." So Marlinchen went to him and said, "Brother, give me the apple." But he was silent, and she gave him a box on the ear, on which his head fell down. Marlinchen was terrified, and began crying and screaming, and ran to her mother, and said, "Alas, mother, I have knocked my brother's head off!" and she wept and wept and could not be comforted. "Marlinchen," said the mother, "what hast thou done? but be quiet and let no one know it; it cannot be helped now, we will make him into black-puddings." Then the mother took the little boy and chopped him in pieces, put him into the pan and made him into black puddings; but Marlinchen stood by weeping and weeping, and all her tears fell into the pan and there was no need of any salt.

678 Then the father came home, and sat down to dinner and said, "But where is my son?" And the mother served up a great dish of black-puddings, and Marlinchen wept and could not leave off. Then the father again said, "But where is my son?" "Ah," said the mother, "he has gone across the country to his mother's great uncle; he will stay there awhile." "And what is he going to do there? He did not even say good-bye to me."

679 "Oh, he wanted to go, and asked me if he might stay six weeks, he is well taken care of there." "Ah," said the man, "I feel so unhappy lest all should not be right. He ought to have said good-bye to me." With that he began to eat and said, "Marlinchen, why art thou crying? Thy brother will certainly come back." Then he said, "Ah, wife, how delicious this food is, give me some more." And the more he ate the more he wanted to have, and he said, "Give me some more, you shall have none of it. It seems to me as if it were all mine." And he ate and ate and threw all the bones under the table, until he had finished the whole. But Marlinchen went away to her chest of drawers, and took her best silk handkerchief out of

the bottom drawer, and got all the bones from beneath the table, and tied them up in her silk handkerchief, and carried them outside the door, weeping tears of blood. Then the juniper-tree began to stir itself, and the branches parted asunder, and moved together again, just as if someone was rejoicing and clapping his hands. At the same time a mist seemed to arise from the tree, and in the center of this mist it burned like a fire, and a beautiful bird flew out of the fire singing magnificently, and he flew high up in the air, and when he was gone, the juniper-tree was just as it had been before, and the handkerchief with the bones was no longer there. Marlinchen, however, was as gay and happy as if her brother were still alive. And she went merrily into the house, and sat down to dinner and ate.

680   But the bird flew away and lighted on a goldsmith's house, and began to sing:

681   "My mother she killed me,
      My father he ate me,
      My sister, little Marlinchen,
      Gathered together all my bones,
      Tied them in a silken handkerchief,
      Laid them beneath the juniper-tree,
      Kywitt, kywitt, what a beautiful bird am I!"

682   The goldsmith was sitting in his workshop making a gold chain, when he heard the bird which was sitting singing on his roof, and very beautiful the song seemed to him.

683   Then the bird flew away to a shoemaker, and lighted on his roof and sang the same song.

684   The shoemaker heard that and ran out of doors in his shirt sleeves, and looked up at his roof, and was forced to hold his hand before his eyes lest the sun should blind him. "Bird," said he, "how beautifully thou canst sing!" Then he called in at his door, "Wife, just come outside, there is a bird, look at that bird, he just can sing well." Then he called his daughter

and children, and apprentices, boys and girls, and they all came up the street and looked at the bird and saw how beautiful he was, and what fine red and green feathers he had, and how like real gold his neck was, and how the eyes in his head shone like stars. "Bird," said the shoemaker, "now sing me that song again." "Nay," said the bird, "I do not sing twice for nothing; thou must give me something." "Wife," said the man, "go to the garret, upon the top shelf there stands a pair of red shoes, bring them down." Then the wife went and brought the shoes.

685 And when he had sung the whole he flew away. In his right claw he had the chain and the shoes in his left, and he flew far away to a mill, and the mill went, "klipp klapp, klipp klapp, klipp klapp," and in the mill sat twenty miller's men hewing a stone, and cutting, hick hack, hick hack, hick hack, and the mill went klipp klapp, klipp klapp, klipp klapp.

686 In the room sat the father, the mother, and Marlinchen at dinner, and the father said, "How light-hearted I feel, how happy I am!" "Nay," said the mother, "I feel so uneasy, just as if a heavy storm were coming." Marlinchen, however, sat weeping and weeping, and then came the bird flying, and as it seated itself on the roof the father said, "Ah, I feel so truly happy, and the sun is shining so beautifully outside, I feel just as if I were about to see some old friend again." "Nay," said the woman, "I feel so anxious, my teeth chatter, and I seem to have fire in my veins." And she tore her stays open, but Marlinchen sat in a corner crying, and held her plate before her eyes and cried till it was quite wet. Then the bird sat on the juniper tree, and sang the same song.

687 Then she was light-hearted and joyous, and she put on the new red shoes, and danced and leaped into the house. "Ah," said she, "I was so sad when I went out and now I am so light-hearted; that is a splendid bird, he has given me a pair of red shoes!" "Well," said the woman, and sprang to her feet and

her hair stood up like flames of fire, "I feel as if the world were coming to an end! I, too, will go out and see if my heart feels lighter." And as she went out at the door, crash! the bird threw down the millstone on her head, and she was entirely crushed by it. The father and Marlinchen heard what had happened and went out, and smoke, flames, and fire were rising from the place, and when that was over, there stood the little brother, and he took his father and Marlinchen by the hand, and all three were right glad, and they went into the house to dinner, and ate.[626]

688   The initial episode resembles that in "Snow White," except that in this tale it concerns a son (in some variants, however, the little sister is the tragic victim).[627] The mother's relationship with the juniper (in Standard German, as Bolte and Polívka explain,[628] the *Machandelbaum*, "almond tree," is called *Wacholder*, "juniper"). In particular, the fact that she eats its berries while she is pregnant recalls the opening episode of "Rapunzel."[629] As it does there, the relationship with the plant denotes the connection with the demonic world: The juniper is also magically involved in the begetting of the boy because the mother expresses her wish to give birth to a child beneath this tree. Yet its berries also kill the mother. In the end, when the juniper stands on her grave, it also personifies, as in "Cinderella,"[630] the mother who has become a ghost. For the boy, it thus represents both the primordial father and the primordial mother; or, put psychologically, the basic principle of life, the totality of the unconscious, which comprises the opposites man-woman, death-life.

---

[626] Commenting on the above version, Hamann (in *Literarische Vorlagen*, p. 11) praises Runge's masterful presentation of this fairytale, which makes it, like "The Fisherman and His Wife," *The Complete Grimm's Fairy Tales*, pp. 103–112), a literary "gem." He adds: "Without burdening the material with subjective elements, he enabled subsequent fairytale writers to follow these examples by deepening and heightening their motifs, by providing richly detailed descriptions, and by precisely observing the rhythm of spoken prose." See the Caucasian variant "Arsuman" (no. 16): The brother, bewitched into a bird, flies away after avenging himself, but without being redeemed. See also "The Dove" (Russia, no. 3) and "The White Dove" (France, vol. 2, no. 41).
[627] Bolte and Polívka, *Anmerkungen*, vol. 1, pp. 415, 417.
[628] See *ibid.*, p. 421.
[629] *The Complete Grimm's Fairy Tales*, pp. 73–77.
[630] *Ibid.*, pp. 121–128.

689     In popular belief, the evergreen juniper has assumed a magical significance since ancient times, in particular among the Germanic peoples. In his entry on *Wacholder* ("juniper"), Bächtold-Stäubli refers to Middle High German *quecholder*, where *queck* means "fresh, alive." He also notes that the juniper is considered a fertility symbol. "When it is fertile, many boys are born." It is also considered "an anti-demonic shrub," which wards off devils, witches, and evil spirits. In Norway, it is said that even during daytime one can see "the top of the shrub glowing or the whole shrub on fire." The pair of siblings represents, as it were, the opposites already latent in the symbol of the tree, although the sister is closer to the maternal principle, which is portrayed as evil. She is said to carry some of the blame for the brother's murder. In the present fairytale, the masculine principle proves to be weaker than that of the destructive evil mother, as indicated by the father's passive, helpless behavior. The masculine principle almost always represents the spirit, that is, consciousness in the proper sense. Here, however, it is unable to assert itself against the supremacy of the chaotic unconscious, which seeks to snatch back its offsprings. The brother's dismemberment recalls the mythical death of the "Great Mother's" "son-lover" in Oriental myths about gods. His relation to plants and the tree, which he temporarily enters in this fairytale, also recurs in the motif of Attis's transformation into a spruce and of Adonis's blood into the *anemone* (windflower).[631] This is the archetypal motif of the son's entanglement, rapture, and enchantment by the terrible mother[632] as the image of the unconscious.

690     The fact that the father, even if unknowingly, participates in the murder in the present fairytale reveals how powerfully he, too, is spellbound by the evil mother. Thus, he represents a too archaic principle of consciousness, which has become almost as destructive as the unconscious. Incidentally, his devouring of the dead son also recalls Mrile consuming his bull (see "The Tale of Mrile," Africa, no. 9): Weakness makes human beings who have fallen under the Great

---

[631] On the relationship between this fairytale and the myth of Osiris, see Otto Rank, *Das Inzest-Motiv in Dichtung und Sage* (Leipzig and Vienna, 1912), p. 317ff.
[632] For a general discussion, see Jung, *Symbols of Transformation*, CW 5.

Mother's spell destroy their creative power or future. While the African fairytale ends tragically, the previously mentioned myths and most variants of the fairytale about the juniper end more hopefully, albeit in varying degrees: Either the murdered son becomes a bird and affirms that he is still alive by singing "I'm still here, I'm still here!"[633] Or, on another level, he also avenges himself on the evil mother. In the Grimm's version, as well as in many of its variants, he is even transformed back into a human being, so that his death and his bewitchment were, so to speak, merely temporary. The fairytale thus conveys the comforting prospect that, ultimately, consciousness is never doomed to perish for good. As so often happens, even the murdered man's "night sea journey" subsequently proves to be enriching: He brings back precious jewels for his father and sister and gains the power to destroy evil.[634]

691   In a Turkestan variant, "The Turtledove on the Mulberry Tree" (no. 16), the bird is retransformed by a complete turn of events; we have already come across this motif in "The King of the Golden Mountain," "Djulek-Batür," and "The Cat." It indicates the direction in which the psyche moves by reversing the previous direction. Thus, in "The King of the Golden Mountain" and "Djulek-Batür," the keeling over of events is followed by the journey and descent into the underworld; in "The Cat," it reveals the anima's oscillation between the otherworld and this world. In "The Turtledove on the Mulberry Tree," this motif expresses the boy's return to this world and symbolically indicates a psychic process that Jung called the *enantiodromia* of Heraclitus.[635] Thus, psychic life, which we can understand as the energetic process taking place between pairs of opposites, after reaching one pole turns round and, turning back on itself, strives toward the other pole. In fairytales, however, reversal does not occur at the turning point, but only after the counter-movement has been initiated, as it were, as its reinforcement and confirmation: After evil and chaos have gained utmost power, the

---

[633] Bolte and Polívka, *Anmerkungen*, vol. 1, pp. 413, 415, 418, 419.
[634] The millstone is round and thus denotes the self. In negative terms, however, the self can exact the most brutal revenge if the human being resists its laws.
[635] Jung, "On the Psychology of the Unconscious," *CW* 7, § 111ff.

counteraction commences with the bird's action (spiritual principle), which eventually culminates in the sudden reversal back into human form.

692    Compared to a number of the other tales discussed previously, this type describes a primitive process in rather broad terms,[636] lending it a special charm, which also arises from its ambiguity: The simpler a myth is told, the more complex are its possible interpretations. Thus, this fairytale might serve the same purpose as the myths about the son of the gods who succumbs to the terrible mother: to depict the tragic threat, the temporary death, and the rebirth of human consciousness, which emerges gradually from the primeval darkness of the unconscious.[637]

693    Yet this tale also contains another motif, which otherwise is only evident in the myth of Osiris: the motif of the *sister* who gathers her brother's remains and assists his rebirth.[638] She embodies the positive, feminine forces of the unconscious, for which no place

---

[636] This is not changed by the fact that the Grimm's version has been revised into a piece of literature; according to Lincke, it "has a very clear organic structure, which attests to the work of a great narrative artist" and exhibits "an unsurpassable psychological penetration of the material" (*Das Stiefmuttermotif*, p. 56).

[637] On the fragmentation, scattering, and regathering of parts in the ancient mysteries, see Mead, *Fragments of a Faith Forgotten* (1931), pp. 439–440; see also Jung, "The Visions of Zosimos," *CW* 13, § 91: "An essential part of the sacrificial act is dismemberment. Zosimos must have been familiar with this motif from the Dionysian mystery-tradition. There, too, the god is the victim, who was torn to pieces by the Titans and thrown into a cooking pot, but whose heart was saved at the last moment by Hera. Our text shows that the bowl-shaped altar was a cooking vessel in which a multitude of people were boiled and burned. As we know from the legend and from a fragment of Euripides, an outburst of bestial greed and the tearing of living animals with the teeth were part of the Dionysian orgy." See further Jung, "Transformation Symbolism in the Mass," *CW* 11, § 400; Silberer, *Probleme der Mystik*, pp. 56ff. See also Marcus Aurelius's interpretation in his *Meditations*: "If thou didst ever see a hand cut off, or a foot, or a head, lying anywhere apart from the rest of the body, such does a man make himself, as far as he can, who is not content with what happens, and separates himself from others, or does anything unsocial. Suppose that thou hast detached thyself from the natural unity—for thou wast made by nature a part, but now thou hast cut thyself off—yet here there is this beautiful provision, that it is in thy power again to unite thyself. God has allowed this to no other part, after it has been separated and cut asunder, to come together again. But consider the kindness by which he has distinguished man, for he has put it in his power not to be separated at all from the universal; and when he has been separated, he has allowed him to return and to be united and to resume his place as a part" (Book 8, Aphorism 34). "Separation" is the mother's curse.

[638] See the "Hymn of Amon-Mose to Osiris," in Roeder, *Urkunden* (Jena, 1923), p. 24: "His sister has protected him; she who drove away the enemies and chased away misfortune; who warded off the adversary by pronouncing magical spells; whose tongue was skillful and who did not lack speech, the excellent commander, Isis, the transfigured one, who protects her brother; who seeks him and does not languish; who passed through this land in mourning, without resting, before finding him; whose feathers cast shadows and whose wings gave birth to wind; who paid praise and clang to her brother (by the collar during the dance of death); who dispelled the weary one's weakness; who received his seed and gave birth to the heir; who nurtured the child alone, without anyone knowing where these events took place"—Trans.

exists in the image of the evil mother. The gathering of bones signifies the reunification of the scattered parts, the preservation of what remains.[639] Just as the unconscious has a dissolving effect (and thus may lead to a person's complete dissociation), so a secret force takes effect in it. Striving toward becoming one, it is embodied in the sister in the present fairytale. Nevertheless, it is not contradictory that she is the evil mother's real daughter: She is, as later transpires, similar in nature. Killing and separating are—and this paradox is difficult to endure—also animating and unifying.

694    This paradox is more evident in fairytales in which the sister, either indirectly or even directly through her sheer existence, causes her brother or brothers to be enchanted. One example of the former case is the well-known fairytale "The Twelve Brothers":

695    Once upon a time there were a king and a queen. They lived happily together and had twelve children, all boys. One day the king said to his wife, "If our thirteenth child, which you are soon going to bring into the world, is a girl, then the twelve others shall die, so that her wealth may be great, and so that she alone may inherit the kingdom." Indeed, he had twelve coffins made. They were filled with wood shavings and each was fitted with a coffin pillow. He had them put in a locked room, and gave the key to the queen, ordering her to tell no one about them.

696    The mother sat and mourned the entire day, until the youngest son—who was always with her, and who was named Benjamin after the Bible—said to her, "Dear mother, why are you so sad?"

---

[639] Lévy-Bruhl provides evidence for the widespread primitive belief that bones contain the power of the soul, the mana, as that part of humankind that lives longest. "But the most essential appurtenance of the dead man ... is undoubtedly his bony framework, especially his skull. The softer parts of the body rapidly decompose and putrefy, particularly in warm, damp climates, unless there is some means of preventing this by embalming the body ... in the communities we are dealing with here, there is no way of preserving the flesh of a corpse indefinitely; therefore the bones are all the more prized. Their very hardness, and the fact that in most regions they are immune from the influences of time, increases the religious aspect in which they are held. Evidently they contain within them much of the *mana* or the *imunu* of the man himself" (*The "Soul of the "Primitive,"* pp. 244–245).

697    "Dearest child," she answered, "I cannot tell you." However, he would not leave her in peace, until she unlocked the room and showed him the coffins, already filled with wood shavings. Then she said, "My dearest Benjamin, your father had these coffins made for you and your eleven brothers. If I bring a girl into the world, you are all to be killed and buried in them." As she spoke and cried, her son comforted her, saying, "Don't cry, dear mother. We will take care of ourselves and run away." Then she said, "Go out into the woods with your eleven brothers. One of you should climb the highest tree that you can find. Keep watch there and look toward the castle tower. If I give birth to a little son, I will raise a white flag. If I give birth to a little daughter, I will raise a red flag, and then you should escape as fast as you can, and may God protect you. I will get up every night and pray for you, in the winter that you may warm yourselves near a fire, and in the summer that you may not suffer from the heat."

698    After she had blessed her children, they went out into the woods. One after the other of them kept watch, sitting atop the highest oak tree and looking toward the tower. After eleven days had passed, and it was Benjamin's turn, he saw that a flag had been raised. It was not the white one, but instead the red blood-flag, decreeing that they all were to die. When the boys heard this they became angry and cried out, "Are we to suffer death for the sake of a girl! We swear that we will take revenge. Wherever we find a girl, her red blood shall flow."

699    Then they went deeper into the woods, and in its middle, where it was darkest, they found a little bewitched house that was empty. They said, "We will live here. You, Benjamin, you are the youngest and weakest. You shall stay at home and keep house. We others will go and get things to eat." Thus they went into the woods and shot rabbits, wild deer, birds, and doves, and whatever they could eat. These they brought to Benjamin, and he had to prepare them to satisfy their

hunger. They lived together in this little house for ten years, but the time passed quickly for them.

700 The little daughter that their mother, the queen, had given birth to was now grown up. She had a good heart, a beautiful face, and a golden star on her forehead. Once on a large washday she saw twelve men's shirts in the laundry and asked her mother, "Whose are these twelve shirts? They are much too small for father." The queen answered with a heavy heart, "Dear child, they belong to your twelve brothers." The girl said, "Where are my twelve brothers? I have never even heard of them." She answered, "Only God knows where they are. They are wandering about in the world." Then she took the girl, unlocked the room for her, and showed her the twelve coffins with the wood shavings and the coffin pillows. "These coffins," she said, "were intended for your brothers, but they secretly ran away before you were born," and she told her how everything had happened. Then the girl said, "Dear mother, don't cry. I will go and look for my brothers."

701 Then she took the twelve shirts and went forth into the great woods. She walked the entire day, in the evening coming to the bewitched little house. She went inside and found a young lad, who asked, "Where do you come from, and where are you going?" He was astounded that she was so beautiful, that she was wearing regal clothing, and that she had a star on her forehead. "I am a princess and am looking for my twelve brothers. I will walk on as long as the sky is blue, until I find them." She also showed him the twelve shirts that belonged to them. Benjamin saw that it was his sister, and said, "I am Benjamin, your youngest brother." She began to cry for joy, and Benjamin did so as well. They kissed and embraced one another with great love. Then he said, "Dear sister, I must warn you that we have agreed that every girl whom we meet must die." She said, "I will gladly die, if I can thus redeem my twelve brothers."

702 "No," he answered, "you shall not die. Sit under this tub until our eleven brothers come, and I will make it right with them."

703 She did this, and when night fell they came home from the hunt. As they sat at the table eating, they asked, "What is new?" Benjamin said, "Don't you know anything?" "No," they answered. He continued speaking, "You have been in the woods while I stayed at home, but I know more than you do." "Then tell us," they shouted. He answered, "If you will promise me that the next girl we meet shall not be killed." "Yes," they all shouted. "We will show her mercy. Just tell us."

704 Then he said, "Our sister is here," and lifted up the tub. The princess came forth in her regal clothing and with the golden star on her forehead, so beautiful, delicate, and fine. They all rejoiced, falling around her neck and kissing her, and they loved her with all their hearts.

705 Now she stayed at home with Benjamin and helped him with the work. The eleven went into the woods and captured wild game, deer, birds, and doves, so they would have something to eat. Their sister and Benjamin prepared it all. They gathered wood for cooking, herbs for the stew, and put the pot onto the fire so a meal was always ready when the eleven came home. She also kept the house in order, and made up the beds white and clean. The brothers were always satisfied, and they lived happily with her.

706 One time the two of them had prepared a good meal at home, and so they sat together and ate and drank and were ever so happy. Now there was a little garden next to the bewitched house, and in it there were twelve lilies, the kind that are called "students." Wanting to bring some pleasure to her brothers, she picked the twelve flowers, intending to give one to each of them when they were eating. But in the same instant that she picked the flowers, the twelve brothers were transformed into twelve ravens, and they flew away above the woods. The house and the garden disappeared as well. Now

the poor girl was alone in the wild woods. Looking around, she saw an old women standing next to her. The old woman said, "My child, what have you done? Why did you not leave the twelve white flowers standing? Those were your brothers, and now they have been transformed into ravens forever." The girl said, crying, "Is there no way to redeem them?"

707 "No," said the old woman, "There is only one way in the world, and it is so difficult that you will never redeem them. You must remain silent for seven whole years, neither speaking nor laughing. If you speak a single word, even if all but one hour of the seven years has passed, then it will all be for nothing, and your brothers will be killed by that one word."

708 Then the girl said in her heart, "I know for sure that I will redeem my brothers." She went and found a lofty tree and climbed to its top, where she sat and span, without speaking and without laughing. Now it came to pass that a king was hunting in these woods. He had a large greyhound that ran to the tree where the girl was sitting. It jumped about, yelping and barking up the tree. The king came, saw the beautiful princess with the golden star on her forehead, and was so enchanted by her beauty that he shouted up to her, asking her to become his wife. She gave him no answer, but nodded with her head. Then he himself climbed the tree, carried her down, set her on his horse, and took her home with him. Their wedding was celebrated with great pomp and joy, but the bride neither spoke nor laughed. After they had lived a few years happily together, the king's mother, who was a wicked woman, began to slander the young queen, saying to the king, "You have brought home a common beggar woman for yourself. Who knows what kind of godless things she is secretly doing. Even if she is a mute and cannot speak, she could at least laugh. Anyone who does not laugh has an evil conscience." At first the king did not want to believe this, but the old woman kept it up so long, accusing her of so many

wicked things, that the king finally let himself be convinced, and he sentenced her to death.

709    A great fire was lit in the courtyard, where she was to be burned to death. The king stood upstairs at his window, looking on with crying eyes, for he still loved her dearly. She had already been bound to the stake, and the fire was licking at her clothing with its red tongues, when the last moment of the seven years passed. A whirring sound was heard in the air, and twelve ravens approached, landing together. As they touched the earth, it was her twelve brothers, whom she had redeemed. They ripped the fire apart, put out the flames, and freed their sister, kissing and embracing her. Now that she could open her mouth and speak, she told the king why she had remained silent and had never laughed. The king rejoiced to hear that she was innocent, and they all lived happily together until they died. The wicked stepmother was brought before the court and placed in a barrel filled with boiling oil and poisonous snakes, and she died an evil death.[640]

710    Another Grimm's tale, "The Seven Ravens," begins similarly:

A man had seven sons, but however much he wished for a daughter, he did not have one yet. Finally, his wife gave him hope for another child, and when it came into the world it was indeed a girl. Great was their joy, but the child was sickly and small, and because of her weakness, she was to be given an emergency baptism. The father sent one of the boys to run quickly to the well and get some water for the baptism. The other six ran along with him. Because each one of them wanted to be the first one to dip out the water, the jug fell into the well. There they stood not knowing what to do, and not one of them dared to go home. When they did not return the

---

[640] *The Complete Grimm's Fairy Tales*, pp. 59–64. See the following parallel versions: "A Sister Redeems Her Brothers" (Balkans, no. 34), which is entirely parallel, and "The Seven Brothers" (France, vol. 2, no. 58), whose initial episode is parallel. See also the aforementioned "The nine brothers who were turned into lambs and their sister" (France, vol. 2, no. 34).

father grew impatient, and said, "They have forgotten what they went after because they were playing, those godless boys." Fearing that the girl would die without being baptized, he cried out in anger, "I wish that those boys would all turn into ravens." He had hardly spoken these words when he heard a whirring sound above his head, and looking up, he saw seven coal-black ravens flying up and away.

711     The parents could not take back the curse, and however sad they were at the loss of their seven sons, they were still somewhat comforted because of their dear little daughter, who soon gained strength and became more beautiful every day. For a long time, she did not know that she had had brothers, for her parents took care not to mention them to her. However, one day she accidentally overheard some people talking about her. They said that she was beautiful enough, but that in truth she was to blame for her seven brothers' misfortune. This troubled her greatly, and she went to her father and mother and asked them if she indeed had had brothers, and what had happened to them. Her parents could no longer keep the secret, but said that it had been heaven's fate, and that her birth had been only the innocent cause. However, this ate at the girl's conscience every day, and she came to believe that she would have to redeem her brothers. She had neither rest nor peace until she secretly set forth and went out into the wide world, hoping to find her brothers and to set them free, whatever it might cost. She took nothing with her but a little ring as a remembrance from her parents, a loaf of bread for hunger, a little jug of water for thirst, and a little chair for when she got tired.

712     She walked on and on—far, far to the end of the world. She came to the sun, but it was too hot and terrible, and ate little children. She hurried away, and ran to the moon, but it was much too cold, and also frightening and wicked, and when it saw the child, it said, "I smell, smell human flesh." Then she hurried away, and came to the stars, and they were

friendly and good to her, each one sitting on its own little chair. When the morning star arose, it gave her a chicken bone, and said, "Without that drumstick you cannot open the glass mountain, and your brothers are inside the glass mountain."

713 The girl took the drumstick, wrapped it up well in a cloth, and went on her way again until she came to the glass mountain. The door was locked, and she started to take out the chicken bone, but when she opened up the cloth, it was empty. She had lost the gift of the good stars. What could she do now? She wanted to rescue her brothers, but she had no key to the glass mountain. The good little sister took a knife, cut off one of her little fingers, put it into the door, and fortunately the door opened. After she had gone inside a little dwarf came up to her and said, "My child, what are you looking for?" "I am looking for my brothers, the seven ravens," she replied. The dwarf said, "The lord ravens are not at home, but if you want to wait here until they return, step inside." Then the dwarf carried in the ravens' dinner on seven little plates, and in seven little cups. The sister ate a little bit from each plate and took a little sip from each cup. Into the last cup she dropped the ring that she had brought with her.

714 Suddenly she heard a whirring and rushing sound in the air, and the dwarf said, "The lord ravens are flying home now." They came, wanted to eat and drink, and looked for their plates and cups. Then one after the other of them said, "Who has been eating from my plate? Who has been drinking from my cup? It was a human mouth." When the seventh one came to the bottom of his cup, the ring rolled toward him. Looking at it, he saw that it was a ring from their father and mother, and said, "God grant that our sister might be here; then we would be set free." The girl was listening from behind the door, and when she heard this wish she came forth. Then the

ravens were restored to their human forms again. They hugged and kissed one another, and went home happily.[641]

715    The plot of the Grimm's "The Six Swans" parallels the previous tales, although here the sister is not guilty, as is suggested elsewhere:

716    A king was once hunting in a great forest, and he chased his prey so eagerly that none of his men could follow him. As evening approached he stopped and looked around, and saw that he was lost. He looked for a way out of the woods, but he could not find one. Then he saw an old woman with a bobbing head who approached him. She was a witch. "My dear woman," he said to her, "can you show me the way through the woods?" "Oh, yes, your majesty," she answered, "I can indeed. However, there is one condition, and if you do not fulfill it, you will never get out of these woods, and will die here of hunger."

717    "What sort of condition is it?" asked the king.

718    "I have a daughter," said the old woman, "who is as beautiful as anyone you could find in all the world, and who well deserves to become your wife. If you will make her your queen, I will show you the way out of the woods." The king was so frightened that he consented, and the old woman led him to her cottage, where her daughter was sitting by the fire. She received the king as if she had been expecting him. He saw that she was very beautiful, but in spite of this he did not like her, and he could not look at her without secretly shuddering. After he had lifted the girl onto his horse, the old woman showed him the way, and the king arrived again at his royal castle, where the wedding was celebrated.

719    The king had been married before, and by his first wife he had seven children, six boys and one girl. He loved them more than anything else in the world. Fearing that the

---

[641] *The Complete Grimm's Fairy Tales*, pp. 137–139.

stepmother might not treat them well, even do them harm, he took them to a secluded castle which stood in the middle of a forest. It was so well hidden, and the way was so difficult to find, that he himself would not have found it, if a wise woman had not given him a ball of magic yarn. Whenever he threw it down in front of him, it would unwind itself and show him the way. However, the king went out to his dear children so often that the queen took notice of his absence. She was curious and wanted to know what he was doing out there all alone in the woods. She gave a large sum of money to his servants, and they revealed the secret to her. They also told her about the ball of yarn which could point out the way all by itself. She did not rest until she discovered where the king kept the ball of yarn. Then she made some little shirts of white silk. Having learned the art of witchcraft from her mother, she sewed a magic charm into each one of them. Then one day when the king had ridden out hunting, she took the little shirts and went into the woods. The ball of yarn showed her the way. The children, seeing that someone was approaching from afar, thought that their dear father was coming to them. Full of joy, they ran to meet him. Then she threw one of the shirts over each of them, and when the shirts touched their bodies they were transformed into swans, and they flew away over the woods. The queen went home very pleased, believing that she had gotten rid of her stepchildren. However, the girl had not run out with her brothers, and the queen knew nothing about her. The next day the king went to visit his children, but he found no one there but the girl. "Where are your brothers?" asked the king. "Oh, dear father," she answered, "they have gone away and left me alone." Then she told him that from her window she had seen how her brothers had flown away over the woods as swans. She showed him the feathers that they had dropped into the courtyard, and which she had gathered up. The king mourned, but he did not think that the queen had done this wicked deed. Fearing that the girl would be stolen away from him as well, he wanted to take her away with him, but she was afraid of her stepmother and begged the king to let her stay just this one more night in the castle in the woods.

720 The poor girl thought, "I can no longer stay here. I will go and look for my brothers." And when night came she ran away and went straight into the woods. She walked the whole night long without stopping, and the next day as well, until she was too tired to walk any further.

721 Then she saw a hunter's hut and went inside. She found a room with six little beds, but she did not dare to get into one of them. Instead she crawled under one of them and lay down on the hard ground where she intended to spend the night. The sun was about to go down when she heard a rushing sound and saw six swans fly in through the window. Landing on the floor, they blew on one another, and blew all their feathers off. Then their swan-skins came off just like shirts. The girl looked at them and recognized her brothers. She was happy and crawled out from beneath the bed. The brothers were no less happy to see their little sister, but their happiness did not last long. "You cannot stay here," they said to her. "This is a robbers' den. If they come home and find you, they will murder you." "Can't you protect me?" asked the little sister. "No," they answered. "We can take off our swan-skins for only a quarter hour each evening. Only during that time do we have our human forms. After that we are again transformed into swans." Crying, the little sister said, "Can you not be redeemed?" "Alas, no," they answered. "The conditions are too difficult. You would not be allowed to speak or to laugh for six years, and in that time you would have to sew together six little shirts from asters for us. And if a single word were to come from your mouth, all your work would be lost." After the brothers had said this, the quarter hour was over, and they flew out the window again as swans.

722

Nevertheless, the girl firmly resolved to redeem her brothers, even if it should cost her her life. She left the hunter's hut, went to the middle of the woods, seated herself in a tree, and there spent the night. The next morning she went out and gathered asters and began to sew. She could not speak with anyone, and she had no desire to laugh. She sat there, looking only at her work. After she had already spent a long time there it happened that the king of the land was hunting in these woods. His huntsmen came to the tree where the girl was sitting. They called to her, saying, "Who are you?" But she did not answer. "Come down to us," they said. "We will not harm you." She only shook her head. When they pressed her further with questions, she threw her golden necklace down to them, thinking that this would satisfy them. But they did not stop, so she then threw her belt down to them, and when this did not help, her garters, and then—one thing at a time—everything that she had on and could do without, until finally she had nothing left but her shift. The huntsmen, however, not letting themselves be dissuaded, climbed the tree, lifted the girl down, and took her to the king. The king asked, "Who are you? What are you doing in that tree?" But she did not answer. He asked her in every language that he knew, but she remained as speechless as a fish. Because she was so beautiful, the king's heart was touched, and he fell deeply in love with her. He put his cloak around her, lifted her onto his horse in front of himself, and took her to his castle. There he had her dressed in rich garments, and she glistened in her beauty like bright daylight, but no one could get a word from her. At the table he seated her by his side, and her modest manners and courtesy pleased him so much that he said, "My desire is to marry her, and no one else in the world." A few days later they were married.

723

Now the king had a wicked mother who was dissatisfied with this marriage and spoke ill of the young queen. "Who knows," she said, "where the girl who cannot speak comes from? She is not worthy of a king." A year later, after the queen had brought her first child into the world, the old woman took it away from her while she was asleep, and smeared her mouth with blood. Then she went to the king and accused her of being a cannibal. The king could not believe this, and would not allow anyone to harm her. She, however, sat the whole time sewing on the shirts, and caring for nothing else. The next time, when she again gave birth to a beautiful boy, the deceitful mother-in-law did the same thing again, but the king could not bring himself to believe her accusations. He said, "She is too pious and good to do anything like that. If she were not speechless, and if she could defend herself, her innocence would come to light." But when the old woman stole away a newly born child for the third time, and accused the queen, who did not defend herself with a single word, the king had no choice but to bring her to justice, and she was sentenced to die by fire.

724    When the day came for the sentence to be carried out, it was also the last day of the six years during which she had not been permitted to speak or to laugh, and she had thus delivered her dear brothers from the magic curse. The six shirts were finished. Only the left sleeve of the last one was missing. When she was led to the stake, she laid the shirts on her arm. Standing there, as the fire was about to be lighted, she looked around, and six swans came flying through the air. Seeing that their redemption was near, her heart leapt with joy. The swans rushed towards her, swooping down so that she could throw the shirts over them. As soon as the shirts touched them their swan-skins fell off, and her brothers stood before her in their own bodies, vigorous and handsome. However, the youngest was missing his left arm. In its place he had a swan's wing. They embraced and kissed one another. Then the queen went to the king, who was greatly moved, and she began to speak, saying, "Dearest husband, now I may speak and reveal to you that I am

innocent, and falsely accused." Then she told him of the treachery of the old woman who had taken away their three children and hidden them. Then to the king's great joy they were brought forth. As a punishment, the wicked mother-in-law was tied to the stake and burned to ashes. But the king and the queen with her six brothers lived many long years in happiness and peace.[642]

725    Some of these initial episodes describe how the later-born girl causes her brothers' downfall. In the first of the tales cited above ("The Twelve Brothers"), the king explains matters as follows: His wealth and kingdom should remain together. Also in "The Seven Ravens," the father's overzealous love of his newly born daughter indirectly leads to the cursing of the brothers.

726    Even if relations in human families serve as a comparison, it is worth emphasizing that fairytales describe events that occur in an *archetypal* family and that their characters are not concrete persons (or only insofar as such individuals sometimes identify psychically with the archetype and live it unconsciously). Rather, they represent various archetypes: the father, the good and the evil mother, the sister (as a concrete woman *and* as the first representative of the man's anima), and the brother (as a youth *and* as the first representative of the woman's animus). For this reason, almost all fairytale characters are more or less magical. This feature, however, is more prominent in some versions than in others. On balance, this type of fairytale describes a psychological condition that corresponds to a certain stage of human development.

727    As Jung explains,[643] human beings may be assumed to experience the archetypes and archetypal situations unthinkingly, at a very primitive stage, at which they perceive no essential distinction between consciousness and the unconscious, and consequently neither between inner and outer psychic reality. At a further stage, the archetypal event is separated from the reality of human

---

[642] *The Complete Grimm's Fairy Tales*, pp. 232–237.
[643] Jung, "The Psychology of the Transference," *CW* 16, esp. § 438, 441.

consciousness insofar as this is lived only by certain individuals, for instance, the king or the magician. Eventually, it is detached completely from concrete life and projected solely onto a divine realm. A further step was taken by Western alchemy, which no longer projected this divine world into a metaphysical space but experienced that projection materially, and thereby (insofar as their body also makes human beings material) once again approached human reality. Alchemy, then, is the precursor of modern psychology, which recognized the same archetypal circumstances as a *psychic* reality. Compared to alchemy, fairytales represent a more archaic stage by still projecting events onto royal or magical-divine figures. However, in that the earlier stage of development always contains, embryonically as it were, future possibilities, we can consider fairytale representations to be a more recent way of capturing and shaping archetypal events, namely, a psychic one, which exists quite independently of matter.

728   As in the Grimm's "The Juniper Tree," mostly male siblings are subject to evil spells and thrust into the deeper layers of the unconscious. Here, however, this part consists not merely of one brother, but of 12 or seven or six (in some variants, also of three) male figures.[644] This splitting concerns the brother who is meant to be redeemed not only in fairytales about sibling redemption. It also occurs frequently in tales where one or several princesses must be redeemed by one or several heroes, or in tales about the hero's journey, where *one* hero is replaced by a group of men who have joined forces as comrades. These two forms include "The Eighteen

---

[644] On similar groups of figures with the same numbers in Gnostic speculation, see Bousset, *Hauptprobleme der Gnosis* (1907), passim, esp. pp. 9–58. On the role of the number seven in the Kabbalah, see Bischoff, "Elemente der Kabbalah" (1913), pp. 199ff. The number seven indicates being bound to fate and is a preliminary stage to the number eight, which signifies wholeness and freedom as a double quadruplicity. On the connection of the number seven with planets and metals, see Silberer, *Probleme der Mystik*, p. 77; see Jung, "The Psychology of the Transference," *CW* 16, § 402: The seven planets or metals are, in an alchemical view, "all as it were contained in Mercurius, since he is the *pater metallorum*. When personified, he is the unity of the seven planets, an Anthropos whose body is the world, like Gayomart, from whose body the seven metals flow into the earth. Owing to his feminine nature, Mercurius is also the mother of the seven, and not only of the six, for he is his own father and mother." The number six is both a precursor of the number seven and half of the number twelve, which represents wholeness in time in the 12 signs of the zodiac.—The most diverse symbolic use of each number is based on the same archetype, despite the different pictorial contexts, and each number is a different manifestation of the self in time and space.

Soldiers"[645] and "How Six Men Got on in the World").[646] Such fairytales also include ones about adept brothers, such as "The Four Skillful Brothers" or "The Three Brothers" (Italy, no. 26).[647] What the brothers or comrades accomplish in these fairytales is no different

---

[645] Zaunert, *Deutsche Märchen seit Grimm*, p. 101. Eighteen soldiers deserted their army and cheated an innkeeper out of his pay. To avenge himself, the man showed them a path that led through an open door into a mountain whose interior was brightly lit. After crossing three drawbridges, the soldiers reached a castle, where the table was laid for 18 men and where eighteen beds had been prepared. When they awoke the following morning, their former outfits and weapons had been exchanged for brand new ones. The sergeant ordered the soldiers to stand guard. After they had lived like this for a while, one day a carriage drawn by six horses arrived, from which a beautiful lady emerged. She told the sergeant that she was a cursed princess whom he should liberate and marry. For 17 days, she said, another princess would come to be redeemed by the other soldiers. Awaiting his turn, the youngest soldier grew impatient and deserted his regiment. But when he reached the first bridge, the devil broke his neck. The eldest princess told the sergeant that the soldier's actions had ruined the redemptive procedure; either an 18th man would be drafted or the other 17 would die. Thereupon, the corporal went out with two men and managed to recruit a poor tradesman's boy. The deceived innkeeper and his wife spotted the recruiters, followed them, and were killed by the devil. Meanwhile, a princess joined the 18 soldiers every day; one night, all the princesses lay down with their sweethearts but were not allowed to move until the *reveille* (i.e., roll call). And thus, redemption succeeded. The sergeant and his princess remained in the castle, which had been abandoned by the devil, while the other soldiers accompanied their brides to their kingdoms. Similar tales include "The Count's Son" (Zaunert, *Deutsche Märchen seit Grimm*, p. 71) and "The Seven Brothers" (Finland, no. 7).

[646] *The Complete Grimm's Fairy Tales*, pp. 344–349. A decommissioned soldier, able to perform all kinds of tricks and poorly paid by the king, went out looking for the right helpers to force the king to hand over his treasures. He found a servant who could uproot six trees like stalks of grain and carry them away; he also found a hunter who could shoot a fly sitting on the branch of an oak tree two miles away; another of his recruits could blow air from his nostrils to make seven windmills turn at a distance of two miles; and a runner who had to unstrap one leg so as not move faster than a bird could fly; his fifth recruit wore his hat on one ear, or else a violent frost would have frozen the birds aloft in the sky. Together, these six fellows came before the king, who wanted to give his daughter only to that fellow who could race faster than her. Being the applicant, the soldier let "his" runner run with both legs. The latter immediately overtook the princess, drew water from the well as required, but lay down to sleep on the way back. The princess caught up with him and poured out his water. But the hunter shot the horse in the skull, which was the sleeping man was using as a pillow, from under his head, waking him up. He rose, returned to fetch some more water, and won the race. Angrily, the king lured the six men into an iron chamber where they were to dine, while he had a fire built underneath to destroy them. But the journeyman straightened his little hat, so that everything froze. When the king wanted to ransom his daughter with gold, the lumberjack had a huge sack made in which he carried away the gold of the whole kingdom. Lamenting his loss, the king dispatched two cavalry regiments to catch the six men. But the blower blew all the men into the air. Finally, the king gave up, and the six men happily shared their loot on their return home.

[647] The first tale is collected in *The Complete Grimm's Fairy Tales*, pp. 580–584. The three sons of a poor man set out to fend for themselves. They promised to return home after 10 years. The eldest son became a general's servant and learned "to scale every wall of a towering castle with a dagger in each hand." The second son became a famous shipbuilder. The third son lived in a forest, learned the language of birds, and turned into a forest man. On the day of their return, when the brothers were reunited in the local inn, the third one heard a bird singing about a treasure hidden in the corner of the inn. They found the treasure and returned a very rich men to their father. One day, the third brother heard another bird singing about Aglaia, a maiden who lived in a marble castle on a distant island in the sea. The entrance was guarded by a fire, a poisonous snake, and a basilisk. Whoever could scale the tower would obtain the treasure and the maiden. The brothers decided to try their luck together. The second brother built a fast sailing ship, the warrior climbed the castle with two daggers, fetched Aglaia and returned laden with treasures. On their return, the brothers began quarreling over the beautiful woman. "The matter has not been settled to this day." See also "The Four Artful Brothers" (Italy, no. 8) and "The Five Sons" (Italy, no. 43). The groups of characters in these tales, insofar as they concern a father with three sons or four brothers (in particular if we consider the professions chosen by the brothers), could be interpreted based on the schema of the four psychic functions. However, the princess is not awarded to any of the heroes, who are all deemed to be equal. However, as this contradicts the nature of the psyche, and as many fairytales subsume a different number of characters in such groups, it is more likely that these splittings can only achieve their goal in unison, as they only form a whole together.

from those examined so far. They acquire riches, defeat evil forces, and redeem or win a beautiful bride. In most cases, however, the necessary capabilities or powers are distributed among many figures, whose interaction makes the desired heroic feat possible in the first place. This becomes plainly evident when such a group of heroes consists of cripples (e.g., in "Djulek-Batür"). Only then do all these one-sided figures constitute *one* single and moreover superior actor. This suggests that these "skillful brothers" or "comrades" represent independent psychic forces, which on a higher level appear as one of the hero's gifts or talents. A transitional form exists when the hero is *a* single figure, but is called, for example, Thirty-from-Paris (in the eponymous fairytale; see France, vol. 2, no. 33) or Hans Vêrtein (in the eponymous Low German fairytale; see Wisser, *Plattdeutsche*, Jena 1922, vol. 1, p. 81).

729    As observed, the anima is often also depicted not as *the* beloved and sought-after magical woman but is divided into multiple figures (e.g., a group of three). We have interpreted this splitting as a manifestation of this psychic image, which is further removed from consciousness. This coincides with the fact that nature demons also appear in multitudes: Fairies, *vilas*, forest women, nymphs, and so on, almost always appear in groups. Matters are similar with groups of heroes: They are similar to giants (distinguished by their strength), hobgoblins (distinguished by their skill), and hunters (see marksmen), and so on. These nature demons symbolize instinctual, unconscious impulses. Their assimilation is characteristic of an undifferentiated and undeveloped individual consciousness. However, in those fairytales where various figures belonging to the same group are differentiated, they might be compared to aptitudes that are only about to form a unified personality. The splitting of the hero into multiple figures therefore represents the state of not-yet being whole. Insofar as the hero represents the self, such fairytales illustrate that the self does not simply exist from the beginning as the germ of primordial oneness. Rather, it is the result of human immaturity, similar to a light that is still refracted through a prism, and only seems to grow together from many into one in the course of human development.

730    In the tales about 12 brothers, seven ravens, and six swans, the characters are not distinguished by particular talents or traits—unlike most of the groups of comrades discussed earlier. One exception, at least in some instances, is the youngest brother, whose disposition connects him to the redeeming sister or who is not completely redeemed. Distinguished by a special trait, he represents the core of the group around which the multitude will gather to form a unity. This is confirmed by medieval sequels to the fairytale about the swan brothers, whose youngest member becomes *one* of the heroes.[648] In Grimm's fairytales, the curse consists mostly in the fact that the hero, who is portrayed as a barely conscious psychic factor due to his division, regresses: either into the hereafter, that is, the realm of the dead (see the episode about the coffins, the attempted murder); or onto the animal level. The difference is not very significant insofar as the passage about the realm of the dead establishes that the dead, according to primitive belief, live on as animals or, more precisely, appear to the survivor as animals.

731    In a parallel Irish tale, "The Three Shirts of Cotton-Grass" (no. 21), the enchanted brothers temporarily wear blue hoods instead of animal clothes and are transformed into black ravens by their sister's wrongdoing: Before the king marries a second time, he sends his three sons to live in an subterranean house. Every day, his daughter brings them food. Yet the stepmother discovers the hiding place and tries to poison the maiden with an apple. When this ruse fails, one day she follows her stepdaughter unnoticed to the underground abode and turns the three brothers into brass candlesticks. The sister takes them home and cleans them every day. Angered, the stepmother turns the three candlesticks into three pieces of grass, which she throws under a bench. But when she sees the girl running after them, she turns them into wolves that run away into the forest.

---

[648] For the sources, see Ninck, *Wodan*, pp. 257–263; on the connection with the story about the Swan Knight, see *ibid.*, pp. 263–267; see further Otto Rank, "Die Lohengrinsage: Ein Beitrag zu ihrer Motivgestaltung und Deutung," in: *Schriften zur angewandten Seelenkunde*, ed. Sigmund Freud (1911), pp. 65–81. See also "The Birth of the Swan Knight" (France, vol. 1, no. 8) and the corresponding note (p. 308 f.), according to which the connection with the Lohengrin saga is secondary. For a discussion, see Bolte and Polívka, *Anmerkungen*, vol. 1, p. 432, and Ninck, "Älteste Märchen von Europa," in: *Sammlung Klosterberg, Europ. Reihe*, ed. H. U. von Balhasar (Basel: Schwabe, 1945), p. 121 ("The Swan's Tale").

The sister follows them in vain and reaches a hut at the edge of the forest. There she is entertained by a kitten and, as is her habit, cuts three pieces of meat for her brothers. Soon afterward, three youths enter the cottage, throw off their blue hoods, and sit down at the table. Knowing that the kitten is their mother, they find the sister and tell her that they are bewitched only during daytime and that the spell will end after seven years. After her brothers have gone to bed, the sister wants to mend their clothes by the light of the fire. She throws the three hoods into the flames, "so that they will give her light." The brothers enter, desperately wringing their hands, and declare that the spell will now weigh on them forever. Now, they add, they will be redeemed only if the sister gathers, spins, and weaves three shirts from cotton-grass within a year, without uttering a word or shedding a tear. Having uttered these words, the brothers fly away as black ravens.[649]

732    The blue hoods place the brothers, as it were, in an intermediate stage: While their form is *still* human, they are enveloped by the dark, midnight unconscious; the hoods make them resemble dwarves or fog spirits. Another kind of enchantment, the transformation into lilies[650] in the forest garden, is described as an intermediate stage in "The Twelve Brothers." We have already encountered this motif, albeit in connection with the fate of the anima-figure. In "A Soldier Redeems a Cursed Tsarina" (Balkans, no. 35), for instance, the maiden pursued by a vampirish ghost became a flower on her own grave, which subsequently transformed back into a girl. The same events unfold in "The Vampire" (Roma, no. 13). Other forms of enchantment include the brass candlesticks and the pieces of grass in the Irish fairytale discussed above.[651] In this case, paralysis occurs, which in other fairytales is expressed by the bewitchment into a glass mountain. Throughout, however, life is not

---

[649] For the continuation of the story, see p. 349 f. below.
[650] Mannhardt, *Wald- und Feldkulte*, vol. 1, p. 39: "The souls of lovers or of the innocently murdered turn into white lilies... ."
[651] On the significant role played by grass in superstition, see Bächtold-Stäubli under *Rasen* (grass, turf); in sum, grass or turf is a "collective phenomenon" and part of the all-birthing and all-absorbing maternal earth, "which is why most magical magical rituals involving grass are performed to bind the earth."

completely extinguished: The candlesticks still shine, the pieces of grass turn green, and the flowers continue to bloom.

733    The most frequent motif in the variants is the transformation into birds, in particular black birds. This recalls the boy's transformation in "The Juniper Tree." In the present tales, the juniper is mostly replaced by a forest, into which the bewitched disappear: Regression into the unconscious results, on the one hand, in evanescence, that is, spiritualization (birds as spiritual beings); and, on the other, in sinking into *hyle* (matter). This paradox is contingent on the antithetical nature of the unconscious. The latter is expressed in other fairytales by the fact that the brothers become forever quarreling animals or, more generally, are cursed to fight an eternal duel (not as animals)[652] and must be redeemed from this curse. In the latter case, the hero's image is torn asunder, not into multiple parts, but into the primordial opposites inherent in the unconscious.

734    Being embroiled in a conflict always signals unconsciousness and therefore amounts to being transformed into an animal. This, incidentally, illumines what in fairytales so often appears as an intermediate episode: The hero settles the dispute between two or more figures; in return, he either receives miraculous objects from them or tricks them out of those things.[653] The previous deliberations suggest that the combatants represent a more unconscious precursor of the hero: Although dissolved in the unconscious, his essence is magical, powerful, and more encompassing; moreover, he

[652] Bolte and Polívka, *Anmerkungen*, vol. 1, pp. 230, 231; see also "The Fighting Brothers" (Finland, no. 83): A man took a witch as his second wife; when his sons fought over which horse was best, their stepmother cursed them to fight all their lives. Their sister set out to look for her brothers. To help her, an old man living in a wooden cabin asked all the animals of the forest about the fighting brothers, but none of them had seen the young men. The old man directed the sister to a similar hut, where another old man asked all the birds in the sky. They had seen the brothers "beyond the land of nine kings, fighting each other with iron clubs on the seashore." The old man gave the girl a little ball with whose help she found the hut where the brothers were living. The mother's ring, hidden in the ball, told them that the sister had arrived, so they called her out of her hiding place and explained that although they lived peacefully in the hut, at a certain hour they were compelled to fight each other. To redeem her brothers, she would have to remain silent for nine years, whatever happened to her. When the brothers started beating each other with their iron clubs, she escaped and fell into a pit, only to be found and married by a King's son. But when she gave birth to a child, her husband's stepmother slandered her for eating the child. The King's son forgave her; but when the same thing happened again, he sentenced her to be hanged. When the nine years ended, the brothers, now rescued, rushed to her. Angels lifted all of them to heaven, but the stepmother was thrown into hell.

[653] See, e.g., "The Drummer" (*The Complete Grimm's Fairy Tales*, pp. 781–791), "The King of the Golden Mountain" (*ibid.*, pp. 425–430), "Strong Hans" (Latvia, no. 9), "The Huntsman and the Swan Maiden" (Zaunert, *Deutsche Märchen seit Grimm*, p. 133), "The Talking Tree" (Finland, no. 23).

must liberate it from its antithetical, tension-fraught state through conscious intervention and unify it with his conscious being. He has gained insight into the eternal dichotomy. By taking an ethical decision, he has integrated his powers, which are fragmented in the unconscious, and thus becomes powerful himself. Often considered immoral, settling a dispute by outwitting others has a deeper meaning: It reveals the superiority of consciousness, which does not allow itself to be torn apart by conflict.

735    Applied to fairytales about the enchanted brothers, this interpretation suggests that the hero, by appearing as a multitude, is easily subjected to the dissolving effect of the unconscious and therefore is also destined to succumb to the parental curse. Enchantment means further evanescence, into ever more indeterminable unconscious spheres (in part, this process unfolds in distinct stages: a distant castle, the middle of a forest, and, eventually, an unknown, remote land). Compared to the brothers, the father-king represents the previous dominant of consciousness, which is unsympathetic or even hostile toward the self (similar to the fairytales featuring a father and three sons). The stepmother is a negative mother-anima, whose profane and magical destructiveness prevails. She represents all those powers that strive to dissolve and thereby prevent concentration and maturation either from without or from within.

736    In "The Six Swans," when the stepmother throws the swan shirts (i.e., skins) over the brothers, we experience, as it were, that process whose outcomes we are familiar with from so many fairytales about animal princes: The enveloping in animal skin, through which the sovereign, inner person becomes darkened and unsightly and sinks into the depths of the unconscious.

737    In "The Seven Ravens," the motif of cursing is further elaborated: When the brothers go to fetch the baptismal water for the little sister, the jug breaks. In Christianity, as well as in other religions, baptism means spiritual rebirth; water not only serves ritual cleansing but also symbolizes the *materia* (matter) from which a person's spirit is renewed. In the present fairytale, baptism is performed in a state of emergency: The barely apparent image of the self as a child, the

anima, threatens to disappear imminently. If the brothers are unable to capture the water in the jug for the sister's baptism, the whole personality is as yet not mature enough to experience the anima-figure as liberated from the psychic, endogamous bond to the unconscious, that is, as "spiritualized."[654] The father, as the hitherto dominant consciousness, and who hopes to attain this advanced stage swiftly through baptism, is forced to realize that too infantile forces still prevent achieving this goal through a lack of conscious restraint.[655] His anger about this predicament manifests in his curse, which reveals that the brothers, as forms belonging to the nucleus of the personality, are still bound to the unconscious, as volatile and fleeting intuitions. These forms enable the vessel housed at the father's castle, which so far has mediated quite adeptly between this world and the hereafter, to slip into the well—away from conscious-ness—without being able to replace it with a new value. Thus, following the curse, the future personality must be arduously liberated from the spell of the unconscious.

738    In all versions, the sister decides to search for and redeem her lost brothers. This is logical: After all, she caused their enchantment, albeit indirectly. We are familiar with the figure of the wandering woman, who redeems an enchanted animal prince by taking suffering on herself, from our discussion of "The Maiden's Quest" (Volume 3), and in particular from the redemption tales about animal princes discussed previously. She represents both the woman's true essence and the man's female psyche. It is in her utmost interest to redeem the bird princes because they are the spirit that is submerged in the depths and without which no psychic life can blossom.

739    Before the actual test or wandering, some versions insert another motif: The sister unwittingly evokes the curse, which subsequently lies heavily and more intensely on the brothers. In "The Twelve Brothers," she picks the 12 lilies in the forest garden, and only afterward do the brothers fly away forever as birds. In "The Three

---

[654] On the spiritualization of the anima-image, see above, p. 304f.
[655] See also the variants in Bolte and Polívka, *Anmerkungen*, vol. 1, pp. 227ff., where the boys also defy the demands of the profane world, albeit differently (by their fondness for sweet things).

Shirts of Cotton-Grass," she throws the brothers' blue hoods into the fire, thus causing them to be enchanted also at night (so far, they were only bewitched during daytime) and extending the seven-year curse forever. This also includes the fact that, in "The Seven Ravens," the little sister loses the drumstick, which she received as a key to the glass mountain, and can only compensate for this loss by making an enormous sacrifice.

740          Once more, we encounter the motif of "premature illumination" (i.e., burning the animal skin too soon), whose meaning we have already discussed. The motif of the lily and that of the little finger have strange variations: In some cases, the lilies are not the brothers, but the sister is threatened by a fiend and sometimes by a female ogre (a cursing witch, bird, dragon, giant, the brothers' stepmother, man-eater), who want to suck blood from her finger or hand. They are slain by the brothers. From their grave grow flowers or herbs, which, when plucked by the girl and offered to the brothers to consume, transform the latter into animals. Thus, in such cases, the flowers contain the essence of the slain demons, and the sister gives them to the brothers (just as in other versions, she hands them the poison given to her by the witch).[656] Common to these tales is that the sister's finger is the "vulnerable spot." (Inasmuch as the little finger is a phallic symbol, in the present context it points to the anima's animus, i.e., a masculine and obfuscating component of the woman's soul-image). The fact that the brothers appear as animals amounts partly to an assimilation to the curser's demonic form. The assimilation (curse) occurs by enjoying the curser's "psychic matter." The sister unconsciously plays the role of a diabolic mediator. Her connection with a vampire, which later wreaks havoc on the male characters, is familiar from "Djulek-Batür" (Turkestan, no. 7) and from "The Son-in-Law from a Foreign Land" (Balkans, no. 39). Obviously, the anima is also still too close to the unconscious in the present group of fairytales and, as such, too volatile when confronted

---

[656] Bolte and Polívka, *Anmerkungen*, vol. 1, pp. 70ff.; another example is "The Three Shirts of Cotton-Grass" (Ireland, no. 21).

with the absorbing, destructive effect of evil spirits. Hence, she is not only the later redeemer but at first very much the corrupter.

741 A characteristic example of the sister as the corrupter of the heroic brother is evident in "The Strong Brother and the Faithless Sister" (Latvia, no. 5):

742 A brother and sister served the same master and "loved each other so much that they were completely inseparable." One day, they were traveling together in a wagon and came to a large forest. As the path lost itself in the undergrowth, the brother told his sister to wait in the carriage until he had found the way. He came to a robbers' den and shot several of the robbers from his hiding place. However, he fettered the last one in the twelfth chamber. He told his sister to come, reported his experiences, and ordered her not to enter the twelfth chamber while he was out hunting. But she was unable to resist the temptation, freed the robber, married him, and decided to kill her brother together with him. On the robber's advice, she pretended to be sick and demanded that the brother fetch some spurge to cure her. She hoped that he would perish in the process, but he brought home what she had asked for, together with a young wolf. The sister asked for bear's milk and thereafter fox's milk, which the brother brought home each time together with a young animal. Now she wanted some pastry from the cellar. But as he was leaving the cellar, the door slammed shut behind him before his animals, who were accompanying him, could follow. His sister offered to scratch his head one last time before her supposed death; after he had fallen asleep, she cut off his hair, which made him lose his strength. The robber tried to stab him, but the animals managed to free themselves and tore the robber apart. To punish his sister, he made her follow him to the birch trees, which "had grown together so that there was an opening in the middle; the brother lifted his sister into the hollow space between the trees, placed a

large vessel of water and another of coals before her, and said, 'When you have consumed this, you shall be free from your torment.' After uttering these words, he left with his animals." He came to a town where a King's daughter was about to be thrown to a nine-headed dragon. He slayed the dragon and took its tongues. The freed princess promised to marry him. The guard collected the dragon's heads, pretended to be a savior, and forced the princess to marry him. At the wedding, the real savior managed to dispose of the false bridegroom. After the wedding, he went to the birch trees and found his sister: She was "as black as a crow and completely starved," but still alive. He appointed her to be a chambermaid, but she joined forces with a magician and put a poisoned wolf's tooth in her brother's bed, which, as he lay down to sleep, pierced his back so that he died. As he lay on the gurney, his animals sniffed at him, removed the tooth, and revived him. The sister and the magician were hanged, but the brother lived happily ever after with the King's daughter.[657]

743    A related tale is "The Pilgrim" (Modern Greece, no. 46), except that the robber whose life has been spared now becomes 40 dragons that all compete for the sister; unlike in the previous tale, where she demands the milk of wild beasts, the water of immortality, she now demands the milk of the wild doe and the apple from the red tree.

---

[657] The same motif occurs, albeit in a much more primitive form, in "The Huntsman and the Seven-Headed Forest Devil" (Siberia, no. 5): A reindeer hunter owned a bear and a wolf, which he used instead of dogs. He ordered his sister not to sweep the floors or comb her hair during his absence. She asked him to leave his animals at home because she was expecting a visitor. This he did, and she tethered the animals, poured tin in their ears, swept the floors, and combed her hair. Thereupon came a seven-headed devil, whom she embraced and who subsequently pursued the brother. The latter saved himself by climbing to the top of a larch, which the devil tried to chop down. A female hare arrived and offered to continue the work while the devil rested. As soon as he was asleep, however, she fortified the tree and subsequently woke the devil, who set to work anew. The vixen and the otter, which arrived next, did the same. Thereupon a sparrow asked the man on the tree what he was doing, and he sent the bird to his house to fetch the animals to help him. The sparrow called them through the chimney. But because their ears were full of tin, they did not hear the summons. When the raven did likewise, the animals heard him, tore themselves from the chain, rushed to their master, and helped him to kill the devil. Thereafter, the reindeer hunter traveled to the prince's town and received his youngest daughter as a wife. But the groom's sister put a tooth of the seven-headed devil under her brother's mattress, so that he died. However, the hare pulled out the tooth and revived the hunter, at whose command the bear and the wolf bit the sister to death. See also "A Raven's Tale" (Siberia, no. 17).

The brother is assisted by a female dragon, who advises and revives him, and whose daughter he ultimately takes as his wife.[658]

744     The same motif is elucidated differently in "The Evil Mother" (no. 15), a Roma tale in which the hero's mother is the corrupter, whose role is commonly played by the sister:

745

> An emperor's son set off on an adventure and came to some houses in a forest that were inhabited by twelve monsters. He found a dagger with which he stabbed the monsters one after the other as they returned home. He only wrestled with the last and smallest dragon for a long time, defeated it, and locked it inside a barrel. One day, he met a girl with whom he fell in love, just as she fell in love with him. "But the girl was a heroine and bigger than the young man," and she said: "You should have killed him. Now you must let him live." When he told her of his intention to live with his old mother, she said: "You will regret it, but go and fetch her and live with her." He allowed his mother to enter all but one of the rooms, to which she agreed. However, when the son was out hunting, she opened the forbidden door and gave the imprisoned dragon a drink of water. He asked: "Do you love me? I will take you as my wife and make you my empress." She replied: "I love you." Whispering, he told her how she could get rid of her son: She should pretend to be sick and, according to an alleged dream, have him fetch her "a piglet from the pig … which lives beyond in the other world." She should tell him that her life depended on this. The son conferred with the maiden, who gave him her twelve-winged horse for the journey and warned him about the pig. When the sun had reached its zenith, he grabbed the piglet and leapt across the crack in the earth back into this world in time. The maiden exchanged the piglet, the mother ate from the other, and claimed to be healthy.

---

[658] See also "Janni und the Drakes" (Johann Georg von Hahn [trans.], *Griechische und albanische Märchen*, vol. 1, Leipzig, 1864, no. 24).

746 After four days, the dragon again whispered in her ear that she should still feign to be sick and that she had had another dream: This time, she needed an apple "from the golden apple tree in the other world" to heal her. Again, the son told the maiden. "The daughter realized that the mother wanted to eat his head, i.e., take his life." Again, the maiden gave the young man her horse and warned him about the apple tree. "He set off, reached the end of the world, let himself down through a crevice in the ground, and reached the apple tree at dawn. The apples were asleep, so he took one and sneaked out. But the leaves sensed this and began to tremble. The apple tree kept running after him and wanted to grab and kill him." But he reached the maiden, who also exchanged the apple. Soon thereafter, the mother asked for "water from the high mountains." Riding the maiden's horse, which had twenty-two wings, he succeeded yet again and the girl exchanged the jug and the water. In order to kill the son nevertheless, the mother, as the dragon had instructed her, asked the son to play cards with her, but with his hands tied, as she had done previously with his father. The son agreed. Yet when he was bound, the mother called the dragon, who cut him into pieces and put them in a bag. He tied the bag to the son's horse, which he chased away with the words: "Little horse, carry him as a dead man wherever you carried him when was alive." The horse rushed to its mistress, who put the pieces together and revived the young man with the help of piglet meat, an apple, and the water of life. He returned home, burned his mother and the dragon and married his beloved.[659]

---

[659] One similar tale is "The Blue Ribbon" (Zaunert, *Deutsche Märchen seit Grimm*, p. 250): A widow wanted to wander with her son to her deceased husband's brother. Along the way, the son (Hans) found a blue ribbon, which he secretly picked up, against his mother's wishes, and tied around his arm, which gave him unusual strength. When they reached a giant's cave, the beast invited them to stay and married the mother. Fearing the son's strength, the giant wanted to dispose of him and told the mother to pretend she was sick and to ask her son to fetch a lioness's milk to cure her. Hans defeated the old lion, milked the lioness, and the whole lion family followed him home. Thereupon, the mother demanded "apples from the garden of the three giants." Hans filled a large sack with apples, and the lions killed the giants who had begun attacking him. In the cellar of their castle, he discovered a princess who had been abducted and fettered. He tore asunder the chains, and the freed woman asked him to follow her to her

747    Here, too, the hero is threatened by a woman's demonic background, by an animus-figure that appears as a dragon, to whose insinuations she succumbs. In these tales, the sister and the terrible mother have an identical function. This archetypal situation (which people sometimes unconsciously enact in concrete reality) depicts the negative effect of the psychological incest with the mother or sister. This consists in the fact that, as a result of the inferior tension between the conscious and the unconscious, the latter has a life-destroying, devouring effect.[660] Yet just as the terrible mother's persecution, in the form of a female demon or stepmother, for example, makes the hero perform extraordinary deeds and thus helps his personality to mature, so the sister's or mother's intrigues also have a beneficial effect: They make the hero search for and gather the elusive treasures, that is, embark on the path of inner development.

748    While in this fairytale the female partner's animus is indistinguishable from the hero's shadow, as an unconscious identity exists in such situations, one interesting variation is "Stojscha and Mladen" (Balkans, no. 24):

749    A tsar's three daughters were carried away by a whirlwind, and so the later-born brother (Stojscha) asked his mother for his deceased father's weapons and horse and for three cloths embroidered by his sisters, so that they would recognize him.

---

father's court. But he asked her to wait because he first had to deliver the apples to his mother. Because the mother could not understand that he was still alive, he told her about the power of the blue ribbon. Thereupon, he took the mother and the giant to the castle, where the latter succeeded in stealing the ribbon from the sleeping man, gouged out his eyes, and chased the blinded man out of the castle. His lions led the princess to the blind man, whom she wished to marry him despite his blindness, and so they set off for her father's castle. In the forest, she watched how a blind hare regained its sight by diving into a stream three times. She persuaded Hans to do likewise. When he also regained his eyesight, they traveled to her father's court. Together with the old king's soldiers and with the lions, Hans confronted the giant in his castle, retrieved the blue ribbon and blinded the giant, so that it had to starve in the forest. The mother was executed. Hans and the princess celebrated their wedding. See also the eponymous Norwegian parallel (no. 47).

[660] Despite completing his journey, the hero, on his return to the profane world, may still succumb to the mother's intents and purposes (which may have a worldly aspect) and thus, in turn, to emotional incest. In "Palermo, the Sorcerer" (Spain, no. 11), a demonic magician's curse means that the hero, after his grandmother embraces him in his sleep, forgets his real bride; in "The Princess of Tiefental" (Zaunert, *Deutsche Märchen seit Grimm*, p. 355), the constable, after redeeming the princess, succumbs to an old woman's ruse, which delays the final union. The hero's weakness, which becomes the main motif in the above fairytales and whose causes are described in a differentiated manner, reflects how emerging higher consciousness struggles to wrest itself from being bound to the magical world.

Thereupon, he set off in search of his sisters. Along the way, he rested by a spring and protected himself from the flies with one of the scarves. He noticed that a woman who was drawing water from a well kept looking at him. It turned out that she recognized him as her brother by the cloth. She told him that, just like her sisters, she had been abducted by one of three dragon-brothers and took him to her palace. There he ate the large portion intended for the dragon, caught the returning dragon's club and hurled it back. After a violent struggle, during which the dragon is defeated, the young man spares the dragon's life and they are reconciled. The dragon showed his savior the way to the second dragon brother-in-law, where events take the same course as with the third one. Stojscha noticed a hole in the courtyard that ran underground and asked what it meant. The dragon replied: "Oh, brother-in-law, I almost can't tell you, I'm so ashamed. There is a dragon-tsar who often wages war with us, and the time will soon come when we must fight; every time we fight, he defeats all three of us, and only what escapes into this cave remains." Stojscha decided to fight the dragon-tsar on his own. At the top of the latter's palace, he spotted a hare and asked the courtiers what it was doing there. They replied: "If the hare could be brought down, it would slaughter, skin, chop, braise, and roast itself; yet no one has dared to do this because of the danger to their life." Stojscha flew up to the top of the palace on his winged steed and brought down the hare, which, as predicted, roasted itself. He challenged the enraged dragon-tsar to a duel in the attic. After a long, undecided struggle, Stojscha asked the dragon his name. The dragon replied: "My name is Young Lord [Mladen]." Stojscha replied: "I am also the youngest child." Thereupon, they let go of each other, befriended each other, and pledged that they would live together as brothers. United, they attacked the three dragon-brothers, chased them into the cave, blocked the exit with straw, and burned them to death. He left their palaces and kingdom to the dragon-tsar, "his covenant brother," returned home to his mother with his sisters and treasures, and ruled the kingdom.

750    The dragon, Mladen, whose name relates him to the hero, represents the actual inner demon, in which the hero's self confronts him enshrouded in a shadow. Confronting the shadow is the great deed that leads the hero to himself. The "brothers-in-law" are Mladen's weaker forms and represent the "animus" in another guise. As the animal of the demonic mother, the hare represents "bewitchedness," the sisters' "guilt," as well as the connection and the bond between the powerful shadow and them.[661] As soon as this animal, which, as a fertility symbol also points to the instinctual sphere, is plucked from the roof (i.e., "dethroned"), the shadow can be confronted and consciously recognized. The unconscious psychic tendencies embodied in the hare are automatically "sacrificed," cleansed by the fire and made edible: Thus, the hare, once it is brought down from its elevated vantage and transformed, becomes a value. After passing this final test, Stojscha becomes superior to his sisters' demonic animus-figures and therefore can return to human life. In terms of the inner level, his soul is thus also purged of its demons.

751    In most fairytales in which the sister corrupts the hero by courting a demon, she is eventually punished and eliminated, with the hero's bride taking her place. What this fairytale depicts as one figure replacing another, others describe as the transformation of one and the same figure: The sister makes amends, more or less unwittingly, for the harm she has caused.[662] Although she does not

---

[661] In "The Dragon and the Tsar's Son" (Balkans, no. 26), a hare lures the hero, who is out hunting, to a dragon in a mill, where an abducted old woman is waiting to be freed. Here, too, the hare connects the natural, maternal world to the demonic world and the hero. Regarding the ambiguity of hare symbolism, note that among South African natives (Frobenius, *Zeitalter*, p. 356) the hare, as a messenger from the moon, brings life or death. In an anthroposophical view, hares symbolize the senses. Thus, when the hero succeeds in tending the king's hares (who would otherwise scatter) with a magic whistle, as in "The King's Hares" (Norway, no. 39) and "The King's Son and the Bear" (Balkans, no. 45), the hares correspond to devoting one's "thoughts" to the sensory world and the tending of hares to spiritual concentration (Meyer, *Weisheit Schweizer*, p. 59f.). These deliberations suggest that the hare sitting on the roof of the dragon's palace in the above fairytale occupies a libidinal, intermediate position with its positive or negative aspect, depending on the prevailing tendency.

[662] To some extent, even if not directly, this also happens in the above fairytale through the transformation of the hare.

do so in the subsequent fairytale, she enables the hero to win the bride, who then saves him.

752  Thus, "The Two Envious Sisters" (Roma, no. 24) goes like this:

> A prince who was looking for a bride came to an emperor's palace, where three girls were sitting. The eldest girl said: "Peter, Peter Fatfrumos, [663] take me as your wife, for I have enough bread to feed your entire army and that of your father." The middle one said: "Take me, because I will spin clothes for all your soldiers from a single thread." The youngest said: "Take me, Peter, because I will bear you two children of silver, with golden teeth and silver hair, and holding two silver apples in their hands." He married this girl. When the young empress became pregnant, her envious sisters had the newborns removed and two little dogs put in their place. The midwife threw the beautiful children to the pigs. However, the pigs did not eat them, but had them suckled by a sow; the horses and oxen behaved in the same way thereafter. The midwife threw the children into the water, but an old man saved them and raised them. He died in their seventh year. The brother and sister built a house on the other side of the river. Later, the midwife followed them and called to the sister from the other bank: "You there, tell your brother to bring you the crown of the great serpent, whose tail is nine years long from its head. May he bring you her crown." The girl called back: "Escape, because when my brother awakes, he will make his white horse kick you." The midwife ran away, but the girl told her brother about the woman's demand in the form of a dream. The brother rode off immediately, came to Mother Monday and thereafter to the serpent's head. He managed to grab the crown and hide from the serpent at Mother Monday's house. The snake promised the woman, her

---

[663] According to Aichele, *Fatfrumos* means "beautiful one" (*Zigeunermärchen*, 1926, p. 93, fn. 1). On this Romanian hero, see also *Archetypal Symbols in Fairytales*, vol. 1, pp. 388–392.

sister, that she would spare the young man if she could see him once more. Impressed by his beauty, she spared him. When he returned home, the sister said: "May you always be blessed by God, for you have brought me what I asked you to bring: 'The serpent's crown.' Brother, not even the emperor has what we have now!" Thereupon, the midwife called out to the girl to demand that her brother take Leana Simziana as his wife. [664] Again she feigned a dream, and the brother rode to one end of the sky. "He came to Leana's pear tree, whose fruits had all been eaten by worms. But the serpent had advised him to eat a pear and say: 'O Lord! Even since my mother gave birth to me, I have never eaten a pear as beautiful and sweet as this one.' What did the pear tree say? It said: 'Brother! Brother! So many who have passed by have reviled me; only you have done me good. You shall be rewarded.'" The young man behaved in the same way when he came to a worm-eaten blackthorn, lake, and well. He entered Leana's home from its cool side, because the warm side was guarded by twelve buffaloes. He grabbed Leana by the hair and beat her until she agreed to marry him. He put her on his horse and rode home with her. Along the way, she begged the fountain, water, blackthorn, and pear tree to take the young man. But they refused to obey their mistress out of gratitude to the young man. When they returned home, the couple married. The midwife whispered in the sister's ear that she should demand a singing tree and a talking bird. When the brother reached the tree on whose top the bird was sitting, the bird called out: "Where are you going, poor thing?" The hero began to climb the tree in silence; the bird called out again and the hero replied: "I'm coming to you." The hero fell from the tree and turned to stone. Leana Simziana suspected his death and set off in a man's clothes to look for her husband. She did not heed the bird's call, but

---

[664] See Aichele, *Zigeunermärchen,* according to whom this figure is a benevolent fairy in Romanian gypsy tales (p. 321).

silently climbed the twelve branches, grabbed the bird, pulled out a feather, climbed down again, and touched her dead husband with it, bringing him back to life. They returned home. "The following morning, the tree with the bird was also there. It had come on its own and was now standing at the door. The midwife could no longer harm them, and so they lived happily ever after."

753    The brother's deeds are familiar from the hero's "Great Journey" and therefore probably require no detailed interpretation. What is remarkable, however, is the peculiar interaction of the sister with the midwife, who replaces the "stepmother" and whose malice is incited by the heroic siblings' envious aunts. The sister recounts the midwife's insinuations as a dream: The evil powers, as it were, take effect through the sister's unconscious; that, so to speak, is the (open) door through which they can enter. Significantly, they cannot cross water; that is, they are otherworldly and separated from the *terra firma* of a newly created consciousness. We are also told that if the brother beheld the midwife himself, he would have his white horse kick her. The brother's instinct is thus immune to the evil mother's bewitched world, but not to the sister-anima, who is close to that world.

754    As in "Ferdinand the Faithful and Ferdinand the Unfaithful" and in "The Two Travelers,"[665] as well as in several other fairytales, the evil powers are ultimately unable to assert their destructiveness. On the contrary, they make the hero perform greater and thus more fruitful deeds. Gaining this higher level of consciousness is encapsulated in the image of the crown being snatched from the serpent as a symbol of the self. The bird sitting in the tree is a familiar image. We should emphasize, however, that Leana Simziana, the anima-figure, redeems the hero from his inertia. In a Spanish variant, "The White Parrot" (no. 34), this deed is attributed to the hero's repentant sister:

---

[665] *The Complete Grimm's Fairy Tales*, pp. 566–571 and 486–496.

755

A count entrusted his pregnant wife to his steward while he was away at war. The man desired her. But when she rejected him, he took revenge and wrote to the count that his wife had given birth to two Negro children. In fact, she had given birth to a boy and a girl, who both bore a star on their forehead. The count ordered the children to be killed and the countess imprisoned. The steward imprisoned the countess, but threw the children into the river in a glass box. An old fisherman pulled out the container and took care of the children with his wife. To prevent the stars from drawing attention to the children, he tied cloths around their foreheads. A while later, the fisherman and his wife died. After the count returned from the war, the steward feared that the bandaged fisherman's children were the count's children and ordered a witch to dispose of them. She approached the girl in her brother's absence, admired the farm, and said that only a spring with silver water was missing. The brother was told to fetch a jug of water, which he should pour into the courtyard and a spring would appear. The sister begged her brother to fetch the water for her; because he loved her, he overcame his reluctance and set off. On the way, he met an old man who warned him about the lion that was guarding the spring. If its eyes were closed, it was awake; if they were open, it was asleep. When the boy arrived, the lion's eyes were open. He filled the jug and poured the water into the yard at home, where a spring of silver water began to gush. The following day, the old woman whispered to the sister that the brother should fetch a branch of an oak tree whose acorns were made of silver and whose calyxes were made of gold. It would grow into a magnificent oak tree in the courtyard. Again reluctantly, the brother complied with his sister's wish. The old man gave him a horse and told him that the snake guarding the oak was asleep when it hid its head. The boy succeeded in cutting the branch at the right moment, and the oak tree appeared in the courtyard. Thereupon, the angry old woman told the girl that the white parrot was still missing;

whoever caught it would be rich and happy all their life. Only with great difficulty did the sister persuade her brother to fulfill this request. Again the boy received advice from the old man: "You must do as I tell you: You will come to a beautiful garden in whose trees you will see many birds. Don't approach them too closely, but wait a little while, because if you do a very beautiful white parrot will appear. It will settle on a round stone, turn around several times, and say: 'Is there no one to grab me? Is there no one to grab me? Well, if no one likes me, let me go, let me go.' Thereupon, it will put its head under its wing and you can grab it. But don't grab it first, because otherwise it will escape and you will be turned into a stone and have to stay there like all those before you." Everything took its course as the old man had predicted: The boy found the garden and saw many stone statues lying on the ground. Eventually, the white parrot put its head under its wings. "As the boy was afraid that the bird might escape, he grabbed it before it had completely hidden its head. The parrot saw the boy and flew away, and the child was turned into a stone." The sister waited in vain for her brother to return, "and she began to weep and blamed herself for what had happened to her brother." The old woman gleefully advised her to look for her brother. She received the same advice from the old man, which she heeded so closely that she grabbed the bird only when it had become completely still. At that moment, all the stone statues came to life. These were the men who had tried to catch the parrot but had failed. One of them was the children's father. They all stopped at their house, and the brother told the guests their story: that they did not know their parents but still had the glass box and the cloths in which they had been wrapped. The count was lost in thought when the parrot, who always stayed with the girl, said: "You are very thoughtful, Count. If you want to know which of your thoughts are true, free your wife from the dungeon. She will be able to tell you who her children are." The countess was fetched, recognized her children, and removed their bandages. The steward was killed and the old woman fled. "The count and countess lived happily ever after with their children, who never separated from their white parrot."

756    This fairytale seems to be based on an Oriental model, to which also "The Story of Two Sisters Who Were Jealous of Their Younger Sister" in *One Thousand and One Nights* goes back.[666] It has spread across the Western world, except in the Spanish version, in many variations and in almost all countries.[667] Therefore, merely a few psychologically more significant transformations of the motif are mentioned here: The bird is sometimes called "L'oiseau de verité" (i.e., bird of truth)[668] or phoenix; or it is bright green.[669] The anima-figure, called Leana Simziana in "The Two Envious Sisters," is elsewhere a "rich maiden," a "fairy queen," the "fairest of the world," "the beautiful one," or the "beauty of the Earth." In Russia, the scheming witch is called Baba Yaga.[670]

757    Of particular interest in this respect is the variant "The Diamond-Spewing Spring" (Roma, no. 32)[671]:

758    One day, a poor laborer's newborn girl (A) disappeared inexplicably and, "enchanted by God," became a diamond-spewing spring. The parents forgot the older girl when a second daughter was born to them (B). After the laborer's wife (C) died, the rich widow (D) of the laborer's daughter's physician (B) persuaded her father to marry her, the widow. He did. The stepmother, however, insisted that her husband cast out his daughter (B). And so he abandoned her in the

---

[666] Littmann, *Tausendundein Nächten* (Leipzig, 1923), 756th night. See also Bolte and Polívka, *Anmerkungen*, vol. 2, pp. 391ff.

[667] See the variants to this fairytale, as variants to "The Three Little Birds" (*The Complete Grimm's Fairy Tales*, pp. 445–449), compiled in Bolte and Polívka, *Anmerkungen*, vol. 2, pp. 380ff.; see also "The Dancing Water, the Singing Apple, and the Bright Green Bird" (Italy, no. 23), "The Envious Sisters" (Balkans, no. 57), "Sun, Moon, and Morning Star" (Modern Greece, no. 58), and "The Bird That Says Everything" (France, vol. 2, no. 21).

[668] Bolte and Polívka, *Anmerkungen*, vol. 2, p. 382.

[669] See "The Dancing Water, the Singing Apple, and the Bright Green Bird" (Italy, no. 23).

[670] See the variants in Bolte and Polívka, *Anmerkungen*, vol. 2, pp. 383–391, and "The Envious Sisters" (Balkans, no. 57).

[671] For the sake of clarity, the female characters have been designated with capital letters.

forest. One night, a thunderstorm bore the desperate woman aloft and set her down in the beautiful garden of an emperor's son. As she wore the moon on her chest and the sun on her back, a glow emanated from her that attracted the emperor's son. He took her to the palace and married her. His mother (E), however, was hostile toward her, and when the young woman gave birth to a boy and a girl (F) while her husband was away, she abandoned the children in a small box in the river, put two young dogs by the young woman's (B) side and slandered her to the emperor's son. He ordered that no action be taken against her until his return. In the meantime, a miller had picked up the box and raised the two children together with his own. When they grew up, however, they no longer got along with the miller's children, so he built a separate dwelling for them by the mill.

<sup>759</sup> In the meantime, the old empress had learned that the children were still alive and sent an old woman to them, who told the sister (F) that the brother could become a great hero if he brought back the diamond spring (A). As soon as he heard this from his sister, he set off. A hare came running towards him in the forest, and he shared his meal with the animal. The hare knew about the spring, in particular that it immediately turned everyone to stone, and so it gave its horse to the young man. "The hare was the spring's future husband. Ever since the girl had gone mad, she had been turned into a spring, so that no one would recognize her. The hare had suffered the same fate. He had also been enchanted; when he had wanted to make the girl his wife, he had been turned into a hare and had stayed in the forest near the spring. When the spell was lifted, he would become the girl's husband. The young hero began to weep. The hare realized that this was a relative who wanted to fetch the girl, the poor man's daughter, who had been turned into a spring. They went to the old mother of the forest. She should take pity on him and not turn him into a rock. She felt sorry for him for his mother's

sake. The mother of the forest was the mother (C) of the poor man's other girl (B). 'Take my horse and also this letter from me. When you have drawn very close to the spring on horseback, take out the letter and read it as you ride towards it.' Thus spoke the mother of the forest. The boy took the letter and set off. He reached the spring. When he was within its sight, he began to read. But the more he read, the more he and the horse turned to stone. Then the spring caught sight of him. 'Oh dear, my relative is coming to me,' she thought, because he had also turned to stone. 'I shall be freed in a moment, but how can I go with him?' While she was thinking this, she had already turned him to stone, as well as the horse.

760    Thereupon, a girl (G) happened to come to the spring and wanted to draw water and sprinkled the stone with water. The stone robe fell from the boy and he was transformed back into a human being." He set off on his journey home with the spring. The hare joined them and made the youth sever its head. The hare turned into a king's redeemed son and accompanied them to the twin sister (F). With her, they traveled to the imperial court, where the siblings' mother (B) had meanwhile been condemned to be spat on by all passers-by. All four refused to do so and were arrested. When the emperor interrogated them, the spring (A) said: "... Does it befit a child (brother and F) to spit on its own mother (B)? How can the sister (A) treat the sister (B), the son the mother (B), the daughter (F) the mother (B) and a brother-in-law (hare) his sister-in-law (B) like this?' The emperor could not believe what the spring was saying. Horrified, he asked her: 'What, how, why? Repeat what you just said.'" She succeeded in proving the empress's innocence by sending for the miller. She was vindicated and the old empress was killed.

761    In all fairytales of this type, the sister causes her brother's undoing by heeding evil forces, behind which stands the evil mother as a rule, and whose insinuations almost always result in immodest claims (i.e.,

unattainable values). This motif expresses a deeper psychological truth than first meets the eye. Because the element that troubles the unconscious, and hence unredeemed, person and sometimes even drives them into outer and inner ruin is basically an unacknowledged desire for inner wholeness. This, however, remains a negative inner thorn as long as the person refuses to take this claim seriously and to embark on the brother's adventurous journey.

762 Thus, the bird is not called "L'oiseau de verité" for no reason. As its name suggests, its primary function is to ruthlessly reveal the truth. The unconscious, and the manifestations of the self at work therein, are the most inexorable mirror of truth in humankind. They are the quiet, yet unsilenceable inner voice, which relentlessly denounces and destroys everything untruthful. Although the brother, in his naive boldness and driven by his sister's aspirations, that is, by his soul's restlessness and intemperance, eventually dares to approach this core of inner truth, he succumbs to the surrounding dangers.[672] As a rule, he turns to stone—the principal motif in almost all variants—because he reaches out prematurely for the bird or because he lets himself be enticed by inner opposition or doubt[673] to turn around instead of steadfastly pursuing the bird. The latter motif is easily understood. Although the unconscious contains the voice of inner truth, it may also assail the human being like a chaotic, corrosive (i.e., disintegrating) polyphony, in particular when a

---

[672] For an example of how the sister can place her brother in mortal danger, see "The Witch and the Sun" (Afanas'ev, *Russische*, vol. 1, no. 13), whose tragic ending, the brother's evasion into the sun, would in fact correspond to a state of madness: A mute tsar's son is warned by his stableboy (i.e., the earthly part of his psyche, his "shadow") that his parents will give him a sister who will devour everything. He flees on horseback: During his escape, two seamstresses tell him that they will have to die after completing their work; an oak-turner [a man able to tear up oaks] tells him that he will have to die after clearing all the oak trees; and a mountain-turner [a man able to tear up moutains] tells him that he will have to die after moving all the mountains (like the stableboy, these figures are also part-souls). The tsar's son reaches the sun, which gives him the means—after the witch's sister has eaten everything in his homeland—to rejuvenate the seamstresses and to create even more oaks and mountains and thus to prolong the life of these figures. Back home, the sister flatters him. Warned by a mouse, he escapes again and once more reaches the sun with the help of seamstresses, oak- and mountain-turners. The pursuing sister instructs the heavier of the two to devour, or rather slay, the lighter one. They mount a pair of scales to decide their fate. The prince is flung up to the sun, while the witch remains on earth. The hero, who longs for immortality and is threatened by the sister, is chased to the sun three times. Accordingly, his consciousness is "too light," and his personality is destroyed forever. See also "The Witch's Sister" (Turkestan, no. 8). In that tale, however, the witch's sister perishes during the hero's magical escape, whereas he returns home and marries.
[673] See "The Story of Two Sisters Who Were Jealous of Their Younger Sister" in Littmann, *Tausendundein Nächten* (756th night) and "The Bird That Says Everything" (France, vol. 2, no. 21).

person has abandoned their *conscious* purposefulness. The unconscious resembles a mirror: It is clear and unambiguous compared to clear and unambiguous human consciousness. It can descend into unbridled chaos when someone is unable to maintain their moral and conscious integrity.

763     The hero's impetuousness springs from a secret fear: Those who are uncertain cannot wait; and those who doubt that they will reach their goal hastily seek solutions. The unconscious, however, imposes on those who wish to grasp its meaning the strictest self-discipline and patience. These qualities enable a person to wait for the fateful moment and to remain calm in tense and crucial situations against the roguish-demonic element adhering to the unconscious as a force of nature. In some versions, not only the hero turns to stone, but also others before him; sometimes even the hero's father is afflicted because the task of maturing into a higher personality is often closely related to hereditary factors or tribal and family problems. Therefore, those who undertake the journey inward almost always encounter their ancestral spirits: One example is Ivan, the hero in "The Maiden Tsar" (Russia, no. 41), who was compelled to follow in his father's footsteps and took to his grandfather's cellar to find the necessary strength.[674]

764     In many hero myths, the hero, who emerges from the belly of the devouring monster, also leads his parents, tribesmen, or ancestors, who were also dead and devoured, back into the light, and thereby into life.[675] Because whenever someone gains higher awareness by battling their way through a conflict to its end, the effect is liberating, and enables new life to emerge around that person; they purify the burdened atmosphere and thus have a redeeming effect. Even past values, which afflicted the unconscious heir, are reinvigorated by a newly gained worldview; hence the idea of redeeming the ancestral spirits. Turning to stone, as an image of being turned away from life and into a demon, is related both to the motif of dying in the monster's belly, and thus to that of animal skin, insofar as that

---

[674] See also "The Strange Boy" (Sock, *Eskimomärchen*, 1921, p. 109).
[675] See, e.g., "Kholomodumo" (Africa, no. 24) and "The Story of the Man-Eating Monster and the Child" (Africa, no. 81).

clothing is made of stone, and to that of being imprisoned in an iron stove or a glass coffin. It aptly expresses the hardening that arises from unresolved inner conflicts and which, in pathological cases, leads to complete paralysis. In common parlance, this state is also called "turning to stone."

765    If paralysis springs from a rashness induced by fear, then, as the present fairytale also recounts, only the anima can bring about transformation. The tale shows how the sister, whose aspirations were only partly meant to endanger her brother, now sets out, remorsefully, to save him again. Thus, the sister becomes the protagonist, as in the fairytales about the seven ravens, the six swans, and the 12 brothers discussed above. In contrast, in "The Strong Brother and the Faithless Sister" (Latvia, no. 5), "The Evil Mother" (Roma, no. 15), and in the aforementioned parallels, the sister perishes as an enemy and is replaced by an "exogamous" anima-figure. Comparing these variants reveals *a very specific* psychic force: the soul-image, which is projected either onto the sister or onto another woman, the "anima." She represents a strangely ambivalent, inner, and unconscious personality of the man, on the one hand entangling him in perilous situations and, on the other, thereby driving him to death and rebirth and to attaining the highest goals. When the evil sister is killed, the evil aspect is stripped away, because the archetype cannot be slain. Thus, if the sister's punishment is death, then this is merely another image of the transformation depicted in other fairytales. The latter is, as it were, the more philosophical conception by which the anima's dual nature is captured. Yet the more primitive account (e.g., in "The Strong Brother and the Faithless Sister" and its variants) fails to grasp, or at least does not express, the secret identity of the corrupting aspect with the healing one.

766    In the fairytales about the 12 brothers, seven ravens, and six swans, the sister-figure who atones for her inadvertent guilt either undertakes a journey, as in "The White Parrot" (Spain, no. 34) and its variants, or seeks to redeem her brothers by becoming a hermit. The journey in "The Seven Ravens" resembles that undertaken by

the heroine in the fairytales discussed previously. Its stations (sun, moon, morning star) correspond to those in "The Singing, Soaring Lark" (i.e., sun, moon, wind).[676] As observed, the glass mountain is also the inaccessible abode of an unredeemed being. Sacrificing the finger is an unequivocal act of atonement, because in some variants the vampirish demon attacks and sucks the sister's finger,[677] that is, that place through which the sister was connected with the evil power. In primitive belief, the little finger, which "tells everything," is the seat of unconscious psychic forces. Therefore, cutting off the sister's finger amounts to severing her secret connection with the dark underworld powers, and thereby enabling her to redeem the brothers.

767     As such archetypal representations indicate, in its negative aspect the anima is not *per se* hostile to life. Rather, she becomes like this by being bound to the even more otherworldly and even more archaic contents of the unconscious. For the man, she thus becomes a key to the unconscious secrets, and Jung therefore calls her a "system of relations to the unconscious."[678] This positive side of the anima, however, only becomes effective when it is freed from its entanglement with the dark elements; rather strangely, in the present fairytale, the anima-figure herself transforms her state of coercion into a "key function." In this sense, she resembles a real woman, who can only have a liberating effect after sacrificing or transforming her masculine-demonic and maternal-demonic aspects.[679]

---

[676] *The Complete Grimm's Fairy Tales*, pp. 399–404.

[677] According to Bächtold-Stäubli under *Finger* (finger), popular belief attributes to the little finger "the gift of magic and divination ... According to the *Minne Regel* of Eberhard of Cersne (v. 3878. 3887ff.), it contains death and life ... Blood is also drawn from the little finger for other magical purposes."

[678] Jung, "The Relations between the Ego and the Unconscious," *CW* 7, § 310.

[679] This, presumably, is the meaning of the fact that, in the second (probably added) part of "King Lindworm" (Denmark, no. 1), the woman must still redeem two kings who have been transformed into birds (swan and crane) before she can live happily ever after with King Lindworm. When he is away fighting a war, she is slandered for giving birth to two dogs and is chased into a forest, while her children are given to a wet nurse. She climbs a mountain, sits down, and squeezes the milk from her breasts into the beaks of a swan and a crane. "And as she sat there, all of a sudden they turned into the two most beautiful princes imaginable, and the mountain became the most beautiful royal castle; with retainers and animals, gold and silver, and everything that befits such a place. They had been so enchanted that they could never be redeemed unless they drank milk from a queen who had previously given birth to two boys." In the meantime, King Lindworm returns from war and goes out to look for his wife. He finds the castle in the forest, where one of the redeemed kings wants to marry the young queen, but she proposes a toast that resolves everything, whereupon she lives happily with King Lindworm.— According to Bächtold-Stäubli under *Glasberg* (glass mountain), "King Swan" belongs in the same group as the swan maidens, while in "Queen Crane" (Sweden, no. 17) a queen by that name appears, whose

768    Fairytales do not distinguish between the archetype of the anima and a real woman because both form a primordial unity on a lower level of consciousness. For this reason, the anima in the fairytale about the seven ravens is described as both unearthly and real (i.e., human). Therefore, her sacrifice would, in terms of the real woman, be a conscious act; in terms of the anima, however, it would constitute a simple reversal of the movement by which what binds becomes what loosens.

769    A new motif, that of silence and work, appears in the two other versions ("The Twelve Brothers" and "The Six Swans"). Other fairytales involving a female protagonist have shown that she tends to strive toward her inner goal more through suffering than by undertaking an adventurous journey. This becomes apparent in the many fairytales in which the heroine humbly performs kitchen duties or, as in "The Girl Without Hands,"[680] spends a long time waiting in a deserted forest. Compared to the present fairytales, however, the motif was never emphasized as a condition for the turn of events. Retreating into a lonely forest is a form of medieval penance. Religiously motivated, this practice dates back, culturally and historically, to ancient anchoritism (i.e., seclusion), which may also be due to Indian influences. This mode of life intends to bring about the greatest possible introversion and to sever all ties with external objects. This results in a corresponding animation of the inner world, which may heighten into auditions, visions, and ecstatic states. The versions of these fairytales discussed here have the same objective: The brothers have dissipated into the diffuse and inaccessible unconscious,[681] and therefore can be brought back to life only by utmost psychic concentration.

---

clan presumably includes "King Crane." In any event, the disenchanted kings in the continuation of "King Lindworm" may be said to be animus-figures because they have the same names as mythical beings, whose deliverance from their demonic imprisonment is the precondition of the queen's human happiness.
[680] *The Complete Grimm's Fairy Tales*, pp. 160–166.
[681] In *Die Sage vom Schwanritter* (1856, pp. 418–440), Wilhelm Müller, to whom Otto Rank's *Lohengrinsage* (1911, p. 82f.) refers, interprets the brothers' appearance as birds as a state of death. This, however, is obvious because the unconscious is always associated with the realm of death, as we have shown in *Archetypal Symbols of Fairytales*, vol. 1, pp. 105–112. This state of death is not concrete but involves a splitting off into the unconscious.

770    As the maiden needs to concretize her brothers, in some variants she must also produce shirts for the lost ones (e.g., "The Six Swans"; "The Three Shirts of Cotton-Grass"). In some variants, however, the shirts are made from nettles, oak leaves, reed grass, or buttercups.[682] Presumably, the common denominator is that these garments are sewn from plants, that making them requires tremendous patience and work, and thus also an intense concentration of consciousness, which is one of the most effective means of resisting the dissolving forces of the unconscious, which induce panic or even madness. According to the law of *similia similibus*, making and wearing such shirts counteracts the stepmother's magic, who bewitches the brothers in several versions by throwing animal skins over them.

771    This motif recalls the redemption scene in "King Lindworm": The maiden must remove Lindworm's animal skin and replace it with some of her shirts, which we have interpreted as a subtle process of transformation. The Lithuanian ghost story "The Suffering Flax" (no. 23) also involves experiencing the effect of the counterspell through concentration, a process that this tale presents dramatically, even thrillingly. Although no flax is woven in this story, the concentrated effort its preparation requires is described in pedantic detail. This proves successful: An old woman wards off two spirits of the dead to protect a maiden who is haunted by them.[683]

772    "The old woman said (to the hustling ghost): 'Wait and don't push so hard! Listen to the agony of the flax! Afterwards you can ...' 'All right, old woman, but tell your tale faster! Not even the flax's torment ceases all at once, but slowly ...' 'I say, old woman, be quick!' 'Now, now! Listen to how they sowed the flax and harvested it, what agony it suffered! When spring is warm, everything happens more quickly; but when it is cold, the flax crawls out of the earth with its last strength; as soon as it has risen, it grows stalks and leaves, unless disease strikes ...' 'Old woman, be quicker!' 'Oh, you fiend, as soon as the flax

[682] See Bolte and Polívka, *Anmerkungen*, vol. 1, pp. 72f., 231.
[683] See Bächtold-Stäubli under *Lein* (flax) on the occasional role of flax in superstition as a means of protection against demons.

rears its head out of the earth, it seems as if it might grow. And yet, as soon as the wind blows over it, it sways and bends, and its little heads bump against each other. 'Faster, old woman!' 'When it has grown a little, all kinds of weeds appear, and the girls pull out the flax, kick and trample its roots, and toss it in all directions. 'Faster, old woman!' 'When it has grown, with difficulty, it is tormented by the wind, exposed to the sun, and eventually ripens. All the farmhands go to the field, pull it out of the ground, tie it together, and place it in almonds. Again, it suffers greatly until it is completely dry, whereupon they bring it back to the farm. The workers gather, lay down planks, and beat its brains out, time and again.' 'Faster, old woman!' 'Thereafter, they take it out to the fields and scatter it. The rain lashes it, and the wind torments it. When it has endured enough torment, they collect and tie it together and bring it back to the barn. They lay it on a trestle and dry it until all its little bones are dry. The workers gather again and keep breaking its bones until nothing but skin is left if this is done properly. 'Faster, old woman!' 'As if that weren't enough. When they bring it back in, they peel off its skin with sharp boards and comb it with wire, so that not a single part of its body remains in one piece. 'Faster, old woman!' 'They weave it into long threads and span these on the loom, one lengthways, the other crosswise, until they have made a fabric. 'Faster, old woman!' 'As if that weren't enough. They spread the fabric out on the field where it must remain in all weathers. It can barely dry because they begin dousing it with water again, tormenting it as much as they can. 'Faster, old woman!' 'Oh, if only that were enough! Thereupon, they sew clothes, which wear them until they tear; when they are torn, they sell them to the Jew. He takes them to the factory where they grind the bones and skins and turn them into paper. The scribes write and write all kinds of stories on it, and when they have written all over it, they tear it up and throw it away, and the wind carries it across the fields.' Then the cock crowed. ..."

773    The evil spirit's impatience impressively reveals the imminent danger of being overrun, of letting oneself be rushed, and of panicking as a result. What helps, as the tale shows, is patiently and quietly concentrating on transforming what is given by nature.

774    Laistner has compiled numerous local legends[684] in which the *Mittagsfrau* (midday woman) quizzes the peasants and bakers who have remained out on the fields over lunch about cultivating flax and weaving with linen. Or, as in the Lithuanian tale, how telling the story wards off the spirits of the dead until the cock crows, that is, until the witching hour is over. Sometimes, the flax is replaced by grain. This motif appears in Scandinavian variants of "Puss in Boots" (France, vol. 1, no. 26), where the tomcat holds off the demonic owner of the castle by telling him the story about the tormented rye until the sun rises and the troll bursts asunder. Thus, the shadow-figure concentrates on protecting consciousness; elsewhere, the loaf of bread tells us how it was made (i.e., came into existence).

775    Presumably, laboriously and patiently making shirts to break the spell in the fairytales considered here has a similar meaning. Once again, it is about counteracting the magical forces—which urge toward dissolution and behind which lurk death and madness—through human effort and being willing to make sacrifices. The variant to "Puss in Boots" cited by Laistner shows that work and concentration involve an *Auseinandersetzung* (confrontation) with the forces of nature.[685] In that story, the "grateful dead man" (who appears as the tomcat) will admit the troll into the castle only if the latter is prepared to endure the rye's entire torment. When the troll discovers that it is going to be ground, it bursts into pebbles. By equating the troll with the grain, the helper realizes that it is a natural being that must be transformed and put in its place, thus eradicating its supremacy.

---

[684] Laistner, *Das Rätsel*, vol. 1, pp. 1–30 and 43.
[685] Laistner, *Das Rätsel*, vol. 1, pp. 26ff.

776     Asters, which sometimes are used to make shirts, also have a symbolic meaning. Ninck amplifies this motif by noting that the sister endeavors to enrapture the swan brothers, or turn them into stars, by making shirts from asters.[686] In Germanic mythology, the fylgja[687] or Valkyrie, whom the sister replaces in the present tale, make such shirts. Psychologically, however, rapture means sinking into the unconscious. This term therefore more aptly describes the initial enchantment by the stepmother, which Ninck has also interpreted similarly:

777     The wicked stepmother artfully sews a spell into "little white silk shirts" ... and throws these over the queen's children, who are immediately transformed into swans. Every evening, however, when they were transformed back into their former state, "they blew off each other's feathers, and their swan skin fell off them like a shirt." Our word "shirt" ... comes from *hamr*, "form, soul, protective spirit, skin, covering, clothing," and from *hamast*, "to change the covering, to become enraged, to be transformed, to be carried away" ... In accordance with this etymology, the Edda always describes the transformation of the Valkyries and gods as wearing a shirt made of feathers. In addition to the shirts and the identical meaning, we found transformation rings in the North, just as the gold chains change with the shirts in the fairytale about the swan.[688]

778     Yet the second spell cast by the shirts has an opposite effect: It restores the brothers to human life. Nevertheless, the connection between the two processes remains palpable. This illustrates a peculiar psychological phenomenon: A person who has been transported too deeply into the unconscious, into the archetypal world, finds their way back. They can accomplish this either by fleeing back into the human world at great sacrifice (this magical

---

[686] Ninck, *Wodan*, p. 286.
[687] Translator's note: These supernatural beings or spirits accompany a person toward their fate or fortune.
[688] See Ninck, *Wodan*, p. 280.

flight requires relinquishing all the miraculous objects received from that world), or by performing a certain feat in that world (e.g., winning the anima, defeating a monster). Correspondingly, they will return enriched (i.e., more conscious), or will eventually—as happens here—undergo a peculiar transformation, remaining "enraptured" to some extent (see the youngest brother's incomplete redemption). This, however, will not prevent them from also leading a human life in this world.

779     Inhabiting two worlds, that person knows that this world reflects the otherworld and that the inner and outer spheres interact in their own particular way in human fate. In terms of profane life, this person is still enraptured. Hence, the redeemed brothers wear the anima's aster robe, which brands them as figures who are connected to the world beyond. On the other hand, they are no longer alienated from the human world, nor powerless in this world, as they were when they wore the stepmother's magical clothing. On the contrary, they are now capable of also intervening in this world. According to Ninck, asters have a rapturous character. And yet, the anima's *work transforms* them, so that they become "human shirts" and can be contrasted with the stepmother's swan shirts.[689] Negativity and magic are defeated with similar means. These shirts have, as it were, transformed the stepmother's. In this way, the soul has once again affiliated the volatile forces that appear in the brothers with this world.

780     Not only must the sister sew the shirts. In most versions (in some variants, this is even the only condition), she is not permitted to speak or laugh for a certain time (e.g., seven years). As so often, redemption is bound to a particular fate. This includes, as in an Italian parallel,[690] that the maiden goes on a pilgrimage to the "Mother of Time." In "The Seven Ravens," the maiden's quest also takes her via the sun and the stars, with which humans measure time. This is often associated with the mother-archetype, for example, in the image of the Parcae (spinners) or the Norns. The

---

[689] Bolte and Polívka, *Anmerkungen*, vol. 1, pp. 433f.
[690] Bolte and Polívka, *Anmerkungen*, vol. 1, p. 71.

forest, and in particular the tree, where the heroine takes refuge to perform her task, also have a maternal meaning. In a certain sense, the heroine is attracted by or assimilated to the mother-archetype. Moreover, she is carried away into the unconscious, although in the opposite sense than her brothers. They enter the aerial or spiritual realm as birds, whereas the sister goes into the forest (*hyle*, matter), into the darkness of the material, feminine principle. Just as the heroine of "The Stepdaughter's and the Maid's Reward" (Finland, no. 53) found her womanhood by seeking the father-archetype and turned fate in her favor in "Mother Holle"[691] by devotedly serving her mother, so sewing (or spinning) in the tree constitutes a period of service. During this time, the heroine must undergo the most extreme female and maternal hardships in order to overcome them. This happens because the maiden, as some introductory episodes to this type of fairytale suggest, is also enslaved to the terrible mother (who, for example, sucks her blood[692]), which might paralyze the woman's feminine instinct. Because the woman, as Jung observes, "can never find herself at all, not even approximately, without a man's help; she has to be literally abducted or stolen from her mother. Moreover, she must play the role mapped out for her for a long time and with great effort, until she actually comes to loathe it."[693] Psychologically, the sister experiences this course of events once the hunting king appears on the scene. Seen thus, the sister redeems the brothers by working on her own unredeemed state until her

781 personality, thus purified, has a redeeming effect on her brothers.

At this juncture, the fairytale changes direction and makes the sister the protagonist. (We will discuss the paradoxical double meaning of the siblings as real symbolical figures later). This is followed by the tragedy of the queen being slandered after giving birth to her children, who are abandoned, persecuted, and eventually freed in utmost distress. This account also exists as a separate

---

[691] *The Complete Grimm's Fairy Tales*, pp. 133–136.
[692] Bolte and Polívka, *Anmerkungen*, vol. 1, pp. 70ff.
[693] Jung, "Psychological Aspects of the Mother Archetype," *CW* 9/I, § 182.

fairytale; sometimes, it forms not the conclusion but the opening episode of the sibling drama (see, e.g., "The White Parrot"[694]).

782

    In the Grimm's versions, the imperative to remain silent brings the queen into a precarious situation; in several variants, however, the precept ceases to apply. Yet the young queen cannot justify her actions for other reasons; the king does not even listen to her. She is slandered by a "false bride," who is usually fused with the figure of the terrible mother. The latter is often—as in the Grimm's versions— the young queen's mother-in-law; she clearly parallels the female demon who appeared as an enemy when the brothers were being enchanted.[695] Thus, in the second phase, the destructive unconscious forces again rear their heads, now as profane slander and intrigue. Yet evil assails the maiden also in the form of the king who goes hunting in the forest, and who recalls the same figure in "Allerleirauh" and in "Brother and Sister."[696] Unlike the brothers, who are split into multiple parts, the king represents the new and unified dominant of the inner events. The king destroys the incest, which

---

[694] On the motif of the mother being slandered and the children abandoned, see "It Comes to Light in the End" (Roma, no. 44): A poor man had three daughters. The eldest said that if the emperor took her as his wife, she would clothe his whole army with a single thread; the middle one said she would feed his army with a loaf of bread; but the youngest wanted to "give him two good and clever sons with golden hair and pearl teeth." The emperor, hearing these words, married the youngest daughter. While he was away fighting a war, she gave birth to two sons, which the maid hid in the pigsty and alleged that the mother had given birth to two small dogs. The pigs not only spared the children but also gave them water; when the maid carried the boys to the stables, the horses behaved in the same way. Thereafter, she buried the children in the dunghill, from which grew two golden fir trees. The maid slandered the empress to her husband who was returning from a military campaign. He had his wife buried up to her waist, made her breastfeed the young dogs, and married the maid. The new empress induced the emperor to cut down the fir trees and make a bed from their wood. One night, after the two boys had complained about the sleeping stepmother from inside the bed, she demanded that the bed be burned. Two sparks escaped through the blocked chimney and fell on two lambs, whose wool turned to gold. The emperor's wife had the lambs slaughtered and the wool washed after she had counted every last thread. But two threads escaped on the water and turned into doves, which in turn became boys again. A widow raised them for seven years. One day, the emperor invited his subjects to a ball and said: "Guess what I have suffered." One of the boys solved the riddle by telling the story of his parents. He said that his brother and he were the emperor's sons; the mother was freed and the stepmother was dragged to death by a wild horse.—See also "Brother and Sister and the Goldilocked Princes" (Finland, no. 15): After their mother had been slandered, a queen's six goldilocked boys were abandoned and subsequently abducted by the devil. The seventh boy, who resembled a peasant's son, was cast into the sea with his mother in a barrel. When they reached land, an old man helped them find a castle. From there the boy set out, freed his brothers from the devil, and brought them to the mother in the castle. One day, when the king lost his way while out hunting, he found refuge in the castle, and the youngest son told him his story: the story of the queen, his mother. She was reinstated and the slanderer punished.—See further "The Bird That Says Everything" (France, vol. 2, no. 21), "The Two Golden Children" (Zaunert, *Deutsche Märchen seit Grimm*, p. 141), "The Goldilocked Children" (Caucasus, no. 9), and "God's Punishment" (Africa, no. 80).

[695] Lincke, "Stiefmutter," p. 68f.

[696] *The Complete Grimm's Fairy Tales*, pp. 326–331 and 67–73.

enables integrating a new piece of the "world" into the soul as a living system, thus fulfilling the precondition for the birth of the "divine child," the actual self. Following the established pattern, however, when salvation approaches, evil unleashes its greatest onslaught. True to the archetype, therefore, the hero-child,[697] and often also the mother, is now threatened. Jung offers a psychological interpretation of this primordial situation in "The Psychology of the Child Archetype." In sum, he argues that the child represents any being's strongest possible urge, "the urge to realize itself." Thus:

783    It is, as it were, an incarnation of *the inability to do otherwise*, equipped with all the powers of nature and instinct, whereas the conscious mind is always getting caught up in its supposed ability to do otherwise. The urge and compulsion to self-realization is a law of nature and thus of invincible power, even though its effect, at the start, is insignificant and improbable. [698]

784    Abandonment, exposure, danger, etc. are all elaborations of the "child's" insignificant beginnings and of its mysterious and miraculous birth. This statement describes a certain psychic experience of a creative nature, whose object is the emergence of a new and as yet unknown content. In the psychology of the individual there is always, at such moments, an agonizing situation of conflict from which there seems to be no way out—at least for the conscious mind, since as far as this is concerned, *tertium non datur*. But out of this collision of opposites the unconscious psyche always creates a third thing of an irrational nature, which the conscious mind neither expects nor understands. It presents itself in a form that is neither a straight "yes" nor a straight "no," and is consequently rejected by both.[699]

---

[697] Otto Rank, "Der Mythus von der Geburt des Helden. Versuch einer psychologischen Mythendeutung," in: *Schriften zur angewandten Seelenkunde*, no. 5 (1922), pp. 15, 21f., 26; see also Bachofen, *Gräbersymbolik* (1859), p. 127f.
[698] Jung, "The Psychology of the Child Archetype," CW 9/I,§ 289 (Jung's emphasis); see also § 288–290.
[699] *Ibid.*, § 285.

In the present fairytale, this becomes evident by the negative powers threatening the becoming of this child in both magical and profane ways.

785      The mother's sole task is to avoid betraying her innermost being at all cost and continue performing the task assigned to her by fate regardless of any confusing events. This requirement corresponds to that in "The Bird that Says Everything" (France, vol. 2, no. 21), a variant of "The White Parrot" (Spain, no. 34): The heroine must seize the bird without being distracted by a host of mocking, skeptical, and distracting voices. Among the undesirable reactions in Grimm's fairytales, laughter is a human and liberating form of expression. In fairytales where the princess must be made to laugh (e.g., "The Golden Goose"[700]), it is a matter of incorporating the anima into human life; when laughter is forbidden in fairytales about the redemption of the brothers, it is about consciously distancing oneself from the "merely human."[701] The silence and seriousness imposed on the heroine in the Grimm's "The Six Swans" and "The Twelve Brothers" indicate that this task is "sacred": Silence and mourning used to be performed by novices in ancient initiation rites.[702] Primitive initiation rites also often involved the precept to maintain silence.[703] In Christian mysticism, silence is also one of the principal

---

[700] *The Complete Grimm's Fairy Tales*, pp. 322–326.

[701] In this connection, note that the Angakoq in "The Flight to the Moon" (North America, no. 2) was forbidden to laugh when he saw the wife of the man in the moon. Magical figures transcend everything human and their demands extend far beyond human ones.

[702] Dieterich, *Mithrasliturgie* (1923), pp. 7 and 43. On the meaning of μυειν (myein) as the root word of mystery, see Kerényi, "Das göttliche Mädchen: Die Hauptgestalten der Mysterien von Eleusis in mythologischer und psychologischer Beleuchtung," in: *Albae Vigiliae*, no. VIII/IX (1941), pp. 62–63. See also Paul Schmitt, "Antike Mysterien in der Gesellschaft ihrer Zeit," *Eranos-Jahrbuch 1944: Die Mysterien*, ed. Olga Fröbe-Kapteyn (1945), pp. 108–109. See further Friedrich Heiler, "Die Kontemplation in der christlichen Mystik," *Eranos-Jahrbuch 1933: Yoga und Meditation im Osten und im Westen*, ed. Olga Fröbe-Kapteyn (1934), p. 303: "In the innermost part of the heart, the mystic, who has closed the outer senses (myein = to close; the root word of mysticism), experiences the presence of the infinite God. Thus, the narrowing of the spiritual field of vision to the bottom of the soul denotes its infinite expansion; *sese angustat ut dilatetur* (it narrows in order to expand), as Gregory the Great aptly says of the soul that concentrates inward (Hom. in Ezech. II 11, 12). Having died to the outer world, the soul comes to life again in the divine inner world; in a characteristic pun, Bernard of Clairvaux speaks of the *vitalis vigilque sopor* ('the living and waking sleep, which enlightens the inner sense' (Cant. 52, 2, 3)."

[703] See Thurnwald, "Primitive Initiationsriten" (1940), p. 333f. On silence as a means of enhancing power, and on its role in magical dealings with the world of demons, see Bächtold-Stäubli under *schweigen* (to remain silent).

religious exercises,[704] whose meaning has probably been described most aptly by Meister Eckhart:

786     Just await this birth within you, and you shall experience all good and all comfort, all happiness, all being and all truth. If you miss it, you will miss all good and blessedness … truth is within, in the ground, and not without. So he who would see light to discern all truth, let him watch and become aware of this birth within, in the ground.[705]

787   In this type of fairytale, the requirement to sever ties with the outside world even surpasses the prohibition of talking and laughing. In "The Three Shirts of Cotton-Grass" (Ireland, no. 21), for instance, the heroine is not permitted to shed a tear when her child dies; thus, suffering is also forbidden. She must, although this makes her seem heartless, demonstrate her unconditional devotion and sub-ordination to the superiority of the unconscious forces and their pressing demands by concentrating exclusively on her task. In particular because the terrible mother lurks as a corrupting force, the heroine must sacrifice her own unconscious, natural mother-liness to be able to realize it on a higher level.

788   Accomplishing redemption by enduring hardship and silence while suffering torment, which has magical and profane causes, is a familiar motif (e.g., "The King of the Golden Mountain"[706] and its variants). In both types of fairytales, the requirements to be fulfilled during silence indicate that, psychologically, the threatening contents of the unconscious appear and can be consciously grasped only when consciousness "remains silent"; that is, when it remains directed inward and enables things to happen.

---

[704] See esp. Heiler, "Kontemplation i. d. christl. Mystik" (1934), p. 308: "Tauler quite rightly states: 'The very best and noblest thing that you can attain in this life is that you remain silent and let God do his work and speak; where works and ideas have been deprived of their power, there this (divine) word is spoken.'" See also *ibid.*, p. 302, and v. d. Leeuw, *Phänomenologie der Religion* (1933), pp. 409ff.

[705] *The Complete Works of Meister Eckhart* (2009), pp. 39 and 41 (Sermons II, on Matthew 2:2). On the same sermon, see also *Archetypal Symbols in Fairytales*, vol. 2, p. 90, fn. 34. On the parallel Eastern idea of insensitivity and silent concentration as saintly conduct, see Przyluski, "Der Lebendig-Erlöste" (1938), pp. 127f. and 132.

[706] *The Complete Grimm's Fairy Tales*, pp. 425–430.

789    In most cases, the heroine is slandered for giving birth to dogs, cats, or other animal children.[707] Behind this accusation lies a religious secret: Both sodomy, which would be a prerequisite for such animal birth, and incest seem to have been a divine prerogative.[708] Regressing to the animal level, which involves humans aligning themselves with animals, or even becoming one with them, is a basic factor of Germanic berserker and werewolf experiences, as well as of the Dionysian mysteries; it is also evident among most primitive peoples. Ninck has therefore related being slandered for giving birth to dogs to the Germanic belief in werewolves. Although such profane statements about one's enemy might initially strike us as malicious lies, closer scrutiny reveals a psychological truth: The heroine's bond with the animal brothers is—analogously to the amplifications of the sibling fairytales considered so far—incestuous; by endeavoring to redeem the animal brothers, the maiden is closely allied to the unconscious as the deepest psychic realm. This, however, is a psychological mystery (hence the imperative to maintain silence). As observed, fairytales about the relationship with the anima reveal that betraying the marriage with one's beloved, who has been transformed into an animal, is met with contempt by the profane sphere and ruins the marriage. This contrast is also evident here: What on the inner level is a sacred event, and should not be betrayed, in a profane light becomes sinful. Therefore, the heroine has *not* committed the crime of which she stands accused in the alleged manner, because she is connected with the animal kingdom on an incommensurable inner level, that is, in psychic reality.

790    By steadfastly pursuing her inner task, and even bearing the profane threat to her children and herself with seeming indifference, the heroine not only achieves the greatest sacrifice and devotion, but thereby also concentrates the psychic forces so much that not only the utmost danger arises but also clarification and liberation. This is symbolized by the heroine being burned almost entirely on the

---

[707] Ninck, *Wodan*, p. 257f.
[708] *Ibid.*, p. 285, according to which Odin consorted with a bitch (i.e., a female dog).

funeral pyre. This greatest possible tension recalls that variant of "Snow White" where the dwarves are supposed to burn the coffin containing the seemingly dead maiden, whereupon the redeeming prince appears at precisely that moment.[709] In discussing the motif of being burned to death,[710] we have interpreted it as an image of the inner fervor or accumulation of passionate forces that is accomplished by immersion, which strongly intensifies the clash of opposites and leads to unexpected *lysis* (disintegration). It is only in such moments, in which human beings, embroiled in conflict, almost consume themselves and seem to be lost, that their inner being (i.e., essence) reveals itself. Once more, we realize why the heroine silently endures all profane persecutions: The brothers unexpectedly return from the unknown sphere into which they had escaped and, moreover, transform into human beings.[711]

791     The components of the self that are displaced by the profane tendencies of the conscious world (which ultimately is driven by the negative-magical side, the devouring unconsciousness, i.e., the evil mother) into the invisible sphere (i.e., entirely into the unconscious), are recalled by the suffering soul, consolidated, and guided back from their animal state (i.e., unconsciousness) into human life. The heroine's children represent the self to the brothers in a new form, as a wholeness attained on a higher level. By comparison, the brothers are preliminary stages. Therefore, melancholy hangs over their redemption: In most cases, a stroke of misfortune prevents the youngest brother from being entirely redeemed; either the goldsmith has broken one of the little rings on his chain,[712] or one of his shirt sleeves has not been completely finished, and so on.

792     This incomplete redemption amounts to an incomplete realization of consciousness. The motif of the ring, evident in many versions,[713] illumines this process more clearly insofar as a ring

---

[709] See *Archetypal Symbols in Fairytales*, vol. 3, p. 259.

[710] See, e.g., "The Girl and the Skull" (Siberia, no. 36).

[711] On mutual redemption, see "The Poor Souls" (France, vol. 2, no. 47): The heroine redeems the poor souls, who in turn liberate her, confirming the notion of intrapsychic figures.

[712] Ninck, *Wodan*, pp. 260–261.

[713] On the various designs and amplifications of this motif, see Ninck, *Wodan*, p. 257ff.; see also his "Älteste Märchen von Europa" (1945), p. 121: "Das Schwanenmärchen" (for the source, see *ibid.*, p. 187).

always symbolizes attachment and connection. This suggests that this connection, with consciousness, is not entirely stable.[714] A last remnant of that mysterious group of brothers escapes realization. Whereas in "The Singing, Soaring Lark" and similar tales the animal prince becomes completely human and takes the heroine into his realm, here matters are different from the outset: The animal prince appears as a multitude and is confronted with a royal, human husband. (The latter motif also occurs in the Grimm's "Brother and Sister"; in such fairytales, the brother is sometimes redeemed, sometimes not, and thus his destiny seems to be uncertain). In fairytales about brothers who must be redeemed, the archetypal image of the royal husband (who must also be redeemed) of the equally archetypal female figure is split, revealing this archetype's complex and mysterious double nature. As the amplifications of the animal prince in "The Singing, Soaring Lark" indicate, this archetype is a psychic content. In other systems, this content appears as a divine primordial human. Often, this figure has a strange double aspect: an animal, demonic, and divine side; *and* a human one, whose hallmark is its "royalty." As we have seen, this archetype represents the self.

793    The twofold manifestation results from the self being experienced in different forms: As a king, it manifests as the superior, dominating, and eternally sublime inner being; as a sorrowfully enchanted animal, on the other hand, it manifests as a part of nature, which has either never been human or used to be human, yet lost its humanity by coming into contact with the dark world of matter before sinking to the lower levels of creation.[715] This reveals the unconscious projection of the self onto cosmic realities, as Jung explains based on Gnostic-alchemical material[716]:

---

[714] One revealing variant is "The Birth of the Swan Knight" (France, vol. 1, no. 8): The chain ensures the brothers' ability to be human and thus symbolizes their connection with the conscious world. The ring that is thrown by the sister into the brothers' cups in the Grimm's "The Seven Ravens" has a similar meaning: It reconnects the fugitives with the human world.

[715] Although the sister's marriage to the king at first appears as an "exogamous" detachment from her brothers, and although versions without a king (e.g., the Grimm's "The Seven Ravens") appear less well-rounded, we should assign the king to the group of brothers, especially because the sister's main task is to redeem her brothers even after she marries the king, and also because the brothers live with the king and queen after being redeemed.

[716] Jung, *Psychology and Alchemy*, CW 12, § 410–411.

794  The idea of the pneuma as the Son of God, who descends into matter and then frees himself from it in order to bring healing and salvation to all souls, bears the traits of a projected unconscious content. Such a content is an autonomous complex divorced from consciousness, leading a life of its own in the psychic non-ego and instantly projecting itself whenever it is constellated in any way—that is, whenever attracted by something analogous to it in the outside world. The psychic autonomy of the pneuma is attested by the Neopythagoreans: in their view the soul was swallowed by matter and only mind— νους (nous)—was left. But the nous is outside man: it is his daemon. One could hardly formulate its autonomy more aptly. *Nous* seems to be identical with the god Anthropos: he appears alongside the demiurge and is the adversary of the planetary spheres. He rends the circle of the spheres and leans down to earth and water (i.e., he is about to project himself into the elements). His shadow falls upon the earth, but his image is reflected in the water. This kindles the love of the elements, and he himself is so charmed with the reflected image of divine beauty that he would fain take up his abode within it. But scarcely has he set foot upon the earth when Physis locks him in a passionate embrace. From this embrace are born the seven first hermaphroditic beings. The seven are an obvious allusion to the seven planets and hence to the metals which in the alchemical view spring from the hermaphrodite Mercurius.[717]

795  He adds:

In such visionary images as the Anthropos glimpsing his own reflection there is expressed the whole phenomenon of the unconscious projection of autonomous contents. These myth-pictures are like dreams, telling us that a projection

---

[717] My note: We find the number seven also in the Grimm's "The Seven Ravens."

has taken place and also what has been projected. This, as the contemporary evidence shows, was nous, the divine daemon, the god-man, pneuma, etc. In so far as the standpoint of analytical psychology is realistic, i.e., based on the assumption that the contents of the psyche are realities, all these figures stand for an unconscious component of the personality which might well be endowed with a higher form of consciousness transcending that of the ordinary human being. Experience shows that such figures always express superior insight or qualities that are not yet conscious; indeed, it is extremely doubtful whether they can be attributed to the ego at all in the proper sense of the word.

796  This interpretation also explains why many fairytales emphasize the "rehabilitation" of the ousted or enchanted animal prince. Psychologically, regaining royal dignity means withdrawing the projection into that human being from whom it had unconsciously emanated. In the projection, the process appears as if the transpersonal psychic content, sunken into the world of evil, reappeared in its original clarity; in fact, the as-yet unconscious person experiences a heightening of their inner being, by intuiting that a higher being is working within them and has chosen them as the vessel in which they will realize themselves in this world. The depicted, yet not entirely successful redemption of the last brother indicates that something mysterious remains, which cannot be integrated in the human realm. However, we should understand the untransformed wing not merely as a disfigurement or as a blemish. It is as much an attribute that brands the youngest brother as it is a demigod. It is therefore no coincidence that tradition has, in the second instance, related this figure to other narratives by associating the swan and Lohengrin with it.[718] In this pair, the two aspects of the

---

[718] See the French version ("The Birth of the Swan Knight"; vol. I, no. 8): Queen Beatrix gave birth to seven children. Matabrune, her mother-in-law, slandered her to King Oriant, her husband, for bearing seven dogs. Because the King refused to take action against his wife, Matabrune had the Queen thrown into a dungeon and ordered her children, six boys and one girl, to be killed. Instead of following orders, her servant abandoned the children in a forest. Each of the children had worn a chain around its neck since birth, which ensured their human form, because otherwise they would have become swans. A

supernatural human, the godlike hero and the animal spirit, are once again presented as a duality.

797     Just as the animal brothers and the royal husband indicate that the archetype of the animal prince is split, so the figure of the heroine is probably also divided, as she, too, is an archetypal figure. Thus, we have a quaternity of figures, which is interrelated crosswise. Such a quaternity is hinted at in the Grimm's "Brother and Sister": The two male figures were the heroine's little stag brother and the royal husband, while the female ones were the heroine and the wicked witch's daughter, whose overcoming determined the little brother's fate. This fourth female figure is thus portrayed as inexorably evil and therefore cannot be included in the group. Analogously, the fourth figure in tales about the 12 brothers and the six swans could be the profane slanderer and the female demon, who

---

hermit raised the children. When Matabrune discovered that the children were alive, she instructed her woodman to tear off their necklaces. Only the child that had gone into the forest with the hermit was spared this brutal ordeal; the others flew as swans to the pond at their father's castle. Matabrune commissioned a goldsmith to make a drinking bowl from the six chains. However, he used only one chain and hid the other five, whose value he recognized, in a safe place. After the young queen had languished in the dungeon for fifteen years, Matabrune ordered that she should be burned at the stake. The barons decided that the execution should take place the following day if no one could be found to defend her. From an angel, the hermit learned about the Queen's impending fate and was instructed to send the last remaining boy to Illefort to defend his mother. Before leaving, he should be baptized as Helias. The young man set out and along the way killed one of Matabrune's servants, who had been dispatched to kill him. He reported to the King, was baptized Helias at his request, and defeated the woodman, who was fighting for Matabrune. The latter fled the castle. Helias healed the blinded servant who had spared the children at the time by breathing life into him, and thereupon gave back to five of his swan brothers their chains and thus their human form. Only the one sibling whose chain had been used by the goldsmith was compelled to remain a swan. The King handed over the kingdom to Helias, who took revenge on Matabrune. Commenting on these events, Tegethoff (France, vol. 1, pp. 308–309) observes that the story about the swan children exists in four versions, of which the one translated here corresponds to the most recent version, "which, however, may still belong to the second half of the 12th century. ... The fairytale on which the saga is based is composed from two originally separate types. One type, about the slandered woman (i.e., the Genovevan type), appears very early in Germanic countries and may safely be claimed to have a Germanic origin. ... The fairytale about the boys who are turned into animals, and who are redeemed by their sister, might have a Celtic origin (note that the final episode in that tale is blurred). The name Helias is most plausibly interpreted from Celtic *ealadh* ("swan"). The Celtic elements include the Circean motif of the animal transformation by the witch (also blurred) and the manifestation of the gods of light as swans ... On a second level, the saga about the swan children was related to the Lohengrin saga, which forms of a group of stories about disrupted marriages." See also the other version of this fairytale collected in Ninck, "Älteste Märchen von Europa" (1945), p. 121, which ends as follows (p. 126): "Only that child on whose chain the goldsmith had broken a little ring could not be transformed back into its present state. He remained a swan and served one of his brothers." On the motif of abandonment, see Ninck, *Wodan*, pp. 258ff., and Rank, "Lohengrinsage" (1911), pp. 19–49, 156f. See also Usener, *Sintfluthsagen* (1899,) esp. pp. 80–108 and112, who links sagas about heroes who are abandoned as children in water with those about heroes who emerge from a bark or ship. (However, as soon as "water" is used to mean the "unconscious," this connection, which otherwise seems to be necessary, becomes superfluous). On the motif of abandonment, see also Frobenius, *Zeitalter* (1904), pp. 224ff. and 240ff.

appears at the beginning, and whose identity seems obvious[719] (the group of brothers is considered to be a single figure for the reasons mentioned above). She represents, as her sister's secret accomplice, the heroine's demonic shadow-figure. This figure is not redeemed but merely defeated and rejected. This is related to the fact that, for the man, she represents that ambiguous, seductive nature of the woman that also ties him to the sensual side of the world, in which, for him, evil is essentially contained.

798    We find an interesting multiplication of these pairs in "The Diamond-Spewing Spring" (Roma, no. 32), even if the psychological conditions are nuanced quite differently in that case. There we have three pairs: first, two cursed figures that are destined for each other (the source of diamonds and the hare); second, the unequal pair that finds each other (the emperor's son and the persecuted sister of the source of diamonds); and third, the siblings who are exposed to slander and exposure, and where the sister almost corrupts the brother, whom she forces to perform impossible tasks. The solicited beheading of the hare renders this figure parallel to the fox in the Grimm's "The Golden Bird" in terms of the hero, who was the "brother" in the third pair. Only two pairs were clearly distinguished: the source of diamonds/hare and the siblings, who eventually appeared at court as a group of *four*.

799    The manifold intersections of meanings and motifs with the previously discussed fairytales suggest that all these pairs are repetitions of the same primordial couple, whose aspects are extended, repeated, and thus nuanced over generations. This pair represents two unredeemed beings that are bewitched in animal form. To some extent, these two beings are siblings—insofar as they have a common origin and are kindred. Eventually, drama, which is aimed at mutual redemption, unfolds between these two figures. In each case, either the woman or the man appears (if all fairytales are considered) closer to humankind and less demonic, and as such

---

[719] Rank, "Lohengrinsage," pp. 73ff.

redeems the other part. In each case, the redeeming part is closer to humankind.[720]

800     The strange possibility of reversing the drama of redemption between the partners is demonstrated by "Brother and Sister" (Zaunert, *Deutsche Märchen seit Grimm*, p. 406). This fairytale coincides largely with that about the swan brothers, except that the roles are reversed: The female part flies away as a bird and is redeemed by the brother:

801     A brother and a sister didn't get along, but the sister was more quarrelsome. When the brother complained about her, their father wished that she became a dove. No sooner had he expressed his wish, the girl flew out of the window. The brother mourned his sister. When he had grown up, he set off to look for her. For his journey, his father gave him a new linen shirt with his sister's name embroidered in the cloth. In a forest, he spent the night in the cottage of the old mother of the winds. She made her son promise not to harm the boy, bid him come out of his hiding place and to make his request. The following day, the wind tried to track down the sister, yet in vain. The boy continued his journey and spent the night with the raven's mother, where events unfolded as they had previously. Thereafter, the young man reached a third cottage, where a beautiful woman, the sun, lived. She succeeded in finding the sister with her glow: In the middle of a large, impassable stretch of water stood a magnificent castle high up on an island. "Stay with me until tomorrow; thereafter, go and buy yourself a black hen, which you shall cook and eat;

---

[720] The Indian rite *bhrātri-sphota* is described by Heinrich Zimmer in "Zur Bedeutung des indischen Tantra-Yoga," *Eranos-Jahrbuch 1933: Yoga und Meditation im Osten und im Westen*, ed. v. Olga Fröbe-Kapteyn (1934), pp. 13–14: "*Bhrātri-sphota* (Bengali *bhai-phota*), i.e., the "sign on the brother's forehead" is observed on the second night of the waxing moon in October. All the sisters of the family convene and invite their brothers; their rite serves to save their brothers from death. It is offered as a sacrifice to overcome death. Other sacrifices are made to worship a god, to win his favor; here no god comes into question; the sacrifice consists in the sister offering herself to death. This is what the only sister of the first man did for her brother Yama. The first man, Yama (i.e., "twin"), had a twin sister Yamunā (who is called "Yamī" in Vedic myth), who overcame death for him. By her sacrificing herself every day to death for him, he became the death-conquering king in the realm of the blessed, and thus became the ruler of the world of the dead. This mythical circumstance is the model for the sisters and repeated through their observance."

but keep the bones. Buy yourself a pot of syrup and walk until you come to the water. You will see a bridge of glass, which rises steeply up to the castle and is so smooth that no one can climb it; but always take a little leg from the hen, dip it in syrup, and lay it on the bridge, and you will be able to step on it, and so scale the heights." When the boy tried to follow these instructions, he lost a leg, which made the last step impossible. And thus, he cut off his little finger and reached the castle. In the first room, he ate a meal and regained his strength. In the second room, fourteen girls, one of whom was his sister, were sleeping in fourteen beds. He placed the linen shirt on her pillow and crossed the third room, which was sky-blue and bright, into the garden. When the girls awoke, the shirt fell off the pillow. The sister exclaimed: "Oh, my brother is here! But if he had only done one more thing, swept an almond (15 pieces) to ashes, I would have been saved; alas, things being as they are, I am doomed to the dark world.' She went out into the garden where he was, but she was not permitted to greet him or speak to him—instead, she passed by him and walked down the bridge and onward into the dark world." He returned to the second room, found the terms of redemption she had written down, took the shirt, and followed his sister to a mill by the sea, on whose side lay the dark world. The miller told him: "Every day a raven comes here to fetch three tons of flour for the dark world; you can sit in a barrel over there and the raven will take you across. But he has a habit: If a barrel is too light, he lets it fall into the sea; if it is too heavy, he returns to fetch another until one of them has the right weight." The young man let himself be carried across the sea in a barrel, but the raven dropped it not far from the shore on the other side because it was "too light." But the wind and the waves drove it to the shore and the young man began walking. Soon, however, he had to crawl on all fours due to the increasing darkness. When he reached the city gates, two pigs ran away horrified when they saw the "Christian"; the same happened with two bears and two donkeys at the second and third gates. Thereupon, the young man crawled over the bridge into the castle and heard a voice say: "Oh, when will we be saved?" Another voice replied: "First someone must come and sweep the almonds lying on top of the hall into pure ashes and carry them to the rampart and throw them into the water; by no means should he look around, even if he is summoned, and even if the water tries to hold him back. There will be a loud crash and we will be saved. But no one will be able to perform this feat." The boy crawled up into the hall and found the brooms, "and when he made the second stroke, the broom turned to ashes; and so did the others. Thereupon, he contemplated how he might carry the ashes to the water. He took his handkerchief, swept them into it, and carried them away. When he done this, a voice behind him called out, seized him by the collar, and threatened to unleash a great misfortune; despite these odds, he advanced without looking back. And when he threw the ashes into the water, there was a terrible crash. He returned, and everything grew ever lighter, and soon there was broad daylight. He entered the castle and found the fourteen girls asleep. He put his sister's shirt on her pillow and left the room. The girls awoke and were redeemed. But the sister saw the shirt and found her brother; and in the castle, where everything was now beautiful and splendid, they lived happily together.

802 Here, in contrast to the fairytales considered above, the brother indirectly causes the cursing of the sister; like the brothers in the Grimm's "The Seven Ravens," she subsequently vanishes as a bird. Just as in that tale the sister follows the brother, so here the brother follows the sister over different stations. Once more, a little bone, which is replaced by a little finger, plays the same role. The psychological meaning of this process arises from inverting the fairytale about the seven ravens. Here, the maiden's transformation

into a bird, as in "The Raven,"[721] means that—although the bird is a dove—she becomes identical with an animalistic psychic component that flies away into the unconscious and therefore must be evaluated negatively. In the Siberian variant, "The Raven" (no. 17), the sister, instead of being transformed, is abducted by the evil raven-man, whom her third brother defeats by journeying to the otherworld, from where he brings home the sister (together with the older brothers previously overcome by the raven-man).

803

Similarly, in the present fairytale, the brother must dare to enter the "dark world" to redeem the sister, who has become a dove. The additional motif, the condition of redemption, is remarkable: The brother must sweep 15 brooms to ashes and throw the ashes into the water to liberate his sister from that world, which is alluded to as hell. Its guardian animals (pigs, bears, and donkeys) point to the chthonic, uncanny nature of that realm. As in "The Golden Castle That Hung in the Air" (Norway, no. 35), the anima is far removed to an elevated position. Afterward, however, she is not only brought down to earth but is also freed from the chthonic realm.

804

Sweeping many brooms to ashes indicates that this act of liberation is an act of purification, comparable to the cleaning of the Augean stables in the myth of Heracles. The anima can only be incorporated into consciousness—in fairytales, into the human world—by disentangling and thus delivering her from the shadow elements. Psychologically, this lengthy and arduous self-examination requires patience. Choosing an "almond," 15 pieces, that is, as the measure of things confirms that this task amounts to self-education: 14 pieces serve the anima-figure, while the 15th serves the hero, who is the 15th member of the group. According to Bächtold-Stäubli (see *kehren*, *Kehricht*, sweepings, refuse), sweeping or sweeping out carries a defensive connotation, in particular as primitive belief considers sweepings a hiding place for evil spirits. "Thus," so Bächtold-Stäubli, "sweeping must be understood from the outset as a cathartic, magical act." In the death rituals and traditions of various peoples, the soul of the deceased, which takes hold in the ground, is

---

[721] *The Complete Grimm's Fairy Tales*, pp. 431–436.

swept out or poured into the grave with the sweepings. On the other hand, sweeping the death room is apotropaic: It helps to prevent the soul from returning as a vampire. The broom is either thrown onto the burial site or burned:

805     In the same way as in the custom of the dead, the repellent and purifying character of sweeping is also evident in traditional ceremonies. At certain times and on certain occasions, the material blessing must be removed by a material act of purification.

806  Thus, among the primitives, the demons are swept out, and the sweepings must be removed. "If you want to banish a spirit or ghost, sweep out the house of spirits with a new broom. ... If you want to cast an evil spell on your enemy, take a broom with which you swept out a dead man, burn it, and sprinkle the ashes of the broom upon your enemy ... ." Sweeping up also means to "gather," "to bring one thing to another." Moreover, "sweepings, as the result of sweeping, assume the character of what defines the action: the quality of 'bringing to(gether).' Thus sweeping and sweepings become the prerequisite for acquisition, for possession, and for happiness in general."

807     In the present fairytale, the broom and the sweepings form a unity. The hero sweeps out the magic spell: Because, as the passage about enchanting an enemy emphasizes, both the broom and its ashes contain the evil spell. Here, sweeping seems to imply gathering, that is, concentrating on redemption. This involves recognizing the hidden fervor of the demonic sphere, transforming it while it is burning and, when it has "extinguished" and become "ashes," once again handing it over to the unconscious (forest, water) in its harmless, transformed form. Thus, the brooms—which here are bearers of demonic characteristics— that become ashes, thus represent the shadow's demonic aspect. The alchemists associated ashes, the product of decomposition in a fire, with corpses and the

body.[722] After all, in the sweeper's hand the broom also becomes part of the sweeper. In "The Comrade" (Norway, no. 7) and other variants, the shadow-figure eventually disappears in its transformed form. Brooms also correspond to the demonic animus, which often bewitches the anima. Thus, the cathartic effect of sweeping is essential here: The demonic element is eliminated, and the sister is restored to human form.

808
Even if redemption assumes a peculiar form and symbolism in these fairytales, in essence they are inverted versions of "The Seven Ravens" and similar tales, where the roles of brother and sister are exchanged. This suggests that these two figures represent two aspects of the same archetype. This assumption seems correct because in some fairytales, one or the other figure exhibits the traits of the opposite sex: Sometimes, the anima is a virago who, dressed in men's clothes, measures herself against the hero and only surrenders to her vanquisher (e.g., in "Born of a Fish," Finland, no. 31; "Beautiful Helena and the Heroic Woman," Caucasus, no. 26; and "Balai and Boti," Caucasus, no. 13). In this tale, a king's three sons set out to defeat a belligerent maiden; the two elder brothers disregard an old man's advice and confront the maiden, who exposes her breast, whereupon the brothers faint and are beheaded by slaves. The youngest brother, on the other hand, listens to the old man's counsel to approach the maiden with his eyes closed.[723] In these examples, her masculinity is her personal secret, which the hero must discover through his cunning. Abandoning the adopted male role (often only at night) is also considered to constitute redemption.[724]

---

[722] Jung, "The Psychology of the Transference," *CW* 16, § 495.

[723] See also "The Girl Soldier" (Russia, no. 31), "The Girl in the Box" (Balkans, no. 56), "The Robber's Bride" (Zaunert, *Märchen aus dem Donaulande*, p. 104). On the idea of the combative maiden (i.e., the belligerent Germanic Valkyrians), see Ninck, *Wodan*, p. 224f.

[724] See "The Twelve Huntsmen" (*The Complete Grimm's Fairy Tales*, pp. 334–336): The first bride of a King's son placed herself and 11 companions as hunters in the service of her bridegroom and thus persuaded him not to marry the King's daughter, whom his father had intended for him. See also "Siebenschön" (Zaunert, *Deutsche Märchen seit Grimm*, p. 146). On "girls wearing men's clothes and the efforts to determine their sex," see Georg Hüsing, "Die Iranische Überlieferung und das arische System," in: *Mythologische Bibliothek*, ed. v. d. Ges. f. vergleichende Mythenforschung, vol. 2, no. 2 (1909), p. 13, fn. 1. See also "How a Girl Became a Boy" (Hertel, *Indische Märchen*, 1925, no. 76), "The Story of the Weeping Pomegranate and the Laughing Quince" (Turkey, no. 4); for an extensive collection of material, compiled from mythology and traditional customs, see Bolte and Mackensen, *Handwörterbuch* (1930/1934) under *Geschlechtswechsel* (change of sex). Interpreting these matters in terms of human psychology (i.e., the subjective experience of the anima or animus) reveals the double,

809    While the reverse motif is more seldom, it is especially evident in "The Cursed Queen of Elves"[725]: For six years, King Oddur, who was popular with his people, killed his winter guest on the first day of summer because he could not answer his guest's question about him that none of his subjects knew the answer to. The seventh winter guest, however, negotiated with the king that he could share his bedchamber. On Christmas night, he followed the king unnoticed to a swamp and plunged into the depths after him. In the underworld, he sees Oddur don women's clothes and become the king's wife. He hears Oddur say that the coming summer will be the last opportunity for him to be redeemed. Should the winter guest fail again, he will never be able to return to his subterranean spouse. On the first day of summer, however, the winter guest is able to point out to Oddur the robe that it is appropriate for him to wear in the underworld, whereupon Oddur transfers the government of the realm to the winter guest and returns home. Here, too, the man's nocturnal transformation into a woman is a secret that amounts to a curse (according to its author's people, whose consciousness was undeveloped when this fairytale was created, in this world the figure of the nocturnal woman is regarded as the proper one rather than that of the king). This motif is even more evident in other fairytales, where the hero temporarily becomes a woman, either voluntarily or involuntarily, as a result of being cursed.[726]

810    These motif combinations reveal that fairytale heroes and heroines have a secret androgynous side. Psychologically, this rests on the fact that the man's anima possesses an inner feminine personality, while the woman's animus has an inner masculine part. Fairytales illumine human circumstances almost exclusively in otherworldly, that is, unconscious and archetypal terms. As such, they distinguish neither the real woman and the man's anima, nor

hermaphroditic aspect of the self. See Bächtold-Stäubli under *Geschlechtswechsel, Geschlechtsverwandlung* (change or transformation of sex) and especially under *Kleidertausch* (changing clothes).
[725] Rittershaus, *Neuisländische* (1902), no. LXXXV I.: "King Oddur."
[726] See "The Man Who Was Transformed into a Woman and Back into a Man" (Modern Greece, no. 56), and also "The Man Who Visited the Polar Bears" (Siberia, no. 41), which describes the transformation into a woman as a consequence of and punishment for marrying a female polar bear. In "The Story of Dschefa and Sefa" (Turkey, no. 11), this motif is modified into that of cunning disguise.

the concrete man and the woman's animus. At best, they depict the anima and animus in two different manifestations, laying the foundations for the subsequent awareness of this distinction.[727] Hence, it is barely surprising that the principal figures—hero and heroine—appear to be interchangeable aspects of one and the same figure. Whereas the monstrous mythological figure of the hermaphrodite is not found in fairytales (unlike, for example, in alchemical imagery), the secret identity of the male and the female figure emerges more often.

811     In conclusion: Who are these two figures? Which archetype do they represent?

812     First of all, these figures can be compared with the alchemical pair of siblings and with the hermaphrodite, and moreover with Gnostic pairs of redeemers. Insofar as fairytale figures are bound in matter, they parallel the Gnostic conception of "'the divine soul imprisoned in the elements,' whom it is the task … to redeem."[728] The anthropos, who descends into matter, and whose mythology is manifold,[729] appears in both male and female form.[730] As fairytales plainly show, the two halves have the same task: to redeem each other. As reported by August Ey, one variant of "The Singing, Soaring Lark," clearly illumines this: In "The Golden Rose,"[731] the heroine speaks to the rose bush: "I shall redeem you, and you shall redeem me." To this corresponds a famous alchemical saying, according to which the stone (which corresponds to the arcane substance) says to the adept: "Protect me and I will protect thee. Give me what is mine that I may help thee."[732] In the latter case, the split is distributed, so that it appears between the adept (i.e., the conscious

---

[727] Appearing or manifesting as a duality is symptomatic of a growing awareness.

[728] Jung, *Psychologie und Alchemie*, CW 12, § 413, esp. § 410f.; see above, pp. 353ff. Similar ideas have also been preserved in the Jewish Kabbalah. According to the Sohar, the souls of the righteous symbolize the Son of God, whom the Father sent down to earth to complete his education. Subsequently, he brings him home by sending his mother, the queen, the Shekhinah (i.e., the presence of God) to him, who brings him home to the father's palace: "The spirit (the higher soul) does not leave the earth until the queen has become one with it, in order to introduce it into the King's palace, where it shall dwell forever"; see Bischoff, "Elemente der Kabbalah" (1913), p. 112.

[729] Bousset, *Hauptprobleme der Gnosis* (1907), pp. 215ff.

[730] On the hermaphroditic nature of primitive humans, see also Bischoff, "Elemente der Kabbalah" (1913), p. 227f., fn. 173.

[731] Ey, *Harzmärchen* (1862), p. 91.

[732] Jung, "The Psychology of Rebirth," CW 9/I, § 238.

real individual) and the arcane substance (i.e., that part of the soul that is projected into the substance and is unconscious). In fairytales, it is distributed between an archetypal man and an archetypal woman. Human consciousness was said to participate in that part that was less enchanted into less human forms. Consequently, the part closer to humankind was considered to be the redeeming one.

813     Considering the role of human consciousness in this archetypal event shows that it is placed, like an instrument, between two opposite positions that meet in the archetypal image of the magical pair. In fairytales, the human being is identical with one or the other archetypal part. This rests on the fact that fairytales depict an archaic stage of human development, where the human ego and the archetypal inner events have not yet been differentiated. Or, if they have, then only rudimentarily. Thus, explaining fairytale material in psychological terms is so extraordinarily difficult, because the connection with today's concrete world seems to be absent; vice versa, the archetypal world often seems so banal that the deeper meaning of fairytales, which are seemingly so "harmless," is easily underestimated.

814     While ancient myths of redemption (of the Gnostic and speculative type) describe a cosmic and therefore superhuman event, medieval alchemical philosophy acknowledges, albeit by un-consciously projecting the same archetype, yet with absolute conviction, that the role of the human being is to redeem the spirit that is concealed in matter. Fairytales are also based on the same archetype, the primordial process involved in the reciprocal relation-ship between the one who redeems and the one who is to be redeemed. Reflected by an as-yet-undeveloped spirit, the ego's psychic experience of the inner Thou identifies, through partici-pation (or projection), with the otherworldly sphere, the observed archetypal fairytale figures. Accordingly, the redeemer corresponds to the human, conscious ego, the one to be redeemed to the higher, yet suffering part of being. In other words, fairytales, whose images reflect the archetype of redemption, depict the human endeavor to liberate the divine spark, which is overgrown with weeds in the soul. The instrumental significance that humankind thus attributes to

itself within this work of redemption reflects its awareness of both its dignity and its responsibility. Because while the archetypal problem of opposites persists forever in the unconscious sphere, fairytales suggest that if that problem can be solved, then on the level of human consciousness, where it can attain a new and fruitful shape through conscious human endeavor.

815        The bond between the one who redeems and the one to be redeemed is, however, merely *one* form of representing the tension between opposites in the psyche and its transformation. As the next volume shows, fairytales contain other images of this problem, ones in which human consciousness is considered to be decisive in terms of the Gnostic power of cognition.

◆

# Bibliography

*MdW* = Märchen der Weltliteratur

Aarne, Antti. *Vergleichende Märchenforschungen.* Helsingfors: Akademische Abhandlung, Druckerei der Finnischen Literatur-gesellschaft, 1908.

Abraham, Karl. "Traum und Mythus: eine Studie zur Völker-psychologie." In *Schriften zur angewandten Seelenkunde,* no. 4, edited by Sigmund Freud. Leipzig and Vienna: Franz Deuticke, 1909.

Abt, Regina, Irmgard Bosch, and Vivienne Mackrel. *Traum und Schwangerschaft: Eine Untersuchung von Träumen schwangerer Frauen.* Einsiedeln: Daimon Verlag, 1996.

Afanas'ev, Alexander N., *Russische Volksmärchen.* Translated by Anna Meyer. Vienna: C. W. Stern (Buchhandlung L. Rosner), 1906.
  – *Russische Volksmärchen.* New edition. Translated by Anna Meyer. Vienna: Verlag Dr. Rud. Ludwig, 1910.
  – *Russian Fairy Tales.* Translated by Norbert Guterman. Toronto: Pantheon Books, 1945.

Aichele, Walther, ed. *Zigeunermärchen.* In *MdW,* edited by Fr. v. d. Leyen and P. Zaunert. Jena: Eugen Diederichs, 1926.

Allberry, Charles R. C. "Symbole von Tod und Wiedergeburt im Manichäismus." In *Eranos-Jahrbuch 1939: Die Symbolik der Wiedergeburt in der religiösen Vorstellung der Zeiten und Völker,* edited by Olga Fröbe-Kapteyn. Zurich: Rhein-Verlag, 1940, pp. 113–149.

Altmann, Christine, ed. *Kleine Märchenzeitung der Schweizerischen Märchen-Gesellschaft SMG,* 3, May 1998.

Angelus Silesius [Johann Scheffler]. *Cherubinischer Wandersmann.* Nach der Ausgabe letzter Hand von 1675 vollst. hrsg. und mit einer Studie "Über den Wert der Mystik für unsere Zeit." Edited by Wilhelm Bölsche. Jena and Leipzig: Eugen Diederichs, 1905.

Apuleius. *The Golden Ass.* Translated by E. J. Kenney. London: Penquin, 2004.

Bachofen, Johann Jakob. *Versuch über die Gräbersymbolik der Alten.* Basel: Bahnmaier's Buchhandlung (C. Detloff), 1859.

– *Das Mutterrecht. Eine Untersuchung über die Gynaikokratie der alten Welt nach ihrer religiösen und rechtlichen Natur.* Stuttgart: Krais & Hoffmann, 1861.

– *Die Unsterblichkeitslehre der orphischen Theologie auf den Grabdenkmälern des Alterthums.* Nach Anleitung einer Vase aus Canosa im Besitz des Herrn Prosper Biardot in Paris, dargestellt von Dr. J. J. Bachofen mit einer Tafel in Farbendruck. Basel: Felix Schneider's Buchhandlung, 1867.

– *Die Sage von Tanaquil. Eine Untersuchung über den Orientalismus in Rom und Italien.* Heidelberg: J. C. B. Mohr, 1870.

Bächtold-Stäubli, Hanns. *Handwörterbuch des deutschen Aberglaubens.* Edited by E. Hoffmann-Krayer et al. Berlin and Leipzig: W. de Gruyter & Co. Vols. I–VII, 1927–1936. Vol. VIII–X, Berlin 1936–1942.

Baumann, Dieter. "Individuation in the Spirit of Love." In *The Fountain of Love.* Edited by E. Kennedy-Xypolitas. Wilmette, Illinois: Chiron Publications, 2006, pp. 167–176.

Bischoff, Erich. "Die Elemente der Kabbalah." Part 1: Theoretische Kabbalah. In *Geheime Wissenschaften: Eine Sammlung seltener älterer und neuerer Schriften über Alchemie, Magie, Kabbalah, Rosenkreuzerei, Freimaurerei, Hexen- und Teufelswesen usw.* Edited by A. v. d. Linden. Vol. 2. Berlin: Hermann Barsdorf Verlag, 1913.

Boehm, Max, and Franz Specht, eds. *Lettisch-litauische Volksmärchen.* In *MdW.* Edited by Fr. v. d. Leyen and P. Zaunert. Jena: Eugen Diederichs, 1924.

Bolte, Johannes, and Lutz Mackensen. *Handwörterbuch des deutschen Märchens.* Vols. 1–2. Berlin and Leipzig: W. de Gruyter & Co., 1930/1934.

– and Polívka, Georg. *Anmerkungen zu den Kinder- u. Hausmärchen der Brüder Grimm.* Vol. 1. Leipzig: Dieterich'sche Verlagsbuchhandlung, Th. Weicher, 1913.

– *Anmerkungen zu den Kinder- u. Hausmärchen der Brüder Grimm.* Vol. 2. Leipzig: Dieterich'sche Verlagsbuchhandlung, Th. Weicher, 1915.

– *Anmerkungen zu den Kinder- u. Hausmärchen der Brüder Grimm.* Vol. 3. Leipzig: Dieterich'sche Verlagsbuchhandlung, 1918.

Botkin, Benjamin Albert, ed. *The Pocket Treasury of American Folklore.* New York: Pocket Books, 1950.

Bousset, Wilhelm. "Die Himmelsreise der Seele." In *Archiv für Religionswissenschaft*. Vol. IV. Tübingen and Leipzig 1901.

– *Hauptprobleme der Gnosis*. Göttingen: Vandenhoeck & Ruprecht, 1907.

Buonaiuti, Ernesto. "Die Erlösung in den orphischen Mysterien." In *Eranos-Jahrbuch 1936: Gestaltung der Erlösungsidee in Ost und West I*. Edited by Olga Fröbe-Kapteyn. Zurich: Rhein-Verlag, 1937, pp. 165–181.

Carus, Carl Gustav. *Psyche: Zur Entwicklungsgeschichte der Seele*. Kröners Taschenausgabe, No. 98. Edited by R. Marx. Leipzig: Alfred Kröner Verlag, 1931.

Cassel, Paulus. *Aus Literatur und Symbolik*. Leipzig: Abhandlungen Wilh. Friedrich, 1884.

Christensen, Arthur. Translated from Persian. *Märchen aus Iran*. In *MdW*. Edited by Fr. v. d. Leyen. Jena: Eugen Diederichs Verlag, 1939.

Cumont, Franz. *Die orientalischen Religionen im römischen Heidentum*. Lectures Delivered at the Collège de France. Based on the Fourth French Edition. Translated by Georg Gehrichs. Edited by Dr. A. Burckhardt-Brandenberg. Leipzig and Berlin: B. G. Teubner, 1931.

Danzel, Hedwig, and Theodor-Wilhelm Danzel, eds. *Sagen und Legenden der Südsee-Insulaner (Polynesien)*. Hagen i. W. and Darmstadt: Folkwang-Verlag, 1923.

Danzel, Theodor-Wilhelm. "Zur Psychologie der altmexikanischen Symbolik." In *Eranos-Jahrbuch 1937: Gestaltung der Erlösungsidee in Ost und West II*. Edited by Olga Fröbe-Kapteyn. Zurich: Rhein-Verlag, 1938, pp. 211–296.

Davids, Rhys. "Zur Geschichte des Rad-Symbols." In *Eranos-Jahrbuch 1934: Ostwestliche Symbolik und Seelenführung*. Edited by Olga Fröbe-Kapteyn. Zurich: Rhein-Verlag, 1935, pp. 153–178.

Deussen, Paul. *Sechzig Upanishad's des Veda*. Translated from Sanskrit. Leipzig: F. A. Brockhaus, 1921.

Dieterich, Albrecht. *Abraxas: Studien zur Religionsgeschichte des spätern Altertums*. Leipzig: B. G. Teubner, 1891.

– *Nekyia: Beiträge zur Erklärung der neuentdeckten Petrusapokalypse*. 2nd edition. Leipzig: B. G. Teubner, 1893.

– *Eine Mithrasliturgie*. Edited by Otto Weinreich. Leipzig and Berlin: B. G. Teubner, 1923.

Dirr, Adolf, ed. *Kaukasische Märchen*. In MdW. Edited by Fr.v. d. Leyen and P. Zaunert. Jena: Eugen Diederichs, 1922.

Dölger, Franz Joseph. *"Ichthys": Das Fischsymbol in frühchristlicher Zeit*. Vol. 1. Freiburg i. Br. and Rome: Buchhandlung Spithover, 1910.

– *"Ichthys": Der Heilige Fisch, in den antiken Religionen und im Christentum*. Vol. 2. Münster i. W.: Verlag der Aschendorffschen Verlagsbuchhandlung, 1922.

Ehrentreich, Alfred, ed. and trans. *Englische Volksmärchen*. In *MdW*. Edited by Fr. v. d. Leyen. Jena: Eugen Diederichs Verlag, 1938.

Erman, Adolf. *Die Religion der Ägypter: Ihr Werden und Vergehen in vier Jahrtausenden*. Berlin and Leipzig: W. de Gruyter & Co., 1934.

Ey, August, ed. *Harzmärchenbuch oder Sagen und Märchen aus dem Oberharze*. Stade: Verlag von Fr. Steudel, 1862.

Fankhauser, Alfred. *Horoskopie*. Zurich and Leipzig, 1939.

Franz, Marie-Louise von, *Zahl und Zeit. Psychologische Überlegungen zu einer Annäherung von Tiefenpsychologie und Physik*. Stuttgart: Ernst Klett Verlag, 1977.

– "Aurora Consurgens," ein dem Thomas von Aquin zuge-schriebenes Dokumentder alchemistischen Gegensatzproble-matik. Ergänzungsband zu C.G. Jung, Mysterium Coniunctionis. CW 14/3. Olten and Freiburg i. Br.: Walter-Verlag, 1971.

– *The Psychological Meaning of Redemption Motifs in Fairy Tales*. Toronto: Inner City Books, 1980.

– *Psychologische Märcheninterpretation*. Küsnacht: Verlag Stiftung für Jung'sche Psychologie, 2012.

– "Marie-Louise von Franz im Film von Françoise Selhofer." In *Jungiana*, Series A, Vol. 2, 1989, pp. 15–30.

Frazer, James. *The Golden Bough: A Study of Magic and Religion*. Abridged edition. London: MacMillan, 1925.

Frobenius, Leo. *Das Zeitalter des Sonnengottes*. Vol. 1. Berlin: Georg Reimer, 1904.

Führer, Maria. *Nordgermanische Götterüberlieferung und deutsches Volksmärchen. 80 Märchen der Brüder Grimm vom Mythus her beleuchtet*. Munich: Neuer Filser-Verlag, 1938.

Gerber, Irene. "Yonec. Zu einer Märchendichtung der Marie de France." In *Jungiana*, Series A, Vol. 9, 2000, pp. 53–96.

Giese, Friedrich, ed. *Türkische Märchen*. In *MdW*. Edited by Fr. v. d. Leyen and P. Zaunert. Jena: Eugen Diederichs, 1925.

Goethe, Johann Wolfgang von. *The Soothsayings of Bakis*. Edited and translated by Harald Jantz. Baltimore: Johns Hopkins Press, 1966.

Grimm, Wilhelm, and Jakob Grimm, eds. *Kinder- und Hausmärchen, gesammelt durch die Brüder Grimm.* In *MdW.* Vol. 1. Edited by Fr. v. d. Leyen. Jena: Eugen Diederichs, 1922.

– *Kinder- und Hausmärchen, gesammelt durch die Brüder Grimm.* In *MdW.* Vol. 2. Edited by Fr. v. d. Leyen. Jena: Eugen Diederichs, 1922.

– *Kinder und Hausmärchen gesammelt durch die Brüder Grimm.* Vol. 3. Göttingen: Verlag der Dieterich'schen Buchhandlung, 1856.

Gubernatis, Angelo De. *Die Thiere in der indogermanischen Mythologie.* Translated by M. Hartmann. Leipzig: Verlag von F. W. Grunow, 1874.

Güntert, Hermann. *Der arische Weltkönig und Heiland. Bedeutungs-geschichtliche Untersuchungen zur indo-iranischen Religions-geschichte und Altertumskunde.* Halle a. S.: Max Niemeyer, 1923.

Hahn, Johann Georg von, ed. and trans. *Griechische und albanesische Märchen.* Vol. 1. Leipzig: Verlag v. Wilhelm Engelmann, 1864.

– *Griechische und albanesische Märchen.* Vol. 2. Leipzig: Verlag v. Wilhelm Engelmann, 1864.

Haltrich, Josef, ed. *Deutsche Volksmärchen aus dem Sachsenlande in Siebenbürgen.* Vienna: Verlag von Carl Graeser, 1882.

Hamann, Hermann. "Die literarischen Vorlagen der Kinder- und Hausmärchen und ihre Bearbeitung durch die Brüder Grimm." In *Palaestra XLVII, Untersuchungen und Texte aus der deutschen und englischen Philologie.* Vol. 47. Edited by Alois Brandl, Gustav Roethe, and Erich Schmidt. Berlin: Mayer & Müller, 1906.

Hambruch, Paul, ed. *Südseemärchen aus Australien, Neu-Guinea, Fidji, Karolinen, Samoa, Tonga, Hawaii, Neu-Seeland u. a..* In *MdW.* Edited by Fr. v. d. Leyen and P. Zaunert. Jena: Eugen Diederichs, 1921.

– *Malaiische Märchen aus Madagaskar und Insulinde.* In MdW. Edited by Fr. v. d. Leyen and P. Zaunert. Jena: Eugen Diederichs, 1922.

Hartlaub, Gustav Friedrich. "Signa Hermetis. Zwei alte alchemi-stische Bilderhandschriften." In *Zeitschr. d. deutschen Vereins f. Kunstwissenschaft.* Vol. 4. Berlin, 1937.

Heiler, Friedrich. "Die Kontemplation in der christlichen Mystik." In *Eranos-Jahrbuch 1933: Yoga und Meditation im Osten und im Westen.* Edited by Olga Fröbe-Kapteyn. Zurich: Rhein-Verlag, 1934, pp. 245–326.

Heinrici, Georg. "Zur Geschichte der Psyche. Eine religions-geschichtliche Skizze." In *Preußische Jahrbücher*. Vol. 90. Edited by Hans Delbrück. Berlin: Verlag von Georg Stilke, 1897, pp. 390–417.

Hertel, Johannes, ed. *Indische Märchen*. In MdW. Edited by Fr. v. d. Leyen and P. Zaunert. Jena: Eugen Diederichs, 1925.

Hertz, Wilhelm. *Der Werwolf. Beitrag zur Sagengeschichte*. Stuttgart: A. Kröner, 1862.

– *Gesammelte Abhandlungen*. Edited by Fr. v. d. Leyen. Stuttgart und Berlin: J. G. Cotta'sche Buchhandlung, 1905.

Hüsing, Georg. "Die Iranische Überlieferung und das arische System." In *Mythologische Bibliothek*. Edited by Ges. f. vergleichende Mythenforschung. Vol. 2, No. 2. Leipzig: J. C. Hinrichs'sche Buchhandlung, 1909.

Huth, Otto. "Wesen und Herkunft des Märchens. Märchen und Gnosis." In *Universitas, Zeitschrift für Wissenschaft, Kunst und Literatur*. 4, No. 6. Edited by S. Maiwald. Stuttgart: Verlag Dr. Roland Schmiedel, 1949, pp. 651–654.

– "Märchen und Megalithreligion." In *Paideuma, Mitteilungen zur Kulturkunde*. Vol. V, October 1950, No. 2. Bamberg: Bamberger Verlagshaus Meisenbach & Co., 1950.

Isler, Gotthilf. "Jung, Carl Gustav." In *Enzyklopädie des Märchens*. Vol. 7. Lieferung 2/3.

– "Franz, Marie-Louise von." In *Enzyklopädie des Märchens*. Vol. 5, Lieferung.

Jung, C. G. *Collected Works*. Edited by Sir Herbert Read, Michael Fordham, and Gerhard Adler. Translated by R. F. C. Hull. Bollingen Series XX. Vols. 1–19. Princeton NJ: Princeton University Press, 1957.

– *Bericht über das Deutsche Seminar von Dr. C. G. Jung, 5.–10. Oktober 1931 in Küsnacht-Zürich*, zusammengestellt von Olga von Koenig-Fachsenfeld, Stuttgart: Privately Printed, 1932.

– *Seminar über Kinderträume und ältere Literatur über Traum-Interpretation, a. d. ETH Zürich*. Edited by Hans H. Baumann. Zurich: Privately Printed, 1936/37.

– "Erlösungsvorstellung in der Alchemie." In *Eranos-Jahrbuch 1936: Gestaltung der Erlösungsidee in Ost und West I*. Edited by Olga Fröbe-Kapteyn. Zurich: Rhein-Verlag, 1937, pp. 13–111.

– *Psychologische Interpretation von Kinderträumen und älterer Literatur über Träume. Seminar a. d. ETH Zürich*. Edited by

Liliane Frey and Riwkah Schärf. Zurich: Privately Printed, 1938/39.

– *Psychologische Interpretation von Kinderträumen und älterer Literatur über Träume. Seminar a. d. ETH Zürich.* Edited by Liliane Frey and Aniela Jaffé. Zurich: Privately Printed, 1939/40.

– and Jarrett, James L., ed. *Nietzsche's Zarathustra: Notes of the Seminar Given in 1934–1939.* Princeton: Princeton University Press, 1988.

Jung, Emma. "Ein Beitrag zum Problem des Animus." In *Wirklichkeit der Seele: Anwendungen und Fortschritte der neueren Psychologie.* Edited by C. G. Jung. Zurich: Rascher & Cie. A.G. 1934.

Jungbauer, Gustav, ed. *Märchen aus Turkestan und Tibet.* In *MdW.* Edited by Fr. v. d. Leyen and P. Zaunert. Jena: Eugen Diederichs, 1923.

Kappes, Alison. "Bibliographie von Marie-Louise von Franz." In *Jungiana,* Series A, Vol. 2, 1989, pp. 33–46.

Keller, Walter, ed. and trans. *Italienische Märchen.* In *MdW.* Edited by Fr. v. d. Leyen. Jena: Eugen Diederichs, 1929.

Kennedy-Xypolitas, Emmanuel, ed. *The Fountain of the Love of Wisdom: An Homage to Marie-Louise von Franz.* Wilmette, Illinois: Chiron Publications, 2006.

Kerényi, Karl. "Das göttliche Mädchen: Die Hauptgestalten der Mysterien von Eleusis in mythologischer und psychologischer Beleuchtung." In *Albae Vigiliae.* No. VIII/IX 1941.

– "Heros Iatros: Über Wandlungen und Symbole des ärztlichen Genius in Griechenland." In *Eranos-Jahrbuch Band XII: Studien zum Problem des Archetypischen.* Edited by Olga Fröbe-Kapteyn. Zurich: Rhein-Verlag, 1945, pp. 34–54.

Koch-Grünberg, Theodor, ed. *Indianermärchen aus Südamerika.* In *MdW.* Edited by Fr. v. d. Leyen and P. Zaunert. Jena: Eugen Diederichs, 1921.

Köhler, Reinhold. "Kleinere Schriften." In *Kleinere Schriften zur Märchenkunde.* Vol. 1. Edited by Johannes Bolte. Weimar: Verlag von Emil Felber, 1898.

Krauss, Friedrich Salomon. *Sagen und Märchen der Südslaven, in ihrem Verhältnis zu den Sagen und Märchen der übrigen indogermanischen Völkergruppen.* Vol. 1. Leipzig: Verlag von Wilhelm Friedrich, 1883.

– *Sagen und Märchen der Südslaven, in ihrem Verhältnis zu den Sagen und Märchen der übrigen indogermanischen Völkergruppen.* Vol. 2. Leipzig: Verlag Wilhelm Friedrich, 1884.

Kretschmer, Paul, ed. *Neugriechische Märchen.* In *MdW.* Edited by Fr. v. d. Leyen and P. Zaunert. Jena: Eugen Diederichs, 1919.

Krickeberg, Walter, ed. *Indianermärchen aus Nordamerika.* In *MdW.* Edited by Fr. v. d. Leyen and P. Zaunert. Jena: Eugen Diederichs, 1924.

– *Märchen der Azteken und Inkaperuaner, Maya und Muisca.* In *MdW.* Edited by Fr. v. d. Leyen. Jena: Eugen Diederichs, 1928.

Kunike, Hugo, ed. *Märchen aus Sibirien.* In *MdW.* Edited by Fr. v. d. Leyen. Jena: Eugen Diederichs, 1940.

Laistner, Ludwig. *Das Rätsel der Sphinx: Grundzüge einer Mythengeschichte.* Vols. 1–2. Berlin: Verlag von Wilhelm Hertz, 1889.

Layard, John. "The Incest Taboo and the Virgin Archetype." In *Eranos-Jahrbuch Band XII: Studien zum Problem des Archetypischen.* Edited by Olga Fröbe-Kapteyn. Zurich: Rhein-Verlag, 1945, pp. 253–307.

Leeuw, Gerardus van der. *Phänomenologie der Religion: Neue theologische Grundrisse.* Edited by R. Bultmann. Tübingen: J. C. B. Mohr (Paul Siebeck), 1933.

– *Der Mensch und die Religion: Anthropologischer Versuch.* Basel: Verlag Haus zum Falken, 1941.

– "Unsterblichkeit." In *Eranos-Jahrbuch Band XVIII: Aus der Welt der Urbilder.* Edited by Olga Fröbe-Kapteyn. Zurich: Rhein-Verlag, 1950, pp. 181–206.

Leisegang, Hans. *Die Gnosis.* Kröners Taschenausgabe, Vol. 32. Stuttgart: Alfred Kröner Verlag, 1941.

– "Das Mysterium der Schlange. Ein Beitrag zur Erforschung des griechischen Mysterienkultes und seines Fortlebens in der christlichen Welt." In *Eranos-Jahrbuch 1939: Die Symbolik der Wiedergeburt in der religiösen Vorstellung der Zeiten und Völker.* Edited by Olga Fröbe-Kapteyn. Zurich: Rhein-Verlag, 1940, pp. 151–250.

Leskien, August, ed. *Balkanmärchen aus Albanien, Bulgarien, Serbien und Kroatien.* In *MdW.* Edited by Fr. v. d. Leyen and P. Zaunert. Jena: Eugen Diederichs, 1919.

Lévi-Strauss, Claude. *Les structures élémentaires de la parenté.* Paris: Presses Universitaires de France, 1949.

Lévy-Bruhl, Lucien. *The "Soul" of the Primitive.* Translated by Lilian A. Clare. London: Allen & Unwin, 1922.

Lincke, Werner. "Das Stiefmuttermotiv im Märchen der germanischen Völker." In *German. Studien.* No. 142. Edited by E. Ebering. Berlin: Verlag Dr. Emil Ebering, 1933.

Littmann, Enno, trans. *Die Erzählungen aus den Tausendundein Nächten.* [German Edition in Six Volumes. Based for the first time on the original Arabic text of the Calcutta edition of 1839]. Leipzig: Insel-Verlag, 1923.

Loepfe, Alfred. *Russische Märchen.* Olten: Verlag Otto Walter AG, 1941.

Löwis of Menar, August von. Ed. and trans. *Russische Volksmärchen.* In *MdW.* Edited by Fr. v. d. Leyen and P. Zaunert. Jena: Eugen Diederichs, 1921.

– Ed. and trans. *Finnische und estnische Volksmärchen.* In *MdW.* Edited by Fr. v. d. Leyen and P. Zaunert. Jena: Eugen Diederichs, 1922.

Lukas, Franz. *Die Grundbegriffe in den Kosmogonien der alten Völker.* Leipzig: Verlag von Wilhelm Friedrich, 1893.

Lum, Peter. *Fabulous Beasts.* New York: Pantheon Books, 1951.

Lüthi, Max. *Das europäische Volksmärchen. Form und Wesen. Eine literatur-wissenschaftliche Darstellung.* Bern: A. Francke, 1947.

– "Psychologie des Märchens. Märchendeutung. Zu einem Buche Hedwig von Beits." In *Neue Zürcher Zeitung, Literatur und Kunst,* Sunday, 12 April, Sheet 4, 1953.

– "Besprechung von Band II. Gegensatz und Erneuerung." In *Neue Zürcher Zeitung,* No. 2806/7, 1957.

– "Hedwig von Beit." In *Enzyklopädie des Märchens.* Vol. 2. Berlin: Walter de Gruyter, 1979.

Mannhardt, Wilhelm. *Wald- und Feldkulte. Band 1: Der Baumkultus der Germanen und ihrer Nachbarstämme. Mythologische Unter-suchungen.* Berlin: Gebrüder Borntraeger, 1875.

– *Wald- und Feldkulte. Band 2: Antike Wald- und Feldkulte aus nordeuropäischer Überlieferung.* Berlin: Gebrüder Borntraeger, 1877.

Marc Aurel. *Selbstbetrachtungen.* Translated by Wilhelm Capelle. Leipzig: Alfred Kröner Verlag, 1933.

Mead, G. R. S. *Fragments of a Faith Forgotten.* London: John M. Watkins, 1931.

Meier, Harri, ed. and trans. *Spanische und portugiesische Märchen.* In *MdW.* Edited by Fr. v. d. Leyen. Jena: Eugen Diederichs Verlag, 1940.

Meinhof, Carl, ed. *Afrikanische Märchen.* In *MdW.* Edited by Fr. v. d. Leyen and P. Zaunert, Jena: Eugen Diederichs, 1921.

Meister Eckhart, *The Complete Works*. Edited and translated by Maurice O'C Walshe. Revised by Bernard McGinn. New York: Crossroad Publishing, 2009.

Meyer, Rudolf. *Die Weisheit der Schweizer Märchen*. Schaffhausen: Columban-Verlag, 1944.

Mogk, Eugen. *Germanische Religionsgeschichte und Mythologie*. Sammlung Göschen. Berlin and Leipzig: Walther de Gruyter & Co., 1927.

Müller-Lisowski, Käte, ed. *Irische Volksmärchen*. In *MdW*. Edited by Fr. v. d. Leyen and P. Zaunert. Jena: Eugen Diedrichs, 1923.

Naumann, Hans, and Ida Naumann, trans. *Isländische Volksmärchen*. In *MdW*. Edited by Fr. v. d. Leyen and P. Zaunert. Jena: Eugen Diederichs, 1923.

Niedner, Felix. "Islands Kultur zur Wikingerzeit." In: Thule, *Altnordische Dichtung und Prosa*, Einleitungsband. Jena: Eugen Diederichs, 1920.

Ninck, Martin. *Wodan und germanischer Schicksalsglaube*. Jena: Eugen Diederichs, 1935.

– "Älteste Märchen von Europa." In *Sammlung Klosterberg*, Europ. Reihe. Edited by H. U. von Balhasar. Basel: Benno Schwabe, 1945.

Novalis, *Fragmente. Erste vollständige, geordnete Ausgabe*. Edited by Ernst Kamnitzer. Dresden: Wolfgang Jess Verlag, 1929.

Panzer, Friedrich, ed. *Die Kinder- und Hausmärchen in ihrer Urgestalt*. Munich: C. H. Beck'sche Verlagsbuchhandlung Oskar Beck, 1913.

Patch, Howard Rollin. *The Other World: According to Descriptions in Medieval Literature*. Cambridge, Mass.: Harvard University Press, 1950.

Peuckert, Will-Erich. *Deutscher Volksglaube des Spätmittelalters*, Sammlung Voelkerglaube. Edited by Claus Schrempf. Stuttgart: W. Spemann Verlag, 1942.

Przyluski, Jean. "Der Lebendig-Erlöste in dem entwickelten Buddhismus." In *Eranos- Jahrbuch 1937: Gestaltung der Erlösungsidee in Ost und West II*. Edited by Olga Fröbe-Kapteyn. Zurich: Rhein-Verlag, 1938, pp. 117–136.

– "Die Mutter-Göttin als Verbindung zwischen den Lokal-Göttern und dem Universal-Gott." In *Eranos-Jahrbuch 1938: Gestalt und Kult der "Grossen Mutter."* Edited by Olga Fröbe Kapteyn. Zurich: Rhein-Verlag, 1939, pp. 35–75.

– "Ursprünge und Entwicklung des Kultes der Mutter-Göttin." In *Eranos-Jahrbuch 1938: Gestalt und Kult der "Grossen Mutter."*

Edited by Olga Fröbe-Kapteyn. Zurich: Rhein-Verlag, 1939, pp. 11–34.

Puech, Henri-Charles. "Der Begriff der Erlösung im Manichäismus." In *Eranos-Jahrbuch 1936: Gestaltung der Erlösungsidee in Ost und West I.* Edited by Olga Fröbe-Kapteyn. Zurich: Rhein-Verlag, 1937, pp. 183–286.

Pulver, Max. "Jesu Reigen und Kreuzigung nach den Johannes-Akten." In *Eranos-Jahrbuch 1942: Das hermetische Prinzip in Mythologie, Gnosis und Alchemie.* Edited by Olga Fröbe-Kapteyn. Zurich: Rhein-Verlag, 1943, pp. 141–177.

Rank, Otto. "Die Lohengrinsage: Ein Beitrag zu ihrer Motivgestaltung und Deutung." In *Schriften zur angewandten Seelenkunde.* Edited by Sigmund Freud. XIII Heft. Leipzig and Vienna: Franz Deuticke, 1911.

– "Das Inzest-Motiv in Dichtung und Sage." In *Grundzüge einer Psychologie des dichterischen Schaffens.* Vienna: Franz Deuticke, 1912.

– "Der Mythus von der Geburt des Helden. Versuch einer psychologischen Mythendeutung." In *Schriften zur angewandten Seelenkunde*, Heft 5. Edited by Sigmund Freud. Leipzig and Vienna: Franz Deuticke, 1922.

Rasmussen, Knud. *Die Gabe des Adlers, Eskimoische Märchen aus Alaska.* Translated and edited by Aenne Schmücker. Frankfurt a. M.: Societäts-Verlag, 1937.

Reitzenstein, Richard. "Das Märchen von Amor und Psyche bei Apuleius." Inaugural Lecture at the University of Freiburg on 22 June 1911. Leipzig and Berlin: Teubner, 1912.

– *Das iranische Erlösungsmysterium. Religionsgeschichtliche Untersuchungen.* Bonn a. Rh.: A. Marcus & E. Weber's Verlag, 1921.

– *Die hellenistischen Mysterienreligionen: nach ihren Grundgedanken und Wirkungen.* 3rd Edition. Leipzig and Berlin: Teubner, 1927.

Rilke, Rainer Maria. *Letters to a Young Poet.* Edited by Ray Soulard. Translated by Stephen Mitchell. Portland, Oregon: Scriptor, 2001.

Rittershaus, Adeline. *Die Neuisländischen Volksmärchen. Ein Beitrag zur vergleichenden Märchenforschung.* Halle a. S.: Max Niemeyer, 1902.

Roeder, Günther. "Urkunden zur Religion des alten Ägypten." In *Religiöse Stimmen der Völker.* Edited by Walter Otto. Jena: Eugen Diederichs, 1923.

Rohde, Erwin. *"Psyche": Seelencult und Unsterblichkeitsglaube der Griechen.* Vols. 1–2. Tübingen: J. C. B. Mohr (Paul Siebeck), 1910.

Róheim, Géza. *Spiegelzauber.* Internat. Psychoanalytische Bibliothek. Vol. 6. Leipzig and Vienna: Internationaler Psychoanalytischer, 1919.

Ruben, Walter. *Die Philosophen der Upanishaden.* Bern: Francke AG, 1947.

Rumpf, Fritz, ed. and trans. *Japanische Volksmärchen.* In *MdW*. Edited by Fr. v. d. Leyen. Jena: Eugen Diederichs Verlag, 1938.

Ruska, Julius. *Tabula Smaragdina. Ein Beitrag zur Geschichte der Hermetischen Literatur.* Heidelberger Akten der von-Portheim-Stiftung 16. Arbeiten aus dem Institut für Geschichte der Naturwissenschaft IV. Heidelberg: Carl Winter's Universitäts-buchhandlung, 1926.

Schmitt, Paul. "Sol Invictus." In *Eranos-Jahrbuch 1943: Alte Sonnen-kulte und die Lichtsymbolik in der Gnosis und im frühen Christentum.* Edited by Olga Fröbe-Kapteyn. Zurich: Rhein-Verlag, 1944, pp. 169–252.

– "Antike Mysterien in der Gesellschaft ihrer Zeit." In *Eranos-Jahrbuch 1944: Die Mysterien.* Edited by Olga Fröbe-Kapteyn. Zurich: Rhein-Verlag, 1945, pp. 107–144.

Schweitzer, Bernhard. *Herakles: Aufsätze zur griechischen Religions-und Sagengeschichte.* Tübingen: Verlag von J. C. B. Mohr (Paul Siebeck), 1922.

Silberer, Herbert. *Probleme der Mystik und ihrer Symbolik.* Vienna and Leipzig: Hugo Heller, 1914.

Siuts, Johannes. *Jenseitsmotive im deutschen Volksmärchen.* Inaugural-Dissertation zur Erlangung der Doktorwürde der hohen philosophischen Fakultät der Königl. Christian-Albrechts-Universität zu Kiel. Greifswald. 1911.

Sock, Paul, trans. *Eskimomärchen.* Berlin: Axel Juncker Verlag, 1921.

Stroebe, Klara, trans. *Nordische Volksmärchen. Band 1 – Dänemark und Schweden.* In *MdW*. Edited by Fr. v. d. Leyen and P. Zaunert. Jena: Eugen Diederichs, 1922.

– *Nordische Volksmärchen, Band 2 – Norwegen.* In *MdW*. Jena: Eugen Diederichs, 1922.

Tegethoff, Ernst. "Studien zum Märchentypus von Amor und Psyche." In *Rhein. Beitr. u. Hülfsbücher z. germ. Philologie u. Volkskunde.* Vol. 4. Edited by Th. Frings, R. Meissner, J. Müller, Kurt Schroeder. Bonn and Leipzig, 1922.

– *Französische Volksmärchen 1: Aus älteren Quellen.* In *MdW*. Edited by Fr. v. d. Leyen and P. Zaunert. Jena: Eugen Diederichs, 1923.

– *Französische Volksmärchen 2: Aus neueren Sammlungen.* In *MdW*. Edited by. Fr. v. d. Leyen and P. Zaunert. Jena: Eugen Diederichs, 1923.

Thimme, Adolf. *Das Märchen. Handbücher zur Volkskunde.* Vol. 2. Leipzig: Verlag von Wilhelm Heims, 1909.

Thurnwald, Richard. "Primitive Initiations- und Wiedergeburtsriten." In *Eranos-Jahrbuch 1939: Die Symbolik der Wiedergeburt in der religiösen Vorstellung der Zeiten und Völker.* Edited by Olga Fröbe-Kapteyn. Zurich: Rhein-Verlag, 1940, pp. 321–328.

Tobler, Otto. *Die Epiphanie der Seele in deutscher Volkssage.* Inaugural-Dissertation, Christian-Albrechts-Universität zu Kiel. Kiel. 1911.

Usener, Hermann. *Die Sintfluthsagen, Religionsgeschichtliche Untersuchungen, dritter Theil.* Bonn: Friedrich Cohen, 1899.

Weicker, Georg. *Der Seelenvogel. In der alten Literatur und Kunst. Eine mythologisch-archaeologische Untersuchung.* Leipzig: B. G. Teubner, 1902.

Wesselski, Albert. "Versuch einer Theorie des Märchens." In *Prager Deutsche Studien*, No. 45. Edited by E. Gierach and H. Cysarz. Reichenberg i. B.: Sudetendeutscher Verlag Franz Kraus, 1931.

Wilhelm, Richard. *The I Ching: The Book of Changes.* Translated by Richard Wilhelm London: Penquin, 1950/2003.

– *The Secret of the Golden Flower: A Chinese Book of Life.* Translated by Cary F. Baynes. Brattleboro, Vermont: Echo Point Books, 1931/2022.

– *Chinesische Märchen.* In *MdW*. Edited by Fr. v. d. Leyen. Jena: Eugen Diederichs Verlag, 1958.

Winthuis, Josef. *Das Zweigeschlechterwesen bei den Zentralaustraliern und anderen Völkern. Lösungsversuch der ethnologischen Hauptprobleme auf Grund primitiven Denkens.* Band 5. Forschungen zur Völkerpsychologie und Soziologie. Leipzig: Verlag von C. L. Hirschfeld, 1928.

Wisser, Wilhelm, ed. *Plattdeutsche Volksmärchen.* In *MdW*. Vol. 1. Edited by Fr. v. d. Leyen and P. Zaunert. Jena: Eugen Diederichs, 1922.

– *Plattdeutsche Volksmärchen, Neue Folge.* In *MdW*. Edited by P. Zaunert. Jena: Eugen Diederichs, 1927.

Wünsche, August. *Der Sagenkreis vom geprellten Teufel.* Leipzig and Vienna: Akademischer Verlag, 1905.

Zaunert, Paul, ed. *Deutsche Märchen seit Grimm.* In *MdW.* Vol. 1. Edited by Fr. v. d. Leyen. Jena: Eugen Diederichs, 1922.

– *Deutsche Märchen aus dem Donaulande.* In *MdW.* Edited by Fr. v. d. Leyen and P. Zaunert. Jena: Eugen Diederichs, 1926.

Zimmer, Heinrich. "'Der König der dunklen Kammer.' In drei Verwandlungen vom Rgveda bis Tagore." In *Zeitschr. d. Deutschen Morgenländischen Gesellschaft.* Edited by G. Steindorff. Leipzig: F. A. Brockhaus, 1929.

– "Zur Bedeutung des indischen Tantra-Yoga." In Eranos-Jahrbuch 1933: Yoga und Meditation im Osten und im Westen. Edited by Olga Fröbe-Kapteyn. Zurich: Rhein-Verlag, 1934, pp. 9–94.

– *Maya der indische Mythos.* Stuttgart and Berlin: Deutsche Verlags-Anstalt, 1936.

– *Weisheit Indiens. Märchen und Sinnbilder.* Darmstadt: L. C. Wittich Verlag, 1938.

– "Tod und Wiedergeburt im indischen Licht." In *Eranos-Jahrbuch 1939: Die Symbolik der Wiedergeburt in der religiösen Vorstellung der Zeiten und Völker.* Edited by Olga Fröbe-Kapteyn. Zurich: Rhein-Verlag, 1940, pp. 251–289.

# Index of Authors

## A

Aarne, A., 263, 282, 286, 397
Abraham, K., 79, 397
Abt, R., 397
Afanas'ev, A., 181
Aichele, W., 82, 213, 357, 358, 397
Allberry, C.R.C., 165, 397
Altmann, C., 397
Angelus, S., 113, 397
Apuleius von Madura., 73, 269, 397, 407

## B

Bachofen, J.J., 22, 46–49, 82, 87, 93, 102, 112, 113, 377, 397
Bächtold-Stäubli, H.B., 21, 33, 34, 49, 59, 62, 63, 79, 81, 82, 99, 112,
    138, 151, 162, 165, 180, 192, 193, 199, 229, 232, 255, 261, 268, 273,
    307, 324, 345, 368, 370, 378, 390, 393, 398
Baumann, D., 398
Bischoff, E., 63, 165, 174, 341, 394, 398
Boehm, M., 32, 398
Bolte, J. and Mackensen, L., 49, 73, 202, 203, 282, 392
Bolte, J. and Polívka, G., 33, 34, 36–38, 41, 50–54, 60, 66, 77, 82, 83,
    87, 88, 91, 94–96, 101, 105, 116–118, 137, 154, 160–162, 165, 170–
    172, 181, 185, 190, 194, 198, 203, 204, 207, 208, 223, 241, 242, 248,
    252, 253, 285, 295, 299, 300, 310, 312, 316, 317, 323, 325, 344, 346,
    348, 349, 362, 370, 374, 375
Bolte, J., 33, 34, 223, 403
Bosch, I., 397
Botkin, B.A., 152, 398
Bousset, W., 61, 157, 165, 166, 252, 341, 394, 399
Brothers Grimm, 11, 53, 219
Buonaiuti, E., 59, 399

◆

# Index of Fairytales

Translator's note: In each section, tales are listed in their order of appearance in Volume 4 of *Archetypal Symbols in Fairytales*. The number indicated after a tale refers to the edition in which that tale was collected. The bibliographic details of those editions and collections are provided after the section heading.

**Brothers Grimm**
*The Complete Grimm's Fairy Tales*, with an introduction by Padraic Colum (New York: Pantheon Books, 1944; Random House, 1972)

**Africa**
Carl Meinhof, ed. *Afrikanische Märchen*, in: *Die Märchen der Weltliteratur*, eds. von der Leyen and Zaunert (1921)

## Caucasus
Adolf Dirr, trans. *Kaukasische Märchen*, in: *Die Märchen der Weltliteratur*, eds. von der Leyen and Zaunert (1922)

## China
Richard Wilhelm, ed. *Chinesische Märchen*, in: *Die Märchen der Weltliteratur*, ed. von der Leyen (1958)

## Danube Region
Paul Zaunert, ed. *Märchen aus dem Donaulande*, in: *Die Märchen der Weltliteratur*, eds. von der Leyen and Zaunert (1926)

## Denmark

Klara Stroebe, trans. *Nordische Volksmärchen*, vol. 1. Denmark and Sweden, in: *Die Märchen der Weltliteratur*, eds. von der Leyen and Zaunert (1922)

## England

Alfred Ehrenteich, trans. *Englische Volksmärchen*, in: *Die Märchen der Weltliteratur*, eds. von der Leyen and Zaunert (1938)

## Eskimo

Paul Sock, trans. *Eskimomärchen* (Berlin, 1921)

## Eskimo (Alaska)

Knud Rasmussen, *Die Gabe des Adlers, Eskimoische Märchen aus Alaska*, trans. Aenne Schmücker (Frankfurt a. Main, 1937)

## Finland

August von Löwis of Menar, trans. *Finnische und estnische Volksmärchen*, in: *Die Märchen der Weltliteratur*, eds. von der Leyen and Zaunert (1922)

## France

Ernst Tegethoff, ed. *Französische Volksmärchen 1: Aus älteren Quellen*, in: *Die Märchen der Weltliteratur*, eds. von der Leyen and Zaunert (1923)

Ernst Tegethoff, ed. *Französische Volksmärchen 2: Aus neueren Sammlungen*, in: *Die Märchen der Weltliteratur*, eds. von der Leyen and Zaunert (1923)

**German (since Grimm)**
Paul Zaunert, ed. *Deutsche Märchen seit Grimm*, vol. 1, in: *Die Märchen der Weltliteratur*, ed. von der Leyen (1922)

**Latvia**
Max Boehm and Franz Specht, eds. *Lettische-litauische Volksmärchen*, in: *Die Märchen der Weltliteratur*, eds. von der Leyen and Zaunert (1924)

The Little White Dog (no. 16), 43
Chuinis (no. 7), 276
Adventures of a King's Son (no. 21), 266
Strong Hans (no. 9), 346
The Strong Brother and the Faithless Sister (no. 5), 350, 367

**Lithuania**
Max Boehm and Franz Specht, eds. *Lettische-litauische Volksmärchen*, in: *Die Märchen der Weltliteratur*, eds. von der Leyen and Zaunert (1924)

The Hedgehog and the King's Daughters (no. 24), 32
A King's Son and an Enchanted Maiden (no. 25), 208
The Suffering Flax (no. 23), 370

**Low German (*Plattdeutsch*)**
Wilhelm Wisser, ed. *Plattdeutsche Volksmärchen*, vol. 1, in: *Die Märchen der Weltliteratur*, eds. von der Leyen and Zaunert (1922)

*De Köni un de Ent*, 316
*De Kopmannssöhn* (The Merchant's Son), 245
*De lütt Ent*, 316
*Hans Vêrtein*, 343

Wilhelm Wisser, ed. *Plattdeutsche Volksmärchen*, vol. 2, in: *Die Märchen der Weltliteratur*, eds. von der Leyen and Zaunert (1927)

*De Eddelmannsdochter in 'n Tôr'n* (The Gentleman's Daughter in the Tower)

**Malaysia**
Paul Hambruch, ed. *Malaiische Märchen aus Madagaskar und Insulinde*, in: *Die Märchen der Weltliteratur*, eds. von der Leyen and Zaunert (1922)

The Half (no. 29), 58

**South Sea Islands**
Paul Hambruch, ed. *Südseemärchen aus Australien, Neu-Guinea, Fidji, u.a.*, in: *Die Märchen der Weltliteratur*, eds. von der Leyen and Zaunert (1921)

The Sun Child (no. 30), 159
Three Stories about the Brothers To Kabinana and To Karwuwu (no. 16), 242
Tolojäla and his Daughter (no. 48), 279
The Journey to the Underworld to Fafá, the Whirlpool Cave (no. 63), 306

**Sweden**
Klara Stroebe, trans. *Nordische Volksmärchen*, vol. 1. Denmark and Sweden, in: *Die Märchen der Weltliteratur*, eds. von der Leyen and Zaunert (1922)

The Old Rattlebag (no. 27), 12
The Werewolf (no. 11), 18, 42
The Lame Dog (no. 13), 74, 76, 82, 85, 104, 106, 163
The Maiden and the Serpent (no. 8), 95
First Born, First Married (no. 12), 136, 144–148, 151, 152, 159, 167
The Princess on the Glass Mountain (no. 16), 139, 205
Lasse, My Servant! (no. 2), 25, 182
Queen Crane (no. 17), 368

**Turkestan**
Gustav Jungbauer, ed. *Märchen aus Turkestan und Tibet*, in: *Die Märchen der Weltliteratur*, eds. von der Leyen and Zaunert (1923)

The Magic Horse (no. 9), 11, 74, 76, 121, 156, 256, 314
Prince Hassan Pascha (no. 4), 25
The Witch and the Golden-Haired Prince (no. 6), 42
Djulek-Batür (no. 7), 144, 232, 309, 325, 343, 349
Prince Shaadot (no. 10), 205
The Poor Stepchildren and the Wicked Harem Women (no. 13), 302
The Turtledove on the Mulberry Tree (no. 16), 325
The Witch's Sister (Turkestan, no. 8), 365

## Turkey

Friedrich Giese, ed. *Türkische Märchen*, in. *Die Märchen der Weltliteratur*, eds. von der Leyen and Zaunert (1925)

# Subject Index

boots, 180, 257

box, 56, 111, 114, 173, 189, 266, 292, 320, 360, 361, 363

boy, 29, 32, 54, 56, 95, 115, 116, 126, 133, 146, 152, 158, 159, 178, 233, 242, 286, 297, 300, 303, 314, 319, 320, 323, 339, 342, 360, 361, 363, 364, 376, 385, 387–389

bread, 187, 191, 197, 199, 204, 209, 223, 333, 357, 372, 376

breast, 392

bride, 15, 39, 53, 54, 60, 62, 65, 71, 72, 121, 123, 126, 128, 146, 170, 172, 177, 179, 186, 190, 198, 207, 208, 242, 245, 273, 280, 285, 286, 294, 299, 305, 307, 331, 343, 354, 356, 357, 392

    false, 15, 20, 24, 27, 37, 53, 56, 93, 102, 114, 120, 122–125, 145–147, 158, 164, 173, 219, 315, 316, 376

bridegroom, 1, 11, 16, 29, 52, 58, 62, 71, 72, 76, 77, 80, 81, 83–85, 87, 94, 96, 111, 115, 123, 189, 191, 285, 392

    false, 282, 286, 287, 351

bridge, 15, 66, 108, 161, 201, 207, 215, 217, 220, 224, 225, 254, 255, 342, 388

broom, 389, 391

brother,

    and sister, 295, 299, 311–313, 350, 357, 392

    animal, 316

    elder, 303

    eldest, 97, 303

    in-law, 209, 220, 293, 355, 364

    little, 152, 299, 300, 302, 303, 316, 317, 323

    older, 291, 292, 295, 302

    redemption of, 378

    younger, 131, 292, 302

    youngest, 97, 193, 212, 329, 344, 381, 384, 392

brothers,

    four, 342

    seven, 333

    three, 97, 193, 207, 220, 247, 344

    twelve, 329, 330, 332

    two, 195

bull, 95, 310, 313, 314, 324

    black, 310, 313

    stomach, 184, 185

calling, 14, 21, 89, 105, 126, 171, 238, 245

candle, 9, 40, 69, 85, 102, 117, 138, 203

candles, 39, 40, 69, 207

honey, 98, 232, 265

horns, 215, 235, 282, 299

horse,

    magic, magical, 76, 121, 314

    white, 26, 64, 206, 226, 227, 230, 240, 243, 357, 359

horses, 25, 31, 45, 53, 77, 89, 143, 148, 150, 179, 191, 262, 271, 342, 357, 376

human, 7, 8, 12, 13, 15, 20, 22–24, 29 , 32, 35, 38, 39, 43, 44, 48, 49, 54, 56–58, 60, 62–66, 68, 70, 71, 73, 78, 80, 82–85, 87, 88, 90, 92, 96, 97, 99, 100, 110–112, 116, 118, 119, 121, 122, 124, 132, 135–138, 143, 144, 146, 151, 153, 154, 156, 157, 160–167, 173, 174, 180, 181, 184, 185, 190–192, 198–201, 203, 205, 206, 209, 214, 215, 218, 223, 226, 228–230, 232, 233, 240, 243, 252, 256, 260, 264, 269, 271, 274, 279, 280, 282–285, 287–289, 293 , 294, 299, 303, 307, 309, 313–315, 317, 324–326, 333–335, 337, 340, 341, 343, 345, 356, 364–366, 369, 372–374, 378, 381, 382, 384, 385, 390, 392, 393, 395, 396

    inner, 49

    primordial, 163–166, 174, 382

humans, 114, 137, 140, 163, 165, 183, 228, 283, 374, 380, 394

husband, 14, 45, 54, 68, 74, 76, 85, 86, 97, 104, 106, 114, 117, 120, 122, 136, 138, 149, 181, 204–206, 209, 210, 212, 276, 279, 281, 289, 291, 303, 318, 339, 358, 359, 362, 363, 376, 382, 384, 385

hut, 8, 9, 11, 18, 97, 106, 115, 187–189, 204, 208, 279, 291, 293, 306, 377, 338, 345, 346

Icelandic, 41, 150, 184, 185, 307

*I Ching, Book of Changes*, 191, 274, 409

idea, 38, 39, 41, 47, 57–59, 61, 62, 89, 99, 102, 103, 117, 121, 129, 130, 145, 154, 157, 162, 171, 174, 182, 196, 197, 203, 208, 225, 244, 245, 267–270, 304, 366, 379, 383, 392

ideas, 12, 23, 69, 78, 85, 103, 163–166, 264, 270, 283, 284, 309, 310, 379, 394

    alchemical, 310

    Christian, 264, 284

    Manichaean, 165

    pagan, 283

illumination, 23, 24, 65, 66, 80, 86, 87, 96, 98, 99–101, 121, 140, 180, 185, 198, 207, 208, 269, 349

    premature, 66, 86, 87, 140, 180, 185, 198, 207, 208, 349

image, 7, 12, 13, 16, 17, 20–24, 26, 28, 37–39, 41, 46–48, 50, 52, 57, 61, 74, 76, 82, 99, 101, 103, 107, 112–114, 118, 120, 121, 138, 139, 142–146,

www.ingramcontent.com/pod-product-compliance
Lightning Source LLC
Chambersburg PA
CBHW030855270326
41929CB00008B/432